Studies in Logic

Volume 15

Logic, Navya-Nyāya & Applications

Homage to Bimal Krishna Matilal

Volume 5
Incompleteness in the Land of Sets
Melvin Fitting

Volume 6
How to Sell a Contradiction. The Metaphysics of Inconsistency
Francesco Berto

Volume 7
Fallacies – Selected Papers 1972-1982
John Woods and Douglas Walton, with a Foreword by Dale Jacquette

Volume 8
A New Approach to Quantum Logic
Kurt Engesser, Dov M. Gabbay and Daniel Lehmann

Volume 9
Handbook of Paraconsistency
Jean-Yves Béziau, Walter Carnielli and Dov Gabbay, editors

Volume 10
Automated Reasoning in Higher-Order Logic. Set Comprehension and Extensional
in Church's Type Theory
Chad E. Brown

Volume 11
Foundations of the Formal Sciences V: Infinite Games
Stefan Bold, Benedikt Löwe, Thoralf Räsch and Johan van Benthem, editors

Volume 12
Second-Order Quantifier Elimination: Foundations, Computational Aspects and Applications
Dov M. Gabbay, Renate A. Schmidt and Andrzej Szałas

Volume 13
Knowledge in Flux. Modeling the Dynamics of Epistemic States
Peter Gärdenfors. With a foreword by David Makinson

Volume 14
New Approaches to Classes and Concepts
Klaus Robering, editor

Volume 15
Logic, Navya-Nyāya and Applications. Homage to Bimal Krishna Matilal
Mihir K. Chakraborti, Benedikt Löwe, Madhabendra Nath Mitra and Sundar Sarukka

Studies in Logic Series Editor
Dov Gabbay dov.gabbay@kcl.ac.uk

Logic, Navya-Nyāya & Applications

Homage to Bimal Krishna Matilal

Edited by

Mihir K. Chakraborty,

Benedikt Löwe,

Madhabendra Nath Mitra

and

Sundar Sarukkai

ISBN 978-1-904987-44-4

College Publications
Scientific Director: Dov Gabbay
Managing Director: Jane Spurr
Department of Computer Science
King's College London, Strand, London WC2R 2LS, UK

http://www.collegepublications.co.uk

Original cover design by Richard Fraser
Created by orchid creative www.orchidcreative.co.uk
Printed by Lightning Source, Milton Keynes, UK

Table of Contents

Preface ... vii

Bimal Krishna Matilal and his contribution to the study of Indian logic and Navya-Nyāya
Jonardon Ganeri ... xi

Rough set theory: A temporal logic view
Mohua Banerjee, Md. Aquil Khan ... 1

Natural logic: A view from the 1980s
Johan van Benthem ... 21

Abhāva: Negation in logic, real non-existent, and a distinctive *pramāṅa* in the Mīmāṃsā
Purushottama Bilimoria ... 43

"Marry your daughter to a handsome person": The Nyāya technique of precisification
Amita Chatterjee, Mihir K. Chakraborty ... 65

Computational Complexity and the expressive power of logics
Anuj Dawar ... 81

Towards a formal regimentation of the Navya-Nyāya technical language I
Jonardon Ganeri ... 105

Towards a formal regimentation of the Navya-Nyāya technical language II
Jonardon Ganeri ... 123

George Bealer's property theories and their relevance to the study of Navya-Nyāya logic
Eberhard Guhe ... 139

Tarski on Padoa's method: A test case for understanding logicians of other traditions
Wilfrid Hodges 155

Other minds in Buddhist epistemology
Hisayasu Kobayashi 171

Marking time
Kamal Lodaya 185

Sense data and *ākāra*
Shinya Moriyama 205

Kauṇḍabhaṭṭa on the *śakyatāvacchedaka* of a meaning of a verb ending
Hideyo Ogawa 217

On relating two traditions of logic
Biswambhar Pahi 235

Reasoning *in* games
R. Ramanujam, Sunil Simon 261

A semiotic interpretation of Indian logic
Sundar Sarukkai 287

Preface

Bimal Krishna Matilal (1935-1991) was one of the few thinkers who devoted a major part of his philosophical career to initiating meaningful dialogues between the philosophical traditions of India and the West. His untimely death deprived the world of an outstanding thinker and philosopher.

The *International Conference On Logic, Navya-Nyāya & Applications*, held 3-7 January 2007 in Kolkata at Jadavpur University, aimed at bringing together the modern logic and traditional Indian systems of logic (especially, the Navya-Nyāya system) in the spirit and in memory of Bimal Krishna Matilal. The conference continued the tradition of the "First Indian Conference on Logic and its Relationship with other Disciplines" that had been held in Mumbai in January 2005.

The conference in Kolkata was an important stepping stone for the development of the *Association for Logic in India* and for the series of scientific events that followed. After the mentioned first conference in January 2005 at IIT Bombay and its follow-up Winter School (January 2006), two events in India were held in January 2007: the conference of which this book is the proceedings volume, and a meeting at IIT Bombay entitled "Second Indian Conference on Logic and its Relationship with other Disciplines" (9–11 January 2007). Many of the international guests travelled from Kolkata to Mumbai to attend this second meeting. At the Kolkata and Mumbai meetings in 2007, the Indian logicians decided to form the *Association for Logic in India* (ALI) which is now responsible for the coordination of the

Indian Logic Conferences and the Logic Winter Schools. In 2008, the Winter School was held at IIT Kanpur. The *Third Indian Conference on Logic and its Applications* will be held at the Institute of Mathematical Sciences, Chennai from 7–11 January 2009.

Organizers and Committees.

The *Chief Patron* of the conference was Gopal Krishna Gandhi (Honourable Governor, West Bengal) and its *President* was D. P. Chattopadhyaya (President, Indian Philosophical Congress).

Advisory Committee. A. N. Basu (Former Vice Chancellor, Jadavpur University), S. K. Sanyal (Vice Chancellor, Jadavpur University), Ratna Datta Sharma (Head, Department of Philosophy, Jadavpur University), J. N. Crossley, H. N. Gupta, D. Dutta Mazumder, J. N. Mohanty, and B. Pahi.

Programme Committee. Mohua Banerjee, Kanpur; Kuntala Bhattacharya, Kolkata; Supratik Chakraborty, Mumbai; Amita Chatterjee, Kolkata; Didier Dubois, Toulouse; Dov M. Gabbay, London; Jonardon Ganeri, Liverpool; Raghunath Ghosh, Darjeeling; Lluis Godo, Barcelona; Chinmoy Goswami, Hyderabad; Amitabha Gupta, Mumbai; Wilfrid Hodges, London; Benedikt Löwe, Amsterdam; Bijoy Mukherjee, Shantiniketan; Piero Pagliani, Rome; Rohit Parikh, New York NY; Sukharanjan Saha, Kolkata; Manidipa Sanyal, Kolkata; Tushar Kanti Sarkar, Kolkata; Sundar Sarukkai, Bengaluru; Hajime Sawamura, Niigata; Jayshankar Lal Shaw, Wellington; Andrzej Skowron, Warsaw; S. P. Suresh, Chennai; Johan van Benthem, Amsterdam.

Convenors. Madhabendra Nath Mitra (Jadavpur University), Mihir K. Chakraborty (University of Calcutta), Rupa Bandyopadhyaya (Jadavpur University), Sadhan Chakraborti (Jadavpur University).

Organizing Committee. Rupa Bandyapadhyay, Sanjukta Basu, Stefan Bold, Arindam Chakrabarti, Sadhan Chakraborti, Badal Chandra Chakraborty, Mihir Kumar Chakraborty, Nirmalya Narayan Chakraborty, Sati Chatterjee, Lopamudra Choudhury, Sujata Ghosh, Amit Konar, Chandan Mazumdar, Madhabendra Nath Mitra, Ranjan Mukhopadhyay, Indrani Sanyal, Prabal Kumar Sen, Ratna Datta Sharma, and Smita Sirker.

Acknowledgements.

We would like to thank Smt. Karabi Matilal for all her support for this conference. Her presence and that of her family during the conference constituted an important link to Bimal Krishna Matilal. In addition, we would like to thank the following institutions for their support: the University Grants Commission of the government of India, the Center for Studies and

Civilizations, New Delhi, Tata Consultancy Services, the Department of Higher Education of the Government of West Bengal, the National Board of Higher Mathematics, the Indian Council of Philosophical Research, the Department of Science and Technology of the Government of India, the Indian Council for Social Science Research, the British Council, Kolkata, United Spirit Limited (UB Group), and —last but not least— Jadavpur University.

The conference was hosted at Jadavpur University, and all students of the Department of Philosophy helped with the organization of the conference. In addition to Jadavpur students, some students from Calcutta University were also involved in the organization. We would like to record our gratitude to those who helped us in various ways. Their names are given below. We apologize to those whose names we may have inadvertently missed:

Amrita Acharyya, Sadidul Alam, Ritaprava Bandyopadhaya, Sanchali Banerjee, Pragya Bhattacharya, Indrani Choudhury, Bikas Das, Mihir Das, Soumitra Das, Ranjan Debnath, Arup Dhar, Buddhadev Gorai, Javad Hassan, Anjan Karmakar, Bikash Mondal, Atreyee Mukherjee, Sunan Nandi, Payal Pakrashi, Mainak Pal, Shalmoli Palit, Debojyoti Roy, Dipankar Roy, Minakshi Roy, Anirban Saha, Debasis Saha, Tamogna Sarkar, Shaoli Seal, Moitreyee Sen, and Deboshree Tarafdar.

This volume.

Over sixty presentations were given at the conference and the editors of this volume invited all speakers to submit a full version of their talk for the proceedings volume. We received many submissions and thoroughly peer-reviewed them: over forty referees helped us maintain the high academic quality of the volume by giving us their opinions on the submissions, and in many cases by actively getting involved in the improvement of the papers. We would like to thank all of the referees without whom we could not have produced this volume.

As is fitting for a volume in memory of Bimal Krishna Matilal, this book contains a short biography of Matilal written by his student Jonardon Ganeri (p. xi–xvii of this volume). We would like to thank Anvita Matilal for providing the pictures of her father that are part of this introductory paper. Apart from the introductory paper, this volume contains sixteen papers by eighteen authors. The diversity of authors and topicsreflect an interesting mix of Indian and Western logic, and the topics range from scholarly questions on Navya-Nyāya to modern computer science. We are convinced that this volume represents the dialogue of philosophical and logical traditions between India and the West that Matilal initiated.

Assisting us with the editorial process, Sujata Ghosh took care of the coordination of the referees. In the later phase, typesetting was done by Edgar Andrade, Pablo Cubides Kovacsics, and V. B. Mariyammal. The LaTeX stylefile we used is an adaptation of Joel Uckelman's `tlg.sty`, and we would like to thank him for his support. Finally, we would also like to thank Jane Spurr of *College Publications* for her support in the early and final phases of our production.

Kolkata, Amsterdam, and Bengaluru, November 2008

M.K.C. B.L. M.N.M. S.S.

Bimal Krishna Matilal and his contribution to the study of Indian logic and Navya-Nyāya

Jonardon Ganeri

Department of Philosophy, University of Sussex, Arts Building B, Brighton BN1 9QN, United Kingdom

E-mail: jonardon@liverpool.ac.uk

Bimal Krishna Matilal (1935-1991) became the Spalding Professor of Eastern Religions and Ethics at the University of Oxford and Fellow of All Souls College in 1976, a position that had earlier been held by the renowned Indian philosopher and later President of India, Sarvepalli Radhakrishnan. He was born in Joynagar, a small town in West Bengal, which

FIGURE 1. Matilal at Kurkushetra, 1975. The person at the podium is the late Gopikamohan Bhattacharya, professor at Kurukshetra University.

he left for Calcutta at the age of fourteen. There he studied many subjects, including mathematics about which he was passionate. As a young man, he was persuaded to take up the study of Navya-Nyāya by Gaurinath Sastri, who, he said, "encouraged me to enter the dense and thorny world of Navya-Nyāya when I was considering more favourably the sunny world of Kāvya and Alaṃkāra". He studied Navya-Nyāya with Anantakumar Tarkatirtha and then, while doing his MA at Calcutta University, with

Mihir K. **Chakraborty**, Benedikt **Löwe**, Madhabendra Nath **Mitra**, Sundar **Sarukkai** (*eds.*). Logic, Navya-Nyāya & Applications. Homage to Bimal Krishna Matilal. College Publications, London, 2008. Studies in Logic 15. pp. xi–xvii.

Received by the editors: 1 May 2007; 14 February 2008.
Accepted for publication: 11 November 2008.

FIGURE 2. Matilal in Toronto, 1976.

Taranatha Tarkatirtha. In 1957 he was appointed as lecturer in the Government Sanskrit College. He continued to study Nyāya with a number of eminent pandits, including Sri Kalipada Tarkacarya and Sri Madhusudana Nyayacarya. Under their guidance, he completed a traditional degree, that of Tarkatīrtha, Master of Logic and Argument, in 1962. Such was his enthusiasm that there are even rumours that he went to his wedding with a volume of Navya-Nyāya in his pocket! For some time prior to this, Matilal had been in correspondence with Daniel Ingalls, who suggested to him the possibility of moving to Harvard in order to acquaint himself with the work being done by W. V. O. Quine in philosophical and mathematical logic. Breaking with traditional patterns Matilal followed this advice, completing his PhD at Harvard in 1965 having attended Quine's classes and continued his studies in mathematical logic with Dagfinn Føllesdal. In his doctoral thesis, *The Navya-Nyāya Doctrine of Negation* [6], published by Harvard University Press in 1968, he gives voice to his growing conviction, emerging from this exposure to contemporary logic, that "India should not, indeed cannot, be left out of any general study of the history of logic and philosophy". This was to be the first statement of a thesis to the defence of which he devoted his academic life, that our philosophical understanding of the fundamental problems of logic and philosophy is enriched if the ideas of the Indian scholars are brought to bear in the modern discussion. His further researches into Navya-Nyāya, as well as into Indian logic more generally, were published in a range of path-breaking books, including *Epistemology, Logic and Grammar in Indian Philosophical Analysis* [5, 3], *Logic, Language and Reality* [7], and *The Character of Logic in India* [8].

It is without doubt very fitting that a conference on Logic, Navya-Nyāya, and its application should therefore be held in Calcutta to commemorate Matilal's enormous contribution to the field. In some ways, this conference has its origins fifty-five years ago, in 1951, when D. H. H. Ingalls published his *Materials for the Study of Navya-Nyāya Logic* [2]. What Ingalls managed to do in this book, above all else, was to 'read' the logical theory of Navya-Nyāya with the benefit of contemporary work in logic, especially the work of his Harvard colleague W. V. O. Quine. He demonstrated, simply but brilliantly, that the distinctions, techniques and concepts that had been developed by the Naiyāyikas were not mere works of hair-splitting sophistry, as they had appeared to the logically untutored indological eye, but were rather sophisticated achievements in logical theory. Before Ingalls, one of the few people who could be said to have achieved something similar was Stanislaw Schayer, the brilliant student of the Polish logician Łukasiewicz, who tried to re-interpret the early Nyāya theory of inference according to modern logic, much as Łukasiewicz had sought to re-interpret the Aristotelian syllogism. Ingalls was himself very much aided in his work, I should add, by the doctoral thesis of the Calcutta scholar Saileswar Sen, published from Wageningen in 1924 under the title *A Study on Mathurānātha's Tattvacintāmani-rahasya* [9]. Saileswar Sen states that

> it was in 1920, when I was a student of the University of Calcutta, that I made up my mind to prosecute research studies in Hindu Philosophy in a Dutch University,

a decision that led him eventually to Amsterdam, where he worked under the supervision of the great Vaiśeṣika scholar, B. Faddegon. It is especially fitting that this link between Amsterdam and Calcutta, forged by a shared devotion to the study of logic, should be continued by this conference with the invaluable dedication of Benedikt Löwe to its organisation and the gracious participation of Johan van Benthem. Another scholar from Amsterdam, Frits Staal, wrote a sequence of break-through articles in Navya-Nyāya logic in the early 1960s, now collected in his book *Universals: Studies in Indian Logic and Linguistics* [10]. Staal also supervised the doctoral work of Cornelis Goekoop, which resulted in an important publication, *The Logic of Invariable Concomitance in the Tattvacintāmaṅi* [1]. It is perhaps not a coincidence that Matilal chose to publish his second book with the Dutch publisher Mouton.

Ingalls' inspirational approach drew Matilal to Harvard a decade later, and I do not think it would be very controversial to say that Matilal soon showed himself to have a finer logical acumen even than Ingalls himself (Ingalls by this time having already returned from Navya-Nyāya to the "sunny world" of poetics and the translation of poetry). Matilal's interest was in logic per se, as a global human intellectual achievement, and in Indian logic and Navya-Nyāya logic in so far as they were very significant but poorly studied components of that achievement. Indian logic was then, and I believe remains today, a tremendously exciting area for someone to work

FIGURE 3. Matilal giving a talk, presumably during a three months stay in Japan (1984) as a guest of the Japanese government working mainly at the University of Kyoto.

in who is by temperament a philosopher, that is, not so much interested in the history of ideas as in the ideas themselves, in the potential and possibilities they can lead to. For philosophers in the past have often had ideas or thought in ways that did not enter the mainstream of historical development, and a return to those neglected pathways in the history of thought is sometimes intellectually enriching as nothing else can be.

To give an example of what I mean, one has only to consider the dominance of Aristotle's logic on the development of logic in the West, and to think, for instance, how we now admire the Stoics for their anticipations of the propositional calculus. If many other forks in the history of logic in the West were only briefly ventured along, which in many cases we can return to now with profit, how much more so will that be true of an entire non-Western history of logic, branches, trunk-roads and all? So when Matilal wrote about the relationship between Aristotelian and Nyāya logic, as he did in [7, 8], he displayed very little interest indeed in the question that would intrigue an historian of ideas, the question of "possible historical influence". Matilal's interest was in the philosophical relationship between Greek and Indian logic; indeed Matilal was perhaps the first to demonstrate conclusively that there are structural differences between the two that go deeper than contingent differences in formulation or emphasis. Matilal's insistence that Indian logic is to be thought of as operating with what he calls a "property-location" model of sentential structure rather than a subject-predicate model, has wide ranging implications that are still being worked out.

FIGURE 4. Matilal talking to students in Oxford, academic year 1986/87.

A similar spirit can be seen at work in Matilal's ground-breaking work on the informal logic to be found in the debating manuals of the Naiyāyikas, Buddhists, Medics and Jainas, in comparison with each other and with works such as Aristotle's *Topica* and *Sophistici Elenchi.* Here I should highlight in particular Matilal's defence and rehabilitation of the so-called vitaṇḍā "refutation-only" style of debate, in which the proponent advances no thesis at all but merely attacks the opponent's counter-thesis. Matilal simultaneously recognised that such debating positions have an important philosophical value in the construction of sceptical arguments, and offered a defence with the help of speech-act theory and the idea of illocutionary negation. In many ways this epitomises Matilal's approach, which resembles the spirit in which philosophers like Vlastos and Irwin have sought to re-appropriate the early Greeks. So when Matilal writes about Nagārjuna's *catuśkoti* or "tetralemma", his question is not "where did this formula come from?" but "how is it logically possibly to deny all four?" This approach is one which he himself describes at various times, as a "re-thinking of the ancient and medieval Indian philosophers in contemporary terms", a re-conceptualisation and re-appropriation of historical ideas which was seen by him as a "prerequisite" of all creative philosophical thinking.

This brings me to Matilal's contribution to the study of Buddhist logic, where again Matilal both saw the philosophical importance and asked the critical philosophical questions, challenging the theory with problems it had not previously had to address. Matilal was not the first to notice, for example, that Diṅnāga's idea of a "triple-condition" or *trirūpa* seems threatened with redundancy problems, but to him we owe the distinction between an epistemic and a realistic reading of conditions, as well as a formal solution to the redundancy problem. To Matilal is due the idea that the Buddhist use of a double negation in its semantic theory incorporates two different negations, which he called "nominally bound" and "sententially bound", thereby avoiding a triviality objection. In the last ten years there have been several workshops and conferences on Buddhist logic and philosophy of language, and it has seemed evident to me that the trajectory of research over this period has been shaped very greatly by Matilal's framing of the issues. Something similar is true in the field of Jaina logic, where again Matilal asked the philosophical question "Is Jaina logic paraconsistent?", a question that has generated a quite lively debate in recent years.

Many of the issues that earlier Indian logicians had wrestled with resurface, sometimes in a rarified form, in Navya-Nyāya. Matilal's work on negation in Navya-Nyāya, both his book [4] and his [6] (appropriately first published in the Festschrift for Ingalls), are, of course, now standard works. Matilal's 'Q' notation, which formed the basis for the later idea of a "property-location" model, has been the subject of much discussion, and Matilal's conjecture that Navya-Nyāya logic is best understood as a three-valued logic is an ongoing topic of debate. In some ways, it seems to me that the field of Navya-Nyāya studies has been slower to take off than some of the other areas of research Matilal's work has opened up, and this is of course both an irony and a pity. But with conferences such as this one, with the gradual publication of better editions and translations, and with the continuing search for appropriate tools and concepts from modern logic to assist in its interpretation, I should confidently predict that Matilal's work on Navya-Nyāya logic may yet well prove to be one of his most enduring legacies. I think we shall be talking about Matilal's ideas, and wrestling with the challenges he has set, for many a good year to come.

References

[1] Cornelis Goekoop. *The Logic of Invariable Concomitance in the Tattvacintāmaṇi: Gangesa's Anumitinirupana and Vyaptivada with Introduction, Translation and Commentary.* D. Reidel, Dordrecht, 1967.

[2] Daniel H. H. Ingalls. *Materials for the Study of Navya-Nyāya Logic*, volume 40 of *Harvard Oriental Series*. Harvard University Press, Cambridge Massachusetts, 1951.

[3] Bimal K. Matilal. *Epistemology, Logic and Grammar in Indian Philosophical Analysis.* Oxford University Press, Oxford, 2nd edition, 2005.

[4] Bimal Krishna Matilal. *The Navya-Nyāya Doctrine of Negation: The Semantics and Ontology of Negative Statements in Navya-Nyāya Philosophy*, volume 46 of *Harvard Oriental Series*. Harvard University Press, Cambridge, Massachusetts, 1968.

[5] Bimal Krishna Matilal. *Epistemology, Logic and Grammar in Indian Philosophical Analysis*. Mouton, The Hague, 1st edition, 1971.

[6] Bimal Krishna Matilal. Double Negation in Navya-Nyāya. In Masatoshi Nagatomi, Bimal Krishna Matilal, Jeffrey Moussaieff Masson, and Edward Dimock, editors, *Sanskrit and Indian Studies. Essays in Honor of Daniel H. H. Ingalls*, volume 2 of *Studies of Classical India*. Reidel, 1980.

[7] Bimal Krishna Matilal. *Logic, Language and Reality: Indian Philosophy and Contemporary Issues*. Motilal Banarsidass, Delhi, 1985.

[8] Bimal Krishna Matilal. *The Character of Logic in India*. Suny Series in Indian Thought, Texts and Studies. State University of New York, Albany, 1998.

[9] Saileswar Sen. *A Study on Mathurānātha's Tattvacintāmaṅi-rahasya*. G. van der Hoogt, Wageningen, 1924.

[10] Frits Staal. *Universals: Studies in Indian Logic and Linguistics*. Chicago University Press, Chicago, 1988.

Rough Set Theory: A Temporal Logic View

Mohua Banerjee, Md. Aquil Khan*

Department of Mathematics and Statistics, Indian Institute of Technology, Kanpur 208 016, India

E-mail: {mohua,mdaquil}@iitk.ac.in

1 Introduction

Rough set theory was introduced by Pawlak [16, 17] in 1982, and since then, work on it has proceeded in many directions. In this paper, we have tried to study rough sets from a temporal viewpoint.

In classical rough set theory, most of the concepts discussed are static, in the sense that time does not play any role. The basic notion is that of an *approximation space*, considered by Pawlak to be a set with an equivalence (*indiscernibility*) relation on it. A practical means of obtaining an approximation space is an *information system*, which is a set of objects with a collection of *attributes*, and an assignment of attribute values to the objects for each attribute. Any information system gives rise to an approximation space, and conversely. A temporal dimension was introduced to the study of information systems by Orłowska, and a *dynamic information system* was defined in [11]. On the side of applications, a notion of *temporal information system* has been used by Synak [14].

Recently, Pagliani [13] has considered *dynamic spaces* to represent different categories of dynamic phenomena. These may be looked upon as "generalized approximation spaces", as they are given by sets with collections of arbitrary binary relations on them. Families of approximation spaces thus form a special case of dynamic spaces. In this article, we are interested in such sequences of approximation spaces over the same domain, and call these *dynamic approximation spaces.* The intention is to study situations where the partition on the domain changes/evolves with time.

In terms of information systems, a partition on the domain may change due to different reasons, e.g., because of variation in the set of attributes of the objects with time, or objects taking different attribute values at different time points, or, a combination of both. It is not difficult to see that addition or deletion of attributes may be required with inflow of information. On the other hand, availability of more information may also warrant enlarging the set of attribute values, due to say, a finer classification of categories.

However, we note that this work does not address the possible reasons behind the change in partitions. Given any partition on the domain, a

*The authors should like to thank the referees for their valuable comments.

Mihir K. **Chakraborty**, Benedikt **Löwe**, Madhabendra Nath **Mitra**, Sundar **Sarukkai** (*eds.*). Logic, Navya-Nyāya & Applications. Homage to Bimal Krishna Matilal. College Publications, London, 2008. Studies in Logic 15. pp. 1–20.

Received by the editors: 28 April 2007; 3 May 2008.
Accepted for publication: 7 September 2008.

subset of objects would be "precisely describable" (*definable*) if it is the union of some equivalence classes. But in general, this may not be the case, and so the subset is termed *rough*. Our focus is on the behaviour of rough sets in dynamic approximation spaces. Objects of the domain may belong to *positive*, *possible*, *boundary* or *negative* regions of a rough set, and with change in the underlying partition, may transit between these regions at various stages of time. Questions such as the following could be raised.

Q1. Does the partition become finer with time?

Q2. Can a time point be reached after which the partition becomes static?

Q3. For each object, is there a time point at which it becomes distinguishable from all other objects?

Q4. Could two rough sets X and Y be related such that each object gets into the positive region of X at some future time point, and before that it is in the negative region of Y?

Q5. Do we have an object such that it is not even in the possible region of a given rough set X at any time point?

Q6. What are the objects that are currently in the boundary region of X, but will get into one of its "certain" (viz. positive/negative) regions in the future?

Q7. Is X, which is currently rough, definable at the next time point, and remain so in all future time? In other words, could its boundary region be erased from the next time point onwards?

Questions like these lead us to identify different patterns of changes of the partition. For example, the gain of information with time may be such that hitherto indistinguishable objects become distinguishable. It is also possible that a stage t is reached after which the partition does not change — e.g., if the attributes deleted are *dispensable*, leading eventually to a *reduct* [17] of the attribute set at stage t. A time point may also be reached where we can distinguish every object from another. Considering this variety of changes, different types of dynamic approximation spaces are defined in § 3. The section also relates dynamic information systems with dynamic approximation spaces. We restrict attention to finite dynamic approximation spaces.

A formal logical approach is adopted here. Many logical systems have been defined to study rough sets in approximation spaces (cf., e.g., [7, 1, 2]). Temporal operators have been brought in by Orłowska [11, 12] to study a logic of dynamic information systems. In this paper, we introduce a propositional modal logic **TRL**, the models of which are based on finite dynamic approximation spaces. The language of this logic has temporal operators as well as modal operators for "necessity" and "possibility". Different types of changes in the partition and questions of the kind mentioned above, are expressible in it. The system and its properties are presented in §§ 4 to 6.

The strong relationship between logics emerging from rough set theory and the modal logic **S5** has been discussed in detail in literature (cf., e.g., [1]). The logic **TRL** provides no exception: it has a strong connection with temporal logic and **S5**. Many proposals of combinations of temporal and other modal logics can be found, e.g., in [3, 4, 5, 6, 8, 9, 15]. But the semantics of **TRL** differs from the systems presented in these, as also from the one presented by Orłowska in [11, 12]. It will be shown that **TRL** semantics is determinable through a combination [5] of temporal and modal semantics thus: a **TRL**-frame can be regarded as the *fusion* of a finite number of binary *product* frames, the latter being composed from a finite temporal frame and a family of **S5**-frames. Moreover, the satisfiability of well formed formulae with respect to a model on the **TRL**-frame can be defined using a kind of *fibring*. We elaborate on this in § 7. The next section presents the requisite preliminaries, and § 8 concludes the article.

2 Preliminaries

We present some basic concepts related to rough set theory. An *approximation space* is a pair (U, R), where U is a non-empty set and R an equivalence relation on it. As mentioned in the Introduction, a subset X of U may not, in general, be exactly described using (the partition induced by) R. It is recognized by the *lower* and *upper approximations* ($\underline{X}_R, \overline{X}_R$ respectively) defined as follows. We denote by $[x]_R$ the equivalence class of the element x.

$$\underline{X}_R := \{x \in U : [x]_R \subseteq X\}; \quad \overline{X}_R := \{x \in U : [x]_R \cap X \neq \varnothing\}.$$

The elements of X are then classified using only the information provided by R. An element $x(\in U)$ is said to be a *positive* or *negative element* of X according as $x \in \underline{X}_R$ or $(\overline{X}_R)^c$. In the former case, we are certain that it is an element of X, while in the latter that is not so. The sets $\underline{X}_R$ and $(\overline{X}_R)^c$ are thus the "positive" and "negative" regions of X respectively. The set $\overline{X}_R$ is the "possible" region, and $\overline{X}_R \setminus \underline{X}_R$ gives the uncertain "boundary" region comprising the *boundary elements* of X. In these terms, X is *definable* in (U, R), provided there is no boundary element of X. A set X is *rough*, if it is not definable.

A practical source of approximation spaces is an *information system* [17]:

Definition 2.1. An information system is a tuple $\mathcal{S} := (U, A, \{\mathrm{Val}_a\}_{a \in A}, f)$ where

- U is a non-empty set of objects;
- A is a non-empty set of attributes;
- Val_a for each attribute a is a non-empty set, the elements of which are called values of attribute a;
- $f : U \times A \to \cup \{\mathrm{Val}_a : a \in A\}$ is such that $f(x, a) \in \mathrm{Val}_a$, for any $x \in U$, $a \in A$.

So f assigns a unique value to each object x for any attribute a. Given an information system $\mathcal{S} := (U, A, \{\mathrm{Val}_a\}_{a \in A}, f)$, the *indiscernibility relation* on $\mathcal{S}$ denoted by $\mathrm{Ind}(\mathcal{S})$ is an equivalence relation on U defined by:

$$x \ \mathrm{Ind}(\mathcal{S}) \ y, \text{ if and only if } f(x, a) = f(y, a) \text{ for all } a \in A.$$

If $x \ \mathrm{Ind}(\mathcal{S}) \ y$, then objects x and y are indiscernible or indistinguishable with respect to the information provided by the information system $\mathcal{S}$. Let $\mathcal{C}$ be a map from the set of all information systems to the set of all approximation spaces defined by $\mathcal{C}(\mathcal{S}) := (U, \mathrm{Ind}(\mathcal{S}))$. It is not difficult to show that $\mathcal{C}$ is onto.

Orłowska [11] extended the notion of an information system by adding the concept of time. A set T of "time points" and a linear order $<$ on T is included to give

Definition 2.2. A tuple $\mathcal{DS} := (U, A, \{\mathrm{Val}_a\}_{a \in A}, T, <, f)$ is called a *dynamic information system*, where

- U, A, Val_a are as in Definition 2.1;
- T is a non-empty set of time points;
- $<$ is a linear order on T;
- $f : U \times T \times A \to \cup \{\mathrm{Val}_a : a \in A\}$ is such that $f(x, t, a) \in \mathrm{Val}_a$, for any $x \in U$, $t \in T$, $a \in A$.

We consider a special case: A dynamic information system $\mathcal{DS} := (U, A, \{\mathrm{Val}_a\}_{a \in A}, T, <, f)$ is said to be *finite time*, if $T := \{1, 2, \ldots, N\}$, N is a natural number and $<$ is the natural linear order on T.

Thus in case of a dynamic information system, the value that f assigns to an object x for any attribute a, becomes dependent on the chosen time point t. Let us note that the attribute set A does not vary with time. In the next section, we formally define finite dynamic approximation spaces, and see that these are related with finite time dynamic information systems in the same way as approximation spaces are related with information systems.

3 Finite dynamic approximation space

Definition 3.1. A *finite dynamic approximation* space is a finite sequence $\mathfrak{F} := \mathcal{F}_1, \mathcal{F}_2, \ldots, \mathcal{F}_N$, where $\mathcal{F}_i := (U, R_i)$, $i = 1, 2, \ldots, N$, are approximation spaces.

From the definition of dynamic information system it follows that corresponding to each time point, there is an information system: for $t \in T$, take the information system $\mathcal{DS}_t := (U, A, \{\mathrm{Val}_a\}_{a \in A}, f_t)$, where $f_t(x, a) = f(x, t, a)$ for all $x \in U$ and $a \in A$. Thus given a dynamic information system $\mathcal{DS}$, we obtain a family of approximation spaces $\{\mathcal{C}(\mathcal{DS}_t)\}_{t \in T}$ ($\mathcal{C}$ as in § 2). In particular, we have:

Observation 3.2. With every finite time dynamic information system, one can associate a unique finite dynamic approximation space such that the ith approximation space in the collection is obtained from the information system corresponding to the ith point in T. We call such a dynamic approximation space *standard*, and denote it $\mathfrak{F}_{\mathcal{DS}}$.

Using the fact that $\mathcal{C}$ is onto, it is easy to see that given a family $\{(U, R_i)_{i \in I}\}$ of approximation spaces with a linear order $<$ on the index set I, there is a dynamic information system $\mathcal{DS} := (U, A, \{\mathrm{Val}_a\}_{a \in A}, I, <, f)$, with the set I indexing time and such that $\mathcal{C}(\mathcal{DS}_i) = (U, R_i)$, $i \in I$.

Thus, given a finite dynamic approximation space $\mathfrak{F}$, we obtain a finite time dynamic information system $\mathcal{DS}$ such that $\mathfrak{F}_{\mathcal{DS}} = \mathfrak{F}$. We have now arrived at:

Proposition 3.3. Every finite dynamic approximation space is a standard dynamic approximation space and conversely.

As remarked in § 1, there may be various kinds of changes in the partition of a domain with time, resulting in different dynamic approximation spaces. For instance, a dynamic approximation space could reflect refinement of partitions on some domain, with the inflow of information. Further, in the ideal situation, the refinement (which may occur after a stage) would lead to the finest possible partition — that with singleton sets. We define the following types of dynamic approximation spaces.

Definition 3.4. Let $\mathfrak{F} := \{\mathcal{F}_1, \mathcal{F}_2, \ldots, \mathcal{F}_N\}$, where $\mathcal{F}_i := (U, R_i)$, $i = 1, \ldots, N$. Then $\mathfrak{F}$ is

- *monotonic refined*, if $R_{i+1} \subseteq R_i$ for all $i \in \{1, 2, \ldots, N-1\}$, $N \geq 2$;
- *eventually monotonic refined*, if there exists a j, $1 \leq j < N$ such that $R_{i+1} \subseteq R_i$ for all $i \in \{j, j+1, \ldots, N-1\}$;

- *eventually discrete*, if $\mathfrak{F}$ has a discrete approximation space $\mathcal{F}_i$ (i.e., R_i is the identity relation), and all $\mathcal{F}_j$, $j > i$, are discrete;
- *saturated*, if there is an $i < N$ such that $R_i = R_j$ for all $j \geq i$; and
- *ideal*, if $\mathfrak{F}$ is monotonic refined and has a discrete approximation space.

The set $\mathfrak{F}$ is clearly saturated if it is eventually discrete or ideal. The only technical restriction is that in the former case, the $\mathcal{F}_i$ in the definition has $i < N$, and in the latter, the discrete approximation space in $\mathfrak{F}$ is some $\mathcal{F}_i$ with $i < N$. Let us observe some simple instances in terms of information systems, where we obtain some of the dynamic approximation spaces defined above.

Example 3.5. Let $T := \{t_1, t_2, \ldots, t_n\}$ be the time points with the ordering $t_1 < t_2 < \ldots < t_n$. In contrast to the case of a dynamic information system, we may have the attribute set varying with time. Suppose no deletion of attributes takes place. Let $\mathcal{S}_{t_i} := (U, A_{t_i}, \{\mathrm{Val}_a\}_{a \in A_{t_i}}, f_{t_i})$ be an information system such that

- $A_{t_i} \subseteq A_{t_{i+1}}$, $i = 1, 2, \ldots n-1$, $(*)$
- if $a \in A_{t_i} \cap A_{t_j}$, we have $f_{t_i}(x, a) = f_{t_j}(x, a)$, for all $x \in U$.

The second condition asserts that if a is found amongst the attributes considered at two different time points, the value assigned for it to any object remains unchanged. So we have the collection of information systems $\mathfrak{S} := \{\mathcal{S}_{t_1}, \ldots, \mathcal{S}_{t_n}\}$. As in Observation 3.2, consider $\mathfrak{F}_{\mathfrak{S}}$. It is easy to see that $\mathfrak{F}_{\mathfrak{S}}$ is monotonic refined. The ideal situation for $\mathfrak{F}$ would of course require that we reach a time point, say t_k, such that for any two objects $x, y \in U$, there exists an attribute $a \in A_{t_k}$ with $f_{t_k}(x, a) \neq f_{t_k}(y, a)$. However, it could also be the case that there exists a j, $2 \leq j < n-1$ such that $A_{t_i} \subseteq A_{t_{i+1}}$, $i = j, j+1, \ldots n-1$, and then $\mathfrak{F}_{\mathfrak{S}}$ would be eventually monotonic refined.

We note that if we do not have the condition $(*)$, i.e., we are also deleting attributes with time (for instance, when some attribute is not considered important enough), then $\mathfrak{F}_{\mathfrak{S}}$ may not be monotonic refined. In fact, there may be coarsening or refinement, or no pattern may be followed at all. If we disallow addition, but allow deletion of attributes, then there would be progressive coarsening of the partitions. In this case, if $\mathfrak{F}_{\mathfrak{S}}$ is saturated after time t_i (say), we know that the attributes deleted from A_{t_i} are *dispensable* [17]. In fact, one may eventually reach a *reduct* of A_{t_i}, i.e., a minimal attribute set preserving the classification due to A_{t_i}.

Example 3.6. Let $\mathcal{DS} := (U, A, \{\text{Val}_a\}_{a\in A}, T, <, f)$ be a dynamic information system. Gain in information may result in a finer classification of categories in the attribute value set, making it change with time. Now suppose the categorization obeys the following for any $x, y \in U,\ a \in A,\ t, t' \in T$:

$$\text{if } f(x,t,a) \neq f(y,t,a), \text{ then for } t < t',\ \ f(x,t',a) \neq f(y,t',a).$$

For instance, at time t there may be categories of possessing "between 2 and 4 moons" and "between 5 and 7 moons", but in a refined categorization one may be able to determine if the objects have exactly 2, 3 or 4 moons. Clearly, $\mathfrak{F}_{\mathcal{DS}}$ is then monotonic refined. As before, if we reach a stage with an attribute such that all objects take different values for it, then $\mathfrak{F}_{\mathcal{DS}}$ would become ideal. But it could also be the case that $\mathfrak{F}_{\mathcal{DS}}$ is not of any of the defined types.

Observation 3.7.

- Suppose $\mathfrak{F}$ is monotonic refined and $x \in U$ is a positive/negative element of $X \subseteq U$ in (U, R_i), for some $i = 1, 2, \ldots, N$. Then x remains so in all the future approximation spaces, i.e., in all (U, R_j), $j = i, i+1, \ldots, N$. Hence if a subset X is definable in some approximation space of $\mathfrak{F}$, it will remain so in all the future approximation spaces.

- Let $\mathfrak{F}$ be eventually discrete. Then every object of U finally becomes a "definite" element, that is, an approximation space is eventually reached where that element is either positive or negative.

In the sequel, we shall see how these properties, among others, may be "formally" expressed.

4 The logic TRL

In this section, we formally present the syntax and semantics of the logic **TRL**. We shall show that questions raised earlier are expressible through well-formed formulae (wffs) of the language, and their validity can be checked.

4.1 Syntax

The language of **TRL** is that of a modal propositional logic, with a unary modal connective $\Box$ (for *necessity*), unary temporal connectives $\oplus$ (*next*), $\ominus$ (*previous*) and the binary temporal connectives $\mathcal{U}$ (*until*), $\mathcal{S}$ (*since*). So wffs are given as:

$$\bot \mid \top \mid p \in \mathcal{P} \mid \neg X \mid X \vee Y \mid \Box X \mid \ominus X \mid \oplus X \mid X\,\mathcal{U}\,Y \mid X\,\mathcal{S}\,Y,$$

where $\bot, \top$ are the logical constants for *false* and *true* respectively, and $\mathcal{P}$ denotes the (countable) set of all propositional variables. Apart from the usual derived connectives $\wedge, \longrightarrow, \longleftrightarrow, \Diamond$ (for *possibility*), there are the following:

- $\mathrm{F}X := \top\, \mathcal{U}\, X$ (*some time in the future*);
- $\mathrm{G}X := \neg\mathrm{F}\neg X$ (*always in the future*);
- $\mathrm{P}X := \top\, \mathcal{S}\, X$ (*some time in the past*);
- $\mathrm{H}X := \neg\mathrm{P}\neg X$ (*always in the past*).

4.2 Semantics

Let $\mathfrak{F}$ be a (standard) finite dynamic approximation space $\mathcal{F}_1, \mathcal{F}_2, \ldots, \mathcal{F}_N$, where $\mathcal{F}_i := (U, R_i)$, $i \in \{1, 2, \ldots, N\}$. A *valuation function* V on $\mathfrak{F}$ is a map from the set $\mathcal{P}$ of propositional variables to 2^U. A **TRL**-*model* is $\mathcal{M}_i := (\mathcal{F}_i, V)$, $i \in \{1, 2, \ldots, N\}$.

The *satisfiability* of a wff X in a model $\mathcal{M}_i$, $i \in \{1, 2, \ldots, N\}$ at $w \in U$ with respect to $\mathfrak{F}$ (in notation $\mathcal{M}_i, w \models_{\mathfrak{F}} X$) is defined inductively:

- $\mathcal{M}_i, w \models_{\mathfrak{F}} \top$ and $\mathcal{M}_i, w \not\models_{\mathfrak{F}} \bot$;
- For each propositional variable p, $\mathcal{M}_i, w \models_{\mathfrak{F}} p \Longleftrightarrow w \in V(p)$;
- The standard definitions for the Boolean cases;
- $\mathcal{M}_i, w \models_{\mathfrak{F}} \Box X \Longleftrightarrow \mathcal{M}_i, w' \models_{\mathfrak{F}} X$ for all w' such that wR_iw';
- $\mathcal{M}_i, w \models_{\mathfrak{F}} \oplus X \Longleftrightarrow i < N$ and $\mathcal{M}_{i+1}, w \models_{\mathfrak{F}} X$;
- $\mathcal{M}_i, w \models_{\mathfrak{F}} \ominus X \Longleftrightarrow i > 1$ and $\mathcal{M}_{i-1}, w \models_{\mathfrak{F}} X$;
- $\mathcal{M}_i, w \models_{\mathfrak{F}} X\, \mathcal{U}\, Y \Longleftrightarrow$ there is a j with $N \geq j \geq i$ such that $\mathcal{M}_j, w \models_{\mathfrak{F}} Y$, and for all k such that $i \leq k < j$, $\mathcal{M}_k, w \models_{\mathfrak{F}} X$;
- $\mathcal{M}_i, w \models_{\mathfrak{F}} X\, \mathcal{S}\, Y \Longleftrightarrow$ there is a j with $1 \leq j \leq i$ such that $\mathcal{M}_j, w \models_{\mathfrak{F}} Y$, and for all k such that $j < k \leq i$, $\mathcal{M}_k, w \models_{\mathfrak{F}} X$.

Observation 4.1. Conditions of satisfiability of the derived connectives F and G are then obtained as follows:

- $\mathcal{M}_i, w \models_{\mathfrak{F}} FX \Longleftrightarrow$ there exists a j with $N \geq j \geq i$ such that $\mathcal{M}_j, w \models_{\mathfrak{F}} X$;
- $\mathcal{M}_i, w \models_{\mathfrak{F}} GX \Longleftrightarrow$ for all j with $N \geq j \geq i$, $\mathcal{M}_j, w \models_{\mathfrak{F}} X$.

The satisfiability of the connectives P and H can be obtained similarly.

Two notions of satisfiability/validity of a wff in a dynamic approximation space may be introduced, according as it is satisfiable in a model of $\mathfrak{F}$, or, in particular, in the first model of $\mathfrak{F}$.

Definition 4.2. Fix $\mathcal{M}_i = (\mathcal{F}_i, V), i \in \{1, 2, \ldots, N\}$.

- A wff φ is said to be *1-satisfiable* in $\mathfrak{F}$ if there exists a valuation function V on $\mathfrak{F}$ such that $\mathcal{M}_1, w \models_{\mathfrak{F}} \varphi$ for some $w \in U$.
- The formula φ is said to be *satisfiable* in $\mathfrak{F}$ if there exists a valuation function V on $\mathfrak{F}$ such that $\mathcal{M}_j, w \models_{\mathfrak{F}} \varphi$ for some $w \in U$ and for some j such that $1 \leq j \leq N$.

Extensions to corresponding notions of validity are made in the usual way. A formula φ is *1-valid under a valuation V in* $\mathfrak{F}$, if for all $w \in U$, $\mathcal{M}_1, w \models_{\mathfrak{F}} \varphi$. It is *1-valid in* $\mathfrak{F}$, if for any valuation function V on $\mathfrak{F}$ and all $w \in U$, $\mathcal{M}_1, w \models_{\mathfrak{F}} \varphi$; and it is *1-valid*, if it is 1-valid in all $\mathfrak{F}$. Similarly, φ is *valid in* $\mathfrak{F}$ if for any valuation function V on $\mathfrak{F}$, all $w \in U$, and all j such that $1 \leq j \leq N$, $\mathcal{M}_j, w \models_{\mathfrak{F}} \varphi$; and finally, φ is *valid*, if it is valid in all $\mathfrak{F}$.

Observation 4.3.

(a) By Proposition 3.3, a wff is (1-)valid if and only if it is (1-)valid in the class of standard dynamic approximation spaces.

(b) If a wff is 1-satisfiable in $\mathfrak{F}$ then it is also satisfiable in $\mathfrak{F}$, but the converse is not true. However, for a given wff φ, φ is satisfiable in $\mathfrak{F}$, if and only if $F\varphi$ is 1-satisfiable in $\mathfrak{F}$.

All the valid wffs of **S5** are valid in **TRL** as well. Some valid temporal wffs are given in the following proposition. As intended, the usual axioms of linear temporal logic [10] are valid here, with modifications to account for finiteness both in the past and future (the last expressed by wffs 2(b) and 2(c) of the Proposition 4.4).

Proposition 4.4.

1. (a) $X \,\mathcal{U}\, Y \longleftrightarrow Y \vee (X \wedge \oplus(X \,\mathcal{U}\, Y))$;
   (b) $X \,\mathcal{S}\, Y \longleftrightarrow Y \vee (X \wedge \ominus(X \,\mathcal{S}\, Y))$;
2. (a)$X \,\mathcal{U}\bot \longrightarrow \bot$; (b) $P\neg\ominus\top$; (c) $F\neg\oplus\top$;
3. (a) $GX \longrightarrow X$; (b) $GX \longrightarrow G\neg\oplus\neg X$;
4. $G(X \longrightarrow Y) \longrightarrow (GX \longrightarrow GY)$; Similarly for H;
5. (a) $X \longrightarrow \neg\oplus\neg\ominus X$; (b) $X \longrightarrow \neg\ominus\neg\oplus X$;
6. $G(X \longrightarrow \oplus X) \longrightarrow G(X \longrightarrow GX)$;
7. (a)$\ominus X \longrightarrow \neg\ominus\neg X$; (b) $\oplus X \longrightarrow \neg\oplus\neg X$.

4.3 Set-theoretic interpretation

Given $\mathfrak{F} := \{\mathcal{F}_1, \mathcal{F}_2, \ldots, \mathcal{F}_N\}$, and a valuation function V on $\mathfrak{F}$, let $V_i(\varphi) := \{w \in W : \mathcal{M}_i, w \models_{\mathfrak{F}} \varphi\}, i = 1, 2, \ldots N$. So $V_i(p) = V(p)$, for any propositional variable p. Following are the set-theoretic interpretations of some **TRL**-connectives and their combinations. (1)(a)-(b) and (3)(a)-(b) give the interpretations in terms of rough sets.

1. (a) $V_i(\Box\varphi) = \underline{V_i(\varphi)}_{R_i}$; (b) $V_i(\Diamond\varphi) = \overline{V_i(\varphi)}_{R_i}$;
2. (a) $V_i(\oplus\varphi) = V_{i+1}(\varphi), i < N$; (b) $V_i(\ominus\varphi) = V_{i-1}(\varphi), i > 1$;
3. (a) $V_i(\oplus\Box\varphi) = \underline{V_{i+1}(\varphi)}_{R_{i+1}}, i < N$;
   (b) $V_i(\ominus\Box\varphi) = \underline{V_{i-1}(\varphi)}_{R_{i-1}}, i > 1$;
4. (a) $V_i(F\varphi) = \bigcup_{N \geq j \geq i} V_j(\varphi)$; (b) $V_i(G\varphi) = \bigcap_{N \geq j \geq i} V_j(\varphi)$;
5. (a) $V_i(P\varphi) = \bigcup_{1 \leq j \leq i} V_j(\varphi)$; (b) $V_i(H\varphi) = \bigcap_{1 \leq j \leq t} V_j(\varphi)$.

Now the questions of the kind posed in the Introduction can be looked upon as questions of (1-)validity/(1-)satisfiability of some **TRL**-wffs. Suppose Q1-Q7 are asked regarding a finite dynamic approximation space $\mathfrak{F}$, where $\mathcal{F}_1$ is considered to be the current time point. We have the following.

- $X, Y \subseteq U$. Let p, q be propositional variables and V a valuation function such that $V(p) := X$ and $V(q) := Y$.
- Q1 and Q2 are about whether $\mathfrak{F}$ is monotonic refined, or saturated (respectively). The wffs for these shall be given in the next section.
- Q3 is equivalent to checking the 1-validity of the wff $F(\Diamond p \rightarrow \Box p)$.
- Q4 is equivalent to checking the 1-validity of $\neg\Diamond q\, \mathcal{U}\, \Box p$ under V.
- Q5 is equivalent to checking the 1-satisfiability of $G\neg\Diamond p$ under V.
- Condition of Q6 is satisfied by those objects o for which we have $\mathcal{M}_1, o \models (\Diamond p \wedge \neg\Box p) \wedge F\ (\Box p \vee \neg\Diamond p)$, where $\mathcal{M}_1 := (\mathcal{F}_1, V)$.
- Q7 is answered by checking if the **TRL**-wff $\Diamond p \wedge \neg\Box p$ is 1-satisfiable and $\oplus G(\Diamond p \rightarrow \Box p)$ is 1-valid under V. A related question is looked at in § 8.

5 TRL and the special dynamic approximation spaces

We can characterize, through the language of **TRL**, the special dynamic approximation spaces of Definition 3.4. The following gives wffs that are (1-)valid *precisely* in the families of the named type. It should be mentioned that the characterizing wffs are chosen in order to work for both notions of satisfiability (cf. Definition 4.2).

Proposition 5.1. Let p be a propositional variable.

1. $G\ (\Box p \longrightarrow (\oplus\Box p \vee \neg\oplus\top))$, characterizes monotonic refined $\mathfrak{F}$, i.e the wff is valid in a dynamic approximation space $\mathfrak{F}$, if and only if $\mathfrak{F}$ is monotonic refined.

2. $F\ominus G\ (\Box p \longrightarrow \oplus\Box p \vee \neg\oplus\top)$ characterizes eventually monotonic refined $\mathfrak{F}$.

3. $F\ (G\ominus(X \longleftrightarrow \oplus X))$, where X does not involve $\oplus, \ominus, \mathcal{U}, \mathcal{S}$, characterizes saturated $\mathfrak{F}$.

4. $G\ (\Box p \longrightarrow (\oplus\Box p \vee \neg\oplus\top)) \wedge F\ (\Box p \vee \Box\neg p)$ characterizes ideal $\mathfrak{F}$.

5. $F\ G\ (\Diamond p \longrightarrow \Box p)$ characterizes eventually discrete $\mathfrak{F}$.

Proof. In each case, we only prove the converse part, i.e., if the given wff is valid in $\mathfrak{F}$ then $\mathfrak{F}$ belongs to the named family.

1. Suppose $\mathfrak{F} = \mathcal{F}_1, \mathcal{F}_2, \ldots, \mathcal{F}_N$ is not monotonic refined where $\mathcal{F}_i := (W, R_i)$. Then there exist R_i and R_{i+1} such that $aR_{i+1}b$ but not aR_ib for some $a, b \in W$. Let us consider a valuation function V such that $V(p) := W \setminus \{b\}$. Then clearly $\mathcal{M}_i, a \not\models_{\mathfrak{F}} \Box p \longrightarrow \oplus\Box p \vee \neg\oplus\top$, where $\mathcal{M}_i := (W, \mathcal{F}_i, V)$ and hence $\mathcal{M}_1, a \not\models_{\mathfrak{F}} G(\Box\alpha \longrightarrow (\oplus\Box\alpha \vee \neg\oplus\top))$.

2. Let $\mathfrak{F}$ be not eventually monotonic refined. So we must have $R_N \not\subseteq R_{N-1}$. Then there exist $a, b \in W$ such that aR_Nb but not $aR_{N-1}b$. Let us consider a valuation function V such that $V(p) := W \setminus \{b\}$. Then clearly $\mathcal{M}_{N-1}, a \not\models_{\mathfrak{F}} \Box p \longrightarrow \oplus\Box p \vee \neg\oplus\top$, where $\mathcal{M}_i := (W, \mathcal{F}_i, V)$ and hence $\mathcal{M}_1, a \not\models_{\mathfrak{F}} F\ominus G(\Box p \longrightarrow \oplus\Box p \vee \neg\oplus\top)$.

3. Suppose $\mathfrak{F}$ is not saturated. Then $R_{N-1} \neq R_N$. So either

   1. there exist $a, b \in W$ such that $(a, b) \in R_{N-1}$ and $(a, b) \notin R_N$, or
   2. there exist $a, b \in W$ such that $(a, b) \notin R_{N-1}$ and $(a, b) \in R_N$.

   Take a valuation V such that $V(p) := W \setminus \{b\}$. Then in both cases we obtain $\mathcal{M}_{N-1}, a \not\models_{\mathfrak{F}} (\Box p \longleftrightarrow \oplus\Box p)$. Hence $\mathcal{M}_1, a \not\models_{\mathfrak{F}} F(G\ominus(\Box p \longleftrightarrow \oplus\Box p)$.

4. Since $G(\Box\alpha \longrightarrow (\oplus\Box\alpha \vee \neg\oplus\top))$ is valid in $\mathfrak{F}$, it must be monotonic refined. If possible let $\mathfrak{F}$ be not discrete. Then we must have $a, b \in W$ such that $b \in [a]_{R_i}$ for all i. Let us consider a valuation function V such that $V(p) := W \setminus \{b\}$. Then $\mathcal{M}_i, a \not\models_{\mathfrak{F}} \Box p$ for all i where $\mathcal{M}_i := (W, \mathcal{F}_i, V)$. Also $\mathcal{M}_i, a \not\models_{\mathfrak{F}} \Box\neg p$ for all i. Thus $\mathcal{M}_1, a \not\models_{\mathfrak{F}} F(\Box p \vee \Box\neg p)$.

5. This can be proved similarly.

Q.E.D.

Instances of valid/satisfiable statements, involving a mixture of the different modalities are given in the following straightforward proposition. Some may be derived as consequences of Proposition 5.1. A formula X is said to be a *propositional wff*, in brief $X \in$ PF, if X involves only Boolean connectives.

Proposition 5.2.

1. $(F\Box X \vee P\Box X) \longrightarrow P(\neg\ominus\top \wedge G\Diamond X)$ is valid for $X \in$ PF.

2. $F(X \longrightarrow \oplus X)$ is satisfied at all worlds, in all models except the last, on any $\mathfrak{F}$ with $|\mathfrak{F}| \geq 2$.

3. $F\Diamond(X \wedge Y) \longrightarrow F(\Diamond X \wedge \Diamond Y)$, for $X, Y \in$ PF, is valid.

4. $\Diamond X\, \mathcal{U}\, (\Diamond X \longrightarrow \Box X)$, for $X \in$ PF, is valid in all eventually discrete $\mathfrak{F}$.

5. The following are valid in all monotonic refined $\mathfrak{F}$, for $X \in$ PF.

   (a) $\neg\oplus\neg G\ominus(\Box X \longrightarrow \oplus\Box X)$

   (b) $(X \longrightarrow \Box X) \longrightarrow G(X \longrightarrow \Box X)$.

   (c) $\Box X \longrightarrow G\Box X$, $\neg\Diamond X \longrightarrow G\neg\Diamond X$.

6. In a monotonic refined $\mathfrak{F}$, if $\mathcal{M}_1, w \models_{\mathfrak{F}} X \longrightarrow F\Box X$ for all $w \in W$, $X \in$ PF, then there exists a j such that $\mathcal{M}_1, w \models_{\mathfrak{F}} \oplus^j(X \longrightarrow \Box X)$ for all $w \in W$.

7. $\Box X \wedge F(\neg\Box X \wedge \Diamond X)$ for $X \in$ PF is satisfiable, but not valid.

8. $F(\Diamond X \longrightarrow \Box X)$ for $X \in$ PF is satisfiable, but not valid.

9. The following are 1-valid:

   (a) $G\Box(X \wedge Y) \leftrightarrow (G\Box X \wedge G\Box Y)$;

   (b) $F\Box(X \wedge Y) \rightarrow (F\Box X \wedge F\Box Y)$.

Let us interpret some of the above: The wff 1 says that if an object is in the lower approximation of a set X at some time (current, past, or future), then it will always be in the upper approximation of X. In $\mathfrak{F}$, the satisfiability of wff 4 at all objects at a time point guarantees that every object will move to a *certain* region of the set X at some future time, and before that it remains in the upper approximation of X. We note that even if $\mathfrak{F}$ has a single discrete approximation space, this wff would be valid in it. The wff 5b expresses the fact that if a set is definable at the current time then it will remain so at all the future times. The wff in 5c expresses that if an object is in a certain region of X, it will remain so at all the future times. Item 6 of the proposition says that if each element of X is an element of the lower approximation of X with respect to some approximation space in $\mathfrak{F}$, then there must be an approximation space in $\mathfrak{F}$ where X becomes definable. A similar result holds if we replace $\Box$ by $\Diamond$. Wff 7 is satisfied by all those elements which are necessarily inside the set X at the current time but which move to the boundary region of X at some future time. In a monotonic refined $\mathfrak{F}$, satisfiability of wff 8 at all objects at a time point means that the set X becomes definable eventually (even if it is rough at that time point). The wff 9a says that an object x is a positive element of the set $X \cap Y$ in all approximation spaces of $\mathfrak{F}$, if and only if it is a positive element of both X and Y in all approximation spaces of $\mathfrak{F}$. But if we replace the operator G by F in the wff, the equivalence does not hold in general. The side that holds is given by wff 9b. In a monotonic refined $\mathfrak{F}$, however, we would have the equivalence.

We note that Observation 3.7 presented earlier, has found expression in the language of **TRL**.

6 Further features of satisfiability

Let the *length* of a formula φ, denoted by $|\varphi|$, be defined as the number of symbols that occur in φ. By $\mathrm{sub}(\varphi)$, we denote the set of all sub-wffs of the wff φ.

Definition 6.1. Let $\mathfrak{F} := \{\mathcal{F}_1, \mathcal{F}_2, \ldots, \mathcal{F}_n\}$ be a dynamic approximation space, where $\mathcal{F}_i := (W, R_i), i = 1, 2, \ldots, n$, and let V be a valuation function on $\mathfrak{F}$. Let $\mathcal{M}_i := (\mathcal{F}_i, V), i = 1, 2, \ldots, n$, and $s \in W$. Then for a wff φ, we have the following notation:

$$[\mathcal{M}_i, s]_{\mathfrak{F},V,\varphi} := \{\beta \in \mathrm{sub}(\varphi) : \mathcal{M}_i, s \models_{\mathfrak{F}} \beta\}.$$

By an easy induction on the complexity of the formula $\beta \in \mathrm{sub}(\varphi)$, we can prove the proposition below. The objects $\mathfrak{F}$, V, and $\mathcal{M}_i$, are as in Definition 6.1.

Proposition 6.2. Let $i, j \in \{1, 2, \ldots, n\}$, $i < j$, and φ be some wff such that

$$[\mathcal{M}_i, s]_{\mathfrak{F},V,\varphi} = [\mathcal{M}_j, s]_{\mathfrak{F},V,\varphi}, \text{ for all } s \in W.$$

Then the following holds:

$$[\mathcal{M}_k, s]_{\mathfrak{F},V,\varphi} = [\mathcal{M}_k, s]_{\mathfrak{F}',V,\varphi},$$

for all $s \in W$ and for all k such that $\mathcal{F}_k \in \mathfrak{F}'$, where $\mathfrak{F}'$ is the dynamic approximation space

$$\{\mathcal{F}_1, \mathcal{F}_2, \ldots, \mathcal{F}_{i-1}, \mathcal{F}_j, \mathcal{F}_{j+1}, \ldots, \mathcal{F}_n\}.$$

We then have

Proposition 6.3. Let φ be a wff that is 1-satisfiable in $\mathfrak{F} := \{\mathcal{F}_1, \mathcal{F}_2, \ldots, \mathcal{F}_\ell\}$, where $\mathcal{F}_i := (W, R_i), i = 1, 2, \ldots, \ell$. Let $|W| = n$. Then there exists a $\mathfrak{F}^*$ with $|\mathfrak{F}^*| \leq f(|\varphi|, n)$ for some function f, such that φ is 1-satisfiable in $\mathfrak{F}^*$.

Proof. By the given condition, there exists a valuation function V on $\mathfrak{F}$ and a $w \in W$ such that

$$\mathcal{M}_1, w \models_{\mathfrak{F}} \varphi,$$

where $\mathcal{M}_j := (\mathcal{F}_j, V), j \in \{1, 2, \ldots, \ell\}$. Let $W := \{w_1, w_2, \ldots, w_n\}$ and $B_{kr} := [\mathcal{M}_k, w_r]_{\mathfrak{F},V,\varphi}, k \in \{1, 2, \ldots, n\}$. With each $\mathcal{M}_k$, we associate an element

$$(B_{k1} \times B_{k2} \times \cdots \times B_{kn})$$

of the set $B^n := \underbrace{B \times B \times \cdots \times B}_{n \text{ times}}$, where $B = 2^{\text{sub}(\varphi)}$. Then we observe that $[\mathcal{M}_k, s]_{\mathfrak{F},V,\varphi} = [\mathcal{M}_t, s]_{\mathfrak{F},V,\varphi}$ for all $s \in W$, if and only if $\mathcal{M}_k$ and $\mathcal{M}_t$ associate to the same element of B^n. Note that $|B^n| \leq 2^{|\varphi|n}$.

Now consider $f(|\varphi|, n) := 1 + 2^{|\varphi|n}$. If $|\mathfrak{F}| \leq 1 + 2^{|\varphi|n}$, then we have nothing to prove. So let $|\mathfrak{F}| > 1 + 2^{|\varphi|n}$. Then we must have $a, b \in \{2, 3, \ldots, \ell\}$ such that

$$[\mathcal{M}_a, s]_{\mathfrak{F},V,\varphi} = [\mathcal{M}_b, s]_{\mathfrak{F},V,\varphi} \text{ for all } s \in W.$$

Therefore, using Proposition 6.2 we obtain a $\mathfrak{F}_1$ such that $|\mathfrak{F}_1| < |\mathfrak{F}|$ and

$$\mathcal{M}_1, w \models_{\mathfrak{F}_1} \varphi.$$

If $|\mathfrak{F}_1| \leq 1 + 2^{|\varphi|n}$, we are done; otherwise we again apply the above arguments on $\mathfrak{F}_1$.

Proceeding in this way, finally we get the desired result. Q.E.D.

Observation 6.4.

(a) Using Observation 4.3 (b), we obtain Proposition 6.3 even in the case that φ is satisfiable in a $\mathfrak{F}$.

(b) If $\mathfrak{F}$ in Proposition 6.2 is monotonic refined (ideal) then the corresponding $\mathfrak{F}'$ is also monotonic refined (ideal), so Proposition 6.3 applies to these classes of $\mathfrak{F}$ as well.

Remark 6.5. The question of decidability of **TRL** is open. However, we note that if one obtains a result of the kind "a **TRL**-wff φ is satisfiable, if and only if it is satisfiable in a $\mathfrak{F}$ with domain of cardinality less than $g(|\varphi|)$ for some function g", decidability would be established using Proposition 6.3.

7 TRL in perspective

As mentioned in the Introduction, a lot of work has been done on investigating modal logics from the temporal angle. Orłowska proposed the logic **DIL** [11, 12] for dynamic information systems. The atomic wffs of **DIL** are of the form (x, a, v), $x \in$ VarOb, $a \in$ VarA, $v \in$ VarV, where VarOb, VarA, and VarV are the sets of object variables, attribute variables and variables of attribute values, respectively. Besides the Boolean connectives, there are the temporal operators F and P. The wffs are evaluated at the time points of a dynamic information system, i.e., the satisfiability relation is a subset of the set $T \times$ Fml, where Fml is the set of all wffs. But it is clear that **DIL** is inadequate for our purpose. There are no modal operators to express lower/upper approximations, and so properties of rough sets cannot be discussed.

Finger and Gabbay [4] introduced a general methodology to combine an arbitrary logical system L with a pure propositional temporal logic T (such as linear temporal logic with "Since" and "Until"). The resultant combined logic is called $T(L)$. We find that the logic $T(\mathbf{S5})$, among all extant relevant systems, is the closest to **TRL**. The main differences are pointed out here.

The wffs of $T(\mathbf{S5})$ form a proper subset of **TRL**-wffs: only those wffs of **TRL** are considered in which temporal operators do not come in the scope of $\Box$. So, for instance, $\Box(\alpha \ \mathcal{U} \ \beta)$ is not a wff of $T(\mathbf{S5})$. Note that if we restrict ourselves to this kind of wffs in **TRL**, it would deprive **TRL** of one of its salient features. We would not be able to compute expressions such as $\underline{(\underline{X}_{R_1})}_{R_2}$, i.e., where there is an iteration of lower/upper approximation operators corresponding to different relations. In **TRL**, the syntactic counterpart (with respect to 1-validity) of the afore-mentioned expression is the wff $\oplus\Box\ominus\Box p$.

The semantics of $T(\mathbf{S5})$ is based on a structure of the form $\mathcal{M}_t :=$ $(T, <, g)$, where $(T, <)$ represents the underlying flow of time and g is a function which associates each time point with a tuple (M_t, w_t). The model

$M_t := (W_t, R_t, V_t)$ is an **S5**-model and $w_t \in W_t$. In order to give the satisfiability relation, **S5**-wffs are divided into two classes: (a) a wff belongs to the set of Boolean combinations, $\mathrm{BC}_{\mathbf{S5}}$, if and only if it is built from other wffs by using one of the Boolean connectives $\neg$ or $\wedge$, or any other connective defined only in terms of those; (b) it belongs to the set of "monolithic" formulae $\mathrm{ML}_{\mathbf{S5}}$ otherwise. The satisfiability relation is defined as follows:

1. $\mathcal{M}_T, t \models \alpha, \alpha \in \mathrm{ML}_{\mathbf{S5}} \Longleftrightarrow M_t, w_t \models \alpha$ where $g(t) := (M_t, w_t)$;
2. $\mathcal{M}_T, t \models \alpha\, \mathcal{U}\, \beta \Longleftrightarrow$ there is an $s \in T$ such that $t < s$ and $\mathcal{M}_T, s \models \beta$ and for every $u \in T$, if $t < u < s$ then $\mathcal{M}_T, u \models \alpha$.

The Boolean and "Since" cases are defined in the standard way. The difference between this semantics and that of **TRL** becomes clear now. In $T(\mathbf{S5})$, for each time point, the world w_t and the model M_t are fixed. So when one moves to a time point t, an **S5**-wff must be evaluated at the world w_t, and across time points, these worlds would vary in general. In **TRL**, however, when one moves across time points using only the $\oplus, \ominus, \mathcal{U}$ or $\mathcal{S}$ operators, the world at which a wff is to be evaluated, remains the same.

TRL as a combination of modal logics

We refer to [5] for the following.

Definition 7.1. Consider two modal frames $\mathcal{F}_1 := (W_1, R_1)$ and $\mathcal{F}_2 := (W_2, R_2)$ with binary accessibility relations. The frame $\mathcal{F}_1 \times \mathcal{F}_2 := (W_1 \times W_2, R_1^*, R_2^*)$ is called their *product*, where $R_1^* := \{((x,z),(y,z)) : xR_1y,\ z \in W_2\}$, and $R_2^* := \{((z,x),(z,y)) : xR_2y,\ z \in W_1\}$.

Definition 7.2. Let $\mathcal{F}_i := (W, R_i)$, $i = 1, \ldots, N$, be a collection of frames over the same set of possible worlds. Their *fusion* is the frame $\mathcal{F}_1 * \mathcal{F}_2 * \ldots * \mathcal{F}_N := (W, R_1, R_2, \ldots, R_N)$.

Let $\{\mathcal{F}_1, \mathcal{F}_2, \ldots, \mathcal{F}_N\}$ be a finite set of **S5**-frames over the same set of possible worlds, say $\mathcal{F}_i := (W, R_i)$, $i \in \{1, 2, \ldots, N\}$. Consider a finite linear temporal frame $T := (\{1, 2, \ldots, N\}, <)$, where $<$ is the natural linear order on $\{1, 2, \ldots, N\}$. Further, let $\mathcal{F}_i^* := T \times \mathcal{F}_i$, $i \in \{1, 2, \ldots, N\}$, and $\mathcal{F} := \mathcal{F}_1^* * \mathcal{F}_2^* * \ldots * \mathcal{F}_N^*$. So $\mathcal{F} = (T \times W, <^*, R_1^*, R_2^*, \ldots, R_N^*)$.

A valuation function V on $\mathcal{F}$, is (as before) a function from the set $\mathcal{P}$ of propositional variables to 2^W. Let us now consider a *selection function* f on $\mathcal{F}$, which is a bijective map from the set T to the set $\{R_1^*, R_2^*, \ldots, R_N^*\}$. Let us call $(\mathcal{F}, f)$ a **TRL**-*structure.*

One can define *satisfiability* of a wff X with respect to a 'model' $\mathcal{M} := (\mathcal{F}, f, V)$ at $(t, w) \in T \times W$ (in notation $(t, w) \models_{\mathcal{M}} X$) inductively, as follows. We omit the Boolean cases.

- For each propositional variable p, $(t, w) \models_{\mathcal{M}} p \iff w \in V(p)$;
- $(t, w) \models_{\mathcal{M}} \Box X \iff (t, y) \models_{\mathcal{M}} X$ for all (t, y) with $(t, x) f(t)(t, y)$;
- $(t, w) \models_{\mathcal{M}} \oplus X \iff$ there is a pair (t', w) such that $(t, w) <^* (t', w)$ and $(t', w) \models_{\mathcal{M}} X$; A similar definition for $(t, w) \models_{\mathcal{M}} \ominus X$;
- $(t, w) \models_{\mathcal{M}} X\mathcal{U}Y \iff$ there exist $(t_1, w), (t_2, w), \ldots, (t_j, w)$ such that $t = t_1$, $(t_1, w) <^* (t_2, w) <^* \ldots <^* (t_j, w)$. Further, $(t_j, w) \models_{\mathcal{M}} Y$, and for all $k = 1, 2, \ldots, j-1$, $(t_k, w) \models_{\mathcal{M}} X$; A similar definition for $(t, w) \models_{\mathcal{M}} X\mathcal{S}Y$.

Here, the role of the selection function f is to pick out the R_i^* with respect to which the $\Box$ modality is to be evaluated. This is the basic idea of *fibring*.

That the above semantics may be identified with that of **TRL**, is established by the following proposition.

Proposition 7.3. There exists a bijective mapping g between the sets of all **TRL** structures and finite dynamic approximation spaces. Moreover, for every wff φ, valuation function V, $\mathcal{M} := (\mathcal{F}, f, V)$, $g((\mathcal{F}, f)) := \mathfrak{F}$, $\mathcal{M}_i, w \models_{\mathfrak{F}} X$, if and only if $(i, w) \models_{\mathcal{M}} X$, using the same valuation function V in both the semantics.

Proof. Given a **TRL** structure $\mathcal{T} = (\mathcal{F}, f)$ where

$$\mathcal{F} = (T \times W, <^*, R_1^*, R_2^*, \ldots, R_N^*)$$

and $T = \{1, 2, \ldots, N\}$, we define a dynamic approximation space $\mathfrak{F}_{\mathcal{T}}$: the ith approximation space in $\mathfrak{F}_{\mathcal{T}}$ is $(W, R_{f(i)}^*)$, $i = 1, 2, \ldots, N$. Let us take $g(\mathcal{T}) := \mathfrak{F}_{\mathcal{T}}$. It is easy to verify that this g is bijective. The other part of the proposition can be proved by a simple induction on the complexity of the wff φ. Q.E.D.

8 Conclusions

A temporal dimension is associated to the theory of rough sets, by considering dynamic approximation spaces. A formal logic **TRL** is proposed, which has as models finite dynamic approximation spaces. It is observed that different kinds of dynamic approximation spaces can be characterized through the language. Properties of **TRL** are presented, and it is put in perspective of related modal systems.

Clearly, there are several issues that need to be addressed now —e.g., a proof procedure for the logic, and the question of its decidability. We have a formulation of the first— that, however, is beyond the scope of this article. The second is answered in case of domains of given finite cardinality. The general problem is open, as remarked earlier.

As mentioned in the Introduction, our focus in this work has been to investigate the behaviour of rough sets when a partition on the domain evolves with time. The logic **TRL** appears appropriate for the purpose. However, with the given semantics, there are problems in expressing some properties. For example, consider statements such as (a) "there is a discrete approximation space in the dynamic approximation space", or (b) "a given set X is definable in some future approximation space". (Note that (b) is a more general form of question Q7 posed in the Introduction.) These would be expressed by wffs of the kind $\mathrm{F}\varphi$. But evaluation of $\mathrm{F}\varphi$ at different objects would give *different* time points where φ would be satisfied, whereas we should like φ to be satisfied at one time point for all objects.
One way out is to add the "all state" modal operator A to the language, defined as:

$$\mathcal{M}_i, w \models_{\mathfrak{F}} AX \Longleftrightarrow \mathcal{M}_i, w' \models_{\mathfrak{F}} X \text{ for all } w'.$$

Then (a) corresponds to the 1-validity of the wff $\mathrm{F}A(\Diamond p \rightarrow \Box p)$, and (b) is equivalent to checking the 1-validity of the same wff under a V, where $V(p) := X$. (p is a propositional variable.)

If one is interested in addressing the *causes* for the changes in partition in terms of information systems, **TRL** is not adequate. We have seen earlier that attribute sets or attribute-value sets may vary with time, or a combination of both may take place to result in a dynamic approximation space. Characterization of these situations would be possible if the language is equipped with expressions for attributes and their values. For instance, we may think of extending the logic **DIL** (cf. § 7). As we want modalities for time as well as for the objects, we can consider atomic wffs to be of the form (a, v) and p. Evaluation of wffs would be done in appropriate information systems, at points of the form (x, t), where x and t are respectively the object and time point. So the wffs of this logic may be given by the following scheme:

$$\bot \mid \top \mid (a, v) \mid p \mid \neg X \mid X \vee Y \mid \Box X \mid \ominus X \mid \oplus X \mid X \, \mathcal{U} \, Y \mid X \, \mathcal{S} \, Y.$$

We leave this issue for future study.

It may be noted here that the equivalence relations R_i defining dynamic approximation spaces, may well be replaced by other binary relations, and collections of binary relations. The semantics for corresponding logics could also be traced out by the combination procedure presented in § 7. These systems would deal with the case of generalized approximation spaces/rough sets. An interesting direction of study now could be the investigation of algebras generated by **TRL** and these logics.

References

[1] Mohua Banerjee and Md. Aquil Khan. Propositional Logics from Rough Set Theory. In James F. Peters, Andrzej Skowron, Ivo Düntsch, Jerzy Grzymała Busse, Ewa Orłowska, and Lech Polkowski, editors, *Transactions on Rough Sets VI*, volume 4374 of *Lecture Notes in Computer Science*, pages 1–25, New York, 2007. Springer.

[2] Mohua Banerjee and Md. Aquil Khan. Formal Reasoning with Rough Sets in Multiple-Source Approximation Systems. *International Journal of Approximate Reasoning*, 49(2):466–477, 2008.

[3] Clare Dixon, Brandon Bennet, Ullrich Hustadt, Enrico Franconi, and Maarten de Rijke. Combinations of Modal Logics. *Artificial Intelligence Review*, 17(1):1–20, 2000.

[4] Marcelo Finger and Dov M. Gabbay. Adding a Temporal Dimension to a Logic System. *Journal of Logic, Language and Information*, 1:203–233, 1992.

[5] Dov M. Gabbay and Valentin B. Shehtman. Product of Modal Logics, Part 1. *Logic Journal of the Interest Group in Pure and Applied Logic (IGPL)*, 6(1):73–146, 1998.

[6] Joseph Y. Halpern, Moshe Y. Vardi, and Ron van der Meyden. Complete Axiomatizations for Reasoning about Knowledge and Time. *SIAM Journal on Computing*, 33(3):674–703, 2004.

[7] Jan Komorowski, Zdzisław Pawlak, Lech Polkowski, and Andrzej Skowron. Rough Sets: A Tutorial. In Sankar K. Pal and Andrzej Skowron, editors, *Rough Fuzzy Hybridization: A New Trend in Decision-Making*, pages 3–98. Springer Verlag, Singapore, 1999.

[8] Richard Ladner and John H. Reif. The Logic of Distributed Protocols. In Joe Y. Halpern, editor, *Proceedings of the 1986 Conference on Theoretical Aspects of Reasoning about Knowledge*, pages 207–221, San Francisco, CA, USA, 1986. Morgan Kaufmann Publishers Inc.

[9] Daniel J. Lehmann. Knowledge, Common Knowledge and Related Puzzles. In Tiko Kameda, Jayadev Misra, Joseph Peters, and Nicola Santoro, editors, *Proceedings of the third annual ACM symposium on Principles of distributed computing, Vancouver, British Columbia, Canada, August 27–29, 1984*, pages 62–67. ACM Press, 1984.

[10] Zohar Manna and Amir Pnueli. *The Temporal Logic of Reactive and Concurrent Systems Specification*. Springer, 1991.

[11] Ewa Orłowska. Dynamic Information System. *Fundamenta Informaticae*, 5:101–118, 1982.

[12] Ewa Orłowska. Kripke Semantics for Knowledge Representation Logics. *Studia Logica*, 49:255–272, 1990.

[13] Piero Pagliani. Pretopologies and Dynamic Spaces. *Fundamenta Informaticae*, 21:1001–1019, 2001.

[14] Piotr Synak. Temporal Feature Extraction from Temporal Information Systems. In Ning Zhong, Zbigniew W. Ras, Shusaku Tsumoto, and Einoshin Suzuki, editors, *Foundations of Intelligent Systems*, volume 2871 of *Lecture Notes in Computer Science*, pages 270–278, Berlin, 2003. Springer.

[15] Michael Wooldridge, Clare Dixon, and Michael Fisher. A Tableau-Based Proof Method for Temporal Logics of Knowledge and Belief. *Journal of Applied Non-Classical Logics*, 8(3):225–258, 1998.

[16] Zdzisław Pawlak. Rough Sets. *International Journal of Computing and Information Sciences*, 11(5):341–356, 1982.

[17] Zdzisław Pawlak. *Rough Sets. Theoretical Aspects of Reasoning about Data.* Kluwer Academic Publishers, Dordrecht, 1991.

Natural Logic: A view from the 1980s

Johan van Benthem

Institute for Logic, Language and Computation, Universiteit van Amsterdam, Plantage Muidergracht 24, 1018 TV Amsterdam, The Netherlands

Department of Philosophy, Stanford University, Stanford CA, 94305, U.S.A.

E-mail: johan@science.uva.nl

"Natural Logic" is a somewhat loose, but popular and suggestive term for recurrent attempts over the last decades at describing basic patterns of human reasoning directly in natural language without the intermediate of some formal system. One main type of inference (though not the only one) where this idea works well is so-called "monotonicity reasoning", involving valid replacement of predicates by predicates with smaller or larger extensions. Essentially, this pattern of inference goes back to the distribution doctrine of traditional logic. With varying motivations, ideas for a simple "surface-syntax" based calculus of reasoning have been rediscovered many times, in such diverse areas as logic, philosophy, linguistics, computer science, and nowadays also cognitive science. In particular, the natural logic program had a certain flowering, going beyond the ubiquitous example of plain monotonicity reasoning, in the formal semantics community in The Netherlands in the 1980s. This paper is the text of a survey lecture given in May 2007 at the request of some colleagues at Stanford University and PARC Research Center, who are working on practical information retrieval from texts by combinations of parsing and simple logical inference. Before re-inventing the wheel (a very common phenomenon in this area), it seems useful to see what rolling stock existed two decades earlier. With a slightly more historical slant, the following text was also presented at the workshop "Logic, Rationality and Interaction" in Beijing 2007. Its purpose is mainly to record the main lines of the work on natural logic done in the 1980s in my own Dutch logic and language environment, and also, to present the broader issues that seemed relevant to us then, and are still so today, even in a broader interdisciplinary environment.

1 Introduction: from classical to modern logic

For beginning logic students in Amsterdam arriving in the late 1960s like the present author, the following "standard example" in our introductory course was supposed to show once and for all how the modern 19th century logic of Boole and Frege came to supersede traditional logic. De Morgan's famous inference runs as follows:

"All horses are animals. So, all horse tails are animal tails."

Mihir K. **Chakraborty**, Benedikt **Löwe**, Madhabendra Nath **Mitra**, Sundar **Sarukkai** (*eds.*). Logic, Navya-Nyāya & Applications. Homage to Bimal Krishna Matilal. College Publications, London, 2008. Studies in Logic 15. pp. 21–42.

Received by the editors: 2 May 2007; 17 March 2008.
Accepted for publication: 17 April 2008.

This is supposed to show the inadequacy of the traditional logic of 'monadic predicates', because binary relations are essential to understand the validity of the inference. And the latter are brought out in the standard first-order logical forms that students are trained in:

$$\forall x(\mathsf{H}x \to \mathsf{A}x) \models \forall x((\mathsf{T}x \wedge \exists y(\mathsf{H}y \wedge Rxy)) \to (\mathsf{T}x \wedge \exists y(\mathsf{A}y \wedge Rxy))).$$

What is more, we can understand the general phenomenon behind this valid first-order inference as follows. Syntactically, we are replacing a predicate "horse" by one with a larger extension "animal" at some position in an assertion: "having a ␣ tail". And what licenses this "upward replacement" in this context is the following semantic property:

Definition 1.1. A formula $\varphi(X)$ is upward monotone with respect to the predicate X if for all models $\mathbf{M}$, if $\mathbf{M}, \mathbf{P}, \mathbf{s} \models \varphi(X)$, and $\mathbf{P} \subseteq \mathbf{Q}$, then $\mathbf{M}, \mathbf{Q}, \mathbf{s} \models \varphi(X)$. Here, we interpret the syntactic predicate X as the set $\mathbf{P}$, while $\mathbf{s}$ is a tuple of objects whose length equals the arity of X.

This property is ubiquitous in first-order logic, but also beyond it in generalized quantifier theory, and the model theory of inductive definitions in logics with fixed-point operator.[1]

Actually, there is another way of looking at the same notion which is closer to the original inferences.[2] One can also think of a formula $\varphi(P)$ with P already interpreted, and then view the inference as replacing this P by some concrete predicate Q with a larger extension. While perhaps a bit less rigorous, this is how most people understand upward monotonicity in practice, and we shall talk this way henceforth. Incidentally, it will be clear that there is also a *downward* version of the preceding notions, allowing for replacement by stronger predicates having a smaller extension. If you own no animals, you own no horses.

This semantic behaviour has a syntactic counterpart, as may be seen in the occurrence of the predicate H in the first-order formula $\mathsf{T}x \wedge \exists y(\mathsf{H}y \wedge Rxy)$. Let us call an occurrence of X in $\varphi(X)$ **positive** if it lies in the scope of an even number of negations, or stated differently, if the formula $\varphi(X)$ is created using only the following inductive syntax rules:

$$\mathsf{H}\text{-free formulas} \mid \wedge \mid \vee \mid \forall \mid \exists.$$

[1] Often, monotonicity is defined looking at all occurrences of the predicate X in $\varphi(X)$. But our definition also works for just one specific occurrence. The single-occurrence based version seems more natural for seeing the fine-structure of inference. Monotonicity inferences can be executed occurrence by occurrence, with no need for more complex "simultaneous replacements".

[2] The observations made in this section may be found with many authors since the 1960s, witness [22, 1], and the sources in [25].

The occurrence of H in $\mathsf{T}x \wedge \exists y(\mathsf{H}y \wedge Rxy)$ is positive in this sense, and in a natural extended sense, so is that of the predicate '*horse*' in the expression '*tail of a horse*'.

Now, it is easy to see that syntactic positive occurrence implies semantic monotonicity (a sort of "soundness", if you wish), by a straightforward induction on the construction of formulas.[3] But it is much less trivial that the converse "completeness" direction holds. Still, it does, witness a well-known model-theoretic result from the 1950s:

Theorem 1.2 (Lyndon's Theorem). A first-order formula is semantically monotone in X if and only if it is equivalent to a formula whose only occurrences of X are positive.

Lyndon's Theorem does not hold for arbitrary extensions of first-order logic, but the above soundness property is quite general: positive occurrence does imply monotonicity in many higher-order logics — and as we shall see, also in natural language. Thus, modern logic provides the right forms for the above family of inferences[4], and it backs these up with important meta-theorems probing the broader extent of the phenomenon.

2 Distribution in traditional logic

But the above De Morgan story is misleading and historically false. Inferences like the one with the horse tail were well within the scope of traditional logic, which was much subtler than many modern critics acknowledge. They blame it for defects it never had — all the way to the invective of Geach [10], who even saw demoniacal political consequences, in his phrase "The Kingdom of Darkness". Indeed, monotonicity inference is closely related to the *Aristotelean Syllogistic*, the main tool of traditional logic. Now the latter is often viewed as a trivial theory of single-quantifier inferences with patterns $\mathsf{Q}AB$ on unary predicates A and B: at best a "fragment of monadic first-order logic". But this modern view in terms of formal systems does no justice to how the Syllogistic really functioned: as a method for *one-step analysis* of statements of any kind into one layer of quantification. In particular, A and B could be predicates with further structure, of whatever expressive complexity (first-order, higher-order, etc.): they are not constrained at all to one fixed formal language. This point may be worth emphasizing. The modern *bottom-up* view of inference as involving formulas constructed explicitly out of atoms is far removed from logical history and from the way we actually reason. We work "*top-down*", unpack some

[3] Again, results for 'negative occurrence' and downward monotonicity are immediate.
[4] It also deals in a dual fashion with "downward monotonic" counterparts.

surface-level quantificational patterns, the fewer the better, and then reason on the basis of those.[5]

Points like the preceding have been made before, and I do not pretend to give a complete history here. The reader is referred to [3] and [22] for some early sources, to [27] for an original computational proposal linking up with automated learning, and to [25] for a more general history. This section is just a brief summary, including my private views about the border line between traditional and modern logic.

Later on, in addition to the syllogistic base system, the medieval scholastics developed the so-called *doctrine of distribution*, a general account of contexts $\varphi(P)$ where the statement was either about "all of P" (the *dictum de omni*), or about "none of P" (the *dictum de nullo*). Again, these contexts could be of any sort of linguistic complexity, where the expression φ might include iterated quantifiers such as "Someone loves every human", or even high-order constructions. Indeed, I should claim that, for the purpose of analyzing ordinary human inference, the modern first-order/higher-order boundary is mainly a mathematical "systems concern" without any clear matching jump in natural reasoning. However this may be, authors like van Eijck, van Benthem, Sanchez Valencia, and Hodges [35, 28, 24, 12] have pointed out in more detail how the distribution principle called *dictum de omni et nullo* corresponded to admissible inferences of two kinds: *downward monotonic* (substituting stronger predicates for weaker ones), and *upward monotonic* (substituting weaker predicates for stronger ones). Traditional logic investigated these phenomena for a wide range of expressions, without any boundary between unary and binary predication — another artifact of viewing history through predicate-logical glasses.

To be sure, this does not mean that all was clear. On the contrary, traditional logic had a major difficulty: providing a systematic account of complex linguistic constructions from which to infer, and in particular, despite lots of valid insights, it wrestled with a good general account of *iterations of quantifiers*. In [4], Dummett makes a lot of this, by saying that Frege's compositional treatment in terms of merely explaining single quantifiers and then letting compositionality do all the rest "solved the problem which had baffled traditional logicians for millennia: just by ignoring it". Again, while there is a kernel of truth to this, there is also a good deal of falsehood. Indeed, as the extensive historical study [25] remarks, it seems more fair to say that De Morgan represents a low point in logical history as far as understanding the scope of monotonicity reasoning is concerned. Things got better after him — but as the author points out tongue-in-cheek,

[5]The top-down view, viewing formal systems as tools for analysis rather than synthesis from atomic components, might be more effective for *teaching* logic as well.

they also got better and better moving back in time to Leibniz and then on to the Middle Ages...

Perhaps not surprisingly then, traditional logicians felt some unfairness when modern logic arrived on the scene, since it attacked a caricature of traditional logic. And indeed, until late in the 20th century, attempts have been made to further develop the Syllogistic into a full-fledged calculus of monotonicity reasoning, witness [26] (going back to versions from the 1960s) and [6]. The claim of Sommers and Englebretsen was that this enterprize provided a viable alternative to first-order logic for bringing out key structures in actual human reasoning in a more congenial way. Still they did not propose turning back the clock altogether. E.g., Sommers's book is up to modern standards in its style of development, providing a systematic account of syntactic forms, an arithmetical calculus for computing positive and negative syntactic occurrence, as well as further inferential schemata generalizing traditional inference patterns like Conversion and Contraposition. While this has not led to a counter-revolution in logic, these points have resonated in other areas, such as linguistics, computer science, and recently also, cognitive science. We now move there.

3 Monotonicity in natural language and generalized quantifier theory

Very similar issues concerning the analysis of reasoning came up in the 1970s and 1980s when linguists and logicians started looking at natural language together (there are several famous joint papers, including Barwise and Cooper's [1]) with fresh eyes, following Richard Montague's pioneering work [17].[6] Suddenly, natural language was no longer 'misleading' as to the correct logical forms, but rather a gold-mine of intriguing insights with remarkable staying power. After all, no one, not even pure mathematicians, has ever seriously switched to predicate logic as a tool of reasoning (but see below). In particular, Montague provided a categorial/type-theoretic analysis of quantifier expressions Q as taking linguistic noun phrases A to noun phrases QA that denote properties of properties B. Deconstructing this forbidding phrasing somewhat, quantifiers may then be viewed semantically as denoting binary relations between predicates, on the pattern

E.g., in this Venn-style diagram format, "All A are B" says that the area $A \backslash B$ is empty, "Some A are B" that the intersection $A \cap B$ has at least one object in it, while the more complex "Most A are B" says that the number of objects in $A \cap B$ exceeds that in $A \backslash B$. Moreover, in addition to judgments of (non-)grammaticality, judgments about valid and invalid inference were now considered relevant to our understanding of natural language, and even

[6]For the state of the art, cf. various chapters in [32].

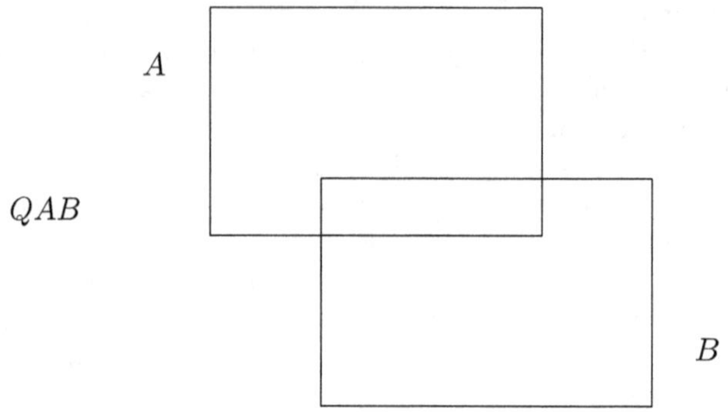

linguists admitted that semantic theories had to account for these.

3.1 Generalized quantifiers and monotonicity

More semantic depth was provided beyond the mechanics of Montague Grammar by Generalized Quantifier Theory: a research program which charted the variety of the quantifier repertoire of natural human languages (cf. [13]), and tried to formulate general laws about expressive power. Again, Monotonicity turned out to play a crucial role across this repertoire. One influential example here was the observation by Bill Ladusaw that so-called "negative polarity items" like "at all", or "ever" flag "negative contexts" in linguistic expressions which allow for downward monotonic entailments from predicates to sub-predicates:

> "If you ever *feel an ache*, I shall cure it" implies "If you ever *feel a headache*, I shall cure it".

As a rule, negative polarity items do not occur in upward entailing positive contexts.

Here are some general facts about monotonicity for basic quantifiers: they can be either upward or downward, in both arguments. E.g., the quantifier "All" is downward monotonic in its left-hand argument, and upward in its right-hand argument, exemplifying the patterns

$$\begin{array}{ll} \downarrow\text{MON} & \text{if } QAB \text{ and } A' \subseteq A, \text{ then } QA'B, \\ \text{MON}\uparrow & \text{if } QAB \text{ and } B \subseteq B', \text{ then } QAB'. \end{array}$$

It is easy to exemplify the other three possible combinations: e.g., "Some" is $\uparrow$MON$\downarrow$. By contrast, a quantifier like "Most" is only MON$\uparrow$, being neither "down" nor "up" on the left. Quantifiers with monotonicity ($\uparrow$ or $\downarrow$) in both arguments are called "doubly-monotonic".

3.2 Conservativity

But Monotonicity is not the only key property found with natural language quantifiers (and NP-forming determiner expressions in general, such as "Mary's"). Here is a further principle which shows how the first argument sets the scene for the second:

$$\text{Conservativity} \quad QAB \text{ if and only if } QA(B \cap A).$$

Conservativity seems to hold in all human languages. One can think of this as a sort of domain or role restriction imposed by the initial predicate A on the predicate B. More generally, the nouns in sentences give us relevant domains of objects in the total universe of discourse, and quantifiers impose a sort of coherence on the total predication expressed.

Taken together, the preceding semantic properties explain what makes particular (logical) notions so special. Generalized Quantifier Theory then charted what sort of expressions pass these tests, getting a grip on what natural languages can say. The following result from [28] is a typical sample, and it shows that the traditional quantifiers may be viewed as the simplest level of *conservative, inference-rich* linguistic expressions, provided we add one more technical condition on denotations saying that the quantifier makes maximal distinctions:

$$\text{Variety} \quad \text{If } A \neq \varnothing, \text{ then } QAB \text{ for some } B, \text{ and } \neg QAC \text{ for some } C.$$

Theorem 3.1. The quantifiers "All", "Some", "No", "Not All" in the *Square of Opposition* are the only ones satisfying Conservativity, Double Monotonicity, and Variety.

But natural language quantifiers can also be classified in other ways, for instance, by means of more algebraic types of inferential property for specific lexical items. A typical example is the rule of "Conversion" already found in traditional logic:

$$\text{Symmetry} \quad QAB \text{ if and only if } QBA.$$

This holds typically for expressions like "Some", "At least n", "No", "All but at most n". Characterizations exist of all quantifiers satisfying Symmetry and other basic properties.

With this bare minimum, we conclude our survey here. For much more detailed information on Generalized Quantifier Theory and its richer agenda, cf. earlier sources like [28, 13], or the recent monograph [20].

4 The "natural logic" program of the 1980s

In the 1980s, the idea arose that the preceding observations had a more general thrust. Natural language is not just a medium for saying and communicating things, but it also has a 'natural logic', viz. a system of simple modules capturing ubiquitous forms of reasoning that can operate directly on natural language surface form without the usual logical formulas. This idea was developed in some detail in [28, 29], whose main proposals we outline here.[7] The main ingredients were to be three modules:

(a) Monotonicity reasoning, or *Predicate Replacement*,

(b) Conservativity, or *Predicate Restriction*, and also

(c) Algebraic laws for inferential features of specific lexical items.

But of course, there are many further natural subsystems in natural language, including reasoning about collective predication, prepositions, anaphora, tense and temporal perspective. The systematic challenge is then to see how much of all this inference can be done directly on natural language surface form, and we shall look at some details below. Another challenge might be how these subsystems manage to *work together* harmoniously in one human mind, and we shall return to this somewhat neglected issue below.

Notice how this way of thinking cuts the cake of reasoning differently from the syntax of first-order logic — redrawing the border-line between traditional and modern logic. E.g., monotonicity inference is both richer and weaker than first- order predicate logic. It is weaker in that it only describes part of all valid quantifier inferences, but it is richer in that it is not tied to any particular logical system, as we observed above (it works for second-order just as well as first-order logic). One intriguing aspect then becomes *where the surplus of first-order logic is really needed.* We shall give two possible answers to this below.

5 Compositional structure, parsing, and free rides for inferences

To get a natural logic going, it is not enough to display single-quantifier inferences of the sort we had before. One also needs to account for the way in which these inferences play in arbitrary *complex sentences*, and here is how this may be done in general, merging ideas from Generalized Quantifier Theory and Categorial Grammar. The earliest source for this calculus seems [28], while our exposition mainly follows [30].

[7] Later on, Sanchez Valencia found an ancestry in the work of C. S. Peirce [24].

5.1 Spreading conservativity

A first example concerns the broader impact of Conservativity. Consider an iterated quantifier sentence of the sort "Every man loves a woman":

$$\mathsf{Q}_1 A R \mathsf{Q}_2 B.$$

Clearly, *both* predicates A and B should have restriction effects. How do they do this? It is not hard to see, and in fact it can be computed in many parsing formalisms, that we have

$$\mathsf{Q}_1 A R \mathsf{Q}_2 B \text{ if and only if } \mathsf{Q}_1 A (R \cap (A \times B)) \mathsf{Q}_2 B.$$

That is, the first predicate restricts the first argument of the binary relation R, while the second predicate restricts the second argument. Based on this and other cases, the semantic and inferential mechanism behind Conservativity might be called *Predicate Restriction*, a first major aspect of natural logic that seems to be at work all through natural language:

Nouns constrain correlated predicate roles.

5.2 Monotonicity in complex sentences

Likewise, to get a full-fledged account of how monotonicity inference functions in complex sentences, we need a grammatical theory that provides an analysis of hierarchical syntactic structure. Just flat strings of words will not do. For instance, I cannot tell whether the occurrence of "women" in

"Johan admires some men and women"

is downward monotonic unless I resolve the scope of the determiner "some". To achieve disambiguation, we can use a logic-friendly grammar formalism, viz. *Categorial Grammar* to obtain a systematic *Monotonicity Calculus.* For a start, consider the sentence

"No mortal man can slay every dragon."

We should like to compute all predicate markings in this sentence, but they cannot be taken at face value. E.g., whether "dragon" is negative depends on the scope of other expressions inside which it occurs. Maybe the reader wants to check that, on the narrow scope reading for "every dragon",[8] readings should come out (intuitively) as follows:

$$\text{“No mortal } \overset{-}{\text{man}} \text{ can slay every } \overset{+}{\text{dragon}}\text{.”}$$

[8]Think of the naturally corresponding first-order formula $\neg\exists x(\mathsf{Mortal\text{-}Man}(x) \wedge \forall y(\mathsf{Dragon}(y) \rightarrow \mathsf{Can\text{-}Slay}(x, y)))$.

E.g., it follows that no mortal *Dutchman* can slay every dragon, or that no mortal man can slay every *animal*. For the wide scope reading of "every dragon" (more artificial, but still acceptable to many people[9]) these markings should come out as follows:

	–		–
"No mortal	man	can slay every	dragon."

But we can be more general. Perhaps surprisingly, other expressions than predicates can also be marked here, when we take a suitably general perspective on sentence construction. For instance, the sentence "*No* mortal man can slay every dragon" clearly implies that "*No or very few* mortal men can slay every dragon". Here the determiner "No or very few" is intuitively weaker than the determiner "No", just as the predicate "animal" is weaker than "dragon". Thus, like predicates, determiners themselves allow for monotonic replacement by suitable items in their linguistic category. This phenomenon is totally general, and the requisite notion of inclusion in arbitrary categories was made precise in the monotonicity calculi of the 1980s, which could handle inferences in arbitrary kinds of expression. Of course, this is best checked against some intuitions. We invite the reader to check that, on the narrow scope reading of "every dragon", markings should come out as follows:

+	–	–	–	–	–	+
"No	mortal	man	can	slay	every	dragon."

5.3 Categorial monotonicity calculus

Speaking generally, we need a linguistic mechanism marking positive/negative occurrences in any category in tandem with the syntactic analysis of given expressions. As it turned out, this can be done quite elegantly in a *categorial grammar*, of the Ajdukiewicz function application type, or the more sophisticated Lambek type which is more like a simple system of function application plus a limited additional operation of ("single-bind") lambda abstraction. For details, we refer to [30, 24]. Here we only state the major rules of the procedure:

Rules come in two kinds:

(a) General rules of composition:

- occurrences in a function head A in applications $A(B)$ retain their polarity,
- occurrences in the body A of a lambda abstract $\lambda x.A$ retain their polarity,

[9] Now think of the formula $\forall y(\mathsf{Dragon}(y) \rightarrow \neg\exists x(\mathsf{Mortal\text{-}Man}(x) \wedge \mathsf{Can\text{-}Slay}(x, y)))$.

though function heads can block the monotonicity marking in their arguments. Notice, e.g., how "Most AB" made its left-hand argument "opaque": it is neither upward or downward. But "Most AB" does pass on monotonicity information in its right-hand argument B, and this demonstrates a second crucial source of information for our calculus:

(b) Specific information about lexical items: e.g., "All" has functional type $e^{-} \to (e^{+} \to t)$.

Here is how the two kinds of information combine. First, in general, a function application $A(B)$ may block the polarity marking of positions in the argument B. E.g., "best (friend)" has no marking left for "friends", as there is no inference to either "best girlfriend" or "best acquaintance". The adjective "best" is highly context- dependent and hence steals the show.

But sometimes monotonicity marking does percolate upwards, when the meaning of the function head A "helps". E.g., "blonde friend" does imply "blonde acquaintance", because the adjective "blonde" has a simple *intersective* meaning forming a Boolean conjunction "blonde $\cap$ B". More generally, if a function head A has type $a \to b$ where the argument type a is marked, the argument position B in applications $A(B)$ will assume that same polarity. This explains how negations switch polarity, how conjunctions just pass them up, and so on. Such markings will normally come from lexical information, but there is one nice twist. They can also be introduced via lambda abstractions $\lambda x_a.M_b$ of type $a \to b$, where the type a gets positive marking. Readers may want to check the semantics for a systematic explanation.

The final ingredient to make this work is the following self- evident rule of calculation. Markings can be computed as long as there is an unbroken string in the parse tree:

(c) *The arithmetic of polarity combination:*

$$\begin{array}{ccccc} ++ & = & + & = & -- \\ +- & = & - & = & -+ \end{array}$$

This is just one mechanism for making natural logic precise. But its basic categorial structure has been rediscovered by many people: it just *is* rather natural! Thus we find one more key aspect of natural logic. Monotonicity marking works in tandem with one's preferred syntactic analysis for natural language — providing fast inferences on the fly.

5.4 Digression: Boolean lambda calculus

For technically inclined readers, here is a summary in terms of *Boolean typed lambda calculus*, the system behind much of the above [30]. Expressions now have "marked types", and we define inductively what it means for an occurrence of a sub-expression to be positive or negative in an expression:

- The occurrence x_a is positive in the term x_a,
- the head M occurs positively in applications $M_{a \to b}(N_a)$,
- if M has type $a^+ \to b$, then N occurs positively in $M_{a \to b}(N_a)$,
- if M has type $a^- \to b$, then N occurs negatively in $M_{a \to b}(N_a)$,
- the body M occurs positively in $\lambda x_a . M_b$, and the resulting type is $a^+ \to b$.

The rest is the earlier computation rule (c), or alternatively, we could have built this feature into the inductive definition. Clearly, this definition can be extended to deal with, not just functional types, but also *product types* $a \cdot b$ allowing for pair formation of objects.

5.5 Meta-theory: Lyndon theorems

This logical perspective raises further issues of its own. One is the "completeness" of the above syntactic marking procedure. Can we be sure that every semantically monotone inferential position will be found in this way? Is there a Lyndon Theorem stating that every semantically monotone occurrence must be positive in the above categorical sense?

This would extend the first-order result. The answer is 'Yes' in the categorial single-bind Lambek Calculus (this is a model-theoretic result proved by brute force in [30]) — but the problem is still open for type theory with Boolean operators in general.

A lambda calculus for natural language has no internal first-/higher-order boundary. The only special thing to first-order quantifiers here is that they have more monotonicity markings than others, in line with our earlier observation about their inferential richness.

5.6 Depth rather than surface after all?

We conclude this section with a worry. When all is said and done, our little "natural logic" turned out to be a rather modern system, requiring a fully-fledged parse of a sentence — just as logics require construction of formulas from the atomic level up. Is not this a "kiss of death" for the natural logic program, that was supposed to work on surface syntax? Now, the above analysis can be twisted to work in a top-down manner [36]. The only thing we need to know for the monotonicity marking of a constituent is the hierarchical structure of the sentence above *it*, leaving all other "side parts" unanalyzed. Even so, I must confess that I am not entirely happy. The categorical monotonicity calculus is definitely not carefree surface analysis, and like much of current linguistics and logic, it analyzes more than the bare minimum which seems involved in natural reasoning. How can we "hit and run" as reasoners, or is that idea just a chimera?

But even with this worry, the main insight from the 1980s remains intriguing. Our natural inferences based on predicate restriction and monotonicity do not need special logical apparatus: they get a free ride on syntactic analysis, a task we have to perform anyway.

6 Descriptive challenges to natural logic

There are many further questions at this stage about the range of our "natural logic" so far.

6.1 Polyadic quantifiers

There is much more to quantifier patterns in natural language than the above single and iterated cases. Through the 1980s, further combinations have come to light which do not reduce to simple iterations, such as *cumulative forms* "Ten firms own 100 executive jets" or *branching patterns* "Most boys and most girls knew each other". These require new forms of monotonicity marking, depending on how one takes their meanings. Also, quantifiers also lead to *collective predication* ("The boys lifted the piano"), as well as *mass quantification* ("the teachers drank most of the wine"), whose inferential behaviour is far from being generally understood — either in linguistic semantics or in modern logic.

6.2 Other fast subsystems

Maybe more interesting is the issue whether there are *other fast surface inference systems* in natural language. I already mentioned the general functioning of Conservativity as a mechanism of general *Role Restriction* for predicates in sentences. And I can think of several other examples, such as "individual positions" X in expressions allowing for arbitrary *distribution over disjunctions*, as in $\varphi(X_1 \wedge X_2) \leftrightarrow \varphi(X_1) \wedge \varphi(X_2)$.[10]

[10] Another candidate came up at the Stanford RTE seminar in 2007: *disjointness of predicates*. Which expressions preserve this? Monotonicity was about inferences of the form: "$P \leq Q$ implies $\varphi(P) \leq \varphi(Q)$". But now, we are now given, not an inclusion premise, but an exclusion premise (note that $P \cap Q = \varnothing$ if and only if $P \subseteq \neg Q$), and we want to know what follows then in the right contexts: "$P \leq \neg Q$ implies $\varphi(P) \leq \neg\varphi(Q)$". In first-order logic, this amounts to stating a monotonicity-like inference between the formula and its dual obtained by working the prefix negation inward switching operators: "$P \leq Q$ implies $\varphi(P) \leq \varphi^{\text{dual}}(Q)$". I think one can find first-order syntax which guarantees precisely this behaviour. More generally, many classical model-theoretic preservation results in first-order logic can be re-interpreted as giving simple special-purpose syntax for specialized inferences.

6.3 Interactions

So much for separate inferential systems. Another issue is of course how these interact with other major features of natural language. E.g., *anaphora* with pronouns can wreak havoc with monotonicity inferences, as in the following example ([28]; but the observation really goes back to Geach [10] and earlier):

> Everyone with a child owns a garden.
> Every owner of a garden waters it. So:
> Everyone who has a child sprinkles it.

Here, the pronoun "it" has picked up the wrong antecedent. Again, information about the total sentence composition is crucial to block these inferences while keeping the correct ones.

6.4 Inference without scope resolution?

Finally, here is a more daunting challenge for surface reasoning. If we are to do inference as close to the linguistic surface string as possible, it would be nice to not have to resolve all quantifier scope ambiguities – and infer as much as possible from ambiguous expressions.[11] This is the way language often comes to us. For instance, in the above two dragon examples with monotonicity markings, note that five out of the seven positions in the string retain the same marking in either scope reading. Can we find a still more surfacy natural logic for inferences unaffected by ambiguity? A stream of recent work on inference with "underspecified" syntax seems relevant here: cf. [34, 35, 7], and subsequent publications.

7 Digression: traditional logic and small inference languages

Here is another direction in current research on natural logic. We saw that the medieval logicians started classifying multi-quantifier inferences. Thus, they were well-aware that

"Some P R all Q" implies "All Q are R-ed by some P"

and that the converse fails. Now the iteration depth in ordinary discourse seems limited (at best three levels, as in "You can fool some people all of the time" seem to occur in practice). Thus it makes sense, *pace* Dummett, to define small special-purpose notations for such combinations, and try to axiomatize them. Moss's [18] is a first attempt in this direction of rehabilitating scholastic efforts, with very appealing sets of valid principles.[12]

[11] This is the view of natural language in Lexical-Functional Grammar; cf. [33].
[12] Admittedly, higher-order quantifiers like "Most" have proved recalcitrant so far.

In addition to this focus on deductive completeness for small languages, Pratt has performed computational complexity analysis on several small decidable fragments of natural language [21]. Here outcomes are a bit more gloomy, in that high complexity can arise — but as so often with bad news of this sort, it remains to be seen what this means in practice.

8 From language to computation

The story of natural logic has also crossed to computer science.

8.1 Efficient information processing

First, it has often been observed that simple reasoning with relational databases only uses small parts of predicate logic, and that monotonicity accounts for most of what is needed. Accordingly, [23] and follow-up publications have come close to the material covered in the above. Likewise, modern research on natural language processing, and in particular, intelligent text analysis appears to be arriving at similar aims and results. Results from the linguistic phase are promoted in [36], using various programming techniques for optimizing the monotonicity calculus and related forms of inference. For an extensive empirical investigation of actual data, cf. [16]. Likewise, polarity calculi for hierarchical marking to extend the scope of natural lexical inferences with factive verbs have been proposed in [19]. Whether all this is really less complex than first-order alternatives is a matter of detailed complexity-theoretic analysis, as said earlier — and the jury is still out.

8.2 Aside: fixed-point logics

The computational setting also suggests natural constructions outside of first-order logic, such as transitive closure (Kleene iteration) and recursive definitions involving *fixed-point operators*. But monotonicity still makes sense here, and indeed, it is crucial. A recursive definition $P\mathbf{x} \leftrightarrow \varphi(P)(\mathbf{x})$ of a new predicate P does not make sense in general — but it does when $\varphi(P)$ is semantically monotone with respect to P [5]. Is this just a technical coincidence, or does this mean something from the perspective of natural logic? Maybe it supports circular definitions?

8.3 AI and default logic: "non-monotonicity calculus"

But there are other, less standard aspects to the computer science connection. In particular, "common sense reasoning" has been analyzed in Artificial Intelligence by John McCarthy and his school. Now this involves not just monotonic inferences, but also *non-monotonic* ones, where inclusion of predicates need not keep the conclusion true. This brings us to the area of default logics, which involve both classical reasoning with rock-solid conclusions, and *defeasible inferences* which can be retracted when new information comes in. For instance, by default "birds fly", but there are exceptions such as penguins, who tend to march? A systematic extension of the above monotonicity calculus to deal also with default implications based on predicate inclusions would be a highly interesting project! Existing logical systems in this area, which already combine material and default conditionals might provide a guide.

8.4 Combination, architecture and complexity

My final computational theme returns to the natural logic program as such, and in particular, to what I myself consider a major open problem not recognized in the 1980s and before. Analyzing natural inference as a large family of simple fast subsystems is not enough! In reality, we are not a bare set of isolated processors. All this information must be combined, and one module must be able to feed quickly into another. So, what sort of "natural" reasoning system are we?

Here, an insidious challenge to the whole enterprize emerges. Much experience with logical systems over the past decade has shown that the analytical strategy of "divide and conquer" does not always hold. The complexity of the total logic is not just a maximum of the complexities of the components. It can explode dramatically, because the additional source of complexity is *the nature of the combination*, i.e., the communication between the different inferential modules. Indeed, several natural examples are known where apparently innocuous combinations of decidable logics create *undecidable* over-all inference systems. Note, this does not have to happen in every case, and the technique of "fibered logics" [9] provides a way out in many cases. But the danger is there.

Our conclusion here is this. Unless we have an additional idea about the *global architecture* of natural logic, claims about its performance may be premature and ill-founded.

9 Cognitive science

A final arena where natural logic is coming up these days is experimental cognitive science. We definitely know that inference in the human brain is not one unified phenomenon, but a joint venture between many modules, some related to our language abilities, some more to immediate visual processing or to schematic representation, and yet others to brain areas dedicated to planning and executive function [14]. Current neuroscience experiments, guided by hypotheses about linguistic data [11] are now beginning to map out how, for instance, monotonicity inference may be located in different parts of the brain than heavy-duty first-order logic (if that is available at all).

10 Conclusion: the case of modern versus traditional logic once more

Natural logic is a proposal for taking a new look at natural inferential systems in human reasoning, not through the lenses of modern logic which see "formal systems" everywhere. I think this is well-worth doing for all the reasons that I mentioned. But let me also be clear that I do not see this as a resumption of warfare between traditional logic and modern logic. If only by this "cheap shot": the only respectable systems of natural logic that I know use thoroughly modern logical techniques and standards of exposition. There is no way back.

10.1 Architecture and transitions

To me, by now, the more interesting question is one of architecture and transitions. Clearly, modern logic provides more subtle tools for analyzing reasoning than traditional logic, and it is of great interest to see where these must come into play. The analysis of mathematical reasoning is of course one clear case in point where traditional logic failed eventually in its accounts of density, continuity, limits, etc. (cf. [8] on Kant's views of mathematics). But the transitions do not lie where De Morgan and many modern teachers claim they lie. Traditional logic was much richer than many people think, and it still deals in attractive ways with large areas of natural language and common sense reasoning. First-order logic probably takes over when explicit variable management and complex object constellations become inevitable. Thus, it seems to me, there is no inevitable conflict between "natural logic" versus modern logic.

10.2 Redefining the issue: mixtures and merges

But again, one cannot just see this peaceful co-existence in sweeping terms like "mathematics is modern logic", "natural language is traditional logic". The more interesting perspective for research may rather be

mixtures of natural and formal language and reasoning!

For instance, it is a telling fact that mathematicians have never abandoned natural language in favour of logical formalisms. Just read any mathematics paper, or go to any mathematics colloquium. The real situation is that mathematicians use mixtures of both, with the logical notation coming in *dynamically* when natural language needs to be made *more precise.* This mixture suggests that "natural logic" and "modern logic" can coexist harmoniously, because both have their place. And modern logic might even learn something from natural logic in combating its "system imprisonment", trying to look for more general systems-free formulations of its basic insights, the same way, say, Monotonicity seems a general insight about human reasoning, which does not really seem to depend on any specific formal language and semantics. But I take this also as a shift in the whole issue. What we really need to understand is how out "natural logic" can be "naturally extended" with formal notations, and other technical inventions which somehow seem to fit our cognitive abilities.

10.3 The price of inferential holism

Here is a final speculation. There might be another role then for modern first-order logic. Maybe modern logic is the only system which really *integrates all separate natural reasoning modules.* And then, as in my story of architecture and module combination, there may be a price to pay. This might be the true reason for the *undecidability* of first-order logic: not because its subsystems are so hard by themselves, but *because their combination is.* This may be seen by linking undecidability to tiling problems and interaction axioms [31], but I shall leave the matter here.

In summary, natural logic seems an inspiring, if not always well-defined, research program into human language and human reasoning which raises many new questions of its own, while helping us rethink the achievements of modern logic in new and unexpected ways.

References

[1] Jon Barwise and Robin Cooper. Generalized Quantifiers and Natural Language. *Linguistics and Philosophy*, 4:159–219, 1981.

[2] Innocentius M. Bocheński. *A History of Formal Logic*. University of Notre Dame Press, Notre Dame, 1997. Translated and edited by Ivo Thomas.

[3] Haskell B. Curry. A Mathematical Treatment of the Rules of the Syllogism. *Mind*, 45:209–216, 1936.

[4] Michael Dummett. *Frege. The Philosophy of Language.* Duckworth Press, London, 1973.

[5] Heinz D. Ebbinghaus and Jörg Flum. *Finite Model Theory.* Perspectives in Mathematical Logic. Springer Press, Berlin, 1996.

[6] George Englebretsen. *Three Logicians: Aristotle, Leibniz, Sommers and the Syllogistic.* Van Gorcum Press, Assen, 1981.

[7] Tim Fernando. Ambiguity under Changing Contexts. *Linguistics and Philosophy*, 20:575–606, 1997.

[8] Michael Friedman. Kant's Theory of Geometry. *The Philosophical Review*, 94(4):455–506, 1985.

[9] Dov M. Gabbay. *Labeled Deductive Systems.* Oxford University Press, Oxford, 1996.

[10] Peter T. Geach. *Logic Matters.* Blackwell, Oxford, 1972.

[11] Bart Geurts and Frans van der Slik. Monotonicity and Processing Load. *Journal of Semantics*, 21(1):97–117, 2005.

[12] Wilfrid Hodges. The Laws of Distribution for Syllogisms. *Notre Dame Journal of Formal Logic*, 39:221–230, 1998.

[13] Edward L. Keenan and Dag Westerståhl. Quantifiers. In Johan van Benthem and Alice ter Meulen, editors, *Handbook of Logic and Language*, pages 837–893. Elsevier Press, Amsterdam, 1997.

[14] Markus Knauff. How our Brains Reason Logically. *Topoi*, 26(1):19–36, 2007.

[15] Fenrong Liu and Jialong Zhang. Some Thoughts on Mohist Logic. In Johan van Benthem, Shier Ju, and Frank Veltman, editors, *A Meeting of the Minds. Proceedings of the Workshop on Logic, Rationality and Interaction*, volume 8 of *Texts in Computer Science*, pages 85–102, London, 2007. College Publications.

[16] Bill MacCartney and Christopher D. Manning. An extended model of natural logic. In *Eighth International Conference on Computational Semantics, IWCS-8, Tilburg, The Netherlands. Proceedings*, 2009. to appear.

[17] Richard Montague. *Formal Philosophy.* Yale University Press, New Haven, 1974.

[18] Larry Moss. Completeness in Natural Logic: What and How. LSA Linguistics Summer Institute Harvard University, 2005.

[19] Rowan Nairn, Cleo Condoravdi, and Lauri Karttunen. Computing Relative Polarity for Textual Inference. In Johan Bos and Alexander Koller, editors, *Inference in Computational Semantics ICoS-5, Workshop Proceedings, Buxton, April 2006*, pages 151–156, 2006.

[20] Stanley Peters and Dag Westerståhl. *Quantifiers in Language and Logic.* Oxford University Press, Oxford, 2006.

[21] Ian Pratt Hartmann. Fragments of Language. *Journal of Logic, Language and Information*, 13(2):207–223, 2004.

[22] Arthur N. Prior. Traditional Logic. In Paul Edwards, editor, *The Encyclopedia of Philosophy*, volume 5, pages 34–45. McMillan Press, London, 1967.

[23] William C. Purdy. A Logic for Natural Language. *Notre Dame Journal of Formal Logic*, 32(3):409–425, 1991.

[24] Victor Sanchez Valencia. *Studies on Natural Logic and Categorial Grammar.* PhD thesis, Universiteit van Amsterdam, 1991.

[25] Victor Sanchez Valencia. The Algebra of Logic. In John Woods and Dov M. Gabbay, editors, *Handbook of the History of Logic. Volume 3, The Rise of Modern Logic: From Leibniz to Frege*, pages 389–544. Elsevier, Amsterdam, 2004.

[26] Fred Sommers. *The Logic of Natural Language.* Clarendon Press, Oxford, 1982.

[27] Patrick Suppes. Variable-Free Semantics with Remarks on Procedural Extensions. In Thomas W. Simons and Robert J. Scholes, editors, *Language, Mind and Brain*, pages 21–31. Lawrence Erlbaum, Hillsdale, 1982.

[28] Johan F.A.K. van Benthem. *Essays in Logical Semantics.* Reidel Press, Dordrecht, 1986.

[29] Johan F.A.K. van Benthem. Meaning: Interpretation and Inference. *Synthese*, 73(3):451–470, 1987.

[30] Johan F.A.K. van Benthem. *Language in Action. Categories, Lambdas and Dynamic Logic.* MIT Press, Cambridge (Mass.), Amsterdam, 1991.

[31] Johan F.A.K. van Benthem. *Exploring Logical Dynamics.* Studies in Logic, Language and Information. CSLI Publications, Stanford, 1996.

[32] Johan F.A.K. van Benthem and Alice ter Meulen (eds.). *Handbook of Logic and Language.* Elsevier Press, Amsterdam, 1997.

[33] Johan F.A.K. van Benthem, Jens E. Fenstad, P. Kristian Halvorsen, and Tore Langholm. *Situations, Language and Logic*, volume 34 of *Studies in Linguistics and Philosophy.* Reidel Press, Dordrecht, 1987.

[34] Kees van Deemter. Towards a Logic of Ambiguous Expressions. In Kees van Deemter and Stanley Peters, editors, *Semantic Ambiguity and Underspecification*, pages 203–237. Cambridge University Press, Cambridge, 1996.

[35] D. Jan van Eijck and Jan O. M. Jaspars. Ambiguity and Reasoning. FRACAS Report CS-R9616, Centrum voor Wiskunde en Informatica, 1996.

[36] Jan van Eijck. A Natural Logic for Natural Language. In Balder ten Cate and Henk W. Zeevat, editors, *Logic, Language, and Computation. 6th International Tbilisi Symposium on Logic, Language, and Computation. Batumi, Georgia, September 12-16, 2005, Revised Selected Papers*, volume 4363 of *Lectures Notes in Artificial Intelligence*, pages 216–230, New York, 2007. Springer.

Appendix A History once more: logic in China

When this material was presented at a lecture in Beijing, some interesting coincidences came to light. As is becoming known by now, logic started simultaneously in at least three geographical areas and cultures: Greece, India, and China. Here are a few telling examples from [15] about Mohist logic (5th century BC), a school of thought clearly manned by logicians. The following inference is straight from the Mohist Canon:

> "A white horse is a horse. To ride a white horse is to ride a horse."

This is clearly the pattern of upward monotonicity. But now, here are two further Mohist examples which seem to contradict this:

> "Robbers are people, but to abound in robbers is not to abound in people."

> "A cart is a wooden object. To ride a cart is not to ride a wooden object."

These examples are subtle, and both highlight a further phenomenon of logical interest. The first seems a failure of upward monotonicity due to *context dependence* of a quantifier. If "Many" just means "more than a fixed threshold value N", it is upward monotonic in both arguments. But if we assume the norm is dependent on the predicate, as seems more likely, "Many" is not upward monotonic in either argument.[13] To manage correct and incorrect inferences here, one would need a dynamic mechanism of "context

[13]Another form of context dependence was brought up during a presentation of this paper at PARC Palo Alto: Does "They verbally attacked the president" imply "They attacked the president"? The conclusion suggests (incorrectly) physical attacks.

management". The second example seems one of *intensionality.* "To ride a cart" may be read extensionally as just "being transported", and then the conclusion does follow by upward monotonicity. But the Mohist colleagues surely meant something more subtle. Intensionally, one rides a cart *as a vehicle*, and read in that way, the stated inference comes out invalid, since one does not ride a wooden object *qua* wooden object. These refinements of the above monotonicity setting are as valid now as they were then. Intensional contexts have been a well-known challenge to simple monotonicity reasoning, ever since Richard Montague made intensional expressions a benchmark for the semantic analysis of natural language.

Mohist logic had many further subtle features than inferences like these. It also includes versions of the Paradox of the Cretans, and very nicely, the following pragmatic paradox of conversation, which was new at least to this author (though one referee of this paper saw an analogy with Buridan's Paradox that "Every proposition is negative"):

> Telling someone that "You can never learn anything" can never be successful.

The somewhat Whorfian question has sometimes been raised how one can ever recognize people in other cultures as colleagues. I should say, with the great historical work [2] that there is no such problem: "*only logicians* worry about crazy things like this".

Abhāva: Negation in logic, real non-existent, and a distinctive pramāṅa in the Mīmāṃsā

Purushottama Bilimoria*

School of International and Political Studies, Deakin University, Geelong Waterfront Campus, Geelong, Victoria, 3127, Australia

School of Philosophy, Anthropology and Social Inquiry, The University of Melbourne, Melbourne, Victoria, 3010, Australia

E-mail: pb1@unimelb.edu.au

The focus of this essay is on the Mīmāṃsās' radical epistemological theory of negation, otherwise known as *abhāva* or "absence", and which may be read as *nāsti* or non-existent. Before we go any further, a word on "Mīmāṃsā" is appropriate, particularly for those who may not be familiar with this particular school of classical Indian thought —perhaps in some ways even pre-classical with its roots in the Brāhmaṇas of the Vedas— and to which also arguably belongs the genesis of the Nyāya school of thought.

The term "*mīmāṃsā*" literally signifies "commeasurement" — from the root "*mān*", "to think" and (with the additional *gaṇ*-prefix *mī*) — "to interpret and align", and this implies, in Zilberman's words,

> "achievement of consistency in reasoning [*naya*, later *nyāya*], as a necessary precondition of making the meanings of words or sentences (for Sanskrit it is all the same) comprehensible [19]".

According to the definition given by Śabara in his *bhāṣya* on *Jaimini-sūtra* I.1.2,

> "... interconnected words or sentences which instruct in methods of cooperation or congruency in actions are known as *pūrva-mīmāṃsā*, or *karma-mīmāṃsā* [19]".

It is in this semantic field where internal consistency is aligned with the normative pragmatic of "what is to be done" (actual or potential actions) — and, counterfactually, what is *not* to be done (i.e., prohibition)— that the doctrine of negation first makes its appearance in Indian philosophical thought. With Kumārila Bhaṭṭa, c. 7th century CE, the doctrine achieves a decisive logical formulation in the dialectical tussles with the Nyāya and

*I should like to extends my thanks to J. L. Shaw, K. T. Pandurangi (my scholastic guru), Frits Staal, Dhirendra Sharma (*in absentia*), and two anonymous referees for their inputs into this paper, which I wish to dedicate to the memory of the ever absently-present, Bimal Krishna Matilal.

Mihir K. **Chakraborty**, Benedikt **Löwe**, Madhabendra Nath **Mitra**, Sundar **Sarukkai** (*eds.*). Logic, Navya-Nyāya & Applications. Homage to Bimal Krishna Matilal. College Publications, London, 2008. Studies in Logic 15. pp. 43–64.

Received by the editors: 7 May 2007; 30 May 2007.
Accepted for publication: 27 August 2008.

Buddhist philosophers. In the background are the rule-based formulations where varieties of negations and self-defeating paradigms within language-uses are schematically dealt with by the —even more vintage— Grammarians, Pāṇini and Patañjali. (By "logical", then, one means not so much formal reasoning as in mathematical logic, but rather ratiocination encompassing linguistics, epistemology and ontology — the Vedanta added "metaphysics" to this developmental *ratio.*)

I have three aims. First I should like to present an outline of the logical theory of negation in the Mīmāṃsā. Second, I shall make a connection of this with the Mīmāṃsā hermeneutic of moral judgments (which for them are inscribed in śruti, the Vedas, in the form of Vedic injunctions, "the ought to do" type of positive propositions or *vidhis.* And finally, we make a further link of these two moves to its epistemological radicalism in standing up for an independent and distinctive pramāṅa, valid instrument of knowing, in respect of "absence" — and that too, on pain of being true to a realist ontology. The most important part of the discussion here is the Mīmāṃsā treatment of negative propositions.

1

As mentioned above, the logical thesis begins with deliberations on rules followed in expressions pertaining to certain actions. The concern is not at all with indicative or purely descriptive expressions (for these are regarded as *arthavāda*, of auxiliary aid to the deliberations). To elaborate on this, I shall use Zilberman's succinct descriptors for action-statements. Actions are divided subjunctively into two classes: prescriptive and prohibitive. Normative injunctions (*vidhis*), derived from the Vedic sentences, which stimulate or are an accomplice to actions can take one of these forms (1) regular, imperative or non-exemptive (*nitya*), i.e., categorically non-conditional; (2) imposed by circumstances (*naimittika*), hence conditional to some greater good; (3) optative, prudentially conditional, i.e., conducive to some desirable award or potential effect (*kāmya*), and is non-prescriptive. These together constitute *dharma*, the normative performatives: this is the Bhāṭṭa a (followers of Kumārila) view; the Prābhākara extend the *kāryatā*, practicum, of *dharma* only to the first two.[1] The inducement or conduciveness toward the requisite effort is communicatively generated, after attention has been roused, in the form of a verbal energy in the so-compelled, excited or inspired initiate by the *vidhi*-proposition, generally of the form: "Let him be induced to do this and that", and it abides in the subjective

[1] *anyākāryatā, anyā ceṣṭasādhanatā ... phalaṃ prati upayātaṃ phalasādhanatvaṃ, kṛtiṃprati pradhānatvaṃ tadadhīnasattākatvam ca kāryatva; ... loke kriyākāryatājñānātpravṛttāvapi kāryatājñānameva pravṛttinimittaḥ.* [11, p. 57]. Cf. also [9, p. 63] where this passage is also cited.

intention (*bhāvana*) much like the subjunctive force of modality. It is rendered by the imperative or optative form of the verb (*liṅ*) and it conceals the deontic modality of the statement which proposes something as hitherto not existent (non-existent), but as due or awaiting to be done (*kāryatā*): the potential or portending action [19, p. 289].

Now, and this is a crux of the argument, the prior *non-existent* (or the facticity of non-existence) is the logical negation of what has not yet been actualised. The relation between the non-existent (or non-existence of the action/thing), *abhāva*, and its counterpositive (*pratiyogī*) is that of incommensurability. In its simplest form this could be expressed as $\neg(p \wedge \neg p)$. All subsequent schools of Indian thought that recognised the ideality of non-existence accepted this formulation of negation. But there are other possible kinds of negations as well; and even more so, the Mīmāṃsā was pressed to argue, in the case of subjunctive propositions, i.e., of the prescriptive, *vidhi*, type. The problem then that faces the philosopher is to interpret all parts of the *vidhis* and the larger passages in which they are embedded, and to sort through the kinds and degrees of permitted (i.e., included), proscribed or prohibited, delimited and bounded qualifications (i.e., inclusive-exclusive), as well as the wholly excluded conditionals governing a particular action (such as, for example, the special sacrifice on the night of equinox). The way this is done is by focusing primarily on the verbal displayment that abides in the impersonal Vedic words (being authorless, there is no question of inquiring into the intentions of the supposed author[4]); and that focus narrows down to the verbal intentionality (*śābdībhāvana*) that presents a specific transcendental function as the specific property of the intension of the verbal meaning.[2] It follows that among the injunctions there may well be resemblances, dissimilarities, or oppositions and defeats; and so generating an order among these becomes of paramount importance.

In the analysis that ensues, two categories become important: affirmative and negative meanings attached to the verbal expressions. Balancing the effects, the consequent, of these would mean first examining their antecedent casual potency (*śakti*) — how much good or damage they can do; this calls for dialectical mediation, and it may mean a recourse to non-formal logic (deontic, subjunctive, subjective, aesthetic, causal, etc.).

It may be noted that, in fact, the Mīmāṃsā were the first to introduce negative kinds of propositions in Indian philosophy. Jaimini-sūtras at VI.5.15, VIII.7,10, specifically discusses *pratiṣedha* and *niṣedha*, and it may be noted that this is well before the Nyāya-Vaiśeṣika and the Jaina and

[2]Here Zilberman cites Maṇḍana Miśra as his authority for this rendering of "*śabda bhāvana*", as he calls it, which otherwise would be *śābdībhāvana*, as "verbal energy" [19, p. 289]. Arindam Chakraborty disputes this is a correct rendering of *śābdībhāvana*, for the *bhāvana* presumably is not in the verbal formation but rather is a disposition within the hearer which propels him forthwith into action.

Buddhists took up these concepts and developed them in rather different and indeed logically rigorous ways. Although it is the case also, as mentioned earlier, that the Grammarian Pāṇiṇi had already laid out some of the terms and rules for interpreting opposition and tensions between contrary expressions or linguistics predicates. The contradiction is recognised to be of the form $(\varphi \wedge \neg\varphi)$. But the grammarian's rules did not embed the same degree of logical articulation, particularly in respect of non-indicative or non-doxastic sentences, which the Mīmāṃsā would herald in. Again, the Mīmāṃsā needed this in order to sort out the different kinds of negative injunctions, which —as already noted— Jaimini set out to do, so that all kinds of *pratibādhya-pratibhandakas* or handicaps, contradictions and incommensurabilities (classed as *vipratiṣedha*, "mutual prohibitions" — in and between the injunctions of equal force, mantras, and their supplementations, i.e., *arthavādas*, and the moot distinctions between these as well) could be put in place. So here is an application of early Indian thinking on negative propositions and how one is to "read" these in respect of their ramifications for the intended purport of the Vedic *codanās* or *vidhis.* For those with an interest in finding other ways to talk about contradictions or self-defeating relations —a divergence from Aristotelian logic— this earliest of Indian classical treatment may well be instructive.

In what follows I shall adopt the notation that Staal used when first discussing the matter [16]. The use of the term "negation" has largely been ignored by modern logicians in favour of sentential negation. The intended reading of $\neg F(x)$, as opposed to $\neg[F(x)]$, is "x is non-F". and is familiar from the discussion of Aristotelian syllogistic logic. The negation of singular terms, as as $F(\neg x)$, however, will strike modern logicians as something unheard of. Its intended reading is "not that x is F". The point of introducing these grades of involvement is not just to stay closer to the grammatical form of the original statements (something modern logic cares preciously little about), but to keep track of the different inferential roles the Mīmāṃsakas attribute to them. All of $\neg[F(x)]$, $\neg F(x)$, and $F(\neg x)$ mean that x is not F, but $\neg F(x)$ additionally carries the information that x is something other than x is F. Granted, these concepts can be formalized using sentential negations (given identity and second order quantification are expressible in logic). However, the exact meaning of the different negations is what is discussed by the Indian philosophers. For example, Staal gives a passage that states that $F(\neg x)$ is to be interpreted as "only x doesn't F [16, p. 64]", prompting a quite different translation into modern logic.

There are four-fold division of negation, as follows (which in much modified form also came to be accepted by the Nyāya-Vaiśeṣika, although they differed on the means of apprehending the stated negations):[3]

[3] *SV*, Abhāva 2–4, p. 336: *kṣīre dadhyādi yannāsti prāgabhāvaḥsa ucyate//2// nāstitā*

1. *prāgabhāva*: antecedent non-existent or prior negation; the "not-yet so" or absence of an effect (e.g., the negation of curd in milk, by its theory of *asatkārya*: an effect is not prior to its cause; the pot's non-existence (*ghaṭābhāva*) before the clay is thrown and its counterpositive, *ghaṭa*, is manifested); this absence is causelessly beginningless but ceases once the effect is produced in temporal space.

2. *dhvaṃsābhāva*: posterior non-existent or deconstructive negation, the "no-more" type of absence due to *destruction* of some being in time: (e.g., the negation of milk in the curd; the destruction of the pot once it falls to the ground and is shattered into pieces; or there is no book *now* on the table; when the Faculty of Arts will all but be destroyed, the *absence* of the Faculty of Arts will be in or haunt the University; when my savings dwindle to zero; and Saddam Hussein is hanged).

3. *anyonyābhāva*: mutual and relational negation; the "not-related" type of absence (x is not in y, e.g., the negation of the horse in the cow, due to the absence of dew-lap; and vice versa; Rāma is not Laxmana (being more honest of the two); Sītā is not Rāvaṇa's wife, as this *rūpīyā* belongs to Rāma; Philosophy is not Cinema Studies; my dogs are not related to the cat in the same house etc.)

4. *atyantābhāva*: absolute negation; the "never-never" or impossible type

---

payaso dadhni pradhvaṃsābhāva iṣyate/ gavi yo'śvādy-abhāvas tu so'nyonyābhāva ucyate//3// śiraso'vayavā nimnā vṛddhikāṭhinyavarjitāḥ/ śaśaśṛṇgaḍirūpeṇa so'tyantābhāva ucyate//4//

In [2, p. 243]; also discussed in [12, pp. 27*sqq*]; compare the Naiyāyika Jagadīśa: "*prāgabhāva-dhvaṃsayorapi uttarapūrvakālāveva*" pointed out by J. L. Shaw in [15, p. 153]. Almost identical classification of these four kinds also appear in Jaina texts, notably *Āptamīmāṃsā* (Kumārila seemed to have been aware of this text), reported in [18, p. 24–25] — interestingly this very thesis on the possibility of the non-existent is built into an example of *syādvāda* in its *saptabhaginaya*, seven-step reasoning, thus:

1. A thing *is* existent — from a certain point of view.
2. It is *non*-existent — from another point of view.
3. It is *both* existent and non-existent *in turn* — from a third point of view.
4. It is *indescribable* (that is, both existent and non-existent simultaneously – from a fourth point of view).
5. It is existent and *indescribable* — from a fifth point of view
6. It *is non*-existent and *indescribable* — from a sixth point of view.
7. It is *both* existent and *non*-existent and *indescribable* — from a seventh point of view.

[18, p. 25]. "*sytā*" means conditional "yes', or more philosophically, it means the same as "*kathamcit*", "in some respect", or "from a certain point-of-view" and "*kadācit*", "somehow" or "sometime"; thus, a proposition, P, could be true or false; if P, then A is B.

of negation in all possible worlds (e.g., absence of hardness in the lower portions of the hare's head, or its likelihood of ever growing horns; Lucy in the sky with diamonds). If absolute nothingness militates against all possible-world emergences, and there is no temporal space for being or things to materialise, ever, then it would be a case of *nityābhāva*, Absence of Presence, eternality of *Nothingness*, Void. This seems to be one sense in which the Mīmāṃsā, especially Kumārila, understood the Buddhist doctrine of *śānyatā*, "non-dependent non-origination", the truth of which he would be persuaded by except that he couldn't condescend to the absence of the timeless *śruti* propositions; even if # 2 above comes to pass, or there is global *pralaya* (Armageddon), mathematical logic has to live on somewhere.

From # 3, following the Grammarian commentator Patañjali, one is able to derive *pratiṣedha*, "mutual prohibition", and *vipratiṣedha* where "two rules with different meaning apply to one (word)"; which could be read as "opposition (between two propositions) of equal force".[4] The question is how to resolve the tension. The Mīmāṃsá for their part begin by grouping the negations into three categories, which I shall call limiting negations. These are now described: *vipratiṣedha*, *pratiṣedha* or *niṣedha*, *paryudāsa*: permissible, prohibited, and excluded, respectively.

The first kind is a contingent opposition, applying to individual instances but is not considered to be universal (for there is no *jāti*, genus, that pervades across the two expressions). When a jar is destroyed, not all jars are destroyed. You may be seen with the umbrella or long-brim hat this morning even though it is not raining, for it may rain in the afternoon (as it always does in Melbourne). Nevertheless, it has more of a force in prescriptive sentences than in indicative or nominal constructions. Strict prohibitions belong to the *pratiṣedha* in its *niṣedha* form.

Negation proper admits of two types, prasajya (mutual prohibition) and paryudāsa (exclusion). Let us take *prasajya* first: "snow is not black" or "there is not-any snow that is black", and it will take the form: $\neg F(x)$. On the other hand, *Paryudāsa*, in its simple form, is exclusion: "the jar is not (here)", "it has not snowed here", $F(\neg x)$; A little more complex form may involve negative implication, "p implies $\neg q$", example of this would be: "if Rāma is a *kṣatriya*, he is not a *brahmin*"; "if it is grey, it is not white", "if y is an *asura*, he is not a god". This is as far as the Grammarians went and they did not bother with what Staal calls the injunctive operator (the obligation conditional), N; where negation is attached either to F (what is) or to N (what is to be done). The latter is compounded and is often a cause for ambiguity when the negation is attached to or pervades the obligatory

[4] Cf. [17, pp. 51–71].

predicate; thus: not-ought, ought-not, ought *not* to, *you*-not ought, you not-ought, etc., etc. So now we shall see how these formulations are transformed and tightened up when the injunctive operator, N, is introduced by the Mīmāṃsā.

Let us take *Prasajya-pratiṣedha* (which is also called *niṣedha*) first and take the injunction "*na bhakṣayet*", "he shall not eat". It is a negation of the positive injunction "*bhakṣayet*", "he shall eat" that is denoted by $N[F(x)]$, where $F(x)$ denotes "he eats" (and modally, "it is necessary that he eats"). Its injunctive force is not in prescribing an action other than eating; rather it simply prohibits eating and so should be rendered as "he shall-not eat" (colloquially, eating is a "no-no"). If "he shall eat" is symbolised by "$N[F(x)]$", its logical negation is symbolised by "$N\neg[F(x)]$" . In this context, as J. L. Shaw notes, the negative injunction has not been symbolised by "$\neg N[F(x)]$" for "in standard deontic logic '$\neg N[F(x)]$' would be equivalent to '$P\neg[F(x)]$', where 'P' stands for the permissibility operator. So '$\neg N[F(x)]$' would not express a negative injunction [14]." In other words, the expression "$\neg N[F(x)]$", even though it appears as a negation of the positive injunction (takes on, as it were, the whole sentence), it *eo ipso* does not have the force of an injunction, and could mean "it is permissible that he does not eat". In that regard, it is more consistent with the second, the *paryudāsa*, or "exclusionary" rather than the strictly prohibitive type of negation, which must strike at a very specific part of the injunction (represented by the verbal ending only, *ākhyāta/lakara-pratyaya*). And this takes us to the second type of negation.

The second type is *paryudāsa*, or "exclusion" negation. Here the negation is connected with either the verbal root or with the noun (the nominal indexical or the predicate object); thus in the injunction, *nekṣeta*[5], "he shall not look", the "not" is attached to the verbal root, so it should be rendered as "he shall not-look"; more positively it prescribes something other than looking (looking away, for instance). Curiously, there is positive injunction here, because there is a preceding phrase "his vows are..." Hence, technically speaking, nothing is prohibited; there is no ikṣana-virodhi (opposition to looking) for he never thought of looking (in the direction of Dharmakīrti's distractingly dancing mistress)! He has not been given a desirous option: the expression is bereft of an optative ending in the negative, which is different from saying you can be enjoined to do W (*kāryatā*), even where W cashes out into $\neg F(x) =$ "**not-look**". You are still doing your work. But the negative could as well strike at the nominal indexical or the predicate object: "**he-shall** not look"; "he shall not **look-at-the-mistress**"; thus someone is excluded or something is occluded from the gaze.[6] Symbolised

[5]Staal takes this from the *Mīmāṃsā-nyāya-prākāśa* in [6].

[6]Whereas Staal takes it to be the opposite and swaps the two. Staal gives the sym-

respectively (per bold qualifiers) by $N[\neg F(x)]$, and $N[F(\neg x)], N[F(x, \neg y)]$.

We could go on and find sentences where one of the nouns is negated (subject, qualia, or object), drawing on #3, the *anyonyābhāva* negation. Thus it could take any one of these forms: $N\neg[F(x)]$, $N[\neg F(x)]$, $N[F(\neg x)]$. If the positive injunction of the expression $F(x, y)$ is $N[F(x, y)]$, [y is contra x, so other than x], its negation or *paryudāsa* is $N[F(\neg x, y)]$, but it still remains positive in its injunctive force (*kāryatā)*.

The difference between the two is that in *paryudāsa*, there is a residue of the essentially positive still lingering on, while the negative is secondary or of second order, a semantic negation that strikes at the last member, not necessarily the verb itself. Whereas in the former, *prasajya*, the essential assertion is of a negation and there need not be any positive residue; it does not apply to the last member of the negative compound but strikes at the verbal ending (*krīyaya saha yatra nañ*) (*nañ* signifies the negation). So the "*paryudāsa*" type of negation may be called "exclusion type of negation"; whereas *prasajya-pratiṣedha* is a "prohibition type" of negation. And this latter is also called "*niṣedha*", which can spell out more radical forms of negation the harder the negative strikes at verbal intension via the N-operator.

In other words, one form of negation may suggest that doing x is not all right at this moment, but it may be permissible at another moment, or by someone else. "He shall not-eat", inscribes into its propositional structure the permissibility of eating at other times.[7] The Mīmāṃsās were interested in delineating the kinds of negation that are prohibitory without a residue of permissibility in any part of the semantic field, for one can easily say, "Do not indulge in sex", but if P got married tomorrow it may become permissible. Likewise, "a Śūdra should not even as much as be permitted to hear the Vedas recited", but it does not necessarily exclude the remaining castes from being present at a sacrifice, and so on. These belong to the exclusionary type. While the Mīmāṃsās are in search of the equivalence of the strictly obligatory of the negative kind.

Clearly the kind of negation in the foregoing examples, if it be admitted as a valid kind of negation (which I presume it would not be in Aristotelian logic, unless one brings in some other operators, like Church's

bolic form of *niṣedha* as "$(\neg N)[F(x)]$, but which does not in deontic modal logic express a negative injunction, so while it admits of permissibility it may or may not reign in prohibition, which *prasajya-pratiṣedha* or *niṣedha* must do. Staal's candidate "$(\neg N)[F(x)]$" would denote there is no injunction or mandate for him to eat — and Staal says as much when he renders "$(\neg N)[F(x)]$" as "there is no mandate for eating"; whereas there is a clear injunction prohibiting any eating: "shall-not"; the negation must strike at the verbal ending not just the N operator. It is not a simple withholding of the taxes but forfeiting the taxes to the taxman.

[7]E.g., crossing communities, it would apply to the Muslim observance of Ramzaan, where eating in the day hours is prohibited, but permitted after sunset.

sūtra (event):	$F(x)$	the door is locked (i)
paryudāsa :	$F(\neg x)$	you may unlock not this, the other door (ii) (not well formed negation; not governed by principle of noncontradiction, as in Quine also)
prasajya-pratiṣedha:	$\neg F(x)$	you may not unlock this door (iii) (negation of the predicate, as in Aristotelean logic; governed by principle of noncontradiction)

FIGURE 1. Grammarian

λ, I suppose), the Mīmāṃsā would classify under *paryudāsa*, "exclusion". *Yatra-uttara-padena nañ*, "where the negative is connected with the next word" — denoting here, "other than the verbal ending", *krīyaya saha yatra nañ*. And the "next word", *uttarapada*, as suggested earlier, denotes the second member of a negative compound (*tatpuruṣa* or *bahuvrihi*, different kinds of nominal compounds in Sanskrit, but not ruling out verbs) can be either a verbal root or a noun, but such a negation does not strike at the core of the injunction (because it excludes the verbal ending), hence it is not properly a negative injunction. In other words, it has a qualificative limiting function rather than an absolute prohibitory function, and therefore it is not consistent with the fourth category of negation either, i.e., *atyantābhāva*.

Bringing this part of the discussion to a close, it should be said that the innovative element in the Mīmāṃsā approach to prohibition and exclusion vis-à-vis the grammarians in respect of the three types of negation, is that negation can be applied to either N or F or all parts of a sentence, which is impossible in grammar. This may not seem very novel from our modern, post-classical point of view in logic, but at a time when logic was totally in the control of a tool used principally by grammarians to structure the determinants of proper speech, this indeed is quite a remarkable break-through. For it attempts to mirror the world outside, while playing with modal possibilities and instantiations — of real *krīyas* and *kāryas*, actions and things, being and events, in speech-forms; and this onto-logic further tries to understand, without compromise, the meaning of certain a priori negations in the Vedic corpus, which the Mīmāṃsā took to be unquestionably valid (because of its *apauruṣeyatva*, freedom from personal errors, including that of a possible deity).

(event)	$F(x)$	the door is locked (iv)
vidhi (positive injunction):	$N[F(x)]$	the door ought to be locked (v)
paryudāsa I (exclusion):	$N[\neg F(x)]$	the door need not-to-be-locked (vi)
paryudāsa II (inclusive-exclusion):	$N[F(\neg x)]$	not this, another door needs to-be-locked (vii)
niṣedha (strict prohibition):	$N\neg[F(x)]$	the door shall-not be locked (viii)
The anomaly or "wild card" here is:	$\neg N[F(x)]$	you told me not to lock the door (ix) (ambiguous)

FIGURE 2. Mīmāṃsā

So we finally give the difference in formal expression in Figures 1 and 2.[8] J. L. Shaw points out that a sharper distinction needs to be drawn between vi/vii and viii, making the former permissible : if we substitute F for eating, then vi/vii renders it permissible that x does not eat (he might not be observing a dietary vow); however, the latter, viii, is an injunction against eating: ought-not to eat. But I believe, from what has been demonstrated above, that the Mīmāṃsa actually achieve this quite successfully.

The Naiyāyikas, from what I understand to be their thinking, reduce negation to two —at most three— main kinds of negation. From the list given earlier by Kumārila Bhaṭṭa, they accept the "not-yet" (*prāgabhāva*), "no-more" (*dhvaṃsa*), and — if J. L. Shaw is right[9] — "never" (*atyantābhāva*). But each of these is based on the fundamental recognition of the self-defeating relation of a thing and its simultaneous absence (*pratibādhya-pratibandhaka bhāva*), which is represented by $(p \wedge \neg p)$; but the pot could

[8] I am grateful to Staal — when I was very confused by the Mīmāṃsā formulations, I went to Staal back in 1981, and we discussed some Mīmāṃsā texts together in Berkeley many moons ago. But I have also modified his formulations with the corrective provided by J. L. Shaw (cf. Footnote 6).

[9] In his [15, pp. 144–145], he classes them under "relational absences", with certain caveats built into the "temporal relation as the limiting relation of the property of being the counterpositive". Although in his other papers on negation, Shaw limits Nyāya negation to two main kinds: relational absence and mutual absence, represented respectively by (1): x is not in y, or x does not occur in y, or the absence of x occurring in y; and (2): x is not y, or x is different from y; where "x" and "y" are non-empty terms, and their counterpositive are: (1') x is in y, or x occurs in y, and (2') x is y. I am indeed grateful to J. L. Shaw for sharing his papers on negation with me, and I have drawn liberally with his permission and kind guidance for the present essay. In particular, his [14] (cf. Footnote 4), [13], and [15, p. 144].

also lack blueness, or there is blueness but no potness, or neither; thus $(p \wedge \neg b)$, $(\neg p \wedge b)$, $(\neg p \wedge \neg b)$, which is really to say, $\neg(p \wedge b) \leftrightarrow \neg p \vee \neg b$.[10] It was also recognised that $\neg p$ rejects p in a way different from that in which p rejects $\neg p$. Or take the simple identity A is A; so A is $\neg A$, and $\neg A$ is A are self-defeating but in quite, even radically, different senses, precisely because the prioricity of absence is marked in a different way in each of the copulas, and one excludes much more than the other.[11] (God is His own Absence, or Nothingness; Eternal Absence or Nothingness is analytically God. The first absence —exclusion— is part of the meaning of God, as the base or *ādhāra*; while Absence in the second conjunct cannot be the base, metaphysically, of God — although a Buddhist might think so!). I leave it to the scholars of Nyāya to elaborate on the Nyāya theory of negation and its difference from the Mīmāṃsaka's theory that I have sketched above, and also to show what the Nyāya owes to the Mīmāṃsaka in developing its particular view in all its symbolic and logical sophistication, particularly when it comes to double negation and contradictions.

Having as it were worked around with the law of non-contradiction without giving it up (but limiting its pragmatic scope), Indian logicians appear to have no hesitation in rejecting the law of excluded middle or "bivalence"; so it turns out on this view to be quite reasonable to say that it is neither true nor false that man will land on Mars by 2020. But to the question of whether man is capable of landing on Mars, the bivalent answer may take this form:

Either it is not in man's power to land on Mars or (given the current state of space-technology) it is not in his power not to land on Mars. It is neither true that man will by 2020 land on Mars (because they never have, and the future owes nothing to the present, as Bradley reminded us), nor is it false that men will land on Mars (given other conditionals). If we replaced "nor" with "and", it will be self-defeating and therefore has to be rejected: $\neg(M \wedge \neg M)$.

But what about $\neg(M \wedge \neg M) \vee \neg(M \vee \neg M)$, given that *paryudāsa* may permit negation of the whole statement, bivalence included? This is where the Buddhists come into the picture. And we may only touch on this intervention before moving onto Section 2 of the paper.

Firstly, the Buddhists also recognise the distinction between *paryudāsa* and *prasajya-pratiṣedha*, but they characterise the distinction in terms of the

[10] Cf. [8].

[11] A point made by K. C. Bhattacharyya in his celebrated essay [3, p. 576]; cf. also, [3, pp. 599–601]. Bhattacharyya asks, what is the denial of "A is either B or C"? Is it "A is either not B or not C"? Bhattacharyya's response is "no" ; he says it that "A is either B or not-B" is the logical negative of "A is either B or C"; but this is the proverbial excluded middle again; however, Bhattacharyya feels strongly that the "indeterminacy" reeking through such negations that evade absolute truth is the "limiting mystery of all philosophy"! Cf. [3, p.601].

different modes of negation involved. In the former, a certain affirmation of a positive entity or event is said to be involved and the negation is more usually than not by implication (*arthāpatti*) rather than by direct reference: so when one means *kṣatriya* he uses the single expression "non-brahmin", and it is implied that he is a *kṣatriya.* Hence the commitment is quite marked, so that even where one is seen to deny "the flower is red", at least he believes the flower to have some colour or that its former red-colour has now withered to a mellow-yellow. While in the case of the latter, *prasajya*, it negates directly whatever the opponent asserts, and there is no implication, nor does it affirm the counterfactual (for other castes are "non-brahmins" too, such as *śūdra, vaiśya*); it simply means he is "not a Brahmin". There is no commitment to anything here, so that when one says "Man is not the creator of the universe", there is no a priori commitment to any creator or for that matter creation. One could as well say, "Nothing exists" (for there never was any-thing).

Using semantics and pragmatics Shaw is able to describe the moves at stake in the view more clearly, and I quote:

> Pragmatics is involved when it is claimed that in *paryudāsa* negation affirmation is primarily intended, but in *prasajya-pratiṣedha* negation affirmation is not primarily intended if there is any affirmation [at all]. Semantics is involved when it is said that both the negative sentence and its implicate describe the same fact in *paryudāsa* negation. The negative sentence "he is not a Brahmin" and its intended implicate "he is a *kṣatriya*" describe the same fact, and the expression "not a Brahmin" and "*kṣatriya*" refer to the same thing. But in the case of *prasajya-pratiṣedha* negation "he is not a Brahmin" and "he is a *kṣatriya*" do not have the same meaning, and the former does not imply the latter. [13, pp. 62–63].[12]

Furthermore, it may be observed that when a *prasajya-pratiṣedha* negation is leveled against the weaker *paryudāsa* negation to which the opponent is bent on committing his adversary (because of its affirmative implicate), despite admitting to the *prasajya-pratiṣedha* alternative (but recall it left the two sentences unconnected), and thereby extract a *position*, both the alternatives are negated and all presuppositions therein also: $G\neg([F(\neg x) \wedge \neg F(x)])$ — where $F(\neg x)$ is *paryudāsa*, and $\neg F(x)$ is *prasajya-pratiṣedha* type of negation, and G is the intended residue qualified by the parenthesis. This makes possible a *prasajya-paryudāsa* type of negation. Space does not permit us to develop this line of thought to its logical culmi-

[12]By the way, the Buddhist view represented in the text here is attributed to one Avalokitavarta, which Shaw finds discussed by Kajiyama; but also cf. [12].

nation in Nāgārjuna's famous *catuṣkoti*, four-cornered dialectic, especially the last premise:*there is neither x nor non-x*; symbolized by "$\neg(p \vee \neg p)$".[13]

2

Now to the last part of the paper. As we have seen, the Mīmāṃsā were inexorably committed to the absoluteness of negation and its manifestation at least in the injunctive mode, initially in Vedic propositions. The *paribhāṣā* ("meta-language") rules became instructive with the development of grammar for its application to more secular speech. The Mīmāṃsās, however, under Kumārila Bhaṭṭa, followed a trajectory laid out in Śabarasvāmin's *bhāṣya*,[14] or even before that in one Upavarṣa[15]; their intuitions on negation is taken a step further and extendedly applied to the perceptual encounter with the objective world as well. In other words, they set out to make a connection between negation and things seen or un-seen, and even to the soteriological end of all perception and knowing: namely, *apavarga* or emancipation. There is a negative underbelly to that as well. Let me explore these insights further, beginning with the foray into the epistemological frontier.

Let us revert back to the fourfold division of negation we began with: antecedent, posterior, mutual, and absolute. Kumārila's argument turns on causality: if one did not admit these four kinds of negation it would not be possible to differentiate between cause and effect (i.e., we would be committing the fallacy of running cause into effect, and vice versa). But what precisely is the ontological status of "negation"? Is it simply a characteristic, *viśeṣa*, of an object whose negation is being effected here, or is it about a phenomenon in its own right? The word used here is "*vastuta*" (not a mere semantic substantive but a "thing-signifying" substantive), substantive entity or object, which I have advisedly called a phenomenon as it could be an event, or an episode, or a substantive absence: an existentially non-existent object, rather an "entitative item" in that sense nevertheless.[16]

In his *adhikaraṇa* on "*Abhāva*", Kumārila observes: there are "those who hold that negation being a non-entity (*avastu*) is not an objective

---

[13] In its expanded form, without collapsing double negation into its positive assertion: $(p \vee \neg p) \wedge (\neg p \vee \neg\neg p))$.

The stifling modern debate of whether this commits the Buddhist to rejecting the excluded middle or, more damagingly, law of noncontradiction is completely beside the point when viewed from the foregoing *logicus negative* genealogy.

[14] *abhāvo'pi pramāṇābhavo nāstītyasyārthayasannikṛṣṭasyeti*, I.i.5; 5.47

[15] Cf. [12, p. 74] with the analysis [12, pp. 26–29] (I have drawn liberally from this discussion). For a useful philological treatment and philosophical discussion of Kumārila's understanding and various possible translations of the key definition (by no means the only telling verse) in *Ślokavārttika* (*abhāvapariccheda* 11), cf. [7].

[16] I think we are entering a Meinongian-Sylvian jungle here.

reality (*tuccha*) and is without a self-existent character (*niḥsvabhāva*)."[17] Adverting to the fore-going classification of negation, he avers that such a classification would not be possible in respect of a non-entity (*avastu*); therefore, he concludes "negation must be an entity". For what is the negation of an effect, other than the absence of the cause.[18] In other words, all effects are non-existent putatively prior to their production; otherwise, under # 1 and # 2, the thing would be always present in time. If there were no *prior* absence of curd in milk, then, we would have to say, curd is present in the milk at all times, and we would not be able to cognise the milk, that is, the cause of the effect (curd). And # 1 is negated in # 2, the counter-entity (*pratiyogin*).

Likewise, with #3: a cow is decisively absent in a horse, and vice versa, even as both are species of the same genus of vertebrates. Thus, "all things are positive from their own standpoint, but negative from that of the other". As for # 4, if the absolute absence of colour were not in the air, or fire in the water, or horns in the hare, smell in the waters, etc, we would be forced to say otherwise.

These may be crude examples, but Kumārila wants to underscore a metaphysical point; he needs a theory of natural kind negation in order to ground the fledgling Mīmāṃsā epistemology of "*Abhāva*". What do I mean by the latter? Among the accepted *pramāṇas* or valid means of knowledge are perception, inference, analogy, and testimony: but these are all in respect of *things* that exist naturally, or perhaps supernaturally. What if perception itself fails to deliver any object? Or any of the *pramāṇa* for that matter? However, where there is perception of absence of any or all of the entities, *padārthas* (to use a Nyāya term), should we bring in absence simply as the failure of cognition of the same or should we say that there is a veridical perception of the *absence* in the locus (*ādhāra*) where the object or entity or event would otherwise have been present? Of course, even this can be interpreted in at least two ways, as we shall see shortly with the Nyāya insisting that there is a perception of something "not there" in a substantive base where it would have otherwise been; but the percept of "absence" is as it were conjunctive rather than disjunctive (though the theory suggests that it is disjunctive but not in the radical sense in which Kumārila would have it, consistent with the trope of *antyantābhāva* or absolute negation). The other way to interpret this absence is to suggest that there is an inference (*via arthāparthi*[19] or implication) made in respect of

[17]This is an intersperse by Pārthasārathi Miśra preceding *SV*, Abhāva 7, p. 336; cf. Footnotes 15 and 19.

[18]Pārthasārathi Miśra in Nyāyaratnākara on *SV* 7–8 (p. 336). We find this also in *Śāstradīpikā*.

[19]Although for Udayana its is more a case of *anumāna*, straight inference than it is of implication.

something "x" in lieu of the substantive base which is perceived as lacking what would otherwise have been there. The "absented x" is epistemically derivative, rather than *sui generis* (*svabhāvic*). Kumārila argues that the failure of perception in this instance, that is "non-perception" itself, constitutes a *karaṇa*, instrument (*reason* = *liṅga*), that warrants the postulation of a separate *pramāṇa*. Kumārila's reasoning for his radical interpretation is partly captured in this passage (it is not the best argument one can make, nevertheless, one can appreciate his motivation and boldness in urging for this warrantability):

> Negation is cognised (*prameyatvācca gamyate*) as an *entity* such as a cow, etc. For it is the object of inclusive and exclusive conceptions and is an object of cognition. It is not merely fortuitous, that it is an (incorrect) imposition or an erroneous notion. Therefore, the fact that (negation defined in terms of) the universal and the concrete particular is not false. (*SV*, Abhāva 8–10, p. 337).

Kumārila's worry is that in order for us to be able to differentiate a particular from all other things and affirm it in its generality, we must first cognise it with its class character and then proceed with the differentiation. The cow is first cognised as the bearer of cow-ness (genus, *ākṛti* = *jāti*), but for the precise cognition of the cow that belongs to Devadatta we must differentiate (*vyāvṛtti*) it from all other cows and from all other objects that are not cows. He believes that such a cognition of affirmation and denial is possible only because every entity (*vastu*) has two-fold reality, namely, that of its class and that of the individual.[20] Moreover, when we cognise the antecedent non-existence of a thing, after having affirmed (*anuvṛtti*) it as belonging to the class of "*abhāva*", we differentiate (*vyāvṛtti*) it from the other three kinds of negation. We also cognise *posterior-negation* as distinct from *antecedent*, *mutual* and the *absolute* negations. In the same way the last two are cognised as distinct from each other and from the rest. So, Kumārila contends that like any other (positive) form of reality negation forms the object of cognition, and that it (negation) can be expressed by affirmative and negative propositions (a move we already encountered in respect of positive and negative injunctions), with M-predicates, for example: "He does nothing", "He eats nothing" — the predicated absence is to be treated as the object of a distinct cognition (*vastu*). This affirmative propositional use of negation indicates a class character (*anuvṛtta-dharma*) Thus, all negative cognitions are members of the class of *abhāva* or absence. And this *abhāva* is a *padārtha* requiring its own *pramāṇa* rather than being simply seen as a *prameya* that can be subsumed under the regular *pramāṇas* — as the Nyāya would have it.

[20]Supplemented with Dhirendra Sharma's translation (with slight modification), [12, pp. 29*sqq*].

Of course, the Buddhist recognise the need to differentiate and affirm; but to them this simply amounts to discrimination and elimination (*apoha*) by virtue of there being positive entities, and it does not warrant bringing this under a separate entitative category, much less a distinctive *pramāṇa* as Kumārila seems to need to ground this perception of the negative entity.

Precisely, Kumārila retorts that he should not be misunderstood as arguing for the existence of *abhāva* in the absence of some positive reality (that would be a sort of Nietzschean nihilism). The *abhāva* inexorably bears relation to its counterpositive (*pratiyogī*), except that it is not known simply via cognition of the counterpositive as his Nyāya counterparts argue for. His point is that when he says "x is its own absence" he means just that, x has both a presence (in regard to its own form, i.e., *svarūpa*) *plus* an absence (in regard to the form of another object, i.e., *pararūpa*) in all possible worlds (*nityaṃsad-asadātmake vastuni*). The two are logically related; but they are also independent, inasmuch as they form the objects respectively of two different cognitions: people sometimes cognise one, sometimes the other (*jñayate kaiścid rūpaṃ kiṅcit kadācana*).(*SV* 12, p. 337).

The realist contention is that "absence of the cloth in the jar" simply means that the cloth *in its non-existent form* inheres in another object, the jar, and as such, produces the cognition of its "non-existent form" in the jar. Furthermore, Kumārila argues:

> A judgment (*nirṇaya*), concerning a (positive) existent (*bhāva*) — such as "this is (the jar) and nothing else"— is not possible without reference to the cognition of absence of everything else. Nor is the knowledge (*saṃvṛitti*) that "it (the jar) does not exist" possible, without reference to the negated thing itself; for there can be no cognition without an objective substratum. (*SV* Abhāva, 15–16, pp. 338–339).

What Kumārila seems to be suggesting in this passage, which is brought out more clearly in a later passage, is that the function of perception is over once our sense-organ fails to make contact with an objective substratum out there (*arthasyendriyasannikṛṣṭasyabādha*) and there thus is non-generation of perception, inference, etc.; instead, there is a stark absence of that object (*nāstītyasyārthasya*); now this "absence" is presented phenomenologically or noetically in the mental grasping, as he comments:

> After the object (*the place where the jar is not present*) has been *perceived*, and the counter-entity (*the jar*) has been *remembered*, then follows the notion that *it (the jar) is not*, which is purely mental (and as such) independent of the sense-organs. (*SV* Abhāva, 27, p. 341).

So, the judgment "p" implies denial of "not-p"; hence, all meaningful positive judgments embed negative cognitive essence — they are not mutually contradictory as Śaṅkara later wanted to argue; when the judgment tilts to the latter, in full view, literally, of the absence of "*p*", we say it in respect of the negative cognitive entity, "not-*p*". There cannot be a cognition without reference to some object or other. Kumārila is being consistently realist, perhaps a naïve negative realist!

In short, from Kumārila's standpoint, negation is not plain "ignorance" (*ajñāna*) but rather "the knowledge of absence" (*abhāvajñāna*), which occurs through the absence of knowledge of the counterpositive; in other words, *pratiyoginaḥ anupalabdhyā abhāvasya upalabdhiḥ*. Another way of putting this is to say that "negation is a cognition of *real* absence in the same way in which affirmation is (a) cognition of real presence". In Stcherbatsky's words: "The Mīmāṃsakas viewed non-existence as a reality *sui generis* (*vastuvantaram*)".[21] The Buddhist objection to this standpoint is that the process of grasping the absence connected with the perception of the bare locus (*kaivalya*) could be explained inferentially as tending towards the exclusive or *paryudāsa* kind of negation. Of course, the neo-Nyāya, railing against the Buddhist reductionism, also came to accept *abhāva* as designating a real which is absent in the locus (entity — hence a *padārtha*); however, the Naiyāyikas denied that its perceptual grasping (albeit, the non-cognition of the otherwise present in the locus of absence) needs to be attributed to an independent *pramāṇa*. The judgment for them is in respect of the cognition of the *locus* devoid of the suggested *relation* with the object negated there, on the epistemic consideration that the negative cognition must refer to positive entities only. The perception of kaivalya, bareness, is in respect of the locus (*ādhāra, adhikaraṇa, āśraya*) and not in respect of the absented object as such to which of course it is related by resemblance (i.e., relationally to its counterpositive). This alternative standpoint that inscribes a relational exclusion was first championed by Prabhākara, and by Śālikanāth Miśra[22] — who set out to refute *abhāvaprāmaṇa*, which brings the Prābhākarans closer to the Buddhists (who re-tool it as *dṛśyānupalabdhi*). The Naiyāyikas seem to have expropriated the qualified reading in Prabhākara in order to qualify the more radical standpoint of Kumārila: on the basis of the non-perception of a perceptible object (*dṛśyādarśana* or *yogyānupalambha*), whence the bare locus, the substratum (*bhūtala*) is cognised, the absence of the object is apprehended through a special inferential trope (*yogyānulapabdhi*). The free-standing reference to *anulapabdhi* is left-out as being otiose, in the Nyāya at least, while for later Mīmāṃsakas, particularly with Pārthasārathi Miśra, *anupalabdhi* comes to replace *abhāva* in naming the distinctive *pramāṇa* that is implicated, rendered it simply as "non-perception of the otherwise

[21] Cited in [12, pp. 35–36]. This means that for these philosophers the "non-existent" is a reality *sui generis* (*vastuvantaram*) and this "knowledge of absence" (not just absence of knowledge) is admitted via *yogya-pratiyogya-anupalabdhi*, though not as an inference (*anumāna*), but a special means of knowing, *pramāṇa*, which they called *abhāva*.

[22] Cf. Footnote 23.

perceptible object because of its absence in the locus". Śālikanātha, whom I just mentioned, invidiously misrepresents the theory of *abhāva* and gives it the Naiyāyika's twist; he writes

> the evidence to prove *abhāva* is the cognition that there is no jar on the ground (*bhūtale ghaṭo nāsti*) [10, p. 265].[23]

As we have seen, Kumārila makes no mention of *bhūtala* (or *ādhāra*, *adhikaraṇa*, *āśraya*); it is prolix for him to introduce the cognition of the substratum and what it is lacking —for the non-existence of the jar becomes a mere attribute of the ground— and the ground would be there even the jar is perceived but we do not necessarily relate the perception of the jar with the perception of the ground, which again is "bare to the bone" but for the presence of the jar! It would be more parsimonious to accept a direct cognition of the non-existence of the jar, regardless, rather than make recourse to its relational counterpositive — which is really a post-*abhāva* intellectual exercise!

The Prābhākarans reject this view because perception would require that there is contact of the senses with the non-existent, which is not possible; the only contact there is *is* with the ground or locus. So absence has to be viewed as the counterpositive (*pratiyogin*) of the *locus* which at another moment flagged that presence. It is not the *pratiyogin* of absence that comes to the cogniser's mind, rather it is the unified cognition of the locus-minus-the-object as *kaivalya* or *bareness*; the absence, if you will, of the relation between the ground and the jar. It is a disjunction built upon a prior conjunction. The disjunction is the non-perception of a positive thing, or it is a perception that underscores a dis-affirmation (literally, *an-upalabdhi*) of a thing, by exclusion (*nivṛtti*), not an affirmation of *no thing* (*tuccha*). It is the mere presence as *bare-boned locus* (*tanmātra*), which means that it is devoid of the relation with the other object: *anupalabdhir hi bhāvanam abhāvaḥ*. It is a denial of the perception of the object (*adṛśyānupalabdhi*; which is like 'inference to the *absence* of the best argument').

However, I contend that in its Bhāṭṭa formulation this doctrine ought not to be reduced to the *pramāṇa* (means of knowing) of *anupalabdhi* (non-cognition) as it only achieves this latter re-naming and articulation with Pārthasārathi Miśra and the Prābhākaran, Śālikanath Miśra. Both these commentators are influenced by and condescended to the criticisms of Buddhist logicians, especially Dharmakīrti (a contemporary of Kumārila, c. 7th century CE) and Prabhākara (the other doyen of the Mīmāṃsā) and indeed

[23] Neither is it a *prameya* nor is it separate *pramāṇa* what we call "non-cognition" is really a perception of the positive entity (the counterpositive), namely that the locus is bereft of a certain entity that otherwise was there — the latter is recalled by memory and thus provides the counterpositive as the positive entity in the apprehension along with the locus that is indeed given in perception.

to the Naiyāyikas. The latter themselves did not begin with the kind of radical doctrine of negation that they end up with, particularly, in Vallabha and Raghunāth Śiromaṇi.

The Buddhists again enter at this juncture and insist that without the bare locus nothing is perceived: or that all cognitions are in relation of one thing to another, and so it is only with reference to the empty ground that the negative judgment, "the jar is not there" is made possible. Dharmottara in *Nyāya-bindu-ṭikā*, puts it thus: "the perception of the *bare* locus with reference to the perceptible jar and the apprehension of this fact are the basis of the negative cognition". "Non-perception is due to the *paryudāsa* type of negation" (which is really Dharmakīrti's position in *Nyāya-bindu*).[24]

It is the Nyāya-Vaiśeṣikas who heed most to this objection, recognising that since there is no direct sense-contact with the non-existent object it cannot properly be said to be a case of perception; however, if we shift the focus to the *locus* —or if the locus is made the focal point of perception— then the onus too shifts from the non-existent to the absence-marking-the-locus, as though the invisible ink- traces of the once-present-but-now-absent object is simmering to the clear-light of the mind that picks up the efflorescence. A negative entity of the kind the Bhāṭṭas of the realist world are hell-bent on positing is not a substance and it therefore cannot come into contact with the senses (*indriyasannikar ṣāyogya*). Thus, on the anti-Bhāṭṭa view circling around, it is far better to hypotheticate a *unique* relation (*viśe ṣaṇatā*) between the so-called negative entity (*nivṛtti*, by default) and the locus or substratum which is at least *pravṛtti*, substantive. Thus, they maintain that the reality of non-existence (*abhāva*) is perceived not as ordinary perception goes but as *qualifying* the locus which is a perceivable substance (Śrīdhara, though it is also in Vallabha). This is tantamount to the return of the *bhūtalamātra* in another guise. Even Raghunātha Śiromaṇi, who bolstered the logical character of negation by redefining *abhāvatva* as *upadhi*, and introducing double negation without regress, could not bring himself to accept the traditional Bhāṭṭa view of "*abhāva*" as an ontological *padārtha* that calls for its own distinctive *pramāṇa*; he accepts *abhāva* as a *prameya*, yes, but only derivatively so. And much has been made of this compromised Navya-Nyāya doctrine in recent literature on Indian philosophy, even as it took the sails out of the more radical Bhāṭṭa view. *Why* then this resistance to condescending to "*abhāva*" as an object (*padārtha*) not in respect of the absent-marked locus as the perceptible object (*prameya*), but of *absence* qua the non-existent itself that is neither perceived nor inferred but is the result of a certain "non-cognition"?

Two implications of the Bhāṭṭa view are worth noting: where there is absolute absence of valid knowledge of something, one can be assured

[24]Notice that *paryudāsa* negation still involves or implies an affirmation, so this is "catch-22" situation from which even the Buddhist could not escape!

that it is absolutely non-existent. The omniscience of the Buddha, and the existence of God, are two such instances. But what if as the Prābhākarans insist, the absence of perception (or non-perception) is a given for non-perceptibles (*adṛśyavastu*), as for some perceptibles too (as in the standard examples of *anupalabdhi*)? The Bhāṭṭa's retort that their theory of *abhāva* does not preclude non-perceptibles — not due to some yogic feat, but by virtue of the possibility of cognition of non-existents in the empirical plane (which does not rule out their existence and positive perception thereof in other possible and real worlds: Martians, for example, seeing green cheese). *Adṛśya* should not be conflated with *anupalabdhi*; something non-existent does not mean it is imperceptible (to the mind, even if not to the senses). Sensory contact was not deemed essential to the perception of absence (and by the time of Gaṅgeśa nor for presence either), why then for other non-existents?

Second, and in concluding this disquisition, the theory of negation has ramifications for a theory of emancipation as well. If the life of *saṃsāra* is full of pain or *duḥkha* as the Buddha also recognised (he wasn't the first to do so, the Śramaṇa and Jainas preceded him), then the eradication of pain or the "absolute non-existence of pain" (*duḥkhātyanta-vomikṣo apavargaḥ*), accordingly to *asatkārya* theory of causality, namely, "non-pre-existent effect" entails that its causes, including its "antecedent non-existence" (*prāgabhāva*), be destroyed (*dhvaṃsa*-ed) by the production of the effect: so this implies a double negation of contraries. Thus, it is clear that apart from the problem of negative judgment, postulation of the negative reality was necessary (also) for their doctrines of Causality and Emancipation. Although, the Mīmāṃsakas' *apavarga* was not as negative, ironically for the *bhūtalamātrikas*, as that of the Naiyāyikas where the end-state of enlightenment was some zombie-like, tirelessly pain-free fiddling in a state of near-boredom[25]; rather for the Mīmāṃsaka, there was at least the rich harvest of the *apūrva*, the transcendental credits or "never-before merits" from the rituals performed and the negative injunctions too carried out equally diligently or with the same inner propulsion of the *śābdībhāvana*, from which a blissful state of *svarga*, or heaven in all worlds could be gleefully drawn upon. Here the empirical world becomes the object of the negative perception of absence, a real negation at that; and realism is not ever compromised: one does not need to run off to or with the temptresses of metaphysical or internal realism of any variety, Indian or Western.

Vive la negation and negative realism of the Mīmāṁsā!

Primary Sources

SV. = *Ślokavārttika*, with Nyāyaratnākara of Pārthasārathi Miśra, in: [1].

[25] Cf. [5].

References

[1] Kumārila Bhaṭṭa. *Ślokavārttika with Nyāyaratnākara of Pārthasārathi Miśra*. Prāchyabhārati Series 10. Tara Publications, Varanasi, 1978.

[2] Kumārila Bhaṭṭa. *Ślokavārttika*. The Asiatic Society, Calcutta, 1985. Translated by Ganganatha Jha.

[3] Krishna C. Bhattacharyya. Some Aspects of Negation. In Gopinath Bhattacharyya, editor, *Krishnachandra Bhattacharyya Studies in Philosophy*, volume I and II. Motilal Banarsidass, Delhi, 1983.

[4] Purushottama Bilimoria. Authorless Voice, Tradition and Authority in the *Mīmāṃsā* — Reflections of Cross-Cultural Hermeneutics. *Nagoya Studies in Indian Culture and Buddhism: Sambhāṣā*, 16:137–160, 1995.

[5] Purushottama Bilimoria. Nyāya. In Helaine Selin, editor, *Encyclopedia of the History of Non-Western Science: Natural Sciences, Technology and Medicine*. Springer-, Dordrecht, 2007.

[6] Franklin Edgerton. *The Mīmāṅsā Nyāya Prakaśa or Āpadevī: A Treatise on the Mīmāṅsā System by Āpadeva. Translated into English, with an Introduction, Transliterated Sanskrit Text, and Glossarial Index*, volume 36 of *Sri Garib Dass Oriental Series*. Sri Satguru Publications, Delhi, 1986.

[7] Birgit Kellner. There are no Pots in the *Ślokavārttika*. *Journal of the Oriental Institute*, 46(3–4):143–168, 1997.

[8] Bimal Krishna Matilal. *The Navya-Nyāya Doctrine of Negation: The Semantics and Ontology of Negative Statements in Navya-Nyāya Philosophy*, volume 46 of *Harvard Oriental Series*. Harvard University Press, Cambridge, Massachusetts, 1968.

[9] Jitendranath N. Mohanty. *Dharma*, Imperatives, and Tradition. In Purushottama Bilimoria, J. Prabhu, and Ramesh Sharma, editors, *Indian Ethics, Classical and Contemporary Challenges*, volume 1. Ashgate Publishers, Aldershot, 2007.

[10] Śālikenātha. *Prakaraṇapañcikā*. Indian Council of Philosophical Research, New Delhi, 2004. with an exposition in English, K. T. Pandurangi.

[11] K.S. Ramaswami Sāstrī, editor. *Rāmānujācārya, Tantrarahasyam*. Oriental Institute, Baroda, 1956.

[12] Dhirendra Sharma. *The Negative Dialectic*. Sterling, Delhi, 1974.

[13] Jayasankar L. Shaw. Negation and the Buddhist Theory of Meaning. *Journal of Indian Philosophy*, 6:59–77, 1978.

[14] Jayasankar L. Shaw. Negation: Some Indian Theories. In Dalsukh Malvania and Nagin J. Shah, editors, *Studies in Indian Philosophy: A Memorial Volume in Honour of Pandit Sukhlalji Sanghvi*, pages 57–78. Institute of 0Indology, Ahmedabad, 1981.

[15] Jayasankar L. Shaw. The Nyāya on Double Negation. *Notre Dame Journal of Formal Logic*, 29(1):139–154, 1989.

[16] Frits Staal. Negation and the Law of Contradiction in Indian Thought: A Comparative Study. In Frits Staal, editor, *Universals : Studies in Indian Logic and Linguistics*, pages 109–128, Chicago, 1988. Chicago University Press.

[17] Frits Staal. *Universals: Studies in Indian Logic and Linguistics*. Chicago University Press, Chicago, 1988.

[18] Satis C. Vidyabhusana. *History of the Medieval School of Indian Logic*. Oriental Books Reprint Corporation, New Delhi, 1977.

[19] David B. Zilberman. *Birth of Meaning in Hindu Thought*. Boston Series in Philosophy of Science. D. Reidel Publishing Co., Dordrecht, 1988.

"Marry your daughter to a handsome person": The Nyāya Techniques of Precisification

Amita Chatterjee, Mihir K. Chakraborty*

Department of Philosophy and Centre for Cognitive Science, Jadavpur University, Kolkata 700 032, India

Department of Pure Mathematics, University of Calcutta, Kolkata 700 019, India

E-mail: amita_ju@yahoo.com, mihirc99@yahoo.co.in

Imprecision and vagueness are ineliminable features of any natural language. Philosophers, logicians and computer scientists are always in search of some effective measure to deal with them. Like logicians and ideal language philosophers of the last century, the Neo-Naiyāyikas also developed a highly technical language between the thirteenth and the eighteenth century (CE) to handle imprecision and uncertainty that often creep in when one addresses some real world problem. The Naiyāyikas are hard core fallibilists. So, they can easily admit the fact that most of our knowledge is incomplete and revisable and any being, who is not omniscient, cannot but act on the basis of incomplete knowledge. They have, therefore, taken some measures to avoid uncertainty and imprecision or neutralize uncertainty factors, if these cannot be eliminated. Surprisingly, discussions on vagueness and sorites-induced difficulties are conspicuous by their absence in the Nyāya and the Buddhist philosophical literature, which is replete with analyses of different types of semantic paradoxes. One may ask, why didn't the Naiyāyikas ever deal with vagueness? It is possible to offer a number of philosophical reasons for that. We are not going to enter into them here. We shall rather address the following counterfactual, what would have been the reaction of the Neo-Naiyāyikas, had anybody raised the issue of vagueness? We have looked into the Nyāya literature meticulously but haven't found any satisfactory answer to the question. In fact, we find a proper example of vagueness only in the famous Grammarian Patañjali's work, *Mahābhāṣya*, where he has introduced the vague predicate "handsome" while discussing an important semantic principle. Though the Naiyāyikas do not always agree with the Grammarians, they do not seem to disagree with the interpretation of this semantic principle. Our main aim in this paper is, therefore, to speculate on the Nyāya attitude to vagueness/ imprecision[1] and possible

*We are extremely grateful to two anonymous referees for their critical comments and important suggestions of improvement. This research is funded by the University Grants Commission under its *University with Potential for Excellence Scheme*.

[1]Here we are using "imprecision" generically without making subtle distinctions

Mihir K. **Chakraborty**, Benedikt **Löwe**, Madhabendra Nath **Mitra**, Sundar **Sarukkai** (*eds.*). Logic, Navya-Nyāya & Applications. Homage to Bimal Krishna Matilal. College Publications, London, 2008. Studies in Logic 15. pp. 65–79.

Received by the editors: 11 May 2007; 22 February 2008, 11 September 2008.
Accepted for publication: 15 October 2008.

remedies thereof with the help of the meagre clue available in the Indian philosophical literature. Matilal's analysis of property and location terms[2], the two main props of Navya-Nyāya logic and epistemology, will help us devising the techniques of precisification within the Nyāya framework.

For convenience of discussion,we have introduced different types of imprecise sentences as examples. A sentence like "Sky-lotus does not exist" is imprecise because its subject term is empty. The sentence "There is bird-contact on the tree" is imprecise because of the peculiar nature of the contact involved. It is difficult to ascribe any definite truth value to the sentence "The milkman's hamlet is on the bank of the river Ganga", because we do not know where the river-bank ends. Again, a sentence involving the predicate "handsome" is vague because there is always some uncertainty about its cases of application. The Naiyāyikas have attempted to deal with such sentences differently and we are just trying to understand these techniques in the light of contemporary tools of precisification. It is not our intention to develop a unified theory of vagueness/imprecision on behalf of the Naiyāyikas.

The paper is divided into five sections. In the first section, we introduce the concept of vagueness and the Nyāya concepts of property, location and delimitor. The second section deals with a version of supervaluational semantics which the Naiyāyikas might have used to handle vague predicates. In the third section, we discuss another plausible way of handling vague expressions, i.e., in terms of comparatives. The fourth section has been devoted to the problems related to vague objects and the final section depicts our conclusion.

1

Before entering into the Nyāya philosophy of language, we need to specify what we mean by vagueness for "vagueness", again, is an imprecise expression. Peirce [13] offered a definition, which could capture the essence of vagueness. Peirce says,

> A proposition is vague when there are possible states of things concerning which it is intrinsically uncertain whether had they been contemplated by the speaker, he would have regarded them as excluded or allowed by the proposition. By intrinsically we mean not uncertain in consequence of any ignorance of the interpreter, but because the speaker's habits of language were indeterminate.

A term is vague à la Peirce, if there are cases in which there is no definite answer as to whether or not the term applies. The term "old", for instance,

amongst different kinds of imprecision.

[2]Cf. [11, Chapter 2] and [10].

is vague. A man over seventy-five is definitely old, a man below forty is definitely not, but what about a man of fifty-five? We are not certain whether the term "old" legitimately applies here or not. So, in the extension of vague terms, there is always a region of uncertainty, which is called the penumbral region. Vague expressions, therefore, lack sharp boundaries. Something is called vague where no natural boundary exists, i.e., when things are naturally arranged in a gradient. Colour predicates are examples of this phenomenon.

Another important feature of vagueness is that vague terms are characterized by tolerance. Here, by "tolerance" is meant that vague terms are immune to small changes; only a big change raises doubt about the application of a term. Consider the predicate "tall". Marginal change in height does not make the predicate inapplicable. But the important question is how much tolerance may a vague term possess? Logically, there is no limit to it. But then a midget will be as tall as a giant is and in that case sorites paradox will follow inevitably.

With this little introduction to the concept of vagueness, we can now move on to the Nyāya theory. Navya-Nyāya logic and epistemology are known to be couched in the language of *dharma* and *dharmin* — two terms, which are very often translated as property and its substratum. Matilal has, however, rightly argued for translating them as "locatee" and "locus". The Naiyāyikas have used "*dharma*" (locatee) in a much wider sense than "property". A locatee is an occurrent entity. It may be either an abstract particular, say, e.g., the property of being *ākāśa*[3] (*ākāśatva*) located in *ākāśa*, a concrete particular, e.g., a pot on a table or a cat on a mat, or an abstract generality like sweetness in honey, or a relational adjective like cup-contact of a table. Nobody usually considers a pot a property of a table or a cat a property of a mat on which it sits. So by relying on the common Sanskritist insight — *vṛttimān dharmaḥ* (a locatee is what is occurrent in something else) Matilal is in favour of using "locatee" in lieu of "property".

Navya-Nyāya logicians expressed any cognitive event in terms of "a locatee in a locus". Hence their basic logical unit is of the form "a has f" or "f-ness in a". Accordingly, the logical universe U of Navya-Nyāya is populated with two types of individuals — locatees and locations or loci. Ontologically speaking, locus and locatee need not be of different types. For, what appears as a locatee in one context may appear as a location in relation to something else. Thus a cup is a locatee in respect of its locus table, but is a locus in respect of the milk it contains. Given any locatee t, it is possible to find a set of locations or loci where t is locatable or present and another set of loci where t is not locatable or absent. For example, smoke,

[3] *Ākāśa* is the fifth material element out of which the world is built, the other four being earth, water, fire and air.

which is located in a mountain, is locatable in a kitchen, in a cowshed, etc., but not locatable in a lake. Here, we must mention an important point. In Navya-Nyāya, "locatibility" was not used in a dispositional sense. In fact, there is a big debate among the modern interpreters of Navya-Nyāya regarding the question whether the concept of possible worlds was at all available as a tool in Navya-Nyāya. However, in spite of the possibility of confusion, we are sticking to "locatibility" because stalwarts like Matilal have used this expression copiously and changing it might lead to greater confusions. The loci where a locatee is locatable is called the presence-range (t_+) of it and all places where that locatee is non-locatable constitute its absence-range (t_-). In case of most locatees both presence-range and absence-range are non-empty, but fictitious locatees like sky-flowers have empty presence-range and ever-present locatees like knowability have empty absence-range. Ordinarily, the Navya-Naiyāyikas consider the presence-range and the absence-range of a locatee mutually disjoint where a locatee is completely occurrent in its locus (*vyāpya-vṛtti dharma*), e.g., the universal pothood is present in a pot in its entirety and not in some of its parts. But these two ranges overlap in case of non-pervasive locatees. (*a-vyāpya-vṛtti dharma*). Thus when a bird sits on a tree, there are places in the tree where there is no contact between the bird and the tree. So the bird is a non-pervasive locatee of the locus tree, since the same tree can be taken as the locus of the bird and the absence of the bird. The obvious casualty of this admission is the classical notion of contradiction. To understand this anomaly, we need to explain the Nyāya notion of relational negation in terms of locus and locatee.[4] A relational negation is nothing but the negation of the occurrence of a locatee in a locus. Consider, for instance, the sentence "the pot is blue". Its negation "the pot is not blue" means "the pot does not possess blue colour" which can be paraphrased as "the pot has the absence of blue colour". So negation here means the negation of a locatee, viz. "absence of blue colour" in a particular locus, viz. the pot. In case of non-pervasive locatees, we have seen that the same locus can be characterised by a locatee and its absence. That is, in such cases, one ascribes and denies the occurrence of the same locatee in the same locus. Isn't it a palpable violation of the principle of non-contradiction? In view of this problem, the Neo-Naiyāyikas rewrite the original problematic sentence by introducing a very effective multi-purpose tool of precisification — the concept of delimitorhood (*avacchedakatva*).

"*Avacchedaka*" (de-limitor) has been used in various different senses. The correlative property, delimitorhood (*avacchedakatva*), has been taken as that property which differentiates an object from other objects. Most

---

[4]Incidentally, the Nyāya-Vaiśeṣika philosophers admit two types of negation — relational negation, e.g., "the pen is not in the pen-holder" and difference, e.g., "a pen is not a pencil".

of the time, it is taken to be a property, which is co-extensive with the defining property of a term. For example, humanity is the property that delimits and thus differentiates humans from non-humans. Again, the term has been used just to refer to the locus of an object, e.g., "There is fire in the base of the hill" (*parvate nitambāvacchedena bahni*), i.e., the base of the hill is the de-limitor here. Another example is, "The bird-contact on the tree is delimited by its branch" (*vṛkṣe śākhāvacchedena pakṣī-saṃyoga*). In a cognitive situation, the delimitor performs the following functions: (1) it states explicitly the mode of presentation of an object, (2) it acts as a quantifier in a content-expressing sentence, and (3) it helps us to determine which pair of sentences is contradictory. Since here we are concerned only with the third point, we shall not explain the first two functions.

To determine which pair of sentences are contradictory to each other, the notion of the "delimitor" has to be used and here we are concerned with the delimitor of the negatum of an absence. By the negatum of an absence is meant that which is being negated, e.g., pot is the negatum of the absence of a pot. An absence is always individuated by its negatum. Now, the cognition of the form, "There is a pot on the floor" is contradicted by the cognition of "There is no pot on the floor", but not by the cognition of the form "There is no substance on the floor". Though a pot is a substance, yet the second negative sentence will not contradict the first affirmative one. To contradict the first cognition the negatum of the absence must be qualified by the same delimitor, which also delimits the qualifier of the affirmative cognition. So to contradict the first cognition the negatum of the absence in the second cognition must be delimited by the property of being a pot *qua* pot and not by the property of being a pot *qua* substance. So to avoid the contradiction between two cognition expressing sentences — "there is a bird on the tree" and "there is no bird on the tree" the locus has to be delimited by two different delimitors. In the first case, the tree is to be delimited by one of its branches, while in the second case it is to be delimited by the tree-trunk. Thus the apparent contradiction can be resolved. It is evident that in case of pervasive or completely occurrent locatees, no such problem will arise because it can never be the case that pot-hood and absence of pot-hood are simultaneously present in the same entity.

2

While logicians have prescribed various ways of regimentation of natural language, the most common tool of uncertainty management found in *Good Old Fashioned Artificial Intelligence* is adoption of multivalent logic, finally honed into fuzzy logic in the inference engine. In connectionist systems too, fuzzy neural nets, fuzzy petri nets, etc., have been introduced to deal with imprecision. Those who are not in favour of multivalent inference engine often use a technique of precisification to handle vague sentences. Instances of such techniques are *supervaluational logic* developed by van Fraassen [16, 17] and *super-truth theory* of Fine [5]. Van Fraassen developed his supervaluational logic with a view to determining the truth value of a sentence containing an empty name or a non-denoting singular term. Let us consider the following sentences

$$\text{Lightning has a white forelock,} \tag{2.1}$$

and

$$\text{Pegasus has a white forelock.} \tag{2.2}$$

The second sentence contains an empty name. If this sentence occurs as a premise of an argument, will the argument ever be valid? Van Fraassen maintains that such an inference will remain valid in spite of the occurrence of the empty name by his theory of supervaluation. Very simply stated, the theory of supervaluation is as follows. A name is always defined in respect of a particular domain, say, D. A name, say, "Lightning" is defined in D if it has a reference in D and any sentence ascribing an appropriate predicate to "Lightning" will be true in this particular domain. If, on the other hand, the name "Lightning" does not have a reference in D, then a sentence like "Lightning has a white forelock" is neither true nor false in D. Next, van Fraassen introduced the notion of classical valuation. A classical valuation is a method of eliminating the truth-value gap by assigning truth-values to indefinite sentences in an arbitrary manner. If there is any name e that has no reference in a given domain, and A is an atomic sentence containing e, then there are at least two classical valuations over this domain; one which assigns T (true) to A and one which assigns F (false) to A. A supervaluation, on the other hand, will assign T (F) to a sentence, if it is assigned T (F) by all classical valuations or else no truth value. The notion can be made clear with the help of the following table.

Let us suppose that a specific language $\mathcal{L}$ contains exactly one monadic predicate F and exactly two names a and b, such that a is non-empty and b is empty. Let us also suppose that there are exactly two classical valuations, v_1 and v_2. Then the supervaluation assigned to sentences will be as follows:

	v_1	v_2	S
Fa	T	T	T
$\neg Fa$	F	F	F
Fb	T	F	—
$\neg Fb$	F	T	—
$Fb \vee \neg Fb$	T	T	T

The table shows that even if there is a truth value gap in the sentences containing an empty name, b, "$Fb \vee \neg Fb$" remains true under supervaluation.

Ermano Bencivenga [1] has captured this spirit of supervaluation perfectly. He writes, "The set of logical truths should be absolutely independent of the philosophy of language we decide to adopt. There will be conventions assigning True to (2.2), again conventions assigning false to it?. Logic can be at best committed to the logical product of all possible conventions, to what is going to be true (or false), no matter what convention you adopt".

The motto of van Fraassen is, therefore, to retain classical truth conditions as far as possible, yet he admits truth-value gap in the context of sentences containing empty names. But the Naiyāyikas do not admit multivalence or truth-value gap in sentences containing empty names. This becomes obvious in their special treatment of negative existential statements, which is reminiscent of Russell's analysis of definite descriptive phrases. First they translate "A does not exist" as "A does not exist in ℓ" (where ℓ is a particular location). Next they will ask whether A stands for a simple word or a compound word. If the former is the case, then they will declare the sentence as meaningless because they do not admit the possibility of any empty simple word. As Matilal writes, "such simple components are always real properties in the sense that they are locatable in some locus or other in our actual world [11]". If, on the other hand, A stands for a compound word like "sky-lotus" or "hare's horn", then they paraphrase the negative existential sentence "Sky-lotus does not exist" as "there is no lotus in the sky" and similarly "there is no horn in a hare" and thus explain away the empty words.

How would a Naiyāyika deal with sentences containing vague terms, say, for instance, "tall"? Like Kit Fine [5], he would try to sharpen the vague predicate by replacing it with a sharp predicate. Let's first look at Fine's proposal. In Fine's theory truth-valuations depend upon an appropriate specification space. A specification space consists of a non-empty set of elements or specification points, and a partial ordering on the set which is reflexive, transitive and antisymmetric. A specification is complete, according to Fine, if it assigns only the definite truth values. A vague sentence is considered true if it is true for all admissible and complete specifications. A specification is admissible if it is appropriate for some precisification. A true sentence is true for all ways of making it precise. A vague sentence might be true at some complete specification point and false at others. Without entering into the technicalities and that is not required for our purpose either, we can say that the crux of Fine's precisification technique consists of distributing the penumbral region of a vague predicate within its complete and admissible specification space in some suitable way. What Fine wanted to convey through spatial metaphors can be narrated in a different language following Mark Sainsbury [14, 15]. In lieu of "precisification", Sainsbury uses "refinement" or "sharpening". A vague predicate can be sharpened if we can replace it by a sharp predicate. This is what Fine means by extending or precisifying a vague predicate. Now what is a sharp predicate? Let's explain it with the help of the vague predicate "tall". Suppose that a person's height is $5'6''$ and it is vague whether somebody of this height can be called tall or not. That means this height falls in the penumbral region of the vague predicate "tall". Sainsbury says that we may precisify or sharpen it by replacing it with a sharp predicate, say, "P-tall" such that heights equal to or above $5'6''$ will fall in its positive extension and all heights below $5'6''$ will fall in its negative extension. Replacing "tall" by "P-tall" is just one way of sharpening. We could have sharpened it by various different ways by shifting the borderline this way or that and by redistributing the instances of the penumbral region to the positive and the negative extension of the new sharp predicates. A vague sentence will be true or false at each sharpenings but it will be true *simpliciter*, if and only if it remains true in all admissible sharpenings. A sharpening is considered *admissible* if the meaning content of the sharpened predicate does not get reduced in accordance with our established linguistic usage.

That the Naiyāyikas would tend to adopt Fine's technique for making a vague predicate precise becomes very much plausible, if we recall how they proposed to handle sentences involving non-pervasive predicates. By introducing the concept of delimitor, they got rid of the contradiction by redrawing the boundary between the presence range and the absence range of the predicate "bird-contact". The original imprecise predicate "bird-contact" was replaced by a sharper predicate "bird-contact delimited by the branch of a tree". Consequently, the presence-range of the new sharp predicate has been restricted and its absence-range has been widened. "Bird-contact" does not seem to be a vague predicate in the same way the predicate "tall" is, nonetheless it is imprecise and the Nyaya approach was to remove this imprecision by gradual precisification of the predicate. Let us explain. Suppose, someone asks, "Is the sentence 'There is a bird-contact on the tree' true?" The answer will depend on how we specify the contact between the bird and the tree. Without any specification the sentence is neither true nor false. Under one specification, it may turn out true and under another it may turn out false. If the sentence is rewritten as "There is a bird-contact delimited by a branch on the tree", it will be true. But if it is specified as "There is a bird contact delimited by the trunk on the tree", it will be false. Let's concentrate on the first way of precisifying the given sentence. This precisification, though admissible, may not be complete and may, therefore, be in need of further specification like "There is a bird-contact delimited by the branch b on the tree". One might still ask, "Where on the branch b is the bird-contact towards the edge or towards the trunk?", etc. These successive precisifications are all admissible specifications and the Naiyāyikas believe that eventually through the process of precisification one is bound to reach a complete specification where the sentence will yield a definite truth value. So, depending on the context, the predicate "bird-contact" will be suitably modified by adding delimitors with a view to narrowing down the penumbral region. The Naiyāyikas are likely to adopt the same technique to successfully accommodate a possible case of truth value gap engendered by a typical vague predicate.

3

Both the old and the new school of Nyāya subscribe to a direct referential theory of meaning and a definite categorial framework in ontology. Hence, according to them, all sentences that are amenable to literal interpretation are either determinately true or determinately false. In our everyday parlance, however, we use sentences, which are to be given extended metaphorical interpretation. One such sentence is: "The milkmen's hamlet is on the river Ganga" (*gangāyām ghoṣaḥ*)[5] which is to be interpreted as "The milkmen's hamlet is just on the bank of the river Ganga". It is, however, entirely indeterminate where the riverbank ends, even though there is unanimity regarding where the riverbank begins. According to the ritualistic practice, any village or town within one mile of the river is to be considered on the riverbank. The nearer the village is to the river the more will it receive the cool breeze and the holier will be its soil. What happens if there are three villages within one mile of the bank of the river Ganga, the second and the third village being more and more away from the bank? We think there will be no difference in respect of their holiness but definitely, the second village will have less cool breeze than the first one and therefore by introducing a criterion of comparative measurement, like "closer to the bank than", the Naiyāyikas will remove the inherent vagueness of the expression "on the river Ganga". For, though "tall" is a vague predicate, everybody admits that "taller than" is not.

The same technique has been indicated in the case of 'Marry your daughter to a handsome person'[6] (*abhirūpāya kanyā pradeyā*). This example, as we have already mentioned, has been taken from Patañjali's *Mahābhāṣya* on Pāṇini's aphorism 1/4/42. The discussion has been initiated in a totally different context. Patañjali was interpreting the phrase 'the most efficient' in the definition of instrumental cause. According to the Grammarians and the Naiyāyikas, one event is generally produced by a collection of causal

[5]See Annaṃbhaṭṭa's *Tarkasamgraha-Dīpikā* in [6].

[6]The translation is by Matilal of Patañjali's *Mahābhāṣya* 1/4/42 [7].

conditions. Of these, the most efficient causal condition is to be taken as the instrumental cause and is to be expressed by using the third case-ending. But which one of the causal conditions is to be taken as the most efficient one? Patañjali suggests that one should follow the principle of the most general interpretation. The principle of the most general interpretation says that when the choice is open, choose the best. So the sentence used as the example should mean, one would get one's daughter married to the most handsome (if he is available), and would not marry her off to one that is not handsome. How is one supposed to judge who is the most handsome? According to the standard dictionaries of technical terms (*kośa*), God is the paradigm of handsome-ness. Surely, God is not available as the groom. So the guardian of the prospective bride must choose the most handsome from among the ordinary mortals. The parent of the girl finds the man from Pataliputra more handsome than one from Samkasya. Therefore, under the circumstances, the man from Pataliputra will be considered more handsome and therefore more eligible. What logical insight can we derive from this example? "Handsome" is a vague predicate and the ideal limits of its applications are determined. God is prototypically handsome and at the other end is placed the definitely ugly. In between these limits, people are assigned graded membership to the set of handsome persons, some being more handsome than the others. Though the Naiyāyikas have not explicitly mentioned of any scale of handsomeness, still their acceptance of the *tara-tama* (more-the most) rule of grammar related to the use of the comparatives and superlatives leads us to believe that they may not be averse to admit graded membership to a set associated with a vague predicate. In fixing the limits, the Naiyāyikas has always followed the scriptural injunctions where available and in other cases they were guided by common usage. They also thought of multiple criteria of handsomeness depending on the context. This becomes obvious in case of the predicate "eligible" (the same term "*abhirūpa*" can be translated as "eligible"). Sometimes, a person is considered eligible, if he is handsome, again, sometimes if he is rich or young or respected in the community. Kaiyaṭa writes in his commentary that the eligibility of the groom depends on for what reason one tries to marry off one's daughter. If the purpose is to ensure happiness of the bride, then some considerations prevail, if, on the other hand, the parent wants to marry off his daughter because of social pressure or soteriological or scriptural consideration, then the parent of the bride would adopt a totally different criterion of eligibility.

4

That vagueness permeates our natural language is an uncontested fact. But some have raised the question: what is the source of vagueness in language?

Is the world itself vague, and vagueness in language reflects the vague nature of reality? Or, is it the case that vagueness is a peculiar feature of human description? Philosophers widely differ among themselves on this issue. Most discussions on ontic vagueness move around the question of the possibility of vague objects. It is commonly held that a vague object is an object with indeterminate or fuzzy spatio-temporal boundaries. Most objects in this world possess fuzzy boundaries in this sense. There is no natural boundary around clouds, mountains, etc. The Naiyāyikas, however, will not hesitate to draw some arbitrary boundary in such cases as is evident from their use of delimitors. There is another familiar way of defining a vague object and that is by associating it with an indeterminate identity condition. Gareth Evans [4] denied the possibility of vague objects by denying the possibility of indeterminate identity, though the legitimacy of this move has been disputed. It appears from their penchant for precisification that the Naiyāyikas will be in favour of conceding a small and manageable amount of fuzzy boundary, which can be rationalised and explained away, rather than tolerating indefinite identity.

There are certain puzzle cases about identity, which have left the followers of Evans quite uneasy. One such case is the now-famous ship of Theseus. The ship got damaged in the mid-sea and was repaired by gradually replacing the old rotten planks with new planks. Is the ship containing the replacement planks the same as the original Theseus's ship? Many think that there is no fact of the matter to decide whether the original ship is identical with the repaired ship. To a Naiyāyika, however, this type of cases will not appear as a puzzle case because they maintain that if you change even one tiny part in a whole, you get a new whole[7]. So, in the Nyāya scheme, the repaired ship is not identical with the original ship of Theseus[8].

The Naiyāyikas' stance on ontic vagueness is so definite because they operate with an entirely determinate categorial framework in their ontology. But can the whole world be classified in neat little pigeonholes, especially when we deal with biological species in the age of genetic engineering? We can have boundary-defying living beings in a large number. How are we going to individuate such beings? A natural kind is generally individuated with the help of the natural sort associated with it. But what about hybrid animals like tigons (a hybrid of tiger and lion) and litigons (a hybrid of tigon and lion), which fall in the penumbra of tiger and lion concepts? The Naiyāyikas have long-drawn arguments on this issue: whether a set of hybrid animals constitutes a new species or not. The oft-used example in this context is that of mule. There is no unanimity among the Naiyāyikas on this issue. However, most Naiyāyikas are not in favour of declaring

[7] Cf. [12].

[8] For a detailed discussion, cf. [2, 3].

a class of hybrid animals a distinct species on the ground of parsimony. So they are reluctant to increase the number of natural sorts admitted in their system in such contexts. In absence of a natural sort corresponding to hybrid animals, the Nyāya scheme of dividing the world in neat little categories is bound to receive a jolt. Most probably, the Naiyāyikas will attempt to individuate such hybrid animals by delimiting them with some arbitrary property (upādhi) related to their functions.

5

It is apparent from the foregoing discussion that the Naiyāyikas would employ various methods to treat different instances of imprecision/ uncertainty/ vagueness. For example, to deal with empty terms, unlike van Fraassen, they would consider atomic sentences with empty term(s) meaningless, while negative existential sentences containing compound empty term(s) would be paraphrased appropriately to explain them away.

Secondly, uncertainties arising out of the use of predicates like "bird-contact" have been handled by introducing delimitors, the essential function of which is precisification. Since the Naiyāyikas have actually used the delimitor to fix the boundary in case of non-pervasive predicates, it appears that their move of handling vague sentences like "This man is tall" or "This blob is pink" would come closest to the super-truth technique. Like the supervaluationists, they would give up the tolerance of vague predicates in the penumbral region and would explain away vagueness instead of explaining it. Again, such monadic vague predicates may be paraphrased in terms of a dyadic crisp comparative predicate, e.g., "is tall" to "is taller than". We have mentioned that this is also a quite plausible approach for the Naiyāyikas to take while dealing with predicates like "handsome groom".

There is, however, one significant point of difference between the Naiyāyikas and the super-truth theorists. While a super-truth theorist would quantify over possible precisifications to *create* truth value gaps, a Naiyāyika would eventually do away with truth value gaps because he believes that one is sure to reach a definite truth value through precisification.

In case of the river-bank example, we have seen that a Naiyāyika depends on the scripture or some well-established convention to assign the limiting values and for the intermediate cases he would take resort to comparison. That means, there is a sort of scale in his mind. One might be tempted to introduce Fuzzy Logic at this point. In fuzzy set theory, the scale usually taken is a linear and dense set $[0, 1]$. If the Naiyāyika's approach is a kind of precisification, so is the fuzzy-set approach [18, 19]. Since, if an object x receives a value $\alpha \in [0, 1]$ in a fuzzy concept A, then one can easily define a crisp concept A_α (i.e., A at least to the extent α), the so-called α-level sets. Each α-level set is a precisification. However, this will not be an admissible reading. For, though comparatives introduce a natural ordering in the given predicate set, that ordering need not be an ordering of truth in the fuzzy way. Hans Kamp has thoroughly worked out how comparatives can be neatly accommodated within supervaluational semantics[9]. Another reason for not imposing fuzzy logic on Nyaya is that while fuzzy logicians question the Law of Excluded Middle, a Naiyāyika will be in favour of retaining it like the supervaluationists. Sainsbury, though not a fuzzy logician, points out what is problematic about retaining LEM uncritically. To show that the sentence 'either he is an adult or he is not' should not be treated as a tautology Sainsbury offers the following argument:

> Either he is an adult or he is not. If he is an adult, then watching the hard-porn movie will do him no harm. If he is not an adult, then he will not understand it... either way, it will do him no harm to watch it.

But Sainsbury observes that watching a hard-porn movie might harm an adolescent for he is in a stage between adulthood and childhood [14]. Making the Law of Excluded Middle artificially true forces us to set aside such instances, although the problem persists. The Naiyāyikas, we guess, will side with the supervaluationists in this respect rather than with Sainsbury.

Some may think that it is possible to compare the Nyāya approach to rough set approach too. We have noted some similarity in these two approaches while delimiting the boundary of a locatee. In rough set approach[10] the extension of a vague concept A is taken to be a pair $\langle A_+, A_- \rangle$ where A_+ is the set of objects to which A definitely applies and A_- is the set of objects to which A definitely does not apply. The set $(A_+)^{\mathsf{C}} \backslash A$ is the boundary region, objects of this region being cases where A is applied as well as is not applied; in other words, A is applied partially. These regions are defined in terms of granules or clusters of objects that are indiscernible relative to available information. While the identity of objects in these regions is determinately of yes/no type, the identity of objects in the boundary may be said to be partially determined. Rough set theorists prefer to use modal operators in their logic rather than opting for many-valuedness as done by fuzzy set theorists. The locatee-ranges t_+ and t_-, as proposed by the Navya-Nyāya, could have been easily interpreted as positive and negative extensions or in rough set-theoretic term the "definite" and "definitely not" part of a rough set, had there been scope for modal interpretation of the content of our cognition within the Nyāya framework, a possibility which

---

[9]Cf. [8]. Of course, Rosanna Keefe has pointed out problems in Kamp's theory and has suggested some important revisions in supervaluational semantics for handling comparatives of vague predicates which we intend to deal with in our future work [9].

[10]Cf., e.g., [20].

has not been admitted by most of the modern interpreters of Navya-Nyāya. There is a similarity between the boundary region of rough sets and the notion that the locatee is and is not in a location. This resemblance should be explored further. The granulation aspect of rough set approach is not found in the Nyāya treatment, though the gradualness aspect is almost visible.

References

[1] Ermanno Bencivenga. Free Logics. In Dov Gabbay and Franz Guenthner, editors, *Handbook of Philosophical Logic*, volume III. D. Reidel, Dordrecht, 1986.

[2] Amita Chatterjee. *Understanding Vagueness.* Pragati Publications, Delhi, 1994.

[3] Amita Chatterjee and Mihir K. Chakraborty. On Representation of Indeterminate Identity via Vague Concepts. *Journal of Applied Non-Classical Logics*, 6(2):191–201, 1996.

[4] Gareth Evans. Can There be Vague Objects? *Analysis*, 38:208, 1978.

[5] Kit Fine. Vagueness, Truth and Logic. *Synthese*, 30:265–300, 1975.

[6] Gopinath Bhattacharya, editor. *Annambhatta, Tarkasaṃgraha-Dīpikā.* Progressive Publishers, Calcutta, 1976.

[7] Jonardon Ganeri, editor. *The Collected Essays of Bimal Krishna Matilal, Volume 1: Mind, Language and World.* Oxford University Press, New Delhi, 2002.

[8] Hans Kamp. Two Theories About Adjectives. In Edward Keenan, editor, *Formal Semantics of Natural Languages*, pages 123–155. Cambridge University Press, 1975.

[9] Rosanna Keefe. *Theories of Vagueness.* Cambridge University Press, Cambridge, 2000.

[10] Bimal K. Matilal. On the Notion of the Locative in Sanskrit. In Jonardon Ganeri, editor, *The Collected Essays of Bimal Krishna Matilal, Volume 1: Mind, Language and World*, pages 326–332. Oxford University Press, 2002.

[11] Bimal Krishna Matilal. *Logic, Language and Reality: Indian Philosophy and Contemporary Issues.* Motilal Banarsidass, Delhi, 1985.

[12] Bimal Krishna Matilal. *Perception: An Essay on Classical Indian Theories of Knowledge.* Clarendon Press, Oxford, 1986.

[13] Charles S. Peirce. Vague. In James M. Baldwin, editor, *Dictionary of Philosophy and Psychology.* Macmillan and Co., London, 1902.

[14] Mark Sainsbury. *Paradoxes.* Cambridge University Press, Cambridge, 1988.

[15] Mark Sainsbury. What Is a Vague Object? *Analysis*, 49:99–103, 1989.

[16] Bas C. van Fraassen. Singular Terms, Truth Value Gaps and Free Logic. *Journal of Philosophy*, 67:481–495, 1966.

[17] Bas C. van Fraassen. Presupposition, Implication and Self-Reference. *Journal of Philosophy*, 69:136–152, 1968.

[18] Lofti A. Zadeh. Fuzzy Sets. *Information and Control*, 8:338–353, 1965.

[19] Lofti A. Zadeh. Fuzzy Logic and Approximate Reasoning. *Synthese*, 30:407–428, 1975.

[20] Zdzisław Pawlak. Rough Sets. *International Journal of Computing and Information Sciences*, 11(5):341–356, 1982.

Computational Complexity and the Expressive Power of Logics

Anuj Dawar

University of Cambridge Computer Laboratory, Cambridge CB3 0FD, United Kingdom
E-mail: anuj.dawar@cl.cam.ac.uk.

1 Introduction

The aim of this paper is to present some ongoing work in the area of descriptive complexity, that ties together the study of the expressive power of languages (or logical formalisms) and the study of computational complexity. Before presenting this work, I shall aim to place it in a wider context of the use of model-theoretic methods in computer science.

This, of course, is itself part of a wider picture of the use of mathematical logic in computer science. It is no exaggeration to say that the second half of the twentieth century has seen an intimate relationship develop between logic and computer science, perhaps greater than was ever the case between logic and mathematics. Indeed, it has been said that logic plays "a fundamental role for computer science similar to that played by calculus for physics" [31].

Some of the most significant work in tying logic and computer science belongs to what one might call the proof-theoretic tradition of logic. This focuses on describing logical deduction through syntactic proof rules and much work in the semantics of programming languages (cf. [39]) seeks to describe the processes of computation in the same terms. It is clear that all programs and data involved in computation can be suitably seen as strings of symbols and hence all computation treated at a purely syntactic level, as in the proof-theoretic view. At the same time, it is often useful, from the conceptual point of view, to distinguish certain of these syntactic constructs and regard them as computational *structures* that provide a semantics for other constructs that we regard as syntactic. This leads to what I term a *model-theoretic* view of computation, which has had much success in recent years in several areas of computer science such as complexity theory, database theory, computer-aided verification and constraint satisfaction problems.

In particular, a connection between logical definability and computational complexity was first established by Fagin [18], who showed that a class of finite structures is definable in existential second-order logic if and only if it is in the complexity class NP. This led to the development of the field of descriptive complexity theory in which a large number of com-

Mihir K. **Chakraborty**, Benedikt **Löwe**, Madhabendra Nath **Mitra**, Sundar **Sarukkai** (*eds.*). Logic, Navya-Nyāya & Applications. Homage to Bimal Krishna Matilal. College Publications, London, 2008. Studies in Logic 15. pp. 81–104.

Received by the editors: 26 May 2007; 28 February 2008.
Accepted for publication: 28 February 2008.

putational complexity classes have been redefined as definability classes in suitable logical formalisms (cf. [25] for a comprehensive treatment). The most important open problem in that field remains to provide a descriptive characterisation of the class P of polynomial time decidability, analogous to Fagin's characterisation of NP.

In the remainder of this paper, we begin with a general overview of the role of logic in computer science (§ 2) and see how it leads to the development of finite model theory, which we consider in § 3. We then focus on the problem of obtaining a descriptive characterisation of polynomial-time computation and in § 4 describe extensions of first-order logic that have been studied in this context. Finally, we shall consider the current state of work on the main open question in § 5.

2 Logic in Computer Science

When I speak of logic, I mean mathematical logic — that is, the trend in logic that drew its inspiration from mathematics. This inspiration takes two important forms. In one sense, if logic is understood to be the formalisation of reasoning, then mathematical logic is particularly concerned with formalising *mathematical* reasoning — i.e., the particular and specialised forms of reasoning that arise in mathematics. The other sense in which mathematical logic is informed by mathematics is that it uses mathematical methods in its study of reasoning. In particular, the elements that are the focus of the study of logic —elements such as proof, proposition, etc.— are turned into first-class mathematical objects in their own right.

For our purposes, it is useful to view mathematical reasoning so formalised as being constituted of three elements: structure, language and proof. Logic gives an account (indeed, various accounts) of each of these elements and the relationships between them. In one standard account, a mathematical *structure* is understood to be an interpretation of a vocabulary consisting of relation and function symbols over some fixed set or universe of discourse. The *language* in which mathematical statements are formulated is first-order predicate logic which is equipped with a *proof* system consisting of axioms and rules of inference. Language and structure are tied together with a Tarskian definition of truth and Gödel's completeness theorem ensures that the proof system is adequate to deriving truth. Of course, a large number of variations of this basic scheme have been investigated, but many of them share these essential elements, each of which is now a precisely defined mathematical object in its own right.

Within this broad view of mathematical logic we can discern two further streams, which we term the proof-theoretic and the model-theoretic lines of investigation. Proof-theoretic considerations focus on the relationship between language and proof. Questions of interest include how the collection of provable statements changes with the choice of axioms and rules of inference, how the lengths of proofs depend on these choices and the development of proof systems for non-standard logic. In contrast, model-theoretic questions are concerned with the relationship between language and structures. Among the central concerns here are issues of definability, dealing with questions such as: what statements are expressible in first-order logic; what structures and relations can be defined in this logic; and how does the expressive power of different logics compare.

Like the relationship between mathematics and logic, that between logic and computation also runs in both directions. One way of understanding this deep relationship is to look at the project of reducing mathematical reasoning to formal symbol manipulation. In this view, by presenting logical inference in terms of symbol manipulation, formal logic reduces reasoning to steps that can be performed mechanically. This naturally raises the question of what operations are permitted as mechanical steps. If the reduction is to have meaning, we need an account of computation that will make sense of the term "symbol manipulation". It is out of just such considerations that the Church-Turing account of computability arose. This account, which grounds the idea of mechanical inference, now forms the theoretical foundation of computer science.

On the other hand, the development of electronic computing machines which are the most concrete application of the theory of computation has allowed the construction of customised mechanical systems of inference. Such "logic engineering" provides one means by which concerns of computer science feed back into the study of logic. In particular, this has led to the consideration of logics and systems of inference far beyond those originally conceived for the purposes of formalising mathematical reasoning.

The dual relationship between logic and computation is nicely summed up in the theorem that the validities of first-order logic are r.e.-complete. One direction, that the validities are recursively enumerable, follows from Gödel's completeness theorem and it tells us that the process of deduction (at least as far as first-order logic is concerned) can, indeed, be carried out by a computational device. On the other hand, the r.e.-hardness of the validities, which follows from Church's proof of the undecidability of first-order logic tells us that any computable problem can be reduced, in a very precise sense, to deciding validity of first-order formulas. Or to put it in other words, any computable problem can be encoded in terms of deduction in first-order logic. Taken together, the results tie logic and computation in a tight embrace. The elegance of this formulation helps to explain, to some extent, the significance attached to first-order logic in the classical development of mathematical logic.

As all programs and data involved in computation are ultimately strings of symbols in a formal system, it is natural to see all computation as consisting of symbol manipulation. Indeed, it can always be seen as inference in a suitable formal system. A paradigmatic example is the view of functional programming which sees programs as constructive proofs of propositions, which themselves represent the types of the programs. The correspondence between proofs and propositions is given by the Curry-Howard isomorphism (cf. [37]). Computation is now seen as a process which transforms a proof into one in normal form through a series of steps.

On the other hand, it is often useful, from the conceptual point of view, to distinguish certain syntactic forms used in computation and regard them as *computational structures* that act as semantic interpretations for a language, i.e., for another set of computational forms that we choose to regard as syntactic. Some examples of the structure/language distinction are: *data structures* and *programming languages* where we often think of the data structure as a structured mathematical object which is referred to by syntactic elements in the languages; *database* and *query language*, where it is common to think of the database as consisting of a set of relations and the query language as a formula in logic that it interprets; *program state space* and *specification language*, in carrying out computer-aided verification it is common to formulate specifications in a logic which is interpreted in the state space of the program. It is interesting to note that the same syntactic form (such as a program in a suitable programming language) may be seen on the language side of this divide (in the first example) or as a description of a structure (in the third example).

The kinds of computational structures that arise in the above examples are of a rather different nature to those that arise in classical model theory. One important respect in which this is so is that the structures involved are often required to be finite. A relational database or a data structure is naturally finite (though there are instances where an infinite database is a useful abstraction) and while the state space of a program may often be thought of as infinite, some of the most successful applications of model-checking have concerned finite-state systems. This is in sharp contrast to classical model theory where infinite structures are the main concern. Model-theoretic questions arising in computer science have led to the development of a model theory specific to finite structures. This is where we next turn our attention.

3 Logic on Finite Structures

Finite model theory has developed as a distinct subject of study over the last three decades or so (cf. [17, 27, 21]). It is not merely the model theory of finite structures as it has evolved a distinctive set of questions, methods and results that are rather different from those that exercise the minds of model theorists. One distinguishing feature is that first-order logic, which plays an important role in model theory, has a somewhat lesser role in finite model theory. Nevertheless, first-order logic will form the starting point of our discussion and we begin with a definition of its syntax. Though the logic is no doubt familiar to all readers, laying out the definition allows us to fix notation which we shall be able to extend later.

3.1 First-Order Logic

Definition 3.1. We are given a vocabulary, which consists of relation symbols $R_1, R_2, \ldots$, each of a fixed arity, function symbols $f_1, f_2, \ldots$, again each of a fixed arity, constant symbols $c_1, c_2, \ldots$ and variable symbols $v_1, v_2, \ldots$. The collection of first order formulas is defined by two successive inductions. First, we define the set of valid terms by:

- any constant or variable is a term; and
- if f is a function symbol of arity n, and $t_1, \ldots, t_n$ are terms, then so is $f(t_1, \ldots, t_n)$.

Secondly, we define the set of formulas by:

- if t_1 and t_2 are terms, then $t_1 = t_2$ is a formula;
- if R is a relation symbol of arity n and $t_1, \ldots, t_n$ are terms, then $R(t_1, \ldots, t_n)$ is a formula;
- if φ and ψ are formulas then so are $(\varphi \wedge \psi)$, $(\varphi \vee \psi)$ and $\neg\varphi$; and
- if φ is a formula and x is a variable, then $\exists x\varphi$ and $\forall x\varphi$ are formulas.

For the rest of this paper, we shall assume that the vocabulary consists of a finite number of relation, function and constant symbols. Formulas of first-order logic are interpreted in a *structure*,

$$\mathbb{A} = (A, R_1, \ldots, R_l, f_1, \ldots, f_m, c_1, \ldots, c_n)$$

where A is a set, $c_i \in A$ for all i and R_i and f_i are interpreted as relations and functions over A of the appropriate arity. The equality symbol $=$ is always interpreted as element identity on A. Here and elsewhere in the paper, we do not distinguish between a symbol in the vocabulary and its interpretation in a structure in the expectation that this will cause no confusion.

First-order logic has been extremely successful for its intended purpose, namely the formalisation of mathematics. Many natural mathematical theories can be naturally expressed through a set of first-order axioms including, perhaps most importantly of all, *set theory*, with its fundamental role in the foundations of mathematics. Moreover, Gödel's completeness theorem tells us that the consequences of a first-order theory can be effectively obtained. This provides another reason why a first-order formalisation of a mathematical theory is seen as an adequate outcome of the reductionist project.

3.2 Finite Structures

If, in the definition of a *structure* given above, we restrict the universe A to be a finite set, a rather different picture emerges. One of the central tools of model theory, the Compactness Theorem, no longer holds and most of its important consequences fail as well. What we mean by this is that it is easy to devise a set S of sentences of first-order logic such that every finite subset of S has a finite model but the set S itself has no finite model. Furthermore, in restricting ourselves to finite structures, we no longer have a completeness theorem. Indeed, Trakhtenbrot has shown [38] that the sentences of first-order logic that are valid on finite structures are not recursively enumerable.

With the vital tools of compactness and completeness no longer available, first-order logic loses much of its significance in finite model theory. Indeed, as this author has said elsewhere [13], when restricted to finite structures, first-order logic is both too strong and too weak.

It is too strong in the sense that the relation of elementary equivalence between structures is trivial on finite structures. A large part of classical model theory can arguably be described as the study of this equivalence relation and the structure of its equivalence classes. Two structures $\mathbb{A}$ and $\mathbb{B}$ are elementarily equivalent if, for every first order sentence φ,

$$\mathbb{A} \models \varphi \text{ if and only if } \mathbb{B} \models \varphi.$$

This is crucial in establishing inexpressibility results. For instance, by proving that all dense linear orders without endpoints are elementarily equivalent, we establish that other properties that might distinguish such orders (such as Dedekind completeness) are not definable.

On finite structures, the elementary equivalence relation is trivial, in that any two elementarily equivalent structures are isomorphic. Indeed, any finite structure is described up to isomorphism by a single sentence. Given a structure $\mathbb{A} = (A, R_1, \ldots, R_m)$ (ignoring function and constant symbols for the moment), where A is a set of n elements, we can construct a sentence

$$\delta_{\mathbb{A}} = \exists x_1 \ldots \exists x_n (\psi \wedge \forall y \bigvee_{1 \le i \le n} y = x_i)$$

where, $\psi(x_1, \ldots, x_n)$ is the conjunction of all atomic and negated atomic formulas that hold in $\mathbb{A}$. Now, for any structure $\mathbb{B}$, $\mathbb{B} \models \delta_{\mathbb{A}}$ if and only if $\mathbb{A} \cong \mathbb{B}$.

This means that first order logic can make all the distinctions that are to be made between finite structures. Still, first-order logic is very weak in terms of its expressive power. For any first-order sentence φ consider the collection of its finite models:

$$\mathrm{Mod}_{\mathcal{F}}(\varphi) = \{\mathbb{A} \mid \mathbb{A} \text{ finite, and } \mathbb{A} \models \varphi\}.$$

It turns out that this class is trivially decidable, in the sense that it can be decided by a deterministic Turing machine working with logarithmic work space. To be precise, to evaluate φ on a structure $\mathbb{A}$ with n elements, the machine needs a register with $\log n$ bits for each variable x that occurs in φ. This allows x to take as value any element of $\mathbb{A}$. On the other hand, there are computationally very simple classes of finite structures which cannot be expressed using a first-order sentence. Among them are two important examples that we shall examine in greater detail:

- the class of sets with an even number of elements; and
- the class of graphs (V, E) that are connected.

The proof that these properties are not definable in first-order logic, even when we restrict our interpretations to finite structures is a simple illustration in the methods of finite model theory (cf., e.g., [17, Chapter 2]).

Essentially, in the model theory of infinite structures, as we classify structures by elementary equivalence, we are looking at the expressive power of theories, i.e., possibly infinite sets of sentences. Two structures that are elementarily equivalent cannot be distinguished by any first order theory. In contrast, any isomorphism closed class C of finite structures is defined by the set of negations of the sentences $\delta_{\mathbb{A}}$, as above, for finite structures $\mathbb{A}$ not in C. Certainly, this theory may have infinite models, but the collection of its finite models is exactly C. In contrast, the expressive power of single sentences is weak. The interesting model-theoretic questions on finite structures have to do with the expressive power of restricted theories where the set of sentences is *regular* in some sense that needs to be made precise. That is, we are interested in *finitely generated* theories.

An alternative way of looking at the same questions is to say that we need to look at definability by single sentences in logics that are more expressive than first-order logic. These single sentences generate first-order theories of a particular regular form.

3.3 Second-Order Logic

In looking for a formalism that is more expressive than first-order logic, it is natural to first consider second-order logic. This is obtained by extending the vocabulary of first-order logic (cf. Definition 3.1) by a collection of relational variables $V_1, V_2, \ldots$ each with an associated arity and adding the following two rules to the definition of the set of formulas.

- if X is a relational symbol of arity n and $t_1, \ldots, t_n$ are terms, then $X(t_1, \ldots, t_n)$ is a formula; and
- if φ is a formula and X is a variable, then $\exists X\varphi$ and $\forall X\varphi$ are formulas.

The semantics of the logic is defined in the natural way: if X is a relational variable of arity a the formula $\exists X\varphi$ is true in a structure $\mathbb{A}$ if there is an interpretation of X as a relation of arity a that makes φ true, and dually for the universal quantifier.

That this language has much richer expressive power than first-order logic can be established by exhibiting sentences that define the properties we earlier noted are not first-order definable, i.e., evenness and connectivity.

Example 3.2. The following sentence is true in a finite structure $\mathbb{A}$ if and only if it has an even number of elements.

$$\begin{aligned}\exists B\exists S \quad & \forall x\exists y B(x,y) \land \forall x\forall y\forall z B(x,y) \land B(x,z) \rightarrow y = z \\ & \forall x\forall y\forall z B(x,z) \land B(y,z) \rightarrow x = y \\ & \forall x\forall y S(x) \land B(x,y) \rightarrow \neg S(y) \\ & \forall x\forall y \neg S(x) \land B(x,y) \rightarrow S(y).\end{aligned}$$

In this formula B and S are bound relational variables, the first being of arity 2 and the second of arity 1. There are no relation symbols other than these bound variables and equality and so the sentence is interpreted in a structure of any vocabulary. The sentence asserts that B is a bijection between the elements in S and those not in S. To be precise, the first line requires B to be a total function, while the second line forces it to be injective (and on a finite structure this is sufficient to ensure that it is a bijection). The third line says that the image under B of any element of S is not in S and the last that the image of any element not in S is in S.

Example 3.3. The following sentence expresses that a graph (i.e., a finite structure interpreting the binary relation symbol E) is connected. That is to say, there is an E-path between any pair of elements of the structure.

$$\forall x\forall y\big[\forall X\big(X(x) \land \forall w\forall z(X(w) \land E(w,z) \rightarrow X(z))\big) \rightarrow X(y)\big].$$

It can be read as stating that for every pair x and y, y is an element of every set that has x as an element and is closed under the binary relation E.

We noted earlier that every property that is definable in first-order logic is decidable by a Turing machine working with a logarithmic amount of work space (that is to say, it is in the complexity class LogSpace). Of the properties expressed in the two examples above, the first one is easily seen to be in LogSpace while for the second one it is a major open problem to prove that it is not in this class (cf. [35]). Still, both properties are easily decidable by machines running in polynomial time and so regarded as *feasibly* decidable. What we have seen, however, is that they do separate the expressive power of first-order logic from second-order logic. Our next example is of a property which we can also show is not definable in first-order logic (or even much stronger *infinitary* logics [12]) but it is easily defined in second-order logic. As the problem is NP-complete [19], whether or not it is in P is the main open problem of complexity theory.

Example 3.4. The following sentence expresses that a graph is 3-colourable, i.e., that we can assign colours to the nodes in the graph, using no more than three colours, such that no edge in the graph has both its endpoints coloured the same.

$$\begin{aligned}\exists R \exists B \exists G \quad & \forall x(R(x) \vee B(x) \vee G(x)) \wedge \\ & \forall x(\neg(R(x) \wedge B(x)) \wedge \neg(B(x) \wedge G(x)) \wedge \neg(R(x) \wedge G(x))) \wedge \\ & \forall x \forall y(E(x,y) \rightarrow (\neg(R(x) \wedge R(y)) \wedge \neg(B(x) \wedge B(y)) \wedge \\ & \qquad \neg(G(x) \wedge G(y))))\end{aligned}$$

The sentence asserts the existence of three sets of nodes (R, B and G which we read as *red*, *blue* and *green*) with: every node belonging to one of the three sets (in the first line); no node belonging to more than one colour (on the second line); and the endpoints of every edge coloured differently (on the third and fourth line).

It is not difficult to see that the class of finite structures satisfying any given second-order sentence is decidable. What we are interested in is the computational complexity of the decision problem. Consider those formulas of second-order logic in which all second-order quantifiers are existential and precede any other operator in the formula. This fragment is denoted Σ^1_1 and called existential second-order logic. Of the examples above, the sentences in Examples 3.2 and 3.4 are formulas of Σ^1_1 while the sentence in Example 3.3 is not (though it is equivalent to a sentence of Σ^1_1). An easy argument establishes that the class of finite models of any sentence in Σ^1_1 is in the complexity class NP. That is, it can be decided by a nondeterministic machine running in polynomial time. For a fixed sentence φ, we consider a machine that when presented with an input structure $\mathbb{A}$ first "nondeterministically guesses" an interpretation of the existentially quantified relational variables and then determines whether the expanded structure satisfies the matrix of φ. The size of the guessed relations is bounded by a fixed polynomial (dependent on φ but not on the structure $\mathbb{A}$). Similarly the deterministic evaluation of the first-order matrix can be carried out in polynomial time as any first-order definable property is in LogSpace and perforce in P. Thus, we can conclude that the total length of the computation of the machine is bounded by a suitable polynomial and hence the property defined by φ is in NP.

Fagin [18] showed that the converse of the above argument also holds. Namely that every class of finite structures that is decidable by a nondeterministic machine running in polynomial time is definable by an existential second-order sentence.

Theorem 3.5 (Fagin)**.** A class of finite structures is definable in Σ^1_1 if and only if it is in NP.

We have seen above an argument why the inclusion holds in one direction: namely that every property defined in Σ^1_1 is necessarily in NP. We now pause to consider what the converse implies. NP can be defined as the class of those decision problems that are decided by a machine that, given an input of size n, first guesses a certificate whose length is bounded by $p(n)$ for some fixed polynomial p and then verifies the certificate in polynomial time. Thus, NP is defined as the class of problems with polynomially-verifiable certificates. It is clear that the existentially quantified relation symbols in our sentence play the role of the certificate. What Fagin's theorem tells us is that polynomial-time verification can be replaced by a first-order definable property. Now, we know that the expressive power of first-order logic is much weaker than polynomial time. What follows from Fagin's theorem is that the second-order quantifiers can compensate for this defect. The first-order verification of polynomial length certificates is just as powerful as polynomial-time verification. It is interesting to place this view in the context of other results that have characterised the class NP in terms of weak (i.e., weaker than polynomial-time) verifiers, such as the celebrated PCP theorem [2].

However, Fagin's theorem has generally been described as a *logical characterisation* of NP, and it is this understanding of it that has had the greatest impact on further developments. It led to the development of the field of descriptive complexity, where we seek to give characterisations of various complexity classes in terms of logical definability. The central open question in this field remains the question of whether there is a descriptive characterisation of the class P, similar in spirit to Fagin's. This question was first posed by Chandra and Harel in 1982 and remains open [8]. If it were the case that P = NP, then second-order logic would be a logic characterizing P. However, assuming these complexity classes are distinct, any logic that characterises P would be intermediate between first-order and second-order logic. It is to such logics that we turn our attention next.

4 Polynomial Time Computation

The computational complexity class P is the class of problems that are decidable by a deterministic machine running in polynomial time. It is generally (though not universally) identified as the class of computational problems we consider to be *feasibly* computable. It is for this reason that a logical characterisation of the class is much sought after as it raises the possibility of designing a language in which one can express all and only the feasibly computable queries. On the other hand, if we could show that no such characterisation is possible, we would have shown that the complexity classes P and NP are different, thus solving the central open problem in theoretical computer science.

One might ask what it would mean to give a negative answer to the question of whether there is a natural logic that characterises the complexity class P. What would count as a natural logic? We shall content ourselves with some very general requirements. As it happens, these lead to the rather precise question of whether the polynomial-time properties of structures are recursively enumerable.

For concreteness, consider graphs, i.e., structures over the signature (E), where E is a binary relation symbol. Clearly, a graph on n nodes can be encoded as a binary string of length n^2. However, the same graph can be encoded in many different ways (up to $n!$) and some machines will accept some encodings of a given graph but not others. We say a Turing machine accepts a graph property if it does not break isomorphism classes of graphs, that is to say it either accepts or rejects all encodings of any given graph. Or, putting it differently, the collection of graphs accepted by the machine is closed under isomorphisms.

Every Turing machine can be converted into a polynomial-time machine by attaching a clock to it that terminates any computation if it exceeds some fixed polynomial time bound. This gives us an enumeration, $(M_i \mid i \in \omega)$ of polynomial-time machines that includes machines that accept any polynomial-time recognisable class of binary strings. The problem of Chandra and Harel can now be framed as follows: can we enumerate a sub-sequence of this list that only includes machines that accept graph properties and includes at least one machine for each graph property accepted by some machine on the original list? An equivalent formulation of the problem was given by Gurevich [22] (cf. also [33] for a recent treatment).

The difficulty in characterising P stems from a mismatch between the descriptive view where a structure is an inherently *unordered* object and the computational view where the structure is represented as a string on the input tape of a machine in some order. This becomes clearer when we consider structures that are *ordered*, i.e., one of their relations is a linear order of the domain. In this restricted case, it is possible to obtain a logic that defines exactly the polynomial-time decidable properties. We turn next to examining such a logic.

4.1 Inductive Definitions

In computer science as well as in logic, many interesting objects and relations are naturally defined *inductively*. The definition of terms and formulas of first-order logic in Definition 3.1 is a typical example. Indeed, the definition of the syntax and semantics of almost any language used in logic and computer science is given inductively as are the definitions of data structures such as trees and lists.

Another classical example is the inductive definition of arithmetic functions. Suppose that we are given the structure $(N, s, 0)$. That is to say, we have a constant symbol for 0, and a symbol for the successor function. There is a natural inductive definition of the addition function in this structure, namely:

$$\begin{aligned} x + 0 &= x \\ x + s(y) &= s(x + y). \end{aligned} \tag{4.1}$$

Though addition is thus inductively defined using very simple formulas, it is not first-order definable. That is to say, there is no first order formula $p(x, y, z)$ with three free variables such that

$$(N, s, 0) \models p[a, b, c] \quad \text{if and only if} \quad a + b = c.$$

To formalise the inductive definition of addition, we say that it is the *least* ternary relation that satisfies the equations in (4.1). Or, equivalently, the equations define a *monotone operator* on the space of ternary relations on the natural numbers and the addition function is the least fixed point of this operator.

Similarly, the definition of first-order terms given in Definition 3.1 can be read as stating that the collection of first-order terms is *the least set* containing all constants, all variables and such that $f(t_1, \ldots, t_a)$ is a term whenever $t_1, \ldots, t_a$ are terms and f is a function symbol of arity a. Once again, fixing a universe S that consists of all strings over a suitable infinite alphabet one can view the definition as giving a monotone operator on the power set of S (ordered by inclusion). The set of terms is then the least fixed point of this operator.

While inductive definitions are ubiquitous in the metalanguage of logic, it is in taking them into the object language that we obtain fixed-point logics. This transfer of fixed-point constructors into the object language is the key insight (originally presented in [1]) that led to the flowering of the study of fixed-point logics in finite model theory.

4.2 Least Fixed Point Logic

The first of the fixed-point logics we consider is LFP, which is the result of adding to first-order logic an operator for forming least fixed points as used in our two examples above. This logic was defined by Chandra and Harel [8]. Least fixed points are, in principle, defined for all monotone operators. However, monotonicity is not a syntactic property (for instance, it is undecidable whether an operator defined by a first-order formula is monotone). Thus, in order to be able to effectively define the syntax of our logic, we allow ourselves only to take fixed-points of operators defined by *positive* formulas. A formula φ is said to be positive in a relation symbol R if R does not occur in φ within the scope of a negation sign.

Formally, the logic LFP is obtained by closing first order logic simultaneously under all the formula forming operations of first order logic along with the rule:

> if R is a k-ary relation variable, $\mathbf{x}$ is a k-tuple of first order variables, $\mathbf{t}$ is a k-tuple of terms and φ is a formula in which R occurs only positively, then
>
> $$[\mathbf{lfp}_{R,\mathbf{x}}\ \varphi](\mathbf{t})$$
>
> is a formula, in which all occurrences of R are bound, and all occurrences of the variables in $\mathbf{x}$ except those occurring in $\mathbf{t}$ are bound.

The intended semantics of this formula formation rule is that, for any structure $\mathbb{A}$, $\mathbb{A} \models [\mathbf{lfp}_{R,\mathbf{x}}\ \varphi](\mathbf{t})$ if and only if $\mathbf{t}^{\mathbb{A}}$ —the tuple of elements of $\mathbb{A}$ defined by the terms $\mathbf{t}$— is in the least fixed point of the monotone operator defined by $\varphi(R, \mathbf{x})$ on A^k.

Example 4.1. The following formula:

$$\forall u \forall v [\mathbf{lfp}_{T,xy}\ (x = y \vee \exists z(E(x,z) \wedge T(z,y)))](u,v)$$

is satisfied in a graph (V, E) if and only if the graph is connected. Indeed, the least relation T that satisfies the equivalence $T(x,y) \equiv x = y \vee \exists z(E(x,z) \wedge T(z,y)))$ is the reflexive and transitive closure of E. This is, therefore, the least fixed point defined by the operator **lfp**. The formula can now be read as saying that every pair u, v is in this reflexive-transitive closure.

As we remarked earlier, the class of connected graphs is not definable by a first-order sentence. Thus, the above example demonstrates that the expressive power of LFP properly extends that of first-order logic.

4.3 Immerman-Vardi Theorem

The importance that is attached to LFP in the realm of finite model theory is explained in part by the Immerman-Vardi theorem. This result was established independently by Immerman and Vardi in 1982.[1] It demonstrates a close relationship between inductive definitions and feasible computation.

Consider only finite structures with a distinguished relation $<$ that is interpreted as a linear order of the universe.

Theorem 4.2 (Immerman-Vardi). A class of finite ordered structures is definable by a sentence of LFP if and only if membership in the class is decidable by a deterministic Turing machine in *polynomial time.*

If we do not restrict ourselves to structures which interpret a linear order, it is still the case that every class of structures definable in LFP is decidable in polynomial time, but the converse fails. There are properties that are easily computable (such as the property of a set having an even number of elements) that are not expressible in the logic. It seems that the order is required if the logic is to be powerful enough to simulate a mechanical computation. For a fuller discussion of these issues, cf. [17].

4.4 Other Descriptive Characterisations

It is worth mentioning at this point that, when we only consider ordered structures and particularly if we confine ourselves to functions over numbers, then there are a number of other descriptive characterisations of polynomial-time computation available. The earliest such is due to Cobham [9], who characterised the collection of polynomial time computable functions on the natural numbers in terms of a recursion scheme (similar to the definition of primitive recursive functions). It turns out that the polynomial time computable functions are exactly the functions that can be defined from certain basic functions: zero, the projection functions, the binary successor functions $s_0(n) = 2n$ and $s_1(n) = 2n + 1$ and the smash function given by $\#(x, y) = 2^{|x||y|}$, where $|x|$ is given by $\lceil \log_2 x + 1 \rceil$, using the operations of composition and *bounded recursion on notation.* We say that the function f is defined by bounded recursion on notation from the functions g, h_1, h_2 and b if:

$$\begin{aligned} f(0, \overline{n}) &= g(\overline{n}) \\ f(s_0(m), \overline{n}) &= h_1(m, \overline{n}, f(m, \overline{n})) \text{ for } m \neq 0. \\ f(s_1(m), \overline{n}) &= h_2(m, \overline{n}, f(m, \overline{n})) \end{aligned}$$

and $f(m, \overline{n}) \leq b(m, \overline{n})$ for all $m, \overline{n}$. Cf. [36] for details of this and many similar characterisations of complexity.

Another characterisation of the polynomial time computable functions on the natural numbers is obtained by looking at weak proof systems of arithmetic. For instance, Buss [6] constructed a proof system for arithmetic, where the induction rule is restricted, and the result is that the

[1] Cf. [24, 40]. A similar result is shown by Livchak [29].

provably total functions are exactly the polynomial time computable functions. Another such proof theoretic characterisation is obtained by Leivant [26], which extends the result from functions on the natural numbers to terms. McAllester (cf. [32]) also obtained a characterisation of polynomial time properties of term structures. This characterisation is based on Horn clauses.

It is worth noting that all these characterisations are over classes of structures (we can think of numbers, terms, lists, etc., as classes of finite structures in an appropriate vocabulary) that are all inherently ordered. In other words, these structures do come with an order built-in and therefore the descriptive characterisations of polynomial time computability on these structures do not carry over to the case of arbitrary finite structures.

4.5 Counting

At one time, Immerman conjectured that adding some mechanism for counting to LFP would suffice to give a logic able to express all properties in P. This was because, at the time, all the examples of polynomial-time properties that were known to be not definable in LFP (such as having an even number of elements) involved counting.

The logic $\mathsf{LFP}+\mathsf{C}$ is built up from the usual set of symbols, except that we have two sorts of variables: $v_1, v_2, \ldots$ ranging over the domain elements of the structure, and $\nu_1, \nu_2, \ldots$ ranging over the numbers. To be precise, when a formula φ is interpreted in a structure $\mathbb{A}$, the number variables occurring in φ are interpreted as ranging over the set $\{0, \ldots, n\}$ where n is the number of elements in $\mathbb{A}$. In addition, we also have second order variables $X_1, X_2, \ldots$, each of which has a type, which is a finite string in $\{\text{element}, \text{number}\}^*$. Thus, if X is a variable of type (element,number), it is to be interpreted by a binary relation relating elements to numbers. The logic allows us to build up *counting terms* according to the following rule:

> if φ is a formula and x is a variable of the first sort, then $\#x\varphi$ is a term.

The intended semantics is that $\#x\varphi$ denotes the number (i.e., the member of the number sort) of elements that satisfy the formula φ.

The formulas of $\mathsf{LFP}+\mathsf{C}$ are now described by the following set of rules:

- all atomic formulas of first-order logic are formulas of $\mathsf{LFP}+\mathsf{C}$;
- if τ_1 and τ_2 are terms of numeric sort (that is each one is either a number variable or a term of the form $\#x\varphi$) then each of $\tau_1 < \tau_2$ and $\tau_1 = \tau_2$ is a formula;
- if φ and ψ are formulas then so are $\varphi \wedge \psi$, $\varphi \vee \psi$ and $\neg\psi$;

- if φ is a formula, x is an element variable and ν is a number variable then $\exists x\,\varphi$ and $\exists\nu\,\varphi$ are formulas; and
- if X is a relation symbol of type σ; $\mathbf{x}$ is a tuple of variables whose sorts match the type σ and $\mathbf{t}$ is a tuple of terms of type σ, then $[\mathbf{lfp}_{X,\mathbf{x},\nu}\varphi](\mathbf{t})$ is a formula.

It can now be proved (cf. [34]) that any formula of LFP + C which has no free variables of number sort can be interpreted in a unique way in a structure $\mathbb{A}$. Thus, a sentence of LFP+C does define a class of structures and we can legitimately ask what the complexity of this class is. Furthermore, this logic can define the class of structures with an even number of elements.

Example 4.3. The following sentence is satisfied in a structure $\mathbb{A}$ if and only if the number of elements of $\mathbb{A}$ that satisfy the formula $\varphi(x)$ is even.

$$\exists\nu_1\exists\nu_2(\nu_1 = [\#x\varphi] \wedge (\nu_2 + \nu_2 = \nu_1))$$

In particular, taking φ to be a universally true formula such as $x = x$, we get a sentence that defines evenness.

Indeed, since there is an order available on the number sort of each structure, and LFP can express all polynomial time properties of ordered structures, it follows that LFP + C can express all the polynomial time properties of structures that are determined purely by cardinality.

It is not difficult to show that any property that is definable in LFP + C is decidable in polynomial time. However, it turns out that there are classes of structures in P that are not definable in LFP + C. This was shown by Cai, Fürer and Immerman [7], refuting the original conjecture by Immerman. The specific polynomial-time decidable property that is shown to be undefinable in LFP + C is not easy to state. Cai, Fürer and Immerman construct an infinite family of pairs of graphs G_k and H_k ($k \in \omega$) such that G_k and H_k are not isomorphic but at the same time they are not distinguished by any formula of LFP + C with fewer than k variables. Since it can be shown that there is a polynomial-time class that contains all G_k and excludes all H_k, it then follows that this class cannot be defined in LFP + C.

As the particular graphs G_k and H_k constructed by Cai, Fürer and Immerman can be chosen to have bounded degree (independent of k), another conclusion that can be drawn from their proof is that the graph isomorphism problem on graphs of bounded degree is also not expressible in LFP + C. While the general graph isomorphism problem is not known to be in P, it is known that there are polynomial time algorithms for solving it in the special case where the degree of graphs is bounded (cf. [30]). Thus, we can take this particular problem as our exemplar of a polynomial-time decidable class that is not definable in LFP + C. Since the algorithm developed by Luks [30] for testing isomorphism of bounded degree graphs relied heavily on group-theoretic machinery, Immerman suggested that a further extension of LFP + C with such operators may be the way to obtain a logic that characterises P. We examine such possibilities and other extensions of the logic in the next section.

5 Further Extensions

Since the result of Cai, Fürer and Immerman established that LFP + C does not capture the full power of polynomial-time computation, there has been a variety of attempts at extending the programme. Several logics have been considered which properly extend the expressive power of LFP + C while still remaining within the complexity class P. We describe several such attempts below. It is worth remarking that for most of them, it remains an open problem to show that the resulting logic does not have the power to express all problems in P. It seems that the sophisticated techniques developed by Cai, Fürer and Immerman to construct polynomial-time properties that are difficult to define have to be extended yet further to deal with these new logics. There have been attempts to obtain such negative results which have met with some success, especially in the context of logics with generalized quantifiers, which we look at first.

5.1 Generalised Quantifiers

One of the most general ways of extending the expressive power of a logic is to add to it suitable generalised quantifiers, in the sense of Lindström [28]. In general, we can associate with any property C (i.e., an isomorphism-closed class of structures) a quantifier Q_C such that adding Q_C to a logic L gives us the least extension of L that is also able to express C and has certain natural closure properties. To be precise, let C be any collection of structures over the signature $\sigma = (R_1, \dots, R_m)$ (where R_i is a relation symbol of arity r_i) that is closed under isomorphism. For a logic L, define the extension $L(Q_C)$ by closing the set of formulas of L simultaneously under the rules of L and under the following formula formation rule: if $\varphi_1, \dots, \varphi_m$ are formulas of $L(Q_C)$ and $\mathbf{x}_1, \dots, \mathbf{x}_m$ are tuples of variables with the length of $\mathbf{x}_i$ being r_i, then $Q_C\mathbf{x}_1 \dots \mathbf{x}_m(\varphi_1, \dots, \varphi_m)$ is a formula of $L(Q_C)$. Here the quantifier $Q_C\mathbf{x}_1 \dots \mathbf{x}_m$ binds only those occurrences of the variables among $\mathbf{x}_i$ which are in φ_i; all other free occurrences of variables remain free. The semantics of the quantifier is given by: $(\mathbb{A}, s) \models Q_C\mathbf{x}_1 \dots \mathbf{x}_m(\varphi_1(\mathbf{x}_1, \mathbf{y}_1), \dots, \varphi_m(\mathbf{x}_m, \mathbf{y}_m))$ if and only if $(|\mathbb{A}|, \varphi_1^{\mathbb{A}}[s_1], \dots, \varphi_m^{\mathbb{A}}[s_m]) \in C$, where $\varphi_i^{\mathbb{A}}[s_i] = \{t \in |\mathbb{A}|^{n_i} \mid \mathbb{A} \models \varphi_i[t, s_i]\}$. For a quantifier Q associated with a class of structures over the signature $(R_1, \dots, R_m)$, the *arity* of Q is $\max(r_1, \dots, r_m)$.

The first systematic consideration of generalised quantifiers in the context of finding a logical characterisation of polynomial-time computation was carried out by Hella [23] who showed that no extension of LFP, or indeed LFP + C, with a collection of quantifiers of bounded arity could capture P. To be precise, he showed that for each bound r on the arity of quantifiers, one can construct a signature σ and a polynomial-time decidable class of σ-structures C that is not definable in the extension of LFP with all quantifiers of arity r. This was established by methods that generalised those of Cai, Fürer and Immerman on LFP + C.

Hella's result leaves open the possibility that on structures of a fixed signature, for instance on finite graphs, there is a collection of quantifiers of bounded arity that can be added to LFP to yield a logic for P. Indeed, this is the case as we can just take one quantifier for every polynomial-time decidable graph property and these quantifiers would all have arity 2. However, this would not yield a reasonable logic in our sense unless this set of quantifiers was itself recursively enumerable which, of course, is equivalent to the original question of whether there is a natural logic for P. Still, it was shown (by entirely different methods) that there is no *finite* set of generalised quantifiers that can be added to LFP that will allow us to capture P [10].

This leaves the case of what infinite collections of generalised quantifiers one could reasonably affix to LFP in the hope of obtaining a logic that captures P or of extending the negative results of Cai, Fürer, Immerman, and Hella. I was able to show [11] that if there is a logic capturing P then there is one that is an extension of LFP by a *vectorised* sequence of quantifiers. This is a particular form of an infinite sequence of quantifiers generated from a single class of structures C in a uniform way. Thus, the question of the existence of such a collection is equivalent to our original question and there is no hope of incrementally extending negative results to this case.

5.2 Algebraic Operations

As we noted above, the proof of Cai, Fürer and Immerman that LFP + C is not powerful enough to express all polynomial-time decidable properties involves a contrived construction of a class of graphs on which the isomorphism problem is solvable in polynomial-time but not in LFP + C. However, the methods developed in that proof have more recently been used to exhibit more natural problems that separate P from the expressive power of LFP + C. In the context of considerations of the definability of constraint satisfaction problems, we show in [3] that the problem of determining the rank of a binary matrix (suitably encoded as a class of finite structures) is not definable in LFP + C. This problem is in polynomial time by a standard Gaussian elimination algorithm. The existence of a natural problem in P that is not definable in LFP + C opens the possibility of finding natural ways of extending the expressive power of LFP + C while remaining within polynomial time. Indeed, the methods of generalised quantifiers discussed above provide one general way of converting any problem into an operator in the logic. Moreover, in the context of algebraic operations such as computing the rank of a matrix, more natural algebraic operators suggest themselves. These remain areas to be explored, not in the expectation that they will yield a logic capturing P but as setting a new challenge to find problems that are not definable in the more expressive logic and thus casting new light on the algebraic structure of P itself.

5.3 Choice

We have seen that when all structures come equipped with a linear order, it is possible to obtain a logic that coincides in expressive power with P. An alternative to having an order in the structure is to have a *choice* operator in the logic. This is an operator that allows one to select an arbitrary member of a defined set. An example is Hilbert's ε-operator. A choice operator in the logic, combined with a recursion mechanism such as that of LFP allows us to construct an order on a structure on the fly. Thus, it is clear that LFP extended with such a choice mechanism can express all polynomial-time properties. However, the mechanism also suffers from the same drawback as allowing an order in the structure, namely it allows us to construct formulas that distinguish between isomorphic structures. It therefore fails our test for a natural logic. Moreover, such a logic may also be able to express properties that are not in P at all. Still, an intriguing question remains whether we can restrict a choice operator in such a way that formulas do not distinguish between isomorphic structures and that enables us to derive polynomial-time algorithms from the formula. An interesting step in this direction was taken by Gire and Hoang [20]. They define a restricted form of choice that only allows one to select an element from a set that is an orbit of the automorphism group of the structure. This guarantees that the properties defined are invariant under isomorphisms. Then, to ensure that the logic still only yields polynomial-time properties, they require that the formula provide explicit automorphisms witnessing that the class from which an element being chosen is indeed such an orbit. Finally, in order for the logic to have reasonable closure properties, they consider a variant with an additional *interpretation* operator. They are able to show that the resulting logic can still only express polynomial-time properties. Moreover, they show that it can express the property that Cai, Fürer and Immerman showed is not definable in $\mathsf{LFP} + \mathsf{C}$. It remains a challenge to show that there is some class of structures in P that is not definable in the logic of Gire and Hoang. However, the very complexity of the definition of the logic makes it difficult to concieve of methods for proving inexpressibility. For some progress in this direction, cf. [14, 15].

5.4 Choiceless Machines

While the addition of some form of constrained choice to LFP offers some candidates for logics that might express exactly P, Blass, Gurevich and Shelah [4, 5] raised the question of exactly how much of P is decidable by algorithms which are forbidden to use any form of choice. They consider a class of machines, called *abstract state machines* that work directly on relational structures but may construct arbitrary data structures on them in the form of hereditarily finite sets. They show that this yields a notion of polynomial-time computation which is more powerful than that expressed by LFP but still unable to express simple cardinality properties. The extension of this with a mechanism for counting (called $\tilde{\mathbf{C}}\mathbf{PT}(\mathbf{Card})$) is the more interesting formalism from our point of view. While it is somewhat removed from our intuitive understanding of what constitutes a logic, it does fall within our more relaxed definition in that it has a concrete syntax and semantics and its sentences do not distinguish between isomorphic structures. Moreover, every definable property is computable in polynomial time and $\tilde{\mathbf{C}}\mathbf{PT}(\mathbf{Card})$ is strictly more expressive than $\mathsf{LFP} + \mathsf{C}$. Indeed, it has recently been shown [16] that the property Cai, Fürer and Immerman used to separate $\mathsf{LFP} + \mathsf{C}$ from P is expressible in $\tilde{\mathbf{C}}\mathbf{PT}(\mathbf{Card})$. On the other hand, we also showed that the expression of this property necessarily requires the use of hereditarily finite sets of unbounded rank. This introduces a new resource measure for measuring the complexity of problems. It also introduces methods for proving lower bounds on these measures which may prove useful in establishing inexpressibility results. As of this writing, it remains an open question whether there is a polynomial-time decidable property that cannot be expressed in $\tilde{\mathbf{C}}\mathbf{PT}(\mathbf{Card})$.

6 Conclusions

We have seen how model-theoretic questions, concerned with determining the expressive power of logical languages arise naturally in computer science. They have a natural connection with questions of computational complexity, one of the central concerns of theoretical computer science but questions about expressive power abound in other areas of computer science as well. One fundamental way in which the model-theoretic questions are different to those studied in classical logic is that first-order logic loses its central role (though it may be also be argued that first-order logic is no longer as important to concerns of infinite model theory as it once was). But perhaps more interesting is the variety of entirely new forms of logical operator that are being considered in the process of trying to match logical expressive power with computational complexity. These range from inductive definitions, which have a well established history in the study of logic, to abstract state machines which are strongly rooted in a computational paradigm and cover such exotic forms as matrix operations and choice operators. In the wake of Fagin's result that existential second-order logic captures the computational power of NP, it was often said that this opens the way for model-theoretic methods to be used to resolve long-standing open questions of complexity theory. Those questions remain open but along the way our notions of logic and logical methods have been greatly enriched.

References

[1] Alfred V. Aho and John D. Ullman. Universality of Data Retrieval Languages. In Alfred V. Aho, Stephen N. Zilles, and Barry K. Rosen, editors, *Proceedings of the 6th ACM SIGACT-SIGPLAN symposium on Principles of programming languages 1979, San Antonio, Texas, January 29–31, 1979*, pages 110–119, New York, 1979. Association for Computing Machinery.

[2] Sanjeev Arora, Carsten Lund, Rajeev Motwani, Madhu Sudan, and Mario Szegedy. Proof Verification and the Hardness of Approximation Problems. *Journal of the Association for Computing Machinery (ACM)*, 45:501–555, 1998.

[3] Albert Atserias, Andrei A. Bulatov, and Anuj Dawar. Affine Systems of Equations and Counting Infinitary Logic. In Ugo Montanari, Jose D.P. Rolim, and Emo Welzl, editors, *Automata, Languages and Programming*, volume 4596 of *Lecture Notes in Computer Science*, pages 558–570, Berlin, 2007. Springer.

[4] Andreas Blass, Yuri Gurevich, and Saharon Shelah. Choiceless Polynomial Time. *Annals of Pure and Applied Logic*, 100:141–187, 1999.

[5] Andreas Blass, Yuri Gurevich, and Saharon Shelah. On Polynomial Time Computation Over Unordered Structures. *Journal of Symbolic Logic*, 67(3):1093–1125, 2002.

[6] Samuel R. Buss. *Bounded Arithmetic.* Bibliopolis, 1986.

[7] Jin-Yi Cai, Martin Fürer, and Neil Immerman. An Optimal Lower Bound on the Number of Variables for Graph Identification. *Combinatorica*, 12(4):389–410, 1992.

[8] Askok K. Chandra and David Harel. Structure and Complexity of Relational Queries. *Journal of Computer and System Sciences*, 25:99–128, 1982.

[9] Alan Cobham. The Intrinsic Difficulty of Functions. In Yehoshua Bar Hillel, editor, *Logic, Methodology and Philosophy of Science: Proceedings of the 1964 International Congress*, Studies in Logic and the Foundations of Mathematics, pages 24–30. North-Holland, 1965.

[10] Anuj Dawar. The Expressive Power of Finitely Many Generalized Quantifiers. *Information and Computation*, 123(2):172–184, 1995.

[11] Anuj Dawar. Generalized Quantifiers and Logical Reducibilities. *Journal of Logic and Computation*, 5(2):213–226, 1995.

[12] Anuj Dawar. A Restricted Second Order Logic for Finite Structures. *Information and Computation*, 143:154–174, 1998.

[13] Anuj Dawar. Types and Indiscernibles in Finite Models. In Johann A. Makowsky and Elena V. Ravve, editors, *Logic Colloquium'95*, volume 11 of *Lecture Notes in Logic*, pages 51–65. Springer, 1998.

[14] Anuj Dawar and David Richerby. Fixed-Point Logics with Nondeterministic Choice. *Journal of Logic and Computation*, 13:503–530, 2003.

[15] Anuj Dawar and David Richerby. Fixed-Point Logics with Symmetric Choice. In Matthias Baaz and Johann A. Makowsky, editors, *Computer Science Logic. 17th International Workshop, CSL 2003, 12th Annual Conference of the EACSL, and 8th Kurt Gödel Colloquium, KGC 2003, Vienna, Austria, August 25-30, 2003, Proceedings*, volume 2803 of *Lecture Notes in Computer Science*, pages 169–182. Springer, 2003.

[16] Anuj Dawar, David Richerby, and Benjamin Rossman. Choiceless Polynomial Time, Counting and the Cai-Fürer-Immerman Graphs: (Extended Abstract). *Electronic Notes in Theoretical Computer Science*, 143:13–26, 2006.

[17] Heinz D. Ebbinghaus and Jörg Flum. *Finite Model Theory*. Perspectives in Mathematical Logic. Springer Press, Berlin, 1996.

[18] Ronald Fagin. Generalized First-Order Spectra and Polynomial-Time Recognizable Sets. In Richard M. Karp, editor, *Complexity of Computation*, volume 7 of *SIAM-AMS Proceedings*, pages 43–73. American Mathematical Society, 1974.

[19] Michael R. Garey and David S. Johnson. *Computers and Intractability: A Guide to the Theory of NP-Completeness.* W.H. Freeman and Company, New York, 1979.

[20] Françoise Gire and H. Khanh Hoang. An Extension of Fixpoint Logic with a Symmetry-Based Choice Construct. *Information and Computation*, 144:40–65, 1998.

[21] Erich Grädel, Phokion G. Kolaitis, Leonid Libkin, Maarten Marx, Joel Spencer, Moshe Y. Vardi, Yde Venema, and Scott Weinstein. *Finite Model Theory and Its Applications.* Texts in Theoretical Computer Science. Springer, 2007.

[22] Yuri Gurevich. Logic and the Challenge of Computer Science. In Egon Börger, editor, *Current Trends in Theoretical Computer Science*, pages 1–57. Computer Science Press, 1988.

[23] Lauri Hella. Logical Hierarchies in PTIME. *Information and Computation*, 129:1–19, 1996.

[24] Neil Immerman. Relational Queries Computable in Polynomial Time. *Information and Control*, 68:86–104, 1986.

[25] Neil Immerman. *Descriptive Complexity.* Graduate Texts in Computer Science. Springer, New York, 1999.

[26] Daniel Leivant. A Foundational Delineation of Poly-Time. *Information and Computation*, 110:391–420, 1994.

[27] Leonid Libkin. *Elements of Finite Model Theory.* Texts in Theoretical Computer Science. Springer, New York, 2004.

[28] Per Lindström. First Order Predicate Logic with Generalized Quantifiers. *Theoria*, 32:186–195, 1966.

[29] Alexander B. Livchak. The Relational Model for Process Control. *Automated Documentation and Mathematical Linguistics*, 4:27–29, 1983.

[30] Eugene M. Luks. Isomorphism of Graphs of Bounded Valence Can be Tested in Polynomial Time. *Journal of Computer and System Sciences*, 25:42–65, 1982.

[31] Zohar Manna and Richard Waldinger. *The Logical Basis for Computer Programming. Vol I: Deductive Reasoning.* Addison-Wesley, Boston, MA, USA, 1985.

[32] David A. McAllester. Automatic Recognition of Tractability in Inference Relations. *Journal of the Association for Computing Machinery (ACM)*, 40(2):284–303, 1993.

[33] Alan Nash, Jeffrey B. Remmel, and Victor Vianu. PTIME Queries Revisited. In Thomas Eiter and Leonid Libkin, editors, *Database Theory — International Conference on Database Theory 2005*, volume 3363 of *Lecture Notes in Computer Science*, pages 274–288, Berlin, 2005. Springer.

[34] Martin Otto. *Bounded Variable Logics and Counting — A Study in Finite Models*, volume 9 of *Lecture Notes in Logic.* Springer, 1997.

[35] Christos H. Papadimitriou. *Computational Complexity.* Addison-Wesley, 1994.

[36] Harvey E. Rose. *Subrecursion: Functions and Hierarchies*, volume 9 of *Oxford Logic Guides.* Clarendon Press, 1984.

[37] Jonathan P. Seldin and J. Roger Hindley, editors. *Essays on Combinatory Logic, Lambda Calculus and Formalism.* Academic Press, 1980.

[38] Boris A. Trakhtenbrot. Impossibility of an Algorithm for the Decision Problem in Finite Classes. *Doklady Akademii Nauk SSSR*, 70:569–572, 1950.

[39] Jan van Leeuwen, editor. *Handbook of Theoretical Computer Science, Volume B: Formal Models and Semantics.* MIT Press, 1990.

[40] Moshe Y. Vardi. The Complexity of Relational Query Languages. In Harry R. Lewis, Barbara B. Simons, Walter A. Burkhard, and Larry Landweber, editors, *Proceedings of the fourteenth annual ACM symposium on Theory of Computing 1982, San Francisco, California, United States, May 05–07, 1982*, pages 137–146. Association for Computing Machinery Press, 1982.

Towards a formal regimentation of the Navya-Nyāya technical language I

Jonardon Ganeri*

Department of Philosophy, University of Sussex, Arts Building B, Brighton BN1 9QN, United Kingdom

E-mail: jonardon@liverpool.ac.uk

Navya-Nyāya is an early modern Indian system of philosophical analysis. It was founded by Udayana (c. 1050 CE), developed by Gaṅgeśa (c. 1200 CE), and reached its peak in the works of authors including Raghunātha (c. 1500 CE), Jagadīśa (c. 1600 CE) and Gadādhara (c. 1650 CE).[1] The school is notable for its development of a technical language, by means of which it clarified many philosophical questions in the traditional Indian debate. This technical language rapidly became the standard idiom for academic works in Sanskrit, not only in philosophy, but in grammar, poetics, law, and other branches of study as well. A careful analysis of the conceptual framework and expressive power of the Navya-Nyāya technical language is therefore of considerable importance in the modern study of the Indian academic literature.

1.1

Ordinary Sanskrit is regarded by Navya-Nyāya as an imperfect vehicle for philosophical discourse, mainly because it is infested with ambiguity. It is not just the presence of ambiguities in the lexicon, homonymous words like *saindhava* (which can mean either salt or a horse), for it is always possible to eliminate such terms in favour of words which are not ambiguous. The greater problem derives from the absence in ordinary Sanskrit of any systematic or compulsory use either of articles or quantifier expressions. In English, the combination of an "applicative" [10, p. 73], that is, an expression like "a", "the", "all", "some", or "most", with a substantival general term such as "pot" or "cow" forms a descriptive or quantified phrase. In Sanskrit, however, an inflected noun or noun phrase occurring by itself often has the same syntactic role. So, for example, the sentence *ghaṭo nīlaḥ* "pot [is] blue" might mean either "the pot is blue", "some pot is blue" or "every pot is blue". Similarly, a phrase like "cause of fire" might signify the cause of a certain fire ("The cause of [the] fire is unknown"), the cause of a fire ("carelessness causes fire"), or the cause of all fire ("a cause of every fire is heat").

*I should like to express my gratitude to the two anonymous referees, whose comments and advice have been invaluable. I should also like to thank Benedikt Löwe.

[1]For the history, cf. [18, 1].

Mihir K. **Chakraborty**, Benedikt **Löwe**, Madhabendra Nath **Mitra**, Sundar **Sarukkai** (*eds.*). Logic, Navya-Nyāya & Applications. Homage to Bimal Krishna Matilal. College Publications, London, 2008. Studies in Logic 15. pp. 105–121.

Received by the editors: 1 May 2007; 28 March 2008, 16 May 2008.
Accepted for publication: 11 November 2008.

1.2

In some contexts then, an inflected noun has the role of a definite description, as for example in "[The] doctor is coming". A classical dispute in Indian philosophy of language is whether the semantic value of "(the) doctor" in a sentence like this is an individual or a universal. These two positions are called Meaning Particularism (*vyaktiśaktivāda*) and Meaning Universalism (*jātiśaktivāda*) respectively. The former view represents a doctrine that nouns have a genuine referring use, and it is within discussions of this view that the theory of reference developed in India. The Universalist, on the other hand, whose approach is in some ways nearer to the standard Russellian treatment of definite descriptions, explains the referential use of nouns by appeal to pragmatic constraints (*lakṣaṇā*) on the interpretation of sentences (for further discussion, cf. [8]).

1.3

In other sentences, a noun can have an existential or universal force; for example "Bring [a] pen" or "[A] cow should not be kicked". Faced with the problem of accounting for this use of nouns, those Indian semanticists who endorsed Particularism argued that a noun has a systematic ambiguity in semantic role, sometimes taking an individual as its value, and sometimes a universal or class. This approach was shared by the early grammarians such as Patañjali as well as the early Naiyāyikas. I shall try to show how this idea comes to be formalised in the Navya-Nyāya technical language.

1.4

When two or more nouns occur in the same sentence, there is a possibility of 'scope' ambiguities. Suppose one forms a phrase "cause of smoke". This might mean cause of a particular body of smoke, cause of a some or other smoke, or else cause of all smoke. Now, when such a phrase is combined with another noun to form a sentence, e.g., "Fire is cause of smoke", the three-fold ambiguity of each noun leads to nine different readings of the sentence. In two of these readings "All fire is (the) cause of some smoke" and "Some fire is (the) cause of all smoke", there is a further ambiguity. The first, for example, might mean "Each fire is (the) cause of some smoke or other" or "There is a body of smoke which is the effect of every fire". This scope ambiguity is not the result of any putative ambiguity in the nouns, but is due to an ambiguity in the syntax of the language.

1.5

When sentences contain relational expressions, there is room for still another sort of ambiguity. Compare the sentences "Pothood is in a pot" and "The cat is in the kitchen". In the first case, the relational expression "in" (or the locative post-noun) indicates the relation of inherence, but in the second it indicates the relation of containment. The English expression "is" is similarly ambiguous, sometimes indicating identity, sometimes existence, and sometimes predication. This kind of ambiguity concerns the semantic role of the relational expression in the sentence [20, p. 136].[2] Naiyāyikas claim that the negation particle *na* "no" suffers from ambiguity in this way: it sometimes indicates a "mutual absence" (*anyonyābhāva*), i.e., the negation of an identity, but sometimes a "relational absence" (*saṃsargābhāva*), i.e., the negation of a predication (cf. [15, p. 94–95]; [14, pp. 54–55]).

2.1

If an ordinary language "with all its ambiguities and abominable syntax" (Russell, quoted in [20, p. 134]) is ill-suited for the careful formulation of philosophical doctrine, the alternative is to construct a formal artificial language free from these defects. This is exactly what Navya-Nyāya does. Authors such as Frege, Russell, and Quine, all of whom introduce artificial or formal languages, differ in their opinions as to the relation between the formal language and ordinary languages, and it is not entirely clear how Navya-Nyāya conceives of the relation between ordinary Sanskrit and its technical language.[3] Minimally, we should suppose it to be such that corresponding to each of the various possible readings of an ordinary Sanskrit sentence, there should be just one sentence in the formal language.

2.2

The Nyāya language includes a small number of logical words, especially "substratum" or "locus" (*adhikaraṇa*, *ādheya*) and its inverse "occurrence" (*vṛtti*), "conditioner" (*nirūpaka*), "delimitor" (*avacchedaka*) and "absentee" or "counterpositive" (*pratiyogin*), together with a non-logical vocabulary of terms and relation-expressions.[4] Accompanying the language, there is a formalised ontology, which is a modified version of the Vaiśeṣika system of categories. Modern interpreters of Nyāya disagree on whether the Nyāya ontology is extensional or intensional (cf. [21, 14, 5, 11, 15]). On the one hand, Nyāya exploits the various abstraction devices in Sanskrit, and speaks of pothood or cause-of-fire-hood where we might speak of the class of pots

---

[2] Or, if we agree with the Nyaya that the relational element is indicated, not by an explicit expression, but by grammatico-syntactic features (*ākāṅkṣā*) of the sentence, we must locate the ambiguity there.

[3] [22, pp. 5–6] usefully distinguishes between three historical positions, according to which the formal language is regarded as an *extension*, an *improvement*, or a *reform*, of natural language. The Navya-Nyāya attitude seems to me to have most in common with the view expressed by the later Wittgenstein [24, § 19], that the relationship between a formal language and natural language is akin to the relationship between a new suburb, "with regular streets and uniform houses" and the ancient city, "a maze of little streets and squares." Cf. also [4, pp. 30-33], [12, pp. 9–15], and [2].

[4] Cf. [14, pp. 28–85], [15, pp. 3–98], [6], [21, pp. 16–35], [12], and [23, pp. 24–35].

or the causes of fire. Yet, when one examines the role of such abstract properties in the theory, it is very often only their extension which is semantically relevant. When developing the Nyāya system, I shall follow the strategy of using a set-theoretic ontology as far as possible. It seems that Nyāya tries in the main to avoid disputes about ontology, and develops a theoretical language which can be used even by those who do not share its ontological dispositions (cf. [16, p. 66], [3, p. 201]). The mention of properties in the Nyāya formal language seems then to be mainly pleonastic. In particular, the abstraction device "*-tva*" is used freely, not restricted to the naming of genuine properties alone: a Naiyāyika happily reparses the sentence "the pot has a long neck and a conch-shaped handle" as "long-neck-conch-shaped-handle-ness is located in the pot". Its commitment to a principle of ontological parsimony prevents Navya-Nyāya from agreeing that every such operation generates the name of a genuine property.[5]

2.3

The Nyāya language is not a symbolic one. It does not, for example, employ variables, although "dummy singular terms" [15, p. 23] like *ghaṭa* ("pot"), as well as the pronouns *tat* "that" and *sva* "own-" sometimes function in the same way. The sentences in the Nyāya language therefore resemble "long-hand" versions of symbolic formulae and as a result are notoriously cumbersome. In principle, however, there is no reason why the Nyāya language cannot be symbolised, and I shall attempt to construct a symbolic notation for a fragment of the language here. We can denote this fragment NN. As long as we restrict our attention to the sentences for which a set-theoretic ontology is sufficient, this fragment should be equivalent to some part of first-order predicate logic, and it will be interesting to find out which part this is.

3.1

I shall now give an informal presentation of the fragment of the Navya-Nyāya language NN, reserving a more formal treatment for [9]. Informally, we can say that syntax for the fragment NN of the Nyāya technical language is built up from the following components:

(1) There is a set of **primitive terms**, such as *ghaṭa* ("pot"), *go* ("cow"),

[5]In [13], Guhe argues that the Navya-Nyāya attitude towards the ontology of properties is similar to that of George Bealer's property theory. Their commitment to a principle of ontological parsimony (which they name *lāghava*; cf. [15, p. 83]) is the reason I doubt if the liberal ontology of Bealer's property theory is necessary for interpreting Navya-Nyāya. It is, however, possible, that a sparser intensional system will be what is needed. My ambition in this paper is to see how much of Navya-Nyāya can be understood on a purely extensionalist basis; we can then ask what is the leanest intensional addition necessary to handle the residue.

etc. i.e., the nouns or uninflected nominal stems (*nāman*, *prātipadika*). We shall use the Roman letters "*a*", "*b*", etc. for these primitive terms.

(2) There is an **abstraction functor** *-tva* or *-tā* ("-ness", "-hood"), the operation of which on a primitive term like *ghadta* "pot" gives rise to an abstract term *ghaṭatva* "pothood". I shall use the Greek letters "α", "β", etc. for abstract terms.

Some Naiyāyikas employ a second abstraction functor — *vyaktitva* ("-individual-hood"), e.g., *ghaṭavyaktitva* "pot-individual-hood". This functor allows us to replace any particular use of a primitive term with a corresponding abstract term. Nyāya sometimes uses this device to eliminate primitive terms from its technical language. It partially resembles Quine's elimination of proper names like "Socrates" in favour of predicates like "x Socratises" [19, p. 181], or rather, "to Socratise".

(3) There is a set of **relational abstract expressions**, such as "locushood", "causehood", "cousinhood", "pervadedness", some logical and some non-logical. There is also a corresponding set of inverse relational abstract expressions, "superstratumhood", "effecthood", etc. I shall use bold letters, e.g., "**R**" for these expressions.

(4) There is a **conditioning operator**, which combines a relational abstract expression with a term (of any kind) to form a term, such as "locushood-conditioned-by-pot" (*ghaṭa-nirūpitādhraṇatā*) or "causehood-conditioned-by-smokehood" (*dhūmatva-nirū-kāraṇatā*). I shall call such expressions "relational terms", because they are terms derived from a relation by specifying its adjunct. Nyaya often abbreviates them to "locushood-to-pot" (*ghaṭīyādhāratā*) etc. (cf. [14, p. 83]). A conditioned relational abstract is represented here by writing the conditioner letter on the right hand side of the relational abstract expression, thus "$\mathbf{R}\beta$".

(5) There are two kinds of **sentence-forming operator**. One combines a relational term "$\mathbf{R}\beta$" with another term to form a sentence "$a.\mathbf{R}\beta$" or "$\alpha.\mathbf{R}\beta$". This operator is named "location" or "residence" (*niṣṭhana*) if the term is primitive, and "delimitation" (*avacchedana*) if it is abstract. For example "locushood-conditioned-by-pot is resident in ground" (*ghaṭa-nirūpitādhāraṇatā sā bhūtalaniṣṭhā*, or *ghaṭa-nirūpitādhāratāśrayaṃ bhūtalam*) or "causehood-conditioned-by-smokehood is delimited by firehood" (*dhūmatva-nirūpita-kāraṇatā sā 'gnitvāvacchinnā*).

The second sentence-forming operator, colocation (*samanadhikaranya*), represented here by a colon, combines an abstract term "α" with a relational term "$\mathbf{R}\beta$" to form a sentence "$\alpha{:}\mathbf{R}\beta$".

(6) There is a **negation functor** "-absence" (*atyantābhāva*), which forms negative terms such as "pot-absence" (*ghaṭābhāva*) from terms. By definition, the negative term "pot-absence" is identical with the relational abstract term "absenthood-conditioned-by-pot" (*ghaṭa-nirūpitānuyogitā*), where "absenthood" (*anuyogitā*) is a logical relational abstract expression. We shall write "absenthood" as "**N**", and negative terms as "*a*-absence" or "**N***a*" etc. There is also a **sentence negation** "not" (*na*). Thus, "causehood-conditioned-by-smokehood is not delimited by firehood" (*dhūmatva-nirūpita-kāraṇatā sā 'gnitvānavacchinnā*). Nyāya avoids sentential negation wherever it can (cf. [17, p. 116]), but cannot eliminate it altogether. I shall isolate the point at which its introduction is necessary below.

The syntax of NN thus consists of relational abstract expressions, various different kinds of term expressions —primitive, relational, abstract, and negative— and a negation particle.

4.1

For the semantics of NN, I shall, as already stated, only draw upon a set-theoretic ontology. Nyāya does not use set-theoretic notions like set inclusion or set membership, but prefers to talk instead of properties occurring in objects, or co-occurring with other properties etc. It is for this reason that it is sometimes said to have a "property-location language". However, since its semantic vocabulary is often clearly extensional (properties which are equipollent (*samaniyata*) are in many cases identified), there is some motivation to using a set-theoretic notation[6]. We can then assign, to each expression in the syntax, an element or set as follows.

(1-2) As noted above, the Nyāya regard nouns sometimes as functioning like singular referring expressions. When thus used, they will share with indexicals the property of taking a different referent depending on the context of use. To each occurrence of a primitive term like "pot" is therefore assigned an object P, such that P belongs to the set p of pots. And to the corresponding abstract term "pothood" is assigned the property pothood. In keeping with our simplifying restriction, let us assign to such an expression the set p of pots[7]. It is now possible for any particular use of an noun-phrase in the ordinary language to be mapped either to a primitive term having a particular value, or else to the corresponding abstract term, whose value is a class.

[6]Note, however, Ingall's reservation [14, p. 50], and [3, p. 290], as well as my comments in Footnote 2 above.

[7]Recall Kātyāyana's aphorism under Pāṇini-sūtra 5.1.119: "the abstraction suffixes [i.e., -hood, -ness, -ity] such as *-tā* and *-tva* (added to nominal stems) 'express' (*abhi* $+\sqrt{}$*dhā*) only those qualities (*guṇa*) on the basis of which the nominal stems are used to refer to things".

Corresponding to each occurrence of a primitive term, there is an abstract term formed by the application of the individuality abstraction functor, for example, the term "pot-individual-hood" (*ghaṭavyaktitva*; cf. [15, p. 57]). If the value assigned to a particular occurrence of the primitive term is P, then the set assigned to this abstract term is the unit set $\{P\}$, i.e., the property of being this very pot.

(3-4) Let us next introduce a number of relations. In set theory a relation is a subset of the Cartesian product of two sets, A and B, the former being the range and the latter the domain of the relation. In other words, a relation is a set of ordered pairs. Naturally, there is a degree of anachronism in using such a notion of relation to explicate the Nyāya system. Yet since the Nyāya claim that a relation is made up of a collection of relation-particulars, each of which is individuated by specifying the two relata (cf. [15, pp. 33–34]), the anachronism may be justifiable. Now given any relation, we can form a series of sets, the extensions of relational properties, as follows. Suppose that an object b is in the domain B of the relation R. Then we can form the set of elements in A which are related by R to b. Similarly, given a set $\beta \in B$, we can form the set of elements in A which are related by R to some element in β. In the standard terminology of relations, this set will be the image of β under the inverse of R. Now, if b is an object assigned to an occurrence of the primitive term "b", or β is the set assigned to an abstract term "b-hood", then we shall say that the set thus formed is the set assigned to the relational abstract term "R-hood-conditioned-by-b(-hood)". For example, the set assigned to the relational abstract term "causehood-conditioned-by-pot-hood" (*ghaṭatva-nirūpita-kāraṇatạ*) comprises those objects which are the cause of a pot. Let such sets be assigned to "$\mathbf{R}b$" or "$\mathbf{R}\beta$".

Given any relation R, it is possible to form an inverse relation R^{-1} such that $yR^{-1}x$ iff xRy.

(5) If "a" is a token of a primitive term, and "$\mathbf{R}\beta$" is a relational abstract term, then the sentence "$\mathbf{R}\beta$ is resident in a" (or equivalently "a is the locus of $\mathbf{R}\beta$"), i.e., "$a.\mathbf{R}\beta$", is true iff the object assigned to "a" is a member of the set assigned to "$\mathbf{R}\beta$". Similarly, if "a-hood" is an abstract term, then the sentence "$\mathbf{R}\beta$ is *delimited by* a-hood", i.e., "$\alpha.\mathbf{R}\beta$", is true iff the set assigned to "a-hood" is contained in the set assigned to "$\mathbf{R}\beta$"[8]. For example, the sentence "causehood-conditioned-by-smokehood is delimited by firehood" is true iff the set of fires is a subset of the set of causes of smoke.

[8]This is the definition of a limitor as "that which occurs in no more [than the abstract]" (*anatirikta-vṛtti*). Cf. [15, p. 76].

The sentence "a-hood is co-located with $\mathbf{R}\beta$" is true iff the intersection of a-hood with $R\beta$ is non-empty, e.g., iff there is a fire which is the cause of smoke.

(6) The Nyāya treatment of negative terms is a little peculiar. Nyāya in fact expands its ontology to include, for every object such as a pot P, an "absentee" or "anti-object" (*abhāva*), an absence of the pot P for example. It expresses the fact that P is not on the table by saying that the anti-object absence-of-P is on the table. Given a token primitive term such as "pot", we can form a negative term "pot-absence" by means of the relational abstract term "absenthood-conditioned-by-pot": the set assigned to "pot-absence" is the set of absences which are absences of the pot P. In fact, since the absence relation is assumed to be one-one, there is only one such absence, and it is called a "specific" absence (*viśeṣābhāva*).[9] Given an abstract term such as "pothood", we can form the negative term "absenthood-conditioned-by-pothood" (unfortunately also written as "pot-absence"), to which is assigned the set of absences which are absences of some pot or other. Nyāya also says that there are "generic absences" (*sāmānyābhāva*), the absence of any pot, for example. We shall see later how such generic readings of "absence of pot" are obtained in the Nyāya language.

4.2

This completes the semantics of NN, but I should like to note a frequently encountered extension. When the conditioner of the relational abstract term "R-hood" is a primitive term "b", Nyāya sometimes reformulates "R-hood-conditioned-by-b" as "R-hood-conditioned-by-R^{-1}-hood-resident-in-b" (e.g., *ghaṭa-niṣṭha-kāryatā-nirūpita-kāraṇatā*). Similarly, when the conditioner is an abstract term "b-hood", Nyāya sometimes reformulates "R-hood-conditioned-by-b-hood" as "R-hood-conditioned-by-R^{-1}-hood-delimited-by-b-hood" (e.g., *ghaṭatvāvacchinna-kāryatā-nirūpita-kāraṇatā*)[10]. The use of the terms "conditioned by", "resident in" and "delimited by" in these neologisms are distinct from, although related to, their use above as term- and sentence-forming operators. The point to these reformulations is as follows. Suppose that an object a is in the domain A of the relation R. Then we can form the set of elements in B which are related by R to a. Similarly, given a set $\alpha \in A$, we can form the set of elements in A which are related by R to an element in α. Now, if a is an object assigned to a token primitive term "a", or a is the set assigned to an abstract term "a-hood", then we shall say that the set thus formed is the set assigned to the relational term "R-hood-resident-in-a" or "R-hood-delimited-by-a-hood", respectively. For example, the set assigned to the relational abstract term

[9] Cf. [14, p. 56].

[10] Cf. [14, p. 46] and [15, p. 80].

"causehood-delimited-by-fire-hood" (*agnitvāvacchinna-kāraṇatā*) comprises those objects which are the effect of a fire. Let such sets be assigned to the terms "$a\mathbf{R}$" or "$\alpha\mathbf{R}$", respectively. The reformulation relies on the identity of $\mathbf{R}b$ with $b\mathbf{R}^{-1}$, and of $\mathbf{R}\beta$ with $\beta\mathbf{R}^{-1}$. Nyāya sometimes calls the notion of delimitation in such a reformulation delimitation-by-conditioning (*nirūpitatva-saṃbandhāvacchinna*), to distinguish it from the sentence forming delimitation-by-residence (*niṣṭhatva-saṃbandhạvacchinna*) introduced earlier[11]. Conditioning delimitors, by contrast, are 'fragments' of a term. The reformulation leads to a pleasant simplification in certain cases. When the relation R is one-one, or when the relation restricted to the sets α and β is itself a sub-relation, then $\alpha.\mathbf{R}\beta$ iff $\beta.\mathbf{R}^{-1}\alpha$. In such a case, we can say that $\mathbf{R}$ as conditioned by $\beta\mathbf{R}^{-1}$ is delimited by α iff $\mathbf{R}$ as conditioned by $\alpha\mathbf{R}^{-1}$ is delimited by β (e.g., *ghaṭatvāvacchinna-kāryatā-nirūpita-kāraṇatā sā daṇḍatvāvacchinnā*, and vice versa). However, I shall ignore this extension in what follows.

5.1

We are now ready to see how an ordinary Sanskrit sentence, e.g., "pot is on table" (or the Nyāya example "*bhutale ghaṭaḥ*"), is disambiguated in the Nyāya technical language. Nyāya resolves the ambiguity of semantic role in the relation expression "on" by saying that contacthood, rather than inherencehood etc. is the "limiting relation" (*avacchedaka-saṃbandha*) of the sentence[12]. Having done that, it needs to distinguish the eleven distinct readings isolated in § 1.4, which it does as follows.

(1) "A particular table t is the locus of a particular pot p". This would be expressed by saying that the relational abstract locushood conditioned by the pot p is resident in the table t. In our symbolic notation, we should write "$t.\mathbf{L}p$", where "t" represents the token primitive term "table" whose value is t, "p" the term "pot" whose value is p, and "$\mathbf{L}$" the relational abstract locushood. "$t.\mathbf{L}p$" is true iff $t \in \mathbf{L}p$, the class of objects on which p is located.

(2) "t is the locus of some pot". The Nyāya paraphrase is: the relational abstract locushood conditioned by pothood is resident in t. Symbolically, "$t.\mathbf{L}\pi$", where "π" represents the class of pots. "$t.\mathbf{L}p$" is true iff $t \in \mathbf{L}\pi$, the class of objects on which some pot is located. A sentence for which (2) might be the most natural construal is "[The] mountain possesses fire" (*parvato vahnimān*).

(3) "t is the locus of all pots". This is turned around to read "Every pot occurs on t", and is paraphrased as: occurrenthood-to-t is limited by pothood, where occurrenthood (*vṛtti, ādheyatā*) is the inverse of locushood.

[11] Cf. [14, p. 50] and [15, p. 75].
[12] Cf. [14, p. 51] and [15, p. 77].

In our notation, this reads as "$\pi.\mathbf{L}^{-1}t$", which is true iff $\pi \subseteq \mathbf{L}^{-1}t$, i.e., the class of pots is a subset of the class of things located on t. Nyāya sometimes says that t is the "generic locus" of pot.[13] Reading (3) is especially natural when absence is involved. As Ingalls notes,

> an absence the [absenteehood (*pratiyogitā*, i.e., the inverse of absenthood)] to which is limited by a generic character or by a property common to several entities is termed a generic absence (*sāmānyābhāva*). Notice that generic absences have the effect of negating all particulars of a given class. [14, p. 56]

Clearly, we should not think of generic loci or generic absences as a special kind of entity.

(4) "Some table is the locus of p" (i.e., "p is on a table"). Nyāya says here that occurrenthood-to-tablehood is resident in p (p possesses the property of occurring on a table.). Symbolically, "$p.\mathbf{L}^{-1}\tau$" ("τ" is the abstract term "tablehood", whose extension is the set τ of tables), which is true iff $p \in \mathbf{L}^{-1}\tau$, the set of objects which occur on a table.

(5) "Every table is the locus of p". Locushood-to-p is limited by tablehood, i.e., "$\tau.\mathbf{L}p$", which is true iff $\tau \subseteq \mathbf{L}p$. We find in the early Naiyāyika Vātsyāyana's discussion of semantics, the sentence "[A] cow should not be kicked [by you]", which may very well serve as an example of this reading.

(6) "Some table is the locus of some pot". Nyāya would say here that locushood to pothood is co-located with tablehood. I.e., "$\tau : \mathbf{L}\pi$", which is true iff $\tau \cap \mathbf{L} \neq \varnothing$.

(7) "Every table is the locus of some pot". This has two readings: (7i) "every table has some pot or other on it", and (7ii) "there is a pot which is on every table". Nyāya expresses the first reading by saying that locushood to pothood is delimited by tablehood, i.e., "$\tau.\mathbf{L}\pi$", which is true iff $\tau \subseteq \mathbf{L}\pi$, (the set of tables is a subset of the set of things with pots on). We might borrow another of Vātsāyana's sentences, "[A] cow is born of [a] cow" to illustrate this reading. It is also a reading closely connected with the Naiyāyikas' notion of pervasion (*vyāpti*). For example, "fire pervades smoke" means that every locus of smoke is also a locus of fire. I shall discuss (7ii) below.

(8) "Some table is the locus of every pot". Again, there are two readings, (8i) "every pot is on some table or another", and (8ii) "there is a table which is the locus of every pot". The first reading is naturally expressed by saying that occurrenthood to tablehood is bound by pothood, i.e., "$\pi.\mathbf{L}^{-1}\tau$". (8ii) requires a similar treatment to (7ii).

[13] Cf. [14, p. 50].

(9) "Every table is the locus of every pot". This too will be discussed below.

6.1

The structure of the Nyāya formal language might be further clarified if we can set up a "translation manual" between NN and some fragment of the predicate logic, presumably a fragment containing dyadic predicates and quantifiers. The examples discussed above suggest the form such a translation manual might take. From readings such as (1), it is clear that each occurrence of a primitive term will translate into an individual constant. Consider now a sentence like "fire causes smoke" (i.e., reading (7i) above). The Nyāya form first the expression "causehood-conditioned-by-smokehood", which translates into the open sentence "$(\exists x : \text{smoke})(y \text{ causes } x)$", where ": f" indicates a restriction on the domain of quantification to things that are f. The original sentence is then paraphrased as "causehood-conditioned-by-smoke is delimited by fire", which translates as

$$\text{“}(\forall y : \text{fire})(\exists x : \text{smoke})(y \text{ causes } x)\text{”}.$$

So a conditioner maps to an existential quantifier, whose domain is restricted to the class assigned to the conditioner, and which binds the second place of a dyadic predicate. Similarly, a delimitor maps to a universal quantifier, whose domain is restricted to the class assigned to it, and which binds the first place of a dyadic predicate. It is clear from the way sentences are constructed in NN that the universal quantifier corresponding to the limitor always has wider scope than the existential quantifier corresponding to the conditioner. Finally, the co-location operator will translate into an existential operator binding the first place of the dyadic predicate, for a sentence like (6), "locushood-conditioned-by-pothood is co-located with tablehood" ("$\tau : \mathbf{L}\pi$") translates to "$(\exists x : \tau)(\exists y : \pi)(x\ L\ y)$". In this way the technical language formalises an ambiguity in the semantics of an ordinary noun-phrase, by translating it into either a token primitive term or an abstract term, and assigning to it either an individual or a class[14].

6.2

The ordinary language Sanskrit sentence rendered as "pot is not in the room" has three distinct readings. It might mean that a certain pot p is not in the room; or that there is a pot which is not in the room; or that no pot is in the room. In everyday Sanskrit, the third reading is usually the most naturally intended one. In NN, we can form from a primitive term

[14]The idea that nouns are ambiguous in this way was first clearly stated by the *tadvat* theorists, Uddyotakara and Jayanta. See their comments under Nyāyasūtra 2.2.66, and [16, pp. 67–69].

"pot", a negative term "pot-absence". We can also form a negative term from the abstract term "pothood", also expressed as "pot-absence". These two terms are by definition equivalent to the relational terms "absenthood-conditioned-by-pot" ("$\mathbf{N}p$") and "absenthood-conditioned-by-pothood" ("$\mathbf{N}\pi$"), where the relation of absence is a one-one relation between any entity and its negative entity or absentee. The first reading is now expressed as "$t.\mathbf{L}(\mathbf{N}p)$", i.e., "$t$ is a member of the set of loci of absences of p", i.e., "$-tLp$". The second reading is expresses as "$t.\mathbf{L}(\mathbf{N}\pi)$", i.e., "$t$ is a member of the set of loci of absences of a pot", i.e., "t is a member of the set of objects which are such that there is a pot for which it is not the locus", i.e., "$(\exists y : \pi)(-tLy)$". Note how this shows that the absence relation, with its corresponding negative terms, is equivalent to a negation which always takes narrowest scope. To catch the third, and most natural, reading of the sentence, i.e., "No pot is on the table" or "The table is the locus of the absence of all pots", Nyāya makes pothood the delimitor of absenteehood (*pratiyogitā*), the inverse of absenthood.[15] The obvious candidate is "$\pi.\mathbf{N}^{-1}(\mathbf{L}^{-1}t)$", i.e., "absenteehood-conditioned-by-superstratumhood-conditioned-by-table is limited by pothood" (*bhūtala-nirūpita-ādheyatā-nirūpita-pratiyogitā sā ghaṭatvāvacchinnā*). This expands as "the set of pots is a subset of absentees for which there is an absence in the set of superstrata of t", i.e., "the set of pots is a subset of the set of objects whose absence is located on t", i.e., "$(x : \pi)(-tLx)$". We might note that, as long as negative terms are only used for the adjunct of another relation, the negative objects are "virtual" entities; they are always quantified out of the final sentence. Matilal exploits this fact to construct a semantics in which every property has a "presence-range" and an "absence-range", corresponding to the set of loci of the property and the set of loci of the absence of the property [17, pp. 112*sqq*].

6.3

The problem of scope ambiguity is usually illustrated by a sentence like "Everybody loves somebody". It is possible to read this sentence in two ways, as saying that given any person, there is someone who loves them, or as saying that there is a person who is loved by everybody. In this second reading, the existential quantifier precedes the universal quantifier. It therefore poses a problem for the Nyāya formal language, in which the universal quantifier or limitor always has widest scope. However, suppose we consider the third 'generic' reading of "pot is not on a table". The NN expression of this is "$\pi.\mathbf{N}^{-1}(\mathbf{L}^{-1}t)$", i.e., "absenteehood-conditioned-by-superstratumhood-conditioned-by-table is limited by pothood", i.e., "the set of pots is a subset of the set of objects whose absence is located on t", i.e.,

[15] Cf. [15, pp. 80–81].

"$(\forall y : \pi)(\exists x : \tau)(-tL^{-1}x)$". If this is *not* true, then there is a table which is not the locus of the absence of any pot, i.e., a table which is the locus of every pot. So the second reading can be expressed as "not $\pi.\mathbf{N}^{-1}(\mathbf{L}^{-1}\tau)$", i.e., "absenthood-conditioned-by-occurrenthood-conditioned-by-pothood is not delimited by tablehood". In the predicate calculus, this result can be expressed via the theorem: $(\exists y : \beta)(\forall x : \alpha)(xRy) = -(\forall y : \beta)(\exists x : \alpha)(-xRy) = -(\forall y : \beta)(\exists x : \alpha)(-yR^{-1}x)$. So with the help of a negation which always takes narrowest scope (the term negation) and one which always takes widest scope (the sentence negation), we can express the mixed readings. An exactly analogous tactic will obtain (9) from (6) where (9) reads "not $\tau : \mathbf{L}(\mathbf{N}\pi)$". It seems that only in such cases is a sentential negation ineliminable.

7.1

The Nyāya language NN is equivalent to a quantified language (NN*) in which each sentence is constructed as follows. (i) There is a dyadic predicate "$\llcorner\ R\ \lrcorner$". (ii) A negation $(-)$ taking narrowest scope optionally occurs next. Thus "$(-)(\llcorner\ R\ \lrcorner)$". (iii) The next step is to fill the second place of the predicate, either with a constant or with a variable bound by an existential quantifier, whose range is restricted to a certain set β. We might, for simplicity, use the individualisation device to eliminate the constants in favour of bound variables. This quantifier has wider scope than the negation in (i) but narrower scope than anything else. Thus "$(\exists y : \pi)(-)(\llcorner Ry)$". (iv) Next, the left hand place is bound, either by a constant, or by a restricted universal quantifier or by a restricted existential quantifier. Thus "$(\forall x : \tau)(\exists y : \pi)(-)(xRy)$" or "$(\exists x : \tau)(\exists y : \pi)(-)(xRy)$". (v) The last step is the optional insertion of a negation which takes largest scope. These five steps correspond to forming a relational abstract, conditioning it with a term (possibly negative) to form a relational term, and forming a sentence using delimitation or co-location (possibly negated). It follows that every sentence in this language (NN*) has the structure $(-)(\forall/\exists)(\exists)(-)(\llcorner R \lrcorner)$. Unlike predicate calculus, the order of the various components is fixed. However, it seems possible to show that every sentence composed from a dyadic predicate, one or two quantifiers, and negation, with no restrictions on the order in which these elements occur, is equivalent to a sentence having the structure of the sentences in NN*. For the formula $(-\forall = \exists-)$ permits any sentence of the form $(\exists\forall)$ or $(\forall\forall)$ to be transposed into one of the form $(\forall\exists)$ or $(\exists\exists)$, respectively, and also permits the transformation of any sentence in which a negation occurs between two quantifiers into one having only narrow or wide scope negation, appropriately inverting the dyadic predicate if necessary. Also, a restricted quantifier can be replaced by an unrestricted quantifier together with an appropriate predicate. So the language NN* is equivalent to that fragment of the predicate calculus whose sentences take the form "$(Fx \wedge Gy \wedge xRy)$", quantified and negated according to taste. Cf. [9] for a more formal treatment.

7.2

The language NN seems to capture some of the logical apparatus used by the Navya-Nyāya authors. I should not claim more than that. The Nyāya authors themselves do not draw such a sharp distinction between terms and sentences as is done in NN, and do not, as far as I am aware, show much interest in the problems of scope ambiguity (and hence understate the need for a sentence negation). There are also many other Nyāya technical notions, for example to do with the concatenation of relations and terms, identity, etc. Moreover, the use of the technical vocabulary varies a little from author to author. And often the language is used in only a semi-formal way, especially when used by non-Nyāya authors. Thus NN is itself a "regimentation" of the Naiyāyikas' technical language.

7.3

One of the ideas which marked the passage from scholastic or medieval logic to the quantifier theory was the realisation that sentences should be seen as constructed in a series of stages, and not as constructed simultaneously from their component elements[16]. The two readings of "Someone loves everyone" are best distinguished if we do not regard the two expressions of generality and the relational expression as simultaneously synthesised; instead, we can see the sentence as built up from the relational expression "␣ loves ␣" in two steps. First, we form a predicate "someone loves ␣" or a predicate "␣ loves everyone", and then we fill in the remaining place. Dummett notes that in an ordinary language, there is an "ad hoc convention", that

> the order of construction corresponds to the inverse order of occurrence of the signs of generality in the sentence [7, p. 12].

This convention works because every sentence has both an active and a passive form, in which the order of the signs of generality are reversed. Thus, the active form "someone loves everyone" and the passive form "Everyone is loved by someone" are most naturally heard as expressing different readings of the sentence (although strictly each is ambiguous).

The Navya-Nyāya technical language seems, as I have tried to show, to encode the insight that sentences are constructed in stages. It is true that their language formalised the "ad hoc convention", and so lacked the elegance or clarity of a quantifier-variable system. Moreover, when a sentence is such that, in the quantifier system, several argument-places are filled by

[16]Cf. [7, pp. 10*sqq*] and [10].

the same bound variable, the Nyāya language resorts, as does ordinary language, to the use of pronouns in order to generate an equivalent sentence in which the sign of generality occurs only in a single place.[17] On the other hand, Dummett's criticism of natural languages, that they

> work by means of principles which are buried deep beneath the surface, and are complex and to a large extent arbitrary, [7, p. 20]

seems less applicable to the Nyāya language than to ordinary Sanskrit, for the principles to which it appeals are generally systematic, explicit, and, most importantly, unambiguous.

References

[1] Dinesh C. Bhattacharya. *History of Navya-Nyāya in Mithilā.* Mithilā Institute of Post-Graduate Studies and Research in Sanskrit Learning, Darbhanga, 1958.

[2] Kamaleswar Bhattacharyya. On the Language of Navya-Nyāya: An Experiment with Precision through Natural Language. *Journal of Indian Philosophy*, 34(1–2):5–13, 2006.

[3] Sibajiban Bhattacharyya. *Doubt, Belief and Knowledge.* Indian Council of Philosophical Research, New Delhi, 1987.

[4] Sibajiban Bhattacharyya. *Language, Testimony and Meaning.* Indian Council of Philosophical Research, New Delhi, 1998.

[5] Innocentius M. Bocheński. *A History of Indian Logic.* Chelsea Publishing Co., New York, 1961. Translated by Ivo Thomas.

[6] Maheśa Chandra Nyayaratna. *Brief Notes on the Modern Nyāya System of Philosophy and its Technical Terms.* Hare Press, Calcutta, 1891.

[7] Michael Dummett. *Frege. The Philosophy of Language.* Duckworth Press, London, 1981. 2nd Edition.

[8] Jonardon Ganeri. *Semantic Powers: Meaning and the Means of Knowing in Classical Indian Philosophy.* Clarendon Press, Oxford, 1999.

[9] Jonardon Ganeri. Towards a formal regimentation of the Navya-Nyāya technical language II. In THIS VOLUME, pages 123–138, 2008.

[17] Cf. [7, p. 13] and [15, p. 23].

[10] Peter T. Geach. *Reference and Generality: An Examination of Some Medieval and Modern Theories.* Cornell University Press, Ithaca, 3 edition, 1980.

[11] Cornelis Goekoop. *The Logic of Invariable Concomitance in the Tattvacintāmaṅi: Gangesa's Anumitinirupana and Vyaptivada with Introduction, Translation and Commentary.* D. Reidel, Dordrecht, 1967.

[12] Dinesh C. Guha. *Navya-Nyāya System of Logic: Some Basic Theories and Techniques.* Bharatiya Vidya Prakasan, Varanasi, 1968.

[13] Eberhard Guhe. George Bealer's Property Theories and their Relevance to the Study of Navya-Nyāya Logic. In THIS VOLUME, pages 139–153, 2008.

[14] Daniel H. H. Ingalls. *Materials for the Study of Navya-Nyāya Logic*, volume 40 of *Harvard Oriental Series.* Harvard University Press, Cambridge Massachusetts, 1951.

[15] Bimal Krishna Matilal. *The Navya-Nyāya Doctrine of Negation: The Semantics and Ontology of Negative Statements in Navya-Nyāya Philosophy*, volume 46 of *Harvard Oriental Series.* Harvard University Press, Cambridge, Massachusetts, 1968.

[16] Bimal Krishna Matilal. *Epistemology, Logic and Grammar in Indian Philosophical Analysis.* Mouton, The Hague, 1st edition, 1971.

[17] Bimal Krishna Matilal. *Logic, Language and Reality: Indian Philosophy and Contemporary Issues.* Motilal Banarsidass, Delhi, 1985.

[18] Karl H. Potter and Sibajiban Bhattacarya, editors. *Encyclopedia of Indian Philosophy. Volume 6: Indian Philososophical Analysis: Nyāya-Vaiśeṣika from Gaṅgeśa to Raghunātha Śiromaṇi.* Motilal BanarsiDass, Delhi, 1993.

[19] Willard V.O. Quine. *Word and Object.* MIT Press, Cambridge, 1960.

[20] Mark Sainsbury. *Russell.* Routledge and Kegan Paul, London, 1979.

[21] Saileswar Sen. *A Study on Mathurānātha's Tattvacintāmaṅi-rahasya.* G. van der Hoogt, Wageningen, 1924.

[22] Martin Stokhof. Hand or Hammer? On Formal and Natural Languages in Semantics. *Journal of Indian Philosophy*, 35(5–6):597–626, 2007.

[23] Toshihiro Wada. *The Analytical Method of Navya-Nyāya.* Egbert Forsten, Groningen, 2007.

[24] Ludwig Wittgenstein. *Philosophical Investigations.* Basil Blackwell, Oxford, 1958.

Towards a formal regimentation of the Navya-Nyāya technical language II

Jonardon Ganeri*

Department of Philosophy, University of Sussex, Arts Building B, Brighton BN1 9QN, United Kingdom

E-mail: jonardon@liverpool.ac.uk

This is the second part of the presentation of a fragment of the Navya-Nyāya language NN. In [1], we gave an informal presentation with a syntax [1, § 3.1] and a set-theoretic semantics [1, § 4.1]. In this paper, I shall attempt to give a more formal treatment of this system.

1 Basic Concepts

The Navya-Nyāya philosophers took certain syntactical features of classical Sanskrit, and used them as the basis of an artificial language for which they devised a sophisticated semantics. The most distinctive features of this artificial language are (i) specialised use of cases, (ii) extensive use of devices for abstraction of noun compounding, (iii) a characteristic treatment of negative terms and negation. The semantic theory derives from a rich collection of concepts and results in set theory, especially the theory of dyadic relations.

1.1 Nominal Sentences

Classical Sanskrit permits the formation of "nominal"' sentences, consisting of a subject and a non-verbal predicate. Such constructions are a feature of many Indo-European languages, but are rather rare in English. When they do occur in English, they are distinguished from sentences merely involving ellipsis of the verb in that their subject is typically enclitic: "shame indeed on me verily for this — that I have foes", "dark the Sun and Moon, and the Almanach de Gotha". Word order is relevant in Sanskrit too, serving there to distinguish a non-verbal predicate from an adjective qualifying the subject. The general rule is that the predicate takes final position:

ghaṭo nīlaḥ
pot+nominative blue+nominative
"the pot is blue"

svalpaṃ ghaṭo nīlaḥ
small+nominative pot+nominative blue+nominative
"the small pot is blue"

*I should like to express my gratitude to the two anonymous referees, whose comments and advice have been invaluable. I should also like to thank Benedikt Löwe.

Mihir K. **Chakraborty**, Benedikt **Löwe**, Madhabendra Nath **Mitra**, Sundar **Sarukkai** (*eds.*). Logic, Navya-Nyāya & Applications. Homage to Bimal Krishna Matilal. College Publications, London, 2008. Studies in Logic 15. pp. 123–138.

Received by the editors: 1 May 2007; 28 March 2008, 16 May 2008.
Accepted for publication: 13 November 2008.

When the predicate is a substantive, however, the subject, as in English, is usually enclitic:

> *ghaṭaḥ saḥ*
> pot+nominative that+nominative
> "that is the pot"

> *svalpaṃ sukhaṃ krodhaḥ*
> small+nominative pleasure+nominative anger+nominative
> "anger is a small pleasure"

A substantive used predicatively can be in a case other than that of the subject:

> *bhūtale ghaṭaḥ*
> ground+locative pot+nominative
> "the pot is on the ground"

The Navya-Nyāya logicians observe that in such cases the relation expressed is never identity. They extrapolate from this and declare that when the predicate has the same case as the subject, a relation of identity is implicitly described.

It will be useful to use numerical superscripts to indicate case (the Sanskrit grammarians themselves number rather than name the cases): 1 nominative; 2 accusative; 3 instrumental; 4 dative; 5 ablative; 6 genitive; 7 locative. So, the above examples will be written pot^1 blue^1, pot^1 ground^7, etc.

1.2 The "genitive + abstract"' construction

In spite of the above, the role of word-order in Sanskrit is generally merely to add emphasis to the term in initial position. Another device is widely used to distinguish between subject and predicate in an nominal sentence. The device is to place the subject in the genitive in apposition with the abstract of the predicate:

> *ghaṭasya nīlatvam*
> pot^6 blue-ness^1
> "of the pot, blueness"

> *brahmaṇaś caturmukhatā*
> Brahman^6 four-faced-ness^1
> "of Brahman, fourfacedness"

Systematic nominal abstraction is achieved by concatenating an abstraction suffix (usually either "-hood", "-ness"' or "-ity"' in English, or "*-tā*"' and "*-tva*"' in Sanskrit) to the term. The use of the abstract is very much wider in Sanskrit than in English, and can be applied to almost any noun phrase, regardless of whether the ensuing abstract noun denotes a natural state or condition. However, we get an English construction near to that of the Sanskrit in "the fact of φ's being ψ".[1]

It is natural to think of a property as being located in its substratum, and so we might expect the subject to be in the locative: ψ-hood in φ. This "locative of residence"' is possible here, but is more widely employed when the sentence is relational (see below).

I shall use capital roman letters as variables over primitive terms, and bold capitals as variables over the corresponding abstract terms. I shall let a semi-colon represent the "genitive + abstract"' construction, dropping the case superscripts. Thus "$A^6\mathbf{B}^1$"' is to be written:

$$A : \mathbf{B}.$$

Apposition is termed in Sanskrit "*sāmānādhikaraṇya*", literally "sameness of location', the reason being that a standard interpretation assigns terms to properties, and an appositional sentence is true if the two properties are colocated. A slightly less standard interpretation assigns terms to classes, sameness of case now signifying class intersection. In either interpretation it is clear that the quantity of the subject is particular not general. The above sentence would translate into English as "A (certain) pot is blue", i.e., to the quantity "some".

1.3 Relational nominal sentences

When the predicate of the nominal sentence is in an oblique case, the sentence is relational. It may also be relational if the predicate is a compound and the second member of the compound is relational:

daśaratho rāma-pitā
Daśaratha^1 Rāma-father^1
"Daśaratha is Rāma's father"

ghaṭo bhūala-ādheyaḥ
pot^1 ground-superstratum^1
"the pot is on the ground"

ākāśaḥ āśrayaḥ
ākāśā^1 sound-locus^1
"*ākāśā* is the locus of sounds"

The Nyāya sometimes transform a relational sentence into a genitive + abstract, with subjunct in the genitive, while the adjunct is placed in the locative:

[1] Cf. Speijer [5, pp. 181*sq*]. Speijer notes that the genitive in such constructions is subjective.

tatprakārakaśābdabodhe śaktijñānasya hetutvam
understanding^{7} knowledge-of-meaning^{6} cause-hood^{1}
"knowledge-of-meaning is the cause of sentence understanding"

ghaḍe ghaṭapadasya śaktir
pot^{7} "pot"^{6} semantic power^{1}
"the semantic power of the word "pot" is in pot"

The locative is used here in the sense of "in the direction of" or "towards". I shall call this the "target" locative in order to distinguish it from the locative of spatio-temporal location.

When the relation is symmetric, the adjunct can be in the instrumental:

sādhyena hetor aikādhikaraṇyaṃ vyāptir ucyate
sādhya^{3} *hetu*^{6} colocatedness^{1} *vyāpti*^{1} it-is-said
"some say that *vyāpti* is the colocatedness of the *hetu* with the *sādhya*"

Frequently, however, the Nyāya use the locative to denote the substratum of the relational abstract, thought of as a property:

daśarathe rāmasya pitṛtā
Daśaratha^{7} Rāma^{6} fatherhood^{1}
"Daśaratha is the father of Rāma"

bhūtale ghaṭa-adhikaraṇatā
ground^{7} pot-substratumhood^{1}
"the ground is the substratum of the pot"

ghaṭe bhūtala-ādheyatā
pot^{7} ground-superstratumhood^{1}
"the pot is the superstratum of the ground"

Here, it is the relation's first term which is in the locative. We may call this the locative of residence (*vṛttitva*), distinguishing it both from the locative of spatio-temporal location (*ādhāratā*) and the target locative. The Nyāya peculiarly call the *first* term in such cases the adjunct (*pratiyogi*), so that, in both cases, it is the adjunct of the relation which is in the locative.

The second term may still be in the genitive, but other syntactic markers are more commonly employed: "on the ground" becomes the compound "superstratum-to-ground" or else "groundy superstratum" (with the suffix *-īya*). When the relation is causehood, the effect takes an accusative with the indeclinable particle *prati* "towards': the causehood in fire is towards smoke. Thus:

agnau dhūmam prati hetutvam
fire^{7} smoke^{2} towards causehood^{1}

Thus the typical form of a relational sentence is either "$A^6B^7\mathbf{R}$" or "$A^7B^2\mathbf{R}$', where, as before, bold indicates abstraction. I shall sometimes denote such a construction by $A\mathbf{R}[B]$.

1.4 The "abstract+instrumental" construction

The Nyāya utilise an important construction to express relational sentences with quantified adjuncts. The adjunct in the locative is replaced by its abstract in the instrumental, $\mathbf{A}^3$. I shall call this the "abstract+instrumental" construction, "by way of being ...". Here is an example, where the locative replaced is a residence locative [3, p. 130]:

> *daṇḍatvena ghaṭa-kāraṇatvam*
> rod-hood^3 pot-causehood^1

Literally, this says that the causehood-to-pot is by way of being a potter's rod. In other words, it says that a potter's rod is the cause of a pot; nothing else is the cause, though the potter's rod may be the cause of other things. In their semantic theory, the Nyāya say that being-the-cause-of-a-pot is *delimited* by rod-hood. The quantifier being described here corresponds, I conjecture, to the English "only": "only potters" rods are the causes of pots". So this construction, and the corresponding notion of a delimitor, represent the introduction of a quantifier into the system.

Here is another example, where the instrumental of the abstract replaces a target locative (*NK*, s.v. "*ādhūnikī*"):

> *ghaṭatvādinā ghaṭādipadasya śaktir*
> pothood^3 "pot"^{6} semantic power^1

Again, the translation is with the quantifier "only" — "the semantic power of the word "pot" is directed only towards a pot". It is the general policy of the Naiyāyikas to exploit an inverse relation transformation to convert such sentences into the first sort:

> *ghaṭatvādinā ghaṭāapad a-śakyatā*
> pothood^3 "pot"-semantic valuehood^1

That is, only a pot has the property of being the semantic value of the word "pot". In their semantic theory, much use is made of inverse relations to this effect.

When the sentence is negative, the construction is again used to introduce generality. An example (*NK*, s.v. "*tṛtīya*"):

> *ghaṭatvena agnir nāsti*
> pot-hood^3 fire^1 is not
> "fire is not any pot"

Here what is denied is the identity of fire, not just with this or that pot, but with any pot at all. Here the construction appears to introduce the quantifier "any" rather than "only". However, the Nyāya treat negation is by reparsing such as statement with an absential term, and under the reformulation we again have the quantifier "only": "only what is different-from-pot is identical with fire" (*aghaṭatvena agnir asti*). Finally, consider

$$\left[\begin{array}{l} \textit{ghaṭatvena bhūtale nāsti} \\ \text{pot-hood}^3 \text{ ground}^7 \text{ is not} \\ \text{"no pot is on the ground"} \end{array}\right.$$

Again, this says the same as "only what is different-from-pot is a superstratum of the ground".

The "abstract+instrumental" construction introduces the forms "$A^6\mathbf{B}^3\mathbf{R}$" and "$\mathbf{A}^3B^2\mathbf{R}$', of which the first is convertible into the second. I shall represent this second form by

$$\mathbf{AR}[B].$$

In their metalinguistic description of the semantics of such structures, they say that the statement is true iff the *relational abstract* $\mathbf{R}$, as restricted to B, is *delimited by* $\mathbf{A}$. These concepts correspond to well-defined set-theoretic notions, as we shall see.

The last example introduced the two words for negation used in the Nyāya language NN. They are the relational negation particle "*na*" (not) and the absential term prefix "*a-*" (non-). I denote the absential term derived from a term "A" by '$\underline{A}$. When the underlying relation in the sentence is identity, as in the above example, the absential term corresponds to something like "thing different from A". However, when the relation is other than identity, it stands for something rather different, "A-absence", which, in the semantic theory, denotes a peculiar kind of absential entity.

NN has a *possessive affix* "-possessing" (*-vat*), which is the inverse of the abstraction affix. The Nyāya accord the following equation an axiomatic status:

$$A = \mathbf{A}\text{-possessing } (\textit{ghaṭo ghaṭatvavān})$$

We shall call this the **Axiom of Possession**.

The possessive suffix may also attach to a non-abstract subject, when the predicate would otherwise take a locative of spatio-temporal location. E.g.,

$$\left[\begin{array}{l} \textit{bhūtale ghaṭam} \\ A^1 B^7 \\ \text{"pot is on ground"} \end{array}\right.$$

$$\left[\begin{array}{l} \textit{bhūtalam ghaṭavat} \\ A\text{-possessing}^1 B^1 \\ \text{"Pot-possessing is ground"} \end{array}\right.$$

bhūtalam ghaṭādhārah
$B^1\mathbf{L}A^1$
"pot-substratum is ground"

where **L** is (spatio-temporal) locushood.[2]

So the Nyāya, by stretching certain features of ordinary Sanskrit, introduce an artificial language with primitive terms, relations, identity, negation, and the quantities "some" and "only". In fact, the Nyāya attempt to indicate all remaining varieties of quantity in NN by means of suitable *modifications of the relation* and by the use of *negative absential terms.*

1.5 The quantifier "just" (*eva*)

Another construction used extensively by the Nyāya involves the modification of either subject and predicate with the indeclinable particle "just" *eva*. The purpose of this construction is again to express sentences with universally quantified subjects or predicates. The important role of "*eva*" in NN is easily overlooked, for the word occurs profusely and its function in ordinary Sanskrit is usually merely emphatic.

Consider the nominal sentence *dravyam guṇavat* "a substance is a possessor of qualities". As it stands, this sentence is ambiguous, for it may mean either that some definite substance is a possessor of qualities, or that every substance possesses qualities, or even that only substances possess qualities. In order to disambiguate the sentence, the Nyāya uses the particle "just" *eva*, which can attach either to subject or predicate. The general significance of "just" is said to be "exclusion from connection with what is other" (see below).

Thus, *dravyam eva guṇavat* "just a substance is a possessor of qualities", is a sentence of the form "$A^1 evaB^1$". The addition of "just" adds to the meaning "exclusion of B from connection with what is other than A". So sentences of this form have the quantity "A and no non-A is B".

This final analysis of "just" ascribes to it the following contribution to logical form:

"just a is G"	(i)	$Ga \wedge (\forall x)(x \neq a \rightarrow {\sim}Gx)$,
or	(ii)	$(\exists x)(x = a \wedge Gx) \wedge (\forall x)(x \neq a \rightarrow {\sim}Gx)$.
"a is just G"	(iii)	$Ga \wedge (\forall x)({\sim}Gx \rightarrow x \neq a)$,
or	(iv)	$(\exists x)(x = a \wedge Gx) \wedge (\forall x)({\sim}Gx \rightarrow x \neq a)$.

We might note that (i) has the same logical form as that given by Russell to "a is the F". Furthermore, we seem to have

[2]Note however that "␣ are two" (*dvau*) does not mean the same as "␣ possesses twoness" *dvitvavān*.

"just F are G"	(v)	$(\exists x)(Fx \wedge Gx) \wedge (\forall x)(\sim Fx \rightarrow \sim Gx)$;
"F are just G"	(vi)	$(\exists x)(Fx \wedge Gx)\&(\forall x)(\sim Gx \rightarrow \sim Fx)$.

2 The Syntax of NN

Our basic vocabulary consists of **primitive terms** ("A', "B', etc.), **primitive relations** ("R', "S', etc.), the identity relation "=', and brackets "(" and ")". In addition to this, we have the following logical constants:

- "␣ is delimited by ␣', written "␣.␣';
- "␣ restricted-to ␣', written "␣[␣]" (usually omitted);
- a term negation "different-from ␣', written "␣′";
- a relational negation "not', written "∼';
- and an abstraction functor "␣-hood', indicated using bold type.

The **abstraction functor** maps terms to (abstract) terms "A-hood" or **A**, and relations to (abstract) relations "R-hood" or **R**. An abstract relation will also be called a relational abstract. The **absence functor** maps terms to (absential) terms "A-absence" or "A^*', and relations to (absential) relations "R-absenteehood" or "R^*". A **relational term** is defined to be the result of concatenating a relational abstract "**R**" with "␣ restricted-to ␣" and then with a term "A': thus "**R**-restricted-to-A". This will be denoted by "**R**[A]" or simply "**R**A". The relation may be an absential relation, but if so, the the restricting term must be an absential term. A **term** is defined to be either a primitive term or a relational term or an abstract term or an absential term.

A **sentence** or wff is defined to be the result of concatenating a relational term "**R**B" with "␣ is-delimited-by ␣" and then with a non-absential term "A', or the result of concatenating a relational term "**R**B" with '␣ is-colocated-with ␣" and then with a non-absential term "A': thus "**R**B is-delimited-by A', written "A.(**R**B)', or "**R**B is-colocated-with A', written "A : (**R**B)".

Technically, then, "␣ restricted-to ␣" is a functor from ordered pairs of relational abstracts and terms to terms, while "␣ is-delimited-by ␣" and "␣ is-colocated-with ␣" are relations between terms and relational terms. The following nomenclature will be used:

R: *English:* relational abstract; *Sanskrit: sambandha.*

R[A]: *English:* **R**-restricted-to-A, A is the restrictor of **R**; *Sanskrit: A-nirūpita-sambandha, A* is a *nirūpaka* of **R**.

$\mathbf{R}^*[A^*]$: *English:* absenteehood-bound-by-**R** A^* is a generic absence; *Sanskrit:* **R**-*sambandhāvacchinna-pratiyogitā*, A^* is a *sāmānyābhāva.*

$A.(\mathbf{R}[\llcorner])$: *English:* **R**-delimited-by-A, A is the delimitor of **R**; *Sanskrit:* A-*avacchinnna-sambandha*, A is an *avacchedaka* of **R**.

$(A):(B)$: *English:* B is colocated with A; *Sanskrit:* B-*samānādhikaraṇa*-A.

I: *English:* identity; *Sanskrit:* *abedha.*

3 Semantics for NN

I shall present an interpretation of NN which preserves the underlying intuitions behind NN, including its reference to a domain of negative entities, but does so in a set-theoretic context. The Naiyāyikas own interpretation differs only in pleonastically assigning properties rather than sets to abstract terms (cf. [2]).

3.1 Primitive Terms and the Axiom of Possession

Let U be a set of objects, the objects in the domain. Assign to each primitive term "A" an object A_i in the subset $\mathbf{A} \subseteq U$. We often write A_i for these objects (instead of x or other letters) to stress that they belong to **A**. Assign to "A-hood" or "**A**" the set **A**.

The axiom of possession "A is A-hood-possessing" asserts that A has A-hood, which we naturally interpret here as stating that A is a member of the class of As. Thus:

$$A_i \in \mathbf{A}.$$

Thus, the locative of residence (*vṛttitva*) will denote the relation "$\in$".

The axiom of possession is true in this interpretation, because each $A_i \in \mathbf{A}$. A different interpretation would have assigned "A" to the class of As, **A**. From one point of view, this would have been a more natural interpretation, as there is no arbitrariness in the assignment of values to terms. Indeed it is a standard interpretation for the Aristotelian syllogistic. However, in order to satisfy the axiom of possession, it would be necessary now to assign to "A-hood" the singleton class $\{\mathbf{A}\}$, and this is counter-intuitive. The Nyāya prefer to tolerate the arbitrariness inherent in assigning particular objects to "pure" occurrences of terms. We may imagine that every occurrence of a term "A" has a suppressed index indicating the particular A to which it is assigned. The value of the index will be determined by contextual factors such as the context of utterance, associated demonstrations or pointing, conversational clues, etc. etc. An object A_i is called a "referent" (*śakya*) of the term "A", and the class **A** was traditionally called the "basis for the application" (*pravṛtti-nimitta*) of the term.

The new Nyāya identify the basis of a term with its "delimitor of referent-hood" (*śakyatāvacchedaka*), the reason being that, by semantic assent, the axiom of possession entails that only an A is the referent of the term "A". In other words, $\mathbf{A}\acute{\mathbf{S}}$"$A$", where $\acute{\mathbf{S}}$ is the referenthood relation.

So for NN, in the statement "pot^1 blue^1", the two terms denote particular objects, a pot and a blue thing, and "blue" does not denote a class or property. The relation between the denotata of an appositional statement is identity:

$$\text{“}A^1B^1\text{” is true iff } A_i = B_j.$$

Although a term denotes a particular, it is not a singular term for any particular. In the metalanguage for NN, singular terms for particulars are introduced via a particularity functor "-particularity" ("*-vyaktitva*'), such that "pot-particularity" denotes the property of being that very pot. Thus, given any term "A', assigned to A_i, let the term "A-singularity" be assigned to the singleton class $\{A_i\}$ or $\mathbf{A}_i$. A pot-singularity is a class having some one pot as its sole member. Jagadīśa supplied the semantics for such terms when he said that "the property of being the singular pot is the property of being identical with that very pot". In other words,

$$\mathbf{A}_i = \{y \mid y = A_i\}.$$

Then $\mathbf{A}_i$ is the basis for the singular term "A_i". When "A" has just one member, A-singularity is the same class as A-hood, a fact which Jagadīśa exploits to avoid the restriction in classical Vaiśesika that the abstraction affix cannot be added to a singly instanced term such as "*ākāśa*". In any context, "*ākāśa*" denotes a member of the class $\{y \mid y = \text{ākāśa}\}$.

3.2 The Residence, Restriction and Delimitation of Relational Abstracts

As with terms, so too with relations. Assign to each occurrence of a primitive relational expression "R" an entity R_{ij} in the set

$$\mathbf{R} \subseteq U \times U.$$

The entity R_{ij} is thus to be identified with an ordered pair $\langle x, y\rangle \in U \times U$. If "$R$" is the relation "father", then $\mathbf{R}$ is the relational abstract father-hood. The Axiom of Possession for relations is:

$$R_{ij} \in \mathbf{R}.$$

It is the practice of the Naiyāyikas to describe R_{ij} as "that $\mathbf{R}$ which is in A_i and of B_j', or "that $\mathbf{R}$ which is of A_i and to B_j". Furthermore,

$$\text{“}A^7\mathbf{R}B^6\text{” is true iff } \langle A_i, B_j\rangle = R_{ij} \in \mathbf{R}$$

and the truth-condition for "$A^7\mathbf{R}B^2$" is the same. The introduction of expressions like "R_{ij} gives rise to a potential confusion between terms and statements (or objects and propositions) of which the Nyāya is often accused. For in describing the pair $\langle A_i, B_j\rangle$ as "R_{ij}", it is presupposed that $\langle A_i, B_j\rangle = R_{ij} \in \mathbf{R}$. Likewise, in describing an object as "A_i", it is presupposed that $A_i \in \mathbf{A}$. Our notation disambiguates terms and propositions and avoids this ambiguity.

Any relation $\mathbf{R}$ induces an image function $\mathbf{R}^{\varepsilon}$ and an inverse image function $\mathbf{R}_{\varepsilon}$ defined by

$$\begin{aligned}\mathbf{R}^{\varepsilon}(\mathbf{A}) &= \{y \mid xRy \text{ for some } x \in \mathbf{A}\},\\ \mathbf{R}_{\varepsilon}(\mathbf{B}) &= \{x \mid xRy \text{ for some } y \in \mathbf{B}\}.\end{aligned}$$

As $\mathbf{R}_{\varepsilon}$ is a function, there is, for any class $\mathbf{B}$, a unique class $\mathbf{A}$ such that $\langle \mathbf{A}, \mathbf{B}\rangle \in \mathbf{R}_{\varepsilon}$. This class is termed "**R**-restricted-to-**B**', (**B**-*nirūpita*-**R**) or simply "**R**-to-**B**". I shall denote $\mathbf{R}_{\varepsilon}(\mathbf{B})$ by $\mathbf{R}[\mathbf{B}]$, the square brackets serving to distinguish between $\mathbf{R}$ and $\mathbf{R}_{\varepsilon}$.

The Nyāya assign such classes to phrases like "$\mathbf{R}^1 B^2$" and to compound terms like "B-$\mathbf{R}^1$". Thus, for example, the compound term "hero-father" stands for some member of the class fatherhood-restricted-to-herohood. A term like "father of a hero" will have as its extension the set each of whose members stands in the "father" relation to some hero, that is, the inverse image of {hero} under the "father" relation. Likewise, "daughter of Daśaratha" has as its extension the class which is the inverse image of {Daśaratha} under the daughterhood relation.

However, there is an ambiguity in NN, which must be resolved here. For when a term like "pot" is the restrictor of a relational abstract, it is ambiguous as to whether the relational abstract is restricted to some definite pot or to all pots. The Nyāya take it that the restriction is by default to all pots, and use the singularity function to indicate when some particular pot is intended. Often, they will write *tattad-ghaṭa-nirūpita-kāraṇatā* "causehood-restricted-to-that very pot", using a reduplicated pronoun to indicate that a particular pot is the restrictor. Thus: Assign to the term "$\mathbf{R}^1 B^2$" or "B-$\mathbf{R}^1$" the class $\mathbf{R}[\mathbf{B}]$.

Now, the sentence "Daśaratha is a hero-father" is given the following truth-condition (*bodha*): fatherhood-restricted-to-herohood is resident in Daśaratha. Thus:

$$\text{"}A^7\mathbf{R}B^2\text{" is true iff } A_i \in \mathbf{R}[\mathbf{B}].$$

We noted that the "abstract+instrumental" construction introduced the quantifier "only": "by way of being a king, fatherhood-to-hero" means "only a king is the father of a hero". The Nyāya here introduce the concept of a delimitor in their semantic theory. The idea is that one class delimits another if it supplies an "upper bound". So we define a delimitor (*avacchedaka*) of $\mathbf{R}_\varepsilon[\mathbf{B}]$ thus: A **delimitor** of $\mathbf{R}[\mathbf{B}]$ is any set D such that $\mathbf{R}[\mathbf{B}] \subseteq D$.

Now, "only a king is the father of a hero" is given the truth-condition: fatherhood-restricted-to-herohood is delimited by kinghood. Once again, when a term "A" functions as a delimitor it is assigned to the class A: here, however, there is no ambiguity, for if some particular is intended, the relational abstract can equally be said either to be resident in the particular or to be delimited by the singleton class. In our set-theoretic reading, the above truth-condition states that the class of things which are fathers of a hero is a subset of the class of kings. Thus:

$$\text{“}\mathbf{A}^3\mathbf{R}B^2\text{” is true iff } \mathbf{R}[\mathbf{B}] \subseteq \mathbf{A}.$$

What about the sentence "A king is the father only of a hero", where the instrumental+abstract replaces a target locative? One way to express the truth-condition would be to say that the image of {king} under fatherhood is a subset of {hero}. Thus:

$$\text{“}A^6\mathbf{R}\mathbf{B}^3\text{” is true iff } \mathbf{R}^\varepsilon(\mathbf{A}) \subseteq \mathbf{B}.$$

However, the Nyāya usually exploit inverse relations:[3] The image and inverse image functions are interdefinable: $\mathbf{R}^\varepsilon = \mathbf{R}_v^{-1} arep$. The truth-condition is then that sonhood-restricted-to-kinghood is delimited by herohood:

$$\text{“}A^6\mathbf{R}\mathbf{B}^3\text{” is true iff } \mathbf{R}^{-1}[\mathbf{A}] \subseteq \mathbf{B}.$$

Before we consider the Nyāya approach to the semantics of negative statements, we must develop further the set-theoretic framework.

3.3 Subjunctity and Adjunctity

Given any $\langle x, y\rangle \in R$, x is the subjunct (*anuyogin*) and y is the adjunct (*pratiyogin*) of the relation. We may therefore define a new pair of relations "subjunctity" ${}^{\mathrm{S}}\mathbf{R}$ and "adjunctity" ${}^{\mathrm{A}}\mathbf{R}$:

$$\langle x, R_{ij}\rangle \in {}^{\mathrm{S}}\mathbf{R} \text{ iff } x \text{ is the subjunct of } R_{ij}$$

$$\langle x, R_{ij}\rangle \in {}^{\mathrm{A}}\mathbf{R} \text{ iff } x \text{ is the adjunct of } R_{ij}$$

It is clear that even if a is a subjunct of R and b is an adjunct of R, it does not follow that aRb. The Nyāya specify the relationship that must obtain between subjunctity and adjunctity for this to be so, by saying that the subjunctity-in-a is conditioned by (*nirūpita*) the adjunctity-in-b. This is a statement of an important result. We derive it as follows.

[3] As usual, the inverse of a relation R is defined by $\langle y, x\rangle \in R^{-1}$ iff $\langle x, y\rangle \in R$.

Given any class $\mathbf{A}$, let $\mathbf{B}$ be a class such that $\langle \mathbf{A}, \mathbf{B} \rangle \in \mathbf{R}_\varepsilon$. There may be many distinct such classes, for different classes can have the same inverse image. However:

Theorem 3.1. Let $\mathbf{A}$ be any class. If $\mathbf{B}$ is such that $\mathbf{A} = \mathbf{R}_\varepsilon(\mathbf{B})$, then $\mathbf{B} \subseteq \mathbf{R}^\varepsilon(\mathbf{A})$.

Proof. Then, given any $y \in \mathbf{B}$, there is an $x \in \mathbf{A}$ such that $x\mathbf{R}y$. So $y \in \{z \mid x\mathbf{R}z \text{ for some } x \in \mathbf{A}\} = \mathbf{R}^\varepsilon(\mathbf{A})$. So $\mathbf{B} \subseteq \mathbf{R}^\varepsilon(\mathbf{A}) = \mathbf{R}_\varepsilon^{-1}(\mathbf{A})$. Q.E.D.

Likewise:

Theorem 3.2. Let $\mathbf{B}$ be any class. If $\mathbf{A}$ is such that $\mathbf{B} = \mathbf{R}^\varepsilon(\mathbf{A})$, then $\mathbf{A} \subseteq \mathbf{R}_\varepsilon(\mathbf{B})$.

Proof. Then, given any $x \in \mathbf{A}$, there is an $y \in \mathbf{B}$ such that $x\mathbf{R}y$. So $x \in \{z \mid z\mathbf{R}y \text{ for some } y \in \mathbf{B}\} = \mathbf{R}_\varepsilon(\mathbf{B})$. So $\mathbf{A} \subseteq \mathbf{R}_\varepsilon(\mathbf{B})$. Q.E.D.

We shall call $\mathbf{R}^\varepsilon(\mathbf{A})$ "$\mathbf{R}$-delimited-by-$\mathbf{A}$" or just "$\mathbf{R}$-by-$\mathbf{A}$', and write it as $(\mathbf{A})\mathbf{R}$. Now,

$$(a)^{\mathrm{S}}\mathbf{R} = \{R_{ij} \mid i = a\} \subseteq \mathbf{R}$$

and

$$(b)^{\mathrm{A}}\mathbf{R} = \{R_{ij} \mid j = b\} \subseteq \mathbf{R}.$$

So

$$A_iRB_i \text{ iff } (a)^{\mathrm{S}}\mathbf{R} \cap (b)^{\mathrm{A}}\mathbf{R} \neq \varnothing \text{ iff } (a)^{\mathrm{S}}\mathbf{R} \equiv (b)^{\mathrm{A}}\mathbf{R} \text{ if either is a function.}$$

Furthermore, $(\mathbf{A})^{\mathrm{S}}\mathbf{R} = {}^{\mathrm{S}}\mathbf{R}^\varepsilon(\mathbf{A}) \subseteq \mathbf{R}$ and $(\mathbf{B})^{\mathrm{A}}\mathbf{R} = {}^{\mathrm{A}}\mathbf{R}^\varepsilon(\mathbf{B}) \subseteq \mathbf{R}$. So A_iRB_i iff $(\mathbf{A})^{\mathrm{S}}\mathbf{R} \cap (\mathbf{B})^{\mathrm{A}}\mathbf{R} \neq \varnothing$. More importantly, the truth-conditions for the "only" sentences can be reformulated thus:

"Only an A is R to a B" $\quad \mathbf{R}_\varepsilon[\mathbf{B}] \subseteq \mathbf{A}$ iff $(\mathbf{B})^{\mathrm{A}}\mathbf{R} \subseteq (\mathbf{A})^{\mathrm{S}}\mathbf{R}$,
"An A is R only to a B" $\quad \mathbf{R}_\varepsilon^{-1}[\mathbf{A}] \subseteq \mathbf{B}$ iff $(\mathbf{A})^{\mathrm{S}}\mathbf{R} \subseteq (\mathbf{B})^{\mathrm{A}}\mathbf{R}$.

Finally, define the relation $\approx$ of "conditioning', such that: $(\mathbf{A})\mathbf{R} \approx (\mathbf{B})\mathbf{R}^{-1}$ iff $(\mathbf{A})^{\mathrm{S}}\mathbf{R} \equiv (\mathbf{B})^{\mathrm{A}}\mathbf{R}$, i.e.,

$$(x)(y)((Ax \wedge xRy \to By) \wedge (By \wedge xRy \to Ax)).$$

Define the conditional composition $\mathbf{R}_1.\mathbf{R}_2$ of two relations $\mathbf{R}_1$ and $\mathbf{R}_2$:

$$\langle x, y \rangle \in \mathbf{R}_1.\mathbf{R}_2 \text{ iff } \langle x, z \rangle \in \mathbf{R}_1 \wedge \langle y, z \rangle \in \mathbf{R}_2 \text{ for some } z.$$

We shall say that $\mathbf{R}_1$ is (compositionally) conditioned by $\mathbf{R}_2$. The term used here for "conditioned" is "*nirūpita*', the term also used for restriction. Yet the two concepts are not quite the same. Note also that conditional composition is symmetric: $\mathbf{R}_1.\mathbf{R}_2 = \mathbf{R}_2.\mathbf{R}_1$.

Theorem 3.3 (Factor Theorem)**.** $\mathbf{R} = {}^{\mathrm{S}}\mathbf{R}.{}^{\mathrm{A}}\mathbf{R}$.

Proof. Let $R_{ab} = \langle a, b\rangle \in \mathbf{R}$. Then $\langle a, R_{ab}\rangle \in {}^{\mathrm{S}}\mathbf{R}$, and $\langle b, R_{ab}\rangle \in {}^{\mathrm{A}}\mathbf{R}$, so $\langle a, b\rangle \in {}^{\mathrm{S}}\mathbf{R}.{}^{\mathrm{A}}\mathbf{R}$. Conversely, if $\langle a, b\rangle \in {}^{\mathrm{S}}\mathbf{R}.{}^{\mathrm{A}}\mathbf{R}$ then there is some z such that $\langle a, z\rangle \in {}^{\mathrm{S}}\mathbf{R}$, and $\langle b, z\rangle \in {}^{\mathrm{A}}\mathbf{R}$. So $z = R_{ay}$ for some y and $z = R_{xb}$ for some x. So $z = R_{ab}$. So aRb just in case the the subjunctity in a is conditioned by the adjunctity in b. Q.E.D.

Here the Naiyāyikas introduce inverse relations (cf. Footnote 3). Thus if y is the adjunct of R_{ij}, then it is the subjunct of R_{ij}^{-1}. Thus ${}^{\mathrm{A}}\mathbf{R} = {}^{\mathrm{S}}(\mathbf{R}^{-1})$. The Factor Theorem therefore becomes: $\mathbf{R} = {}^{\mathrm{S}}\mathbf{R}.{}^{\mathrm{S}}(\mathbf{R}^{-1})$. Thus, if Daśaratha is the father of Rāma, we may say that fatherhood-subjunctity resident in Daśaratha is conditioned by sonhood-subjunctity resident in Rāma. Since $\langle x, y\rangle \in \mathbf{R}$ iff $\langle x, R_{xy}\rangle \in {}^{\mathrm{S}}\mathbf{R}$, x is a subjunct of $\mathbf{R}$ iff x is a subjunct of $\mathbf{R}$-subjunctity. So we may say simply that fatherhood resident in Daśaratha is conditioned by sonhood resident in Rāma.

Notice that the operation of conditioning of one relation by another is reducible to the usual notion of relation composition $\otimes$ by

$$\mathbf{R}_1.\mathbf{R}_2 \text{ iff } \mathbf{R}_1 \otimes \mathbf{R}_2^{-1}.$$

So another reformulation of the Factor Theorem is: $\mathbf{R} = {}^{\mathrm{S}}\mathbf{R} \otimes ({}^{\mathrm{S}}(\mathbf{R}^{-1}))^{-1}$. Likewise, we may define two relations ${}^{\mathrm{S}}\mathbf{R}_{\varepsilon}$ and ${}^{\mathrm{A}}\mathbf{R}_{\varepsilon}$, such that $\langle x, R_{A,B}\rangle \in {}^{\mathrm{S}}\mathbf{R}_{\varepsilon}$ iff x is a subjunct of $R_{A,B}$ and $\langle y, R_{A,B}\rangle \in {}^{\mathrm{A}}\mathbf{R}_{\varepsilon}$ iff y is an adjunct of $R_{A,B}$. A second factor theorem now follows:

$$\mathbf{R}_{\varepsilon} = {}^{\mathrm{S}}\mathbf{R}_{\varepsilon}.{}^{\mathrm{A}}\mathbf{R}_{\varepsilon}.$$

The Nyāya advance further instances to deal with quantified sentences; e.g., causehood-delimited-by-rodhood is conditioned by effecthood-delimited-by-pothood.

3.4 Negation

In Nyāya semantic vocabulary, a negative relational statement "$\sim aRb$" is interpreted as follows. The object a is said to possess an "absence" (*abhāva*). An "absence" is thought of as an object of a certain peculiar type. Let us denote the absence which a possesses when $\sim aRb$ by n^*. The absence n^* is said to take b as its "counter-positive" (*pratiyogin*), and the counter-positivity is said to be delimited by R. So two new relations emerge here. One is the relation between an object and the absence it "possesses": this is described as a relation of "absential particular qualification" (*abhāvīya-viśe aṇat ā-viśe a-sambandha*) or as a "self-linking absential relation" (*abhāvīya-svarūpa-sambandha*). We interpreted the notion of possession by means of the set-membership relation; so let us here interpret the notion of "possession of an absence" by a relation of absential set-membership "$\in^*$". Thus,

$$a \in^* n^* \text{ iff } a \text{ absentially possesses } n^*. \tag{N1}$$

The other relation is that between an absence n^* and the object of which it is the absence, b. The proper description of this relation, say the Nyāya, requires that we state the relation R by which b relates, or rather does not relate, to a. A pot might be present on the ground by the relation of contact but absent by the relation of inherence. Thus,

$$b \text{ is the counter-positive of } n^* \text{ by } R. \tag{N2}$$

Notice that the term for the counter-positivity relation, between an absence and the thing of which it is an absence, is "*pratiyogitā*". In the above theory of relations, this same term was used to denote the relation of adjunctity. That suggests the way to interpret the above theory. Define the relation $R' \subset U \times U$ such that $xR'y$ iff $\sim xRy$. Now b is an adjunct of R'. Let us call ${}^{\mathrm{A}}\mathbf{R}'$ the **absential adjunctity to** R (*R-sambandhā vacchina-abhāvīya-pratiyogitā*). Now, the Factor Theorem tells us that

$$\mathbf{R}' = {}^{\mathrm{S}}\mathbf{R}'.{}^{\mathrm{A}}\mathbf{R}'.$$

In other words, $\langle a, b\rangle \in \mathbf{R}'$ iff for some entity z, $\langle a, z\rangle \in {}^{\mathrm{S}}\mathbf{R}'$ and $\langle b, z\rangle \in {}^{\mathrm{A}}\mathbf{R}'$. But notice that if we interpret "counterpositiveness" as meaning "absential adjunctity', then (N2) says that

$$\langle b, n^*\rangle \in {}^{\mathrm{A}}\mathbf{R}'. \tag{N2*}$$

This suggests that we interpret N1 as follows. Define the absential possession relation "$\in^*$" so that $x \in^* y$ iff $\langle x, y\rangle \in {}^{\mathrm{S}}\mathbf{R}'$. Then (N1), $a \in^* n^*$, is equivalent to:

$$\langle a, n^*\rangle \in {}^{\mathrm{S}}\mathbf{R}' \tag{N1*}$$

(N1*) and (N2*) jointly imply that a is the subjunct of that token of $\mathbf{R}'$ for which b is the adjunct, i.e., that $\sim aRb$. What then is n^*? Clearly, in this interpretation it is nothing other than R'_{ab}. So we can interpret the Nyāya statement that a absentially-possesses an absence the counterpositiveness to which is resident in b and delimited by $\mathbf{R}$, as asserting that a is the absential subjunct of $\mathbf{R}$ whose absential adjunctity is resident in b.

This interpretation has as a consequence that we identity Nyāya absences with certain ordered pairs rather than a peculiar new type of entity. Alternatively, we may construe discussions about the ontological status of absences as pertaining to the irreducibility or otherwise of ordered pairs. For it is certainly strange to say that the ordered pair $\langle a, b\rangle$ "exists" only iff $\sim aRb$.

Primary Sources

NK. = Bhimacharya Jhalakikar, *Nyāyakośa*, in: [4].

References

[1] Jonardon Ganeri. Towards a formal regimentation of the Navya-Nyāya technical language I. In THIS VOLUME, pages 105–121, 2008.

[2] Eberhard Guhe. George Bealer's Property Theories and their Relevance to the Study of Navya-Nyāya Logic. In THIS VOLUME, pages 139–153, 2008.

[3] Bimal Krishna Matilal. *The Navya-Nyāya Doctrine of Negation: The Semantics and Ontology of Negative Statements in Navya-Nyāya Philosophy*, volume 46 of *Harvard Oriental Series*. Harvard University Press, Cambridge, Massachusetts, 1968.

[4] Vasudeva Abhyankara Sastri, editor. *Bhimacharya Jhalakikar, Nyāyakośa or Dictionary of Technical Terms of Indian Philosophy*. Bhandarkar Institute, Pune, 1928.

[5] Jacob S. Speijer. *Sanskrit Syntax*. Motilal Banarsidass, Delhi, 1988.

George Bealer's Property Theories and their Relevance to the Study of Navya-Nyāya Logic

Eberhard Guhe

Institut für Indologie, Johannes Gutenberg-Universität Mainz, Friedrich-von-Pfeiffer-Weg 5, 55099 Mainz, Germany
E-mail: guhe@uni-mainz.de

The purpose of the present paper is to show that some interesting problems in Navya-Nyāya logic can be analysed by means of a Quine-Morse-style extension of Bealer's property calculus T1. There is already an account of the basic ideas of this approach in my dissertation on the Upādhidarpaṇa (*UD*) and in an article in "Berliner Indologische Studien" (cf. [5, 6]). The *UD* is an anonymous early Navya-Nyāya treatise on the inferential undercutting condition (*upādhi*). It might have been composed between the 13th and 14th century and probably predates the time when the great Navya-Nyāya philosopher Gaṅgeśa flourished. My dissertation contains the first edition and translation of the *UD* and also a formal analysis of logical problems discussed by the author. For that purpose I chose Bealer's calculus as a logical framework. In [6], I applied this methodological device in order to analyse some other logical problems in Gaṅgeśa's Tattvacintāmaṇi and in the works of Navya-Nyāya commentators such as Mathurānātha etc. The present paper is divided into the following sections:

In § 1, we discuss the discovery of the intensional character of the logic of Navya-Nyāya and B. K. Matilal's attempt to formalize intensional entities in Navya-Nyāya by means of property terms; then in § 2, we describe Bealer's property calculus T1, and discuss the *tattvavat tad eva*-principle and its liability to yield a contradiction in § 3 (where we analyse the principle in terms of a Quine-Morse-style extension T1+ of Bealer's property calculus T1). In § 4, we give a proof of the identity of the absence of difference from x with x-ness (and similar identities) by applying T1+, and then examine Gaṅgeśa's proof of the existence of universal properties by means of T1+ in § 5. Finally, in § 6, we discuss the defining property of the inferential undercutting condition according to the *UD*.

1

Some decades ago, Matilal and Bocheński already talked about intensional tendencies in the logic of Navya-Nyāya.[1] This impression is owing to the fact that logical inquiries in Navya-Nyāya are mostly concerned with property terms ending in abstract suffixes like *-tva* or *-tā* which can be translated by

[1]Cf. [8, pp. 67 & 74], [9, p. 169], [2, pp. 513 & 517].

Mihir K. **Chakraborty**, Benedikt **Löwe**, Madhabendra Nath **Mitra**, Sundar **Sarukkai** (*eds.*). Logic, Navya-Nyāya & Applications. Homage to Bimal Krishna Matilal. College Publications, London, 2008. Studies in Logic 15. pp. 139–153.

Received by the editors: 30 April 2007; 17 December 2007.
Accepted for publication: 31 January 2008.

English abstract suffixes like "-ness" or "-hood". In some cases circumlocutions by means of the word "being" may also be feasible as translations. So, the Sanskrit words *ghaṭatva* and *kṛtatva*, which derive from *ghaṭa* ("pot") and *kṛta* ("created"), can be translated by "potness" and "being created" respectively. Matilal's idea was to formalize such property terms by using Quine's notation for intensional contexts:

If we write $P(x)$ for "x is a pot", then $x[P(x)]$ (which can be read as "being an x such that x is P") is an analytical expression for "potness".

The function of the variable x in front of this term is to bind the free occurrence of x in $P(x)$. The square brackets around $P(x)$ indicate an intensional context. If we substitute an expression within the bracketed part by another one which is extensionally equivalent we might change the reference of the property term. Such restrictions concerning the substitutability of extensionally equivalent expressions generally distinguish intensional from extensional logical systems.

Matilal once pointed out that Navya-Nyāya philosophers were also aware of this specific intensional feature of property terms, because they regarded "being created" (*kṛtatva*) and "being non-eternal" (*anityatva*) as distinct properties, although the predicates "... is created" and "... is non-eternal" were supposed to refer to the same set of objects (cf. [9, p. 131]).

The fact that the properties "being created" and "being non-eternal" cannot be identified becomes obvious when we compare the following propositions:

(a) "being non-eternal" is a property which characterizes something by way of a negation.

(b) "being created" is a property which characterizes something by way of a negation.

(a) is of course true, whereas (b) is false. One might be tempted to attribute the difference in truth value to a second order predication. But the phrase "... is a property which characterizes something by way of a negation" turns out to be a first order predicate if we regard properties as individuals. This approach is actually closer to the Navya-Nyāya viewpoint.

2

When I came across the book [1] by G. Bealer, it occurred to me that his property theory can be used to elaborate Matilal's formal analysis of Navya-Nyāya logic. Bealer never thought about such an application of his theory. He wants to explicate his realist notion of properties, relations and concepts, which is supposed to open up new vistas in analytical philosophy, especially in the realm of semantics, philosophical logic, philosophy of mind and philosophy of mathematics. For that purpose Bealer designed three calculi called "T1", "T2" and "T2′". T1 is especially suited to the treatment of modal matters, whereas T2 serves to check epistemic arguments. T2′ is a synthesis of T1 and T2. The calculus T1 can also be used as a basis for a formal analysis of the logic of properties in Navya-Nyāya, as we shall see.

The language of T1 consists of the following primitive symbols: Logical operators such as &, $\neg$, $\exists$; predicate letters such as $=$, F_1^1, F_2^1, $\ldots$, F_p^q; variables such as x, y, z, $\ldots$; and finally the brackets (,), [, and].[2] As usual, we give the simultaneous inductive definition of terms and formulas:

1. All variables are terms.
2. If t_i and t_j are terms, then $t_i = t_j$ is a formula.
3. If $t_1, \ldots, t_j$ are terms, then $F_i^j(t_1, \ldots, t_j)$ is a formula.
4. If A and B are formulas and v_k a variable, then $(A \,\&\, B)$, $\neg A$ and $(\exists v_k)A$ are formulas.
5. If A is a formula and $v_1, \ldots, v_m$ $(0 \leqslant m)$ distinct variables, then $[A]_{v_1 \ldots v_m}$ is a term.

Let us remark that in 4., A is an arbitrary formula, in which the variable v_k need not occur. Similarly, in 5. we do not require the variables $v_1, \ldots, v_m$ to be components of A. If they do occur in A they are bound by the index variables. Generally speaking an occurrence of a variable v_i is bound (free) if and only if it lies (does not lie) within a formula of the form $(\exists v_i)A$ or a term of the form $[A]_{v_1 \ldots v_i \ldots v_m}$.

Moreover, the symbols $\forall$, $\supset$, $\vee$ and $\equiv$, which can be defined in terms of $\exists$ and &, are included in the language of T1. The modal operator $\Box$ is another addendum to the linguistic inventory of T1 introduced by way of a definition (which will be explained subsequently) as

$$\Box A :\equiv [A] = [[A] = [A]].$$

As usual, the corresponding dual operator will be denoted by $\Diamond$.[3]

Instead of going into the formal details of the semantics for the language of T1 I shall only explain the meaning of the "exotic" expressions in an informal way: A term of the form $[A]_{v_1 \ldots v_m}$ denotes

[2] Cf. [1, p. 43].

[3] For those readers who are afraid that modal logic might be incompatible with Navya-Nyāya logic as regards ontological presuppositions it is important to note that there is no possible world construction in Bealer's calculus. Modality is simply defined by means of the square brackets.

a) a proposition, if $m = 0$ ("that A").

b) a property, if $m = 1$ ("being a v_1 of which A is true").

c) an m-ary relation, if $m \geqslant 2$ ("the relation which holds between $v_1, \ldots, v_m$ *iff* A applies to them").

Note that case a) is also crucial for a proper understanding of the definition of the modal operator $\Box$: A is necessarily true according to this definition *iff* the proposition "that A" is identical to a trivial necessary truth. There may be "trivial necessary truths" other than tautological propositions like $[[A] = [A]]$ depending on the presupposed concept of necessity (such as analytical or physical necessity etc.). Furthermore, the term $[A]_{v_1 \ldots v_m}$ can be regarded as a counterpart of the class term $\{\langle v_1, \ldots, v_m \rangle | A\}$.

Bealer shows that T1 can be axiomatized in such a way that we get a sound and complete calculus (cf. [1, p. 58]):

A1: Truth-functional tautologies.

A2: $(\forall v_i)A(v_i) \supset A(t)$, where t is free for v_i in A, i.e., no free occurrence of v_i in A lies within the scope of a quantifier or a sequence of index variables in a term $[\ldots]_{v_1 \ldots v_m}$ which would bind a variable occuring in t.

A3: $(\forall v_i)(A \supset B) \supset (A \supset (\forall v_i)B)$, where v_i is not free in A.

A4: $v_i = v_i$.

A5: $v_i = v_j \supset (A(v_i, v_i) \equiv A(v_i, v_j))$, where $A(v_i, v_j)$ is a formula that arises from $A(v_i, v_i)$ by replacing some (but not necessarily all) free occurrences of v_i by v_j, and v_j is free for the occurrences of v_i that it replaces.

A6: $[A]_{u_1 \ldots u_p} \neq [B]_{v_1 \ldots v_q}$, where $p \neq q$.

A7: $[A(u_1, \ldots, u_p)]_{u_1 \ldots u_p} = [A(v_1, \ldots, v_p)]_{v_1 \ldots v_p}$, where these two terms are alphabetic variants.

A8: $[A]_{u_1 \ldots u_p} = [B]_{u_1 \ldots u_p} \equiv \Box \forall u_1 \ldots \forall u_p (A \equiv B)$.

A9: $\Box A \supset A$.

A10: $\Box(A \supset B) \supset (\Box A \supset \Box B)$.

A11: $\Diamond A \supset \Box \Diamond A$[4].

[4] As Bealer wants to integrate the modal logic S5 in T1, there is obviously a blunder in his deviant formulation of A11, which reads as follows: $\Box A \supset \Box \Diamond A$.

R1: If $\vdash A$ and $\vdash (A \supset B)$, then $\vdash B$.

R2: If $\vdash A$, then $\vdash (\forall v_i)A$.

R3: If $\vdash A$, then $\vdash \Box A$.

Axioms A1 to A5 along with R1 and R2 constitute an axiomatization of first order predicate logic including identity. Axioms A6 to A8 tell us how to deal with the intensional abstracts in T1. It is important to note that A8 furnishes a criterion for the identification of intensional abstracts. In this sense it has the same function as the axiom of extensionality in set theory. Finally, axioms A9 to A11 and R3 constitute an axiomatization of the propositional modal logic S5.

3

Bealer further suggests certain extensions of T1 which may function as an alternative to set theories such as ZF or NBG. For that purpose he introduces a binary relation Δ, which serves as a counterpart of the $\in$-relation in set theory (cf. [1, p. 82]). The relation Δ can be used to create formulas such as $a \, \Delta \, [A(x)]_x$.[5] This is supposed to be a counterpart of the set theoretic expression $a \in \{x|A(x)\}$ and can be read as: "a possesses (or is a locus of) the property 'being an x such that A is true of x'."

If we admit individuals other than properties as elements of the universe of discourse, the Δ-relation can be interpreted in such a way that it applies to relations of location in general.[6] In this sense a variable can be used in connection with the Δ-relation as a means to formalize a property abstraction rule in Navya-Nyāya logic, which constitutes a counterpart to the naive

[5] Cf. [1, p. 96].

[6] A specific case, which Navya-Nyāya philosophers often take into account, is the partial location of an entity together with its absence in one and the same place. When a monkey is sitting on a branch of a tree for example, only a part of the tree, namely that particular branch, is actually a locus of contact with a monkey, whereas the roots of the tree are a locus of absence of contact with a monkey. So, in a sense the monkey is present and absent on the tree. Modern interpreters like Matilal, who identify absence with negation, have argued that this is a violation of the principle of the excluded middle (cf. [9, pp. 120*sq*]). Therefore they suggest a many-valued formal reconstruction of Navya-Nyāya logic. I should like to challenge this view. First of all, we shall see that the Navya-Nyāya concept of absence must not be confounded with the propositional operation of negation. Secondly, the assumption that an object a can be simultaneously present and absent in one and the same locus ℓ need not be regarded as contradictory within a two-valued logical framework. If we specify the exact part ℓ_i of ℓ, where a is present, and differentiate it from the part ℓ_j ($\neq \ell_i$) of ℓ, where a is absent, then there is no contradiction between $\ell_i \, \Delta \, a$ and $\neg \ell_j \, \Delta \, a$. Matilal himself notices that there is a similar strategy to avoid the contradiction in Navya-Nyāya logic, namely the introduction of so-called "delimitors" (*avacchedaka*) as a means to restrict a locus to the area which is actually involved in the relation of location (cf. [9, pp. 127*sq*]).

class abstraction rule in set theory, namely *tattvavat tad eva* — "Anything which possesses the property 'being that' is that."[7] In order to see how this rule works we can replace the Sanskrit word *tat* ("that"), which has the same function as a variable here, by words like *ghaṭa* ("pot"). *ghaṭatvavān ghaṭa eva* means: "Anything which possesses the property 'potness' is a pot." The *tattvavat tad eva*-rule can be formally represented in the following way:

$$a \,\Delta\, [A(x)]_x \equiv A(a), \text{ where } a \text{ is free for } x \text{ in } A \text{ and vice versa.} \qquad (*)$$

My interpretation of the *tattvavat tad eva*-rule as an equivalence is confirmed by Matilal, who characterizes the specific style of Navya-Nyāya texts in the following way:

> Simple predicate formulations, such as 'x is F' are noted, but only to be rephrased as 'x has *F-ness*' (where *F-ness* stands for the property derived from 'F'). [9, p. 115]

Apart from property abstraction relational abstraction (which I am not going to deal with in the present paper) also plays an important role in Navya-Nyāya logic (cf. [7, pp. 44*sq*] and [9, pp. 170*sq*]). The above-mentioned T1-terms of the form $[A]_{v_1 \ldots v_m}$ can be used to formalize relational abstracts such as *vṛttitva* ("being resident in"), *vyāpyatva* ("being pervaded by"), etc.

Now, let us replace the word *tat* ("that") in the *tattvavat tad eva*-rule by *asvavṛttitva* ("being not resident in itself"). This property can easily be formalized. If we admit $x \,\Delta\, x$ as a formal equivalent of "x resides in itself", "being not resident in itself" can be expressed by $[\neg x \,\Delta\, x]_x$. Let us abbreviate this property by r.

The Navya-Nyāya logicians were not aware that r can be used to derive a variant of the Zermelo-Russell antinomy from the *tattvavat tad eva*-rule (cf. [5, p. 22] and [6, p. 109]):

(a) If r is resident in itself (i.e., if it is *svavṛtti*), then the property "being not resident in itself" (*asvavṛttitva*) resides in r. Therefore (according to the *tattvavat tad eva*-rule) r is not resident in itself (i.e., it is *asvavṛtti*). Contradiction!

The following is the formal counterpart of the argument: $r \,\Delta\, r$ implies $r \,\Delta\, [\neg x \,\Delta\, x]_x$. We apply $(*)$ with $a = r$ and $A(x) :\equiv \neg x \,\Delta\, x$, to get $\neg r \,\Delta\, r$.

(b) If r is not resident in itself (i.e., if it is *asvavṛtti*), then (according to the *tattvavat tad eva*-rule) the property "being not resident in itself" (*asvavṛttitva*) resides in r. Therefore r is resident in itself (i.e., it is *svavṛtti*). Contradiction!

---

[7] Cf. [7, p. 36].

The following is the formal counterpart of the argument: Substitute $\neg r \, \Delta \, r$ for $A(a)$ in $(*)$ to get $r \, \Delta \, [\neg x \, \Delta \, x]_x$. This implies $r \, \Delta \, r$.

The arguments **(a)** and **(b)** together yield the following variant of the Zermelo-Russell antinomy:

$$r \, \Delta \, r \equiv \neg r \, \Delta \, r$$

In order to modify $(*)$ in such a way that its paradoxical consequence disappears we can try to imitate the strategies which were used by the founders of set theories in order to safeguard the naive class abstraction rule against the Zermelo-Russell antinomy. The systems ZF (Zermelo-Fraenkel), NBG (Neumann-Bernays-Gödel) and QM (Quine-Morse — sometimes also called Morse-Kelley) are all equipped with an axiom of comprehension which replaces the naive class abstraction rule. But let us see if there is a remedy for the antinomy which does not interfere with basic tenets of the Navya-Nyāya system.

A ZF-style modification of $(*)$ is undesirable because the ZF-comprehension axiom excludes the existence of a universal set. *Mutatis mutandis* universal properties would not exist according to T1 combined with a similar modification of $(*)$. However, the majority of Navya-Nyāya philosophers advocates the existence of universal properties. An NBG-style modification of $(*)$ would not interfere with such ontological biases. But it is still too restrictive, as we shall see (cf. § 4).

A property adaptation of the QM comprehension axiom (cf. [4, p. 138]) is associated with a wider range of instantiations than the NBG variant. Therefore the modification of $(*)$ should rather ensue from QM, which is identical with NBG except for the fact that the QM comprehension axiom is impredicative.

An important feature of QM (and also of NBG) is the distinction between sets and classes, whereas in ZF we are only dealing with sets. Every set is a class. But only classes which are elements of classes are sets. The universal class for example is not a set but a class. A class which is not a set is called "proper class". In QM capital letters (X, Y, Z etc.) as individual variables refer to proper classes and sets, whereas small letters (x, y, z etc.) as individual variables refer to sets.

In our property-adaptation of QM we introduce a similar distinction between properly class-like properties and set-like properties. Only a property which is a locus of a property is a set-like property. On the analogy of the universal set universal properties like "being namable" (*abhidheyatva*) are not set-like. We can call them "properly class-like". Following the example of QM we shall use capital and small letters as individual variables in order to distinguish between the two types of properties.

Now we are prepared to formulate a QM-style modification of (*):

$$(\forall x)(x \,\Delta\, [A(Y)]_Y \equiv A(x)), \text{ where } x \text{ is free for } Y \text{ in } A, \text{ \& vice versa.} \quad \text{(C)}$$

The equation (C) is called "impredicative", because the domain of any quantifier which might occur in A is not restricted to set-like properties. Such a restriction would be necessary in order to get an NBG-style modification of (*). But the impredicative variant (C) is preferable, because it includes instantiations which are important for the study of Navya-Nyāya logic (cf. § 4).

Note that since x is a variable referring to set-like properties, we cannot eliminate the universal quantifier in (C) by substituting any property term for x. It is easy to see that this restriction serves as a remedy against the aforementioned antinomy. Consider the following instantiation of (C):

$$(\forall x)(x \,\Delta\, [\neg y \,\Delta\, y]_y \equiv \neg x \,\Delta\, x).$$

In order to derive the antinomy from this formula we should have to eliminate the universal quantifier by substituting $[\neg y \,\Delta\, y]_y$ for x. This is only admissible, if $[\neg y \,\Delta\, y]_y$ is set-like. However, the antinomy which derives from this substitution proves that $[\neg y \,\Delta\, y]_y$ is properly class-like and cannot be substituted for x.

Although there is no counterpart of the concepts "set-like property" and "properly class-like property" in Navya-Nyāya philosophy the preceding strategy to get rid of the antinomy is probably the best compromise with basic Navya-Nyāya tenets.

We can also add the property adaptations of the other QM axioms to T1. Only the QM axiom of extensionality is obsolete for our purposes, because there is already a criterion for the identification of properties in T1, namely A8.

Bealer presents entire NBG-style and ZF-style extensions of T1 (cf. [1, pp. 96*sq* & 265]). A QM-style extension would be identical with the NBG-style variant except for the different counterparts of the comprehension axioms in NBG and QM. Let us denote the QM-style extension of T1 by T1+. For the proofs which I am going to demonstrate we shall need only one more axiom of the QM-style extension, namely the property adaptation of the axiom of regularity:

$$(\forall X)((\exists y)y \,\Delta\, X \supset (\exists y)(y \,\Delta\, X \,\&\, (\forall z)(z \,\Delta\, X \supset \neg z \,\Delta\, y))). \quad \text{(R)}$$

4

Navya-Nyāya philosophers like Mathurānātha advocate the following identity (cf. [7, p. 71] and [9, pp. 152*sq*]):

> The absence (*abhāva*) of difference (*bheda*) from anything which is F is identical with F-ness. (Id)

According to (Id) the absence of difference from a pot (*ghaṭabhedābhāva*) is identical with potness (*ghaṭatva*).

In modern studies on Navya-Nyāya logic "absence" and "difference" are mostly treated like negations (cf. [9, p. 147]). Matilal abbreviates "absence" by "$\sim$", "difference" by "$-$" and "x-ness" by x_1. Thereby he arrives at the following formal expression of (Id):[8]

$$\sim -x = x_1.$$

This formula looks like a violation of the principle *duplex negatio affirmat*. According to my interpretation of (Id) no violation of *duplex negatio affirmat* is involved here. I shall show that in T1+ "absence" and "difference" can be represented as property terms. With these formal representations I shall prove (Id) in T1+. First of all, the "difference from anything which is F" should be rendered by

$$[\neg F(x)]_x.$$

The "absence of anything which is F" can be regarded as a property which characterizes something as being devoid of (or: no locus of) anything which is F.[9] If the predicate F invariably refers to properties we can represent this absence by means of the Δ-relation:

$$[\neg(\exists Y)(F(Y) \,\&\, x \,\Delta\, Y)]_x.$$

In order to obtain a formal representation of the absence of difference from a pot we specify $F(Y)$ as

$Y = [\neg P(x)]_x$, where $P(x)$ is used in the sense of "x is a pot".

Then we can formalize the absence of difference from a pot as

$$[\neg(\exists Y)(Y = [\neg P(x)]_x \,\&\, x \;\Delta\; Y)]_x$$

("being no locus of anything which is identical with the difference from a pot"). Now we are able to express (Id) as a T1+ proposition:

Theorem 4.1. $[P(x)]_x = [\neg(\exists Y)(Y = [\neg P(x)]_x \,\&\, x \;\Delta\; Y)]_x$

Proof.

$P(x) \equiv \neg\neg P(x)$ (A1)

$P(x) \equiv \neg x \,\Delta\, [\neg P(x)]_x$ (C)

[8] Cf. [9, pp. 152*sq*].

[9] Navya-Nyāya philosophers often add the word *atyanta* ("absolute") to the word *abhāva* ("absence") in order to emphasize that they are talking about the absence of *anything* which is F and not just about the absence of a particular object which is F prior to its production (*prāgabhāva*) or posterior to its destruction (*dhvaṃsābhāva*).

$$P(x) \equiv \neg(\exists Y)(Y = [\neg P(x)]_x \,\&\, x \,\Delta\, Y) \qquad \text{(First order predicate logic)}$$
$$\Box(\forall x)(P(x) \equiv \neg(\exists Y)(Y = [\neg P(x)]_x \,\&\, x \,\Delta\, Y)) \qquad \text{(R2, R3)}$$
$$[P(x)]_x = [\neg(\exists Y)(Y = [\neg P(x)]_x \,\&\, x \,\Delta\, Y)]_x \qquad \text{(A8, R1)}$$

Q.E.D.

Similarly, we can prove that

> the absence of the absence of any pot is identical with the property "being a locus of a pot". (Id′)

The proof of (Id′) is analogous to the preceding one. We can start with the T1+ tautology $(\exists Y)(P(Y) \,\&\, x \,\Delta\, Y) \equiv \neg\neg(\exists Y)(P(Y) \,\&\, x \,\Delta\, Y)$.

(Id′) is another identity which would be endorsed by most Navya-Nyāya logicians, although they formulate it in a slightly different way. Since every locus of the property "being a locus of a pot" is a locus of a pot and vice versa, it was customary in Navya-Nyāya to regard expressions like *ghaṭa-vattva* ("being a locus of a pot") and *ghaṭa* ("pot") as interchangeable (cf. [9, p. 115]). So, most Navya-Nyāya logicians would go a step further by reducing the expression "the property 'being a locus of a pot'" in (Id′) to "pot" (cf. [9, pp. 148*sq*]).

5

In his work Tattvacintāmaṇi the Navya-Nyāya philosopher Gaṅgeśa contradicts an opponent who claims that the property "being nameable" cannot be universal, because it is a property and properties are always incompatible with some loci (cf. *TC* 553f). According to Gaṅgeśa the opponent's argument is inconclusive.

> *vyāvṛttatvasyāvyāvṛttatve vyāvṛttatvam eva kevalānvayi, vyāvṛttatve yata eva vyāvṛttaṃ vyāvṛttatvaṃ tad eva kevalānvayīti dharmatvasyānaikāntikatvāt, evam atyantābhāvapratiyogitvasyātyantābhāvāpratiyogitve 'tyantābhāvapratiyogitvam eva kevalānvayi, atyantābhāvapratiyogitve yanniṣṭhātyantābhāvapratiyogy atyantābhāvapratiyogitvaṃ tad eva kevalānvayi.* (*TC* 555f)

> "(α) [No], because 'being a property' is not a conclusive [inferential mark] insofar as the property "being incompatible with some locus" is a universal property, if the property "being incompatible with some locus" is not incompatible with any locus. If it is incompatible with some locus then that with which the property "being incompatible with some locus" is incompatible is a universal property. (β) Similarly, if the property "being a counterpositive of an absolute absence" is not a counterpositive of an absolute absence, then the property "being a counterpositive of an absolute absence" is a universal property. If [the property "being a counterpositive of an absolute absence"] is

a counterpositive of an absolute absence, then the property "being a counterpositive of an absolute absence" is a counterpositive of an absolute absence residing in that which is a universal property."

This passage contains two (tantamount) formulations (signified as (α) and (β)) of an attempt to prove the existence of universal properties. If we understand by "universal property" a property which resides in any entity except for properly class-like properties, there is a direct evidence of the existence of such universal properties in T1+: According to (C), we have $(\forall z) z \ \Delta \ [x = x]_x$. Hence,

$$(\exists Y)(\forall z) z \ \Delta \ Y. \qquad (\dagger)$$

Gaṅgeśa's argument is less straightforward, but it can be confirmed by T1+. It is interesting to note that he tries to prove (†) in a nonconstructive way, i.e., without showing that a specific property is universal. He starts by introducing a property which need not be universal, namely "being incompatible with some locus" (*vyāvṛttatva*) in (α) or "being a counterpositive of an absolute absence" (*atyantābhāvapratiyogitva*) in (β).

If we interpret both expressions in the sense of "being a property which is not universal" we can represent them as $E := [\neg(\forall y) y \ \Delta \ X]_X$. Now Gaṅgeśa argues in the following way: Either E is universal or not. (In the latter case it is *avyāvṛtta* or an *atyantābhāvāpratiyogi*). So, we are faced with the following alternatives:

$$(\forall z) z \ \Delta \ E; \text{ or} \qquad \text{(a)}$$

$$\neg(\forall z) z \ \Delta \ E. \qquad \text{(b)}$$

The statement (†) is confirmed if it proves to be true on the assumption of (a) and (b) alike. From (a) (†) can be directly inferred. In case (b) Gaṅgeśa argues in the following way: If E is not universal, then there is something which is not a locus of E, i.e., there is something which is **not** a locus of the property "being a property which is **not** universal". If we cancel the two negations in bold type we get (†). This argument can be verified in T1+:

$\neg(\forall z) z \ \Delta \ [\neg(\forall y) y \ \Delta \ X]_X$	(b)
$(\exists z) \neg z \ \Delta \ [\neg(\forall y) y \ \Delta \ X]_X$	(First order predicate logic)
$(\exists z) \neg\neg(\forall y) y \ \Delta \ z$	(C)
$(\exists z)(\forall y) y \ \Delta \ z$	(A1)

It is important to note that at the beginning of this proof one of the two negations which Gaṅgeśa cancels appears within a property term, whereas the other one is exterior to it. In Gaṅgeśa's formulation we can easily miss this important point and Gaṅgeśa was probably not aware that his proof does not work without further provisions. Only by applying axiom (C) the initial formula can be reshuffled in such a way that we obtain two adjacent negations, which can be cancelled then. In order to facilitate the application of (C) the range of the first universal quantifier in (b) has to be restricted to set-like loci and we need the same restriction in (a), because (b) is supposed to be the negation of (a). So, our formal reconstruction of Gaṅgeśa's proof gives only evidence of the existence of something which is resident in all set-like entities. Maybe Gaṅgeśa would not have agreed to the idea that residence in all set-like entities is enough to classify a property as universal. But without specifying the meaning of the word "universal" in this way his argument would become inconsistent.

6

In the *UD* (cf. fol. 1r, 1–2v, 2 and fol. 4r, 2–4) the so-called "inferential undercutting condition"[10] is defined as a property (*dharma*), i.e., as something which —unlike the ether and other eternal substances— resides in a particular locus.[11] Moreover, it does not pervade the inferential mark (*sādhanāvyāpaka*), whereas it is coextensive with the probandum (*sādhyasamavyāpta*). As it does not pervade the inferential mark, it cannot be universal. Therefore every inferential undercutting condition is endowed with the defining property (*sāmānyalakṣaṇa*) "being a *dharma* which is not universal" (*atyantābhāvapratiyogidharmatva*). This expression can be formalized in the following way:

$$U := [\, \underbrace{(\exists y) y \,\Delta\, X}_{X \text{ is a } dharma} \;\&\; \underbrace{\neg(\forall y) y \,\Delta\, X}_{X \text{ is not universal}} \,]_X .$$

In the first part of the *UD* an opponent argues that U applies to itself. After all, it does apply to actual undercutting conditions, but not to eternal substances, because they are not *dharmas*. Hence, the defining property of inferential undercutting conditions is a *dharma* which is not universal. Therefore it should be a locus of itself. "Self-dependence" is, however, generally regarded as an absurdity in Indian philosophy. The Nyāya philosopher

[10]This is the translation of *upādhi* suggested in [10] owing to the fact that an *upādhi* vitiates or "undercuts" a false inference such as the inference of smoke (= probandum) from fire (= inferential mark). In this case (which is just the reversal of the correct inference of fire from smoke) wet fuel serves as an *upādhi*, because it was supposed to be a necessary precondition for the production of smoke. With regard to a locus like molten metal, where the *upādhi* is missing, smoke cannot be inferred from fire.

In the *UD* the concept of *upādhi* is defined in such a way that the occurrence of an *upādhi* also entails the occurrence of the probandum of the respective false inference. According to this definition it would be more appropriate to say that wet fuel in conjunction with fire functions as an *upādhi* concerning the inference of smoke from fire, because wet fuel yields smoke only when it is set to fire.

[11]Cf. the following definition of the term *dharma* ("property"): *dhriyate tiṣṭhati vartate yaḥ sa dharmaḥ. ... yatra yo vartate sa tasya dharmaḥ.* — "What is fixed [somewhere], stands [somewhere or] is resident [somewhere] that is a property. ... Whatever is resident somewhere that is a property of that [locus where it is resident]." (*BN* 8, 9–11)

Varadarāja, for example, explicitly rejects looping chains of dependence relations consisting of one member (*ātmāśraya* — "self-dependence"), two members (*anyonyāśraya* — "mutual dependence") or more than two members (*cakraka* — "circularity"). (Cf. *TR* 234f) Regarding these phenomena as counterintuitive would mean to accept the idea of foundation, which is expressed in the above-mentioned axiom of regularity (R).

Such a tool was, however, not available to the proponent in the *UD*. He subscribes to the view that U is also a *dharma* which is not universal, but he cannot convincingly explain why this does not mean to admit a case of self-dependence. Since his argument is rather clumsy, I shall not reproduce it here. The opponent can be defeated much more convincingly by arguing on the basis of T1+. The mistake in his argument consists in an unwarranted application of the naive property abstraction rule. Granting that U is a *dharma* which is not universal we can only conclude that it is a locus of itself, if it is set-like. But in T1+ we can prove that set-like properties are never loci of themselves. This results as a corollary from the following more general theorem (which shows that *anyonyāśraya* and *cakraka* cannot apply to set-like properties either).

Theorem 6.1. $\neg(x_1 \,\Delta\, x_2 \,\Delta \ldots \Delta\, x_n \,\Delta\, x_1)$.

Proof. As an instantiation of (C) we obtain:

$$(\forall y)(y \,\Delta\, \underbrace{[z = x_1 \vee \cdots \vee z = x_n]_z}_{\equiv:x} \equiv y = x_1 \vee \cdots \vee y = x_n) \qquad \text{(a)}$$

Let us make the following indirect assumption:

$$x_1 \,\Delta\, x_2 \,\Delta \ldots \Delta\, x_n \,\Delta\, x_1 \qquad \text{(b)}$$

From (a) we can conclude that $x_1 \,\Delta\, x$, …, $x_n \,\Delta\, x$. So, we obtain:

$$(\exists y) y \,\Delta\, x. \qquad \text{(c)}$$

Now we can apply the property adaptation of the axiom of regularity:

$$(\forall X)((\exists y) y \,\Delta\, X \supset (\exists y)(y \,\Delta\, X \,\&\, (\forall z)(z \,\Delta\, X \supset \neg z \,\Delta\, y))) \qquad \text{(R)}$$

The elimination of the first universal quantifier in (R) by substituting x for X yields: $(\exists y) y \,\Delta\, x \supset (\exists y)(y \,\Delta\, x \,\&\, (\forall z)(z \,\Delta\, x \supset \neg z \,\Delta\, y))$. By applying (c) this formula can be reduced to:

$$(\exists y)(y \,\Delta\, x \,\&\, (\forall z)(z \,\Delta\, x \supset \neg z \,\Delta\, y)) \qquad \text{(d)}$$

According to (a) any y such that $y \,\Delta\, x$ must be one of the elements x_1, …, x_n. As y also occurs in the sequence in (b) it must have a predecessor

z. So, $z \Delta y$. Moreover, we can conclude from (a) that $z \Delta x$, because z is one of the elements $x_1, \ldots, x_n$. As a result we obtain $(\exists z)(z \Delta x \,\&\, z \Delta y)$, in contradiction to (d). Q.E.D.

Primary Sources

BN. = Maheśa Chandra Nyāyaratna, Brief Notes on the Modern Nyāya System of Philosophy and its Technical Terms. In: [3].

TC. = The Tattva-Chintāmaṇi by Gangeśa Upādhyāya, in: [11].

TR. = *tārkikarakṣā. śrīmadācāryavaradarājaviracitā. tatkṛtasārasaṅgrahā-bhidhavyākhyāsahitā. mahopādhyāyakolācaśrīmallināthasūriviracitayā niṣkaṇṭakākhyayā vyākhyayā jñānapūrṇanirmitayā laghudīpikākhyayā ṭīkayā samanvitā.* Pandit Reprint. Varanasi 1903

UD. = Upādhidarpaṇa, in: Bhandarkar Oriental Research Institute, Modern Schoolman (Ms.) 6, 1898–99.

References

[1] George Bealer. *Quality and Concept.* Clarendon Press, Oxford, 1982.

[2] Innocentius M. Bocheński. *Formale Logik.* Orbis Academicus, Freiburg/Munich, 1956.

[3] Maheśa Chandra Nyayaratna. *Brief Notes on the Modern Nyāya System of Philosophy and its Technical Terms.* Hare Press, Calcutta, 1891.

[4] Abraham A. Fraenkel, Yehoshua Bar Hillel, and Azriel Levy. *Foundations of Set Theory*, volume 67 of *Studies in Logic and Foundations of Mathematics.* North-Holland, 1973.

[5] Eberhard Guhe. *Die Lehre von der zusätzlichen Bestimmung (upādhi) im Upādhidarpaṇa.* PhD thesis, Universität Wien, 1999.

[6] Eberhard Guhe. Intensionale Aspekte der Indischen Logik. *Indologische Studien*, 13–14:105–116, 2000.

[7] Daniel H. H. Ingalls. *Materials for the Study of Navya-Nyāya Logic*, volume 40 of *Harvard Oriental Series.* Harvard University Press, Cambridge Massachusetts, 1951.

[8] Bimal Krishna Matilal. *The Navya-Nyāya Doctrine of Negation: The Semantics and Ontology of Negative Statements in Navya-Nyāya Philosophy*, volume 46 of *Harvard Oriental Series*. Harvard University Press, Cambridge, Massachusetts, 1968.

[9] Bimal Krishna Matilal. *Logic, Language and Reality: Indian Philosophy and Contemporary Issues*. Motilal Banarsidass, Delhi, 1985.

[10] Stephen Phillips. *Gaṅgeśa on the Upādhi, the "Inferential Undercutting Condition"*. Council of Philosophical Research, Delhi, 2002. Introduction, translation and explanation with N.S. Ramanuja Tatacharya.

[11] Gangeśa Upādhyāya. *The Tattva-Chintāmaṇi. Part II. Anumāna Khaṇḍa. From Anumiti to Bādha. From the Commentaries of Mathurānātha Tarkavāgīśa*, volume 98 of *Bibliotheca Indica*. Kāmākhyānātha Tarkavāgīśa, Calcutta, 1892.

Tarski on Padoa's method: a test case for understanding logicians of other traditions

Wilfrid Hodges*

School of Mathematical Sciences, Queen Mary, University of London, London E1 4NS, United Kingdom

Herons Brook, Sticklepath, Okehampton EX20 2PY, Devon, United Kingdom

E-mail: w.hodges@qmul.ac.uk

1 Padoa's method and Tarski's version of it

Suppose T is a formal theory and R is a relation symbol in the language L of T. In 1900 Alessandro Padoa announced that the following condition is sufficient to show that no definition of R in terms of the other nonlogical symbols of L can be deduced from T:[1]

> ... to find an interpretation of the primitive symbols [of L] which makes all the axioms [of T] true and continues to make them true when one suitably changes the meaning of [the symbol R]. [11] (1.1)

The use of some version of Padoa's condition is now standard, and one calls it *Padoa's method.*

Around 1930 Alfred Tarski published two papers [17, 13] in which he claimed to give a "theoretical base" for Padoa's method. The first paper is jointly by Tarski and Adolf Lindenbaum, reporting a joint talk of the two authors. The second is by Tarski alone, and it is a writeup of the first with a few extensions.

Before we report Tarski's "theoretical base", we need to explain some of his terminology. A *deductive theory* is a formal apparatus with three components. The first component is a set of logical axioms or axiom schemas, together with a set of logical rules of inference. Together these form what today we call a *logic* (for example first-order logic with identity — though around 1930 Tarski would have mentioned a higher-order logic first). We write $\mathcal{L}$ for logics. We say that $\mathcal{L}$ is *sound* if it never derives a falsehood from a truth.

*This paper is an offshoot of a study of Alfred Tarski's theory of definitions [7]. It is based on a self-contained talk given at the logic conference in memory of Bimal Krishna Matilal in Kolkata in January 2007, and it can be read as a self-contained paper. The Kolkata logic conference was hugely stimulating; my warm thanks to the organisers.

[1]My translation; cf. [20, p. 122] for the full text. Like almost all logicians around 1900, Padoa takes "meaning" and "make true" —or "*signification*" and "*vérifier*" in his French— as informal and undefined terms.

Mihir K. **Chakraborty**, Benedikt **Löwe**, Madhabendra Nath **Mitra**, Sundar **Sarukkai** (*eds.*). Logic, Navya-Nyāya & Applications. Homage to Bimal Krishna Matilal. College Publications, London, 2008. Studies in Logic 15. pp. 155–169.

Received by the editors: 1 May 2007; 6 November 2007.
Accepted for publication: 29 January 2008.

The second component of a deductive theory is a formal language L. This language has formulas; it is closed under the logical operations of $\mathcal{L}$ (which will typically include conjunction and disjunction of two formulas, negation of a formula, universal and existential quantification over first-order variables and maybe also higher-order variables). It can contain equality $=$, and we shall assume that it does. If it contains nothing else, then L is the *pure language* of logic $\mathcal{L}$. But L can also contain some *primitives*, also known as *nonlogical symbols*; these are symbols with fixed meanings referring to some particular subject matter (for example the real numbers).

The third component of a deductive theory is a set T of *nonlogical axioms*; these are sentences of L which are taken to be true about the particular subject matter. When it is clear or irrelevant what $\mathcal{L}$ and L are, we sometimes refer to T as a *theory*. If there are no primitives then there is no particular subject matter and this third component is empty; we say then that $(\mathcal{L}, L)$ form a *pure deductive theory*.

Now given a deductive theory $(\mathcal{L}, L, T)$ and a formula φ of L, we write

$$T \vdash_{\mathcal{L}} \varphi$$

to mean that there is a formal derivation in which the axioms are either logical axioms of $\mathcal{L}$ or sentences in T, the inference steps are all by rules of $\mathcal{L}$, and the conclusion is φ. We write

$$T \nvdash_{\mathcal{L}} \varphi$$

to express that there is no such derivation. When there is such a derivation, we say that φ is *derivable in* the deductive theory.[2]

In the two papers [17, 13], Tarski gave his "theoretical base" for Padoa's method in several slightly different versions. One version, from [17], runs as follows. We assume we have a deductive theory $(\mathcal{L}, L, T)$ where R is a primitive relation symbol. We introduce a new primitive R' of the same syntactic type as R, and we write T' for the theory that comes from T when we replace every occurrence of R by R'. Instead of Padoa's hypothesis (1.1), Tarski puts the condition:

$$T \cup T' \nvdash_{\mathcal{L}} \forall \bar{x}(R\bar{x} \leftrightarrow R'\bar{x}). \tag{1.2}$$

In terms of deductive theories, Padoa's conclusion states: no definition of R in terms of the other primitives of L is derivable in the deductive theory $(\mathcal{L}, L, T)$. From Tarski's discussion in [17, p. 112] we can read off the form that Tarski expects a definition to have, and hence the following precise version of Padoa's conclusion:

[2]The notation $\vdash$ is standard today but didn't appear in these two papers of Tarski.

There is no formula $\varphi(\bar{x})$ of the language L such that R doesn't occur in φ, and $T \vdash_{\mathcal{L}} \forall\bar{x}(R\bar{x} \leftrightarrow \varphi(\bar{x}))$. (1.3)

Tarski notes that for the relevant kinds of deductive theory, (1.2) is equivalent to (1.3). The deductive theories that he has in mind are higher-order — we shall be more specific about this in a moment.

So in brief, Tarski replaces Padoa's implication (1.1) $\Rightarrow$ (1.3) by the implication (1.2) $\Rightarrow$ (1.3).

2 The problem

Now the curious thing is that Padoa's condition (1.1) is clearly not the same thing as Tarski's (1.2). Padoa's condition is model-theoretic: it speaks of interpretations that make the sentences of T true. Tarski's condition is in terms of formal deducibility and makes no use of model-theoretic ideas such as a symbol having an interpretation or a sentence being true in a structure. It's not hard to see that if $\mathcal{L}$ is sound then Padoa's (1.1) implies Tarski's (1.2). But the converse implication from (1.2) to (1.1) is hopeless in general, because higher-order logics don't have a completeness theorem.

For example, take some standard definition of the natural numbers in a standard pure higher-order deductive theory $(\mathcal{L}, L)$ whose set of derivable formulas is recursively enumerable. Let L' be the language that comes by adding to L a 1-ary relation symbol R. Gödel-numbering the formulas of L, we can write an axiom stating that if Rx holds then x is the Gödel number of a derivation of $(0 = 1)$ in $(\mathcal{L}, L)$; let T consist of this axiom. Assuming that $\mathcal{L}$ is consistent, the only possible interpretation of R making T true is that R is empty. So Padoa's condition (1.1) fails for R and T. But if Tarski's condition (1.2) fails, then we have a proof of the consistency of $(\mathcal{L}, L)$ in the deductive theory $(\mathcal{L}, L', T)$, and this is easy to convert to a proof in $(\mathcal{L}, L)$ by replacing Rx by $x \neq x$ throughout. So by Gödel's theorem Tarski's condition (1.2) must hold. Thus we have a counterexample to the implication from (1.2) to (1.1), even if we restrict T to be finite.

So there is a problem for a historian of logic — or indeed for any mildly critical reader. What can Tarski have thought he was doing when he offered the implication (1.2) $\Rightarrow$ (1.3) as a "theoretical base" for Padoa's method? As Tarski himself said later [15], this implication is "mathematically ... rather trivial". Today it seems that the main interest of Padoa's method lies precisely in its model-theoretic hypothesis; Tarski has completely removed the model theory and left only a trivial syntactic implication.

In [7] I gave evidence for the following answer. Tarski was always happy to use model-theoretic methods, but at least up until 1936 he didn't regard them as mathematics. Instead he saw them as informal descriptions of manoeuvres that could at least sometimes be carried out in mathematics. Up to 1936 (and perhaps even later) he regarded mathematics as consisting of derivations in deductive theories; in fact he believed that this was the generally accepted view in foundations of mathematics.

So when Tarski wrote these papers, he must have seen Padoa's condition (1.1) as no more than an informal hint of how to construct, in a suitable deductive theory, a derivation that established Tarski's own condition (1.2).

Today a model theorist would say that (1.1) implies (1.2) at once, assuming that the logic $\mathcal{L}$ is sound. But Tarski couldn't use that argument, because it takes (1.1) as a premise, and Tarski didn't regard (1.1) as mathematical.

It's worth noting that instead of turning (1.1) into syntax, we can turn (1.3) into model theory as follows:

There is no formula $\varphi(\bar{x})$ of the language L such that R doesn't occur in φ, and $T \models \forall\bar{x}(R\bar{x} \leftrightarrow \varphi(\bar{x}))$. (2.1)

Here $\models$ is the model-theoretic entailment relation: $T \models \varphi$ means that every model of T is also a model of φ. The condition (2.1) implies (1.3) for any sound logic $\mathcal{L}$. Also a straightforward model-theoretic argument shows that Padoa's condition (1.1) implies (2.1). So if we are prepared to accept model-theoretic arguments, there is a strong case for us to think of the implication (1.1) $\Rightarrow$ (2.1) as the essence of "Padoa's method". The case is all the stronger because the model-theoretic conditions are absolute, in the sense that they don't refer to a particular proof calculus. We shall come back to this later.

3 The reconstruction

In the rest of this paper I reconstruct an example of what Tarski in the years around 1930 would have counted as a proper use of Padoa's method. The example that I take is a theorem of Lindenbaum. Lindenbaum announced this result in the paper [17] and Tarski mentioned again in [13].

But before we go to the details of Lindenbaum's result, there are some general considerations that apply to any application of Padoa's method.

Suppose we think we have good reason for believing Padoa's condition (1.1) for some particular T and R. In Tarski's picture of the situation, there are two steps from this acceptance of (1.1) to a proof of (1.3).

- The first step is to convert (1.1) into a formal proof, within a deductive theory, which establishes (1.2).
- The second step is to derive (1.3) from (1.2). This step is the triviality that occupies Tarski in the papers [17, 13].

It should strike us as curious that Tarski says almost nothing about what is involved in the first step. Unlike the second step, the first is generally not at all trivial. The most likely reason for Tarski's silence is that he regarded the first step as "business as usual" — any competent mathematical logician would know what was needed.

The rest of this section will make a preliminary analysis of this first step.

1. A deductive theory has meaningful axioms which we believe are true. So it's not enough for the mathematician to suppose that some structure, say A, is a model of T. The mathematician must have in mind a particular structure A, and must believe that A is in fact a model of T.

2. Condition (1.2) is equivalent to the following condition:

   If $\psi(R)$ is the conjunction of a finite number of sentences of T, and $\psi(R')$ is the same sentence but with R' in place of R, then

   $$\psi(R) \nvdash_{\mathcal{L}} \psi(R') \to \forall\bar{x}(R\bar{x} \leftrightarrow R'\bar{x}). \tag{3.1}$$

   This equivalence follows from the deduction theorem and the fact that any derivation from $T \cup T'$ must use just finitely many of the axioms in $T \cup T'$. (A similar argument can be used to justify Tarski's assumption that T is finite when he derives (1.3) from (1.2) in [13].)

3. Conditions (1.2) and (3.1) don't say that something is formally deducible; they say that something is *not* formally deducible. But mathematics supposedly consists of formal derivations. So we need to give a derivation that will show that something else is not derivable. The only general method for doing this is to fall back on the consistency of the underlying theory. Tarski points to this route, but only in the details of a geometric example in [13].[3]

For Padoa's method it will suffice to prove

If $\psi(R)$ is the conjunction of a finite number of sentences of T, then

$$T^\star \vdash_{\mathcal{L}} \exists S\ (\psi(S) \wedge \neg\forall\bar{x}(R\bar{x} \leftrightarrow S\bar{x})). \tag{3.2}$$

where S is a relation variable of the same type as the relation symbol R, and $T^\star$ is a true theory that extends T. Then (3.1) will follow from (3.2) together with the assumption that $T^\star$ is consistent.

[3]Cf. [8, p. 306].

In general the condition (3.2) doesn't follow from (1.1), even assuming that the proof calculus is sound. Yet it —or something like it— seems to be essential for carrying out Tarski's intentions. My guess is that if pressed, Tarski would have justified it by the following methodological argument. Suppose we have a reason for believing Padoa's condition (1.1). Then in particular we have a reason for believing that the old and new interpretations of the primitive R that we have in mind are not the same. If we want this reason to stand up, we have to be prepared to give a mathematical proof of it in some deductive theory. The proof could conceivably use a logic $\mathcal{L}'$ which is stronger than $\mathcal{L}$. But then there is no harm in replacing $\mathcal{L}$ by $\mathcal{L}'$ throughout, since any definition of R that was derivable using $\mathcal{L}$ would also be derivable using $\mathcal{L}'$. For the same reason there would be no harm if the proof used a set of axioms $T^\star$ which extends T. Since we believe the proof, we presumably believe that the axioms of $T^\star$ are true, and hence consistent.

Tarski assumed in [17] and [13] that the logic $\mathcal{L}$ is some form of higher-order type theory. Logics of this kind tend to be very strong, and they allow us to prove a good deal of what today we would prove in set theory. So if our reasons for believing (1.1) were set-theoretic, then there is a good chance that we can carry them over into the theory of finite types with suitable axioms. Tarski and Lindenbaum themselves note that for Lindenbaum's result the deductive theory will need to include the axiom of choice among its logical axioms.

To summarise what seems to have been Tarski's position: suppose we think we have sound reasons for believing Padoa's condition (1.1). Then as mathematicians we should aim to show that they can be converted into formal derivations which establish (3.1); the derivations should be in some acceptable deductive theory using a set $T^\star$ of axioms that may extend T. If we succeed, then Padoa's conclusion —that no definition of R in terms of the remaining primitives is derivable from the formal system— follows by the trivial syntactic manipulations described in [17] and [13]. So we reach Padoa's conclusion (1.3) by a genuinely mathematical argument.

4 Lindenbaum's Theorem

We turn to Lindenbaum's application of Padoa's method. On the field $\mathbb{R}$ of real numbers with order relation $<$ and modulus $|\text{\textvisiblespace}|$, define two relations R and M as follows:

$$\begin{aligned} &R(x,y,z) \equiv (x<y<z \vee z<y<x);\\ &M(x,y,z,w) \equiv |x-y| = |z-w|. \end{aligned} \tag{4.1}$$

In the paper [17], Lindenbaum makes the following statements:[4]

> ... for the term R to be independent of the term M, it is necessary and sufficient that there is a real-valued function F of a real variable, which is not Lebesgue measurable and which satisfies certain conditions. With the help of the axiom of choice one can show that such a function F exists, and hence that the term R *is independent* of the term M. But if one rejects for example the existence of non-measurable sets, *one can write down* (effectively) a correct *definition* of the term R in terms of M. (4.2)

Lindenbaum's note doesn't mention Padoa. But Tarski [13] tells us that the result on the independence of R from M is proved by Padoa's method, and presumably this was the reason for combining Tarski's work with Lindenbaum's in the joint paper [17]. Lindenbaum never published the details of the independence proof. But Tarski reconstructed the main idea in a letter to Schwabhäuser around 1978; Givant published an edited version of Tarski's letter in [19].

The argument that Tarski reports in [19, § 6] is essentially as follows. By the axiom of choice there is a well-ordered basis $B = (b_i : i < 2^\omega)$ of the reals $\mathbb{R}$ as vector space over the field of rationals $\mathbb{Q}$. Without loss of generality suppose

$$b_0 < b_1 < b_2.$$

Let F_0 be the permutation of the basis B which transposes b_1 and b_2, and fixes the remaining basis elements. Let $F : \mathbb{R} \to \mathbb{R}$ be the $\mathbb{Q}$-linear extension of F_0.[5] If x and y are any real numbers then

$$F(x - y) = F(x) - F(y)$$

since F is a linear transformation. Suppose $x - y = z - w = u$. Then

$$F(x) - F(y) = F(x - y) = F(u) = F(z - w) = F(z) - F(w).$$

With a little juggling this shows that for all reals x, y, z, w,

$$M(F(x), F(y), F(z), F(w)) \Leftrightarrow M(x, y, z, w).$$

Hence F is an automorphism of the structure $(\mathbb{R}, M)$. Define R' on the reals by

$$R'(F(x), F(y), F(z)) \Leftrightarrow R(x, y, z).$$

[4] My translation from Lindenbaum's French, with slight changes of notation; his italics.

[5] There exists a unique such extension since B is a basis of $\mathbb{R}$; cf., e.g., [3, § 4.2] for the finite-dimensional case, which generalises straightforwardly.

Then F is an isomorphism from the structure $(\mathbb{R}, M, R)$ to the structure $(\mathbb{R}, M, R')$. So the two structures $(\mathbb{R}, M, R)$ and $(\mathbb{R}, M, R')$ satisfy the same sentences in any formal language that we use to talk about them.

The two structures $(\mathbb{R}, M, R)$ and $(\mathbb{R}, M, R')$ are both models of T. But they differ in the interpretation of the primitive R, since

$$R(b_0, b_1, b_2) \text{ but not } R'(b_0, b_1, b_2).$$

So Padoa's condition (1.1) holds.

In the next section we formalise this argument so that it becomes an application of Padoa's method in the sense that Tarski must have intended.

5 The formal derivation

We need a deductive theory in which the only primitive symbols are R and M. Around 1930 and in Poland, the natural first choice for such a deductive system would be the system of *Principia Mathematica* with certain changes: (a) The individuals are to be the real numbers. (b) Instead of the ramified type hierarchy, we use the hierarchy of simple relational types of finite order; we drop *Principia*'s Axiom of Reducibility. (c) We take as axioms the axiom of extensionality, the comprehension axioms and the axiom of choice. Tarski describes this setup in his paper [12]. He refers to Carnap's textbook [2] of 1929, which discusses higher-order logic; he could have referred to Hilbert and Ackermann [5] too, from 1928.

Tarski and Lindenbaum don't say what the set T of nonlogical axioms is. This won't matter; we can take the axioms to be any set of true statements about the real numbers, using only the primitives R and M. Since we are concerned with formal deductions, there will be no loss in assuming that T is finite. It will be convenient to go one trivial step further and assume that T is a single sentence $\alpha(R, M)$ (where we show the occurrences of R and M). The theory $T^\star$ will extend T.

Lindenbaum's argument assumes the reals are a vector space over the rationals. But to use this assumption, he needs to have symbols for the rationals and for the vector space operations. These symbols obviously can't be defined in terms of the two primitives R and M (for example because the map $x \mapsto x+1$ preserves R and M but wrecks the vector space operations). So how can Lindenbaum feed this information into the system?

The solution is to write down a statement saying

> There exist 3-ary relations X_+ and $X_\star$ which are the graphs of functions $+$ and $\star$ on the domain of individuals, so that this domain is a complete ordered field under the reflexive ordering relation $\exists z(y - x) = z^2$, R is the betweenness relation with respect to this ordering, and $M(x, y, z, w)$ is the relation $(b - a) \star (b - a) = (d - c) \star (d - c)$. (5.1)

One can write (5.1) as a single sentence $\exists X_+ \exists X_\star \text{Realfield}(X_+, X_\star)$ where X_+ and $X_\star$ are relation variables. We take this sentence as an axiom $\beta(R, M)$ of $T^\star$.

Next, suppose $\text{Realfield}(X_+, X_\star)$ holds. Then in terms of X_+ and $X_\star$ we can define numbers 0 and 1 in a field structure on the domain $\mathbb{R}$ of individuals. We define Q to be the smallest set of individuals containing 0 and closed under $x \mapsto x + 1$ and $x \mapsto x - 1$, and under $x \mapsto x/y$ whenever $0 \neq y \in Q$. We can show that Q is a field and that $\mathbb{R}$ is a vector space over Q. Using a standard representation of the natural numbers in higher-order logic, we can show that Q is countably infinite. All this can be written out as a formal proof of a theorem of the form

$$\forall X_+ \forall X_\star (\text{Realfield}(X_+, X_\star) \to \exists Q \ \text{Space}_1(X_+, X_\star, Q)) \tag{5.2}$$

within the theory of finite relational types together with the axiom $\beta(R, M)$.

Since the axiom of choice is one of the logical axioms of $\mathcal{L}$, we can go on to infer that there is a well-ordered sequence B of individuals which forms a basis of $\mathbb{R}$ over Q, with the first three elements increasing in the sense of the ordered field structure on $\mathbb{R}$. Further deductions show the existence of a linear transformation F on $\mathbb{R}$ which is related to B as in the previous section. There exists a 3-ary relation S on the set of individuals, such that for all individuals x, y, z,

$$S(F(x), F(y), F(z)) \leftrightarrow S(x, y, z). \tag{5.3}$$

So we can expand the formal proof of (5.2) to a formal proof of a theorem of the form

$$\begin{aligned} &\forall X_+ \forall X_\star (\text{Realfield}(X_+, X_\star) \to \\ &\exists Q \exists B \exists F \exists S \ \text{Space}_2(X_+, X_\star, Q, B, F, S)) \end{aligned} \tag{5.4}$$

which expresses all this.

Now within the deductive theory assume

$$\text{Realfield}(X_+, X_\star) \wedge \text{Space}_2(X_+, X_\star, Q, B, F, S).$$

Then as in the previous section we can infer

$$\neg \forall \bar{x} (R\bar{x} \leftrightarrow S\bar{x}).$$

From the same assumptions together with the axiom $\alpha(R, M)$ we can also prove $\alpha(S, M)$ as follows.

Proposition 5.1.

$$\alpha(R, M) \vdash_{\mathcal{L}} \text{Space}_2(X_+, X_\star, Q, B, F, S) \to \alpha(S, M).$$

Proof. The main argument is to show, by induction on the complexity of γ, that $\mathrm{Space}_2(X_+, X_\star, Q, B, F, S)$ entails

$$\forall x_1 \dots \forall x_n\ (\gamma(S, M, F(x_1), \dots, F(x_n)) \leftrightarrow \gamma(R, M, x_1, \dots, x_n)). \quad (5.5)$$

whenever $\gamma(R, M, x_1, \dots, x_n)$ is a subformula of $\alpha(R, M)$.

- If $\gamma(R, M)$ is $R(x_1, x_2, x_3)$ then $\gamma(S, M)$ is $S(x_1, x_2, x_3)$ and (5.5) follows from the definition of S (which is included in the formula Space_2).
- If $\gamma(R, M)$ is $M(x_1, \dots, x_4)$ then $\gamma(S, M)$ is the same formula as $\gamma(R, M)$, so that (5.5) holds trivially.

The other cases are standard logic.

When the induction is complete, we have proved (5.5) in the case where $\gamma(R, M, x_1, \dots, x_n)$ is $\alpha(R, M)$. Then we call on the axiom $\alpha(R, M)$ and (5.5) to deduce $\alpha(S, M)$. Q.E.D.

Proposition 5.1 is a special case of [9, Theorem 1], a joint paper of Tarski and Lindenbaum that dates from 1935. Tarski says in a footnote that it belongs to the "same circle of ideas" as [17, 13]. As the paper [9] points out, Proposition 5.1 is a metatheorem, i.e., a theorem that can be proved formally in a deductive theory about deductive theories. So its proof is not a formal derivation in the deductive theory that we are using for Lindenbaum's theorem. Instead, the proof shows that a derivation of the required form can be constructed in that deductive theory.

Note that the idea behind Proposition 5.1 is a very simple model-theoretic notion: isomorphisms preserve satisfaction of all formulas. But Tarski can't use this notion as it stands. Instead he has to convert it into a metatheory demonstration that a proof of the equivalence of two formulas can be carried out in a certain deductive theory. No model-theoretic notions occur in the proposition or its proof, either in the metatheory used for the proof or in the deductive theory itself. The proposition on its own is a striking example of how Tarski in this period uses model theory as an informal prompt for mathematical work that is thoroughly un-model-theoretic.

To return to the main argument: by Proposition 5.1 and the remarks before it, we have

$$\begin{aligned}\alpha(R, M), \beta(R, M) \vdash_{\mathcal{L}} \quad & \mathrm{Realfield}(X_+, X_\star) \wedge \mathrm{Space}_2(X_+, X_\star, Q, B, F, S) \\ & \rightarrow \alpha(S, M) \wedge \neg \forall \bar{x}(R\bar{x} \leftrightarrow S\bar{x}).\end{aligned}$$

Also the definition of $\beta(R, M)$ and the argument for (5.4) tell us

$$\begin{aligned}\beta(R, M) \vdash_{\mathcal{L}} \quad & \exists X_+, X_\star, Q, B, F, S(\mathrm{Realfield}(X_+, X_\star) \wedge \\ & \mathrm{Space}_2(X_+, X_\star, Q, B, F, S)).\end{aligned}$$

Putting these together gives

$$\alpha(R, M), \beta(R, M) \vdash_{\mathcal{L}} \exists S(\alpha(S, M) \wedge \neg \forall \bar{x}(R\bar{x} \leftrightarrow S\bar{x})).$$

Comparing with (3.2), this completes the proof.

It remains to show that the theory $T^\star$ is acceptable. In 1936 Tarski stated conditions for the acceptability of a deductive theory. In his words, the system should have primitives that "seem to us to be immediately understandable", and axioms "whose truth appears to us evident". [6]

Consider first the sentence $\beta(R, M)$, where R and M are given the interpretation described at the beginning of section 4 above. Why does the truth of $\beta(R, M)$ appear to us evident? The answer is that we can prove it from other things that we regard as evidently true, as follows.

In the pure logic of finite relational types we can define "real number" and the arithmetical operations on the reals, and we can prove their basic properties. There is a sketch of these definitions and proofs in the final section of the second (1938) edition of Hilbert and Ackermann [6]. It is not in the first edition of 1928 [5]; but the procedure was probably common knowledge already in the late 1920s, soon after the mathematical logic community adopted unramified type theory in 1926.

Now we can add to the definitions in Hilbert and Ackermann a formula $\rho(x_1, x_2, x_3)$ defining Lindenbaum's relation R on the reals, and a formula $\mu(x_1, x_2, x_3, x_4)$ defining his relation M. Write $\beta(\rho, \mu)$ for the sentence got by replacing all occurrences of the symbols R, M in $\beta(R, M)$ by occurrences of ρ, μ respectively. Then $\beta(\rho, \mu)$ can be proved as a theorem of pure type theory. So the assumption $\beta(R, M)$ can be justified by showing that its translation $\beta(\rho, \mu)$ is provable.

The sentence $\alpha(R, M)$ was by definition something that we believe about the real numbers. Most of our information about the real numbers is derivable in pure type theory. If we want to believe $\alpha(R, M)$ for some other reason, so be it.

6 Some later remarks of Tarski

As we saw earlier, Tarski noted that (1.2) and (1.3) are equivalent in standard higher order logics. The argument from (1.3) to (1.2) depends on the existence of higher order variables and quantifiers, so it fails in first order logic. Nevertheless in 1953 Evert Beth [1] succeeded in proving the remarkable fact that the implication from (1.3) to (1.2) does still hold for first order logic. By the completeness theorem for first-order logic, (1.1) is

[6] This is from [14, § 32], a book that later appeared in an expanded form under the title "Introduction to Logic and to the Methodology of the Deductive Sciences".

equivalent to (1.2) and (1.3) is equivalent to (2.1). So in the case of first-order logic, Beth's theorem shows the purely model-theoretical result that (1.1) is equivalent to (2.1). In fact that is how it is usually stated today.

Beth's theorem reached Tarski in early 1953, and Tarski wrote to Beth in May 1953 as follows:[7]

> ... It seems to me that your result is primarily syntactical, but that by Gödel's [completeness] theorem, it admits of a semantical interpretation since it applies to the first order logic. In fact, if I were you, I would start with a syntactical formulation (which is simpler) and only later would give a semantical translation. ... (6.1)

So for Tarski the syntactic version of Beth's theorem was "primary" and "simpler". It's true that Beth's proof was largely syntactic; but Tarski's comment seems to be about the theorem, not about its proof.

Already in 1953 Tarski's view was hardly sustainable. Thanks to the model-theoretic notions that Tarski himself published in [18] and [16], the model-theoretic version of Beth's theorem is just as simple to state as the syntactic version. It is also more fundamental in two ways. First, as we noted earlier, the syntactic version refers to a particular proof calculus, whereas the model-theoretic version is absolute. Second, applications of Padoa's theorem normally start from the model-theoretic assumption (1.1) — this is true even for Lindenbaum's theorem as Tarski presents it in [19]. So the statement that undefinability can always be proved from (1.1) is more relevant to mathematical practice than the statement that undefinability can always be proved from (1.2).

So again we can ask why Tarski in 1953 said what he did say to Beth. Perhaps in spite of his path-breaking work in model theory, he still had a lingering feeling that the model-theoretic version of Beth's theorem couldn't be real "mathematics". Perhaps his earlier conviction that the equivalence between (1.2) and (1.3) was the "theoretical base" of Padoa's method made it hard for him to adjust to other views of the matter. Perhaps he had some other reason. I doubt if we have the evidence to settle the matter.

A recent preprint of Solomon Feferman [4] discusses Tarski's reaction to Beth's theorem. Feferman's paper is particularly valuable because Feferman himself was working with Tarski at the time, and took part in the correspondence with Beth. Feferman says "From Tarski's point of view, since the statement of Beth's definability theorem is model-theoretic, there ought to be a model-theoretic proof ...". This seems to be a separate point from the one Tarski is making in (6.1), and I am not clear how the two points should be reconciled.

---

[7]Van Ulsen quotes this on [22, p. 136]. [22] also contains a thorough discussion of the background to Beth's theorem — my thanks to Johan van Benthem for directing me to it.

For completeness I should mention a note of reservation in [19]. Discussing Lindenbaum's use of Padoa's method, Tarski says

> ... we apply here essentially Padoa's method, with this difference however, that we do not construct the function ... and the model ... explicitly, but only prove their existence with the help of the axiom of choice. [19, p. 206]

I can make no sense of this. Tarski's own account of Padoa's method in [17] and [13] says nothing about explicitly constructing the models.

7 Conclusion

One thing that comes clear from this reconstruction is that model theory has made life easier. Today we infer Lindenbaum's theorem almost at once from the arguments given in §4 above, without needing any of the hills and detours of §5.

Beyond the details of this particular example, what can the historian of logic take home from this study? I suggest two points.

First, of course we can ask, given a precise result R and a particular person P in the history of logic, whether P was aware of R or could prove it. This is to pose our own questions to P, and there is no harm in it (though we should be prepared for answers like "Not in those terms"). But we miss something essential if we say only how P might have answered our questions, and neglect to find out what questions P himself asked. Tarski's logical research in the 1920s and 1930s was driven by his interest in drawing the boundaries between informal metatheory, formal metatheory and "mathematics". For most of us today these are dead questions, so they are not the ones we would have brought to Tarski from our own experience in logic.

Second, the 1930s are still within the adult lifetime of people alive today. So one would think that the interests of that period would have reached us at least through some kind of folk memory in the logic community. But with a few rare exceptions, they haven't.

Bimal Krishna Matilal has claimed:

> [I]t is extremely difficult, though not impossible, to transfer the philosophical and logical problems from the narrow confines of Sanskrit to the modern philosophical audience in general. [10, p. 201]

I hope I have shown:

> It is extremely difficult, though not impossible, to transfer the logical problems from the narrow confines of 1920s and 1930s Polish to the modern logical audience in general.

Matilal's claim is of course a corollary.

References

[1] Evert W. Beth. On Padoa's Method in the Theory of Definition. *Indagationes Mathematicae*, 15:330–339, 1953.

[2] Rudolf Carnap. *Abriss der Logistik mit besonderer Berücksichtigung der Relationstheorie und ihrer Anwendungen.* Springer, Vienna, 1929.

[3] Paul M. Cohn. *Algebra*, volume 1. Wiley, London, 1974.

[4] Solomon Feferman. Harmonious Logic: Craig's Interpolation Theorem and Its Descendants. *Synthese*, 164(3):341–357, 2008.

[5] David Hilbert and Wilhelm Ackermann. *Grundzüge der Theoretischen Logik.* Springer, Berlin, 1st edition, 1928.

[6] David Hilbert and Wilhelm Ackermann. *Grundzüge der Theoretischen Logik.* Springer, Berlin, 2nd edition, 1938.

[7] Wilfrid Hodges. Tarski's Theory of Definition. In Douglas Patterson, editor, *Alfred Tarski: Philosophical Background, Development, and Influence.* Oxford University Press, forthcoming.

[8] John Corcoran, editor. *Logic, Semantics, Metamathematics, Papers from 1923 to 1938, by Alfred Tarski, translated by J. H. Woodger.* Hackett Publishing Company, Indianapolis, 1983.

[9] Adolf Lindenbaum and Alfred Tarski. Über die Beschränktheit der Ausdrucksmittel deduktiver Theorien. In Karl Menger, editor, *Ergebnisse eines Mathematischen Kolloquiums*, volume 7, pages 15–22, Wien, 1934. Springer. Translated as "On the limitations of the means of expression of deductive theories" in [8, pp. 384–392].

[10] Bimal Krishna Matilal. Introducing Indian logic. In Jonardon Ganeri, editor, *Indian Logic: A Reader*, pages 183–221. Richmond Surrey, 2001.

[11] Alessadro Padoa. Essai d'une théorie algébrique des nombres entiers, précédé d'une introduction logique à une théorie déductive quelconque. *Bibliothèque du Congrès international de philosophie*, 3:309–365, 1902. Translated in part as "Logical introduction to any deductive theory" in [20, pp. 118–123].

[12] Alfred Tarski. Sur les ensembles définissables de nombres réels. I. *Fundamenta Mathematicae*, 17:210–239, 1931. Translated as "On definable sets of real numbers" in [8, pp. 110–142].

[13] Alfred Tarski. Einige methodologische Untersuchungen über die Definierbarkeit der Begriffe. *Erkenntnis*, 5:80–100, 1935. Translated as "Some methodological investigations on the definability of concepts" in [8, pp. 296–319].

[14] Alfred Tarski. *O logice matematycznej i metodzie dedukcyjnej*, volume 3–5 of *Biblioteczka Matematyczna*. Lwów & Warsaw, 1936.

[15] Alfred Tarski. Letter to Evert W. Beth. quoted in [22, p. 136], 1953.

[16] Alfred Tarski. Contributions to the Theory of Models I. *Indagationes Mathematicae*, 16:572–581, 1954.

[17] Alfred Tarski and Adolf Lindenbaum. Sur l'indépendance des notions primitives dans les systèmes mathématiques. *Annales de la Société Polonaise de Mathématique*, 5:111–113, 1926.

[18] Alfred Tarski, Andrzej Mostowski, and Raphael M. Robinson. *Undecidable Theories*. Studies in Logic and the Foundations of Mathematics. North Holland, Amsterdam, 1953.

[19] Alfred Tarski and Steven Givant. Tarski's System of Geometry. *Bulletin of Symbolic Logic*, 5:175–214, 1999.

[20] Jean van Heijenoort, editor. *From Frege to Gödel*. Harvard University Press, Cambridge, 1967.

[21] Paul van Ulsen. *E. W. Beth als Logicus*. PhD thesis, Universiteit van Amsterdam, 2000. ILLC Publications DS-2000-04.

[22] Paul van Ulsen. E. W. Beth als Logicus, 2001. ILLC Publications DS-2000-04; updated electronic version of [21].

Other Minds in Buddhist Epistemology

Hisayasu Kobayashi*

Hiroshima University, 1-2-3 Kagamiyama, Higashi-Hiroshima 739-8522, Japan
E-mail: `hkoba@u-gakugei.ac.jp`

1 Introduction

If external objects did not exist, then how could it be established that one state of consciousness is not limited to just one person but experienced by many alike, so that a number of people see the same thing at a given place and time? This is one of the serious objections raised by realists against the Yogācāra idealistic doctrine, mentioned by Vasubandhu (c. 400-480) in his *Viṃśatikā* (*Viṃś*).[1] Vasubandhu justifies the non-privacy of our ordinary experiences by referring to the example of the river of filth, in which all the *pretas* can see the river of filth at a given place and time, even if it is not externally existent.[2]

Irrespective of whether external objects exist or not, however, one has to clear up the following questions: Can we say that others see the same thing as we see? How can we know other minds?

There are two independent treatises on the problem of knowing other minds in the Buddhist epistemological tradition: one is the *Santānāntara-*

*I wish to express my gratitude to Brendan S. Gillon for helpful comments on the draft of this paper.

[1] *Viṃś* 3,10–17: *yadi vinā rūpādyarthena rūpādivijñaptir utpadyate na rūpādyarthāt kasmāt kvacid deśa utpadyate na sarvatra / tatra eva ca deśe kadācid utpadyate na sarvadā / taddeśakālapratiṣṭhitānāṃ sarveṣāṃ santāna utpadyate na kevalam ekasya / yathā taimirikāṇāṃ santāne keśādyābhāso na anyeṣāṃ / kasmād yat taimirikaiḥ keśabhramarādi dṛśyate tena keśādikriyā na kriyate na ca tadanyair na kriyate / yad annapānavastraviṣāyudhādi svapne dṛśyate tena annādikriyā na kriyate na ca tadanyair na kriyate / gandharvanagareṇāsattvān nagarakriyā na kriyate na ca tadanyair na kriyate / tasmād arthābhāve deśakālaniyamaḥ santānāniyamaḥ kṛtyakriyā ca na yujyate /* Matilal explains the objections raised by realists in the *Viṃśatikā* as follows: "If external objects did not exist and hence were not related causally to our consciousness of them, then (a) what determines the fact that we have one particular consciousness at a given place and time; (b) how is it that one state of consciousness is not limited to just one person but experienced by many alike (e.g., why a number of people can see that there is a chair in this room), and (c) how can a non-existent object function as it is expected to function (e.g., how can a non-existent apple satisfy hunger, or an absent woman evoke amorous feelings)? [9, p. 232]"

[2] *Viṃś* 3,23–4,6: ***pretavat punaḥ / santānāniyamaḥ;*** (k.3bc) *siddha iti vartate pretānām iva pretavat kathaṃ siddhaḥ samam /* ***sarvaiḥ pūyanadyādidarśane*** // (k.3cd) *pūyapūrṇā nadī pūyanadī / ghṛtaghaṭavat / tulyakarmavipākāvasthā hi pretāḥ sarve api pūyapūrṇāṃ nadīṃ paśyanti na eka eva / yathā pūyapūrṇām evaṃ mūtrapurīṣādipūrṇāṃ daṇḍāsidharaiś ca puruṣair adhiṣṭhitām ity ādigrahaṇena / evaṃ santānāniyamo vijñaptīnām asaty apy arthe siddhaḥ /*

Mihir K. **Chakraborty**, Benedikt **Löwe**, Madhabendra Nath **Mitra**, Sundar **Sarukkai** (*eds.*). Logic, Navya-Nyāya & Applications. Homage to Bimal Krishna Matilal. College Publications, London, 2008. Studies in Logic 15. pp. 171–183.

Received by the editors: 1 May 2007; 31 March 2008; 29 October 2008.
Accepted for publication: 10 November 2008.

siddhi, written by Dharmakīrti (c. 600-660), and the other *Santānāntara-dūṣaṇa*, by Ratnakīrti (c. 1000-1050). As the titles suggest, in the former Dharmakīrti makes an attempt to establish the existence of other minds from the standpoint of the Vijñānavādins,[3] in the latter Ratnakīrti tries to deny it from the same standpoint. While, according to Dharmakīrti, other minds can be known by inference, according to Ratnakīrti, their existence cannot be known by inference.

This paper looks at Prajñākaragupta (c. 750-810), who must have flourished between Dharmakīrti and Ratnakīrti. As will be shown below, Prajñākaragupta's arguments against the inference of other minds clearly reflect his theory of *svasaṃvedanamātra*, that is, his theory that there is nothing real other than the fact that a cognition is self-cognized.

2

Before discussing Prajñākaragupta's view of other minds, it will be useful to give an overview of the basic arguments for and against the inference of other minds, adduced by Dharmakīrti and Ratnakīrti.

2.1

As I mentioned above, Dharmakīrti considers that other minds are inferable. The process of inferring other minds, shown by Dharmakīrti, can be summed up as follows: Observing in ourselves that bodily and verbal actions are preceded by the activity of minds, we establish the causal relation between the activity of minds and the actions; we see the bodily and verbal actions of others; then, we infer other minds from these actions.[4]

As Matilal points out, the method by which idealists would prove the existence of other minds is not much different from the method by which realists would hope to establish the existence of other minds [9, p. 238]. As the realists could introduce as evidence the bodily and verbal actions belonging to others, so also Dharmakīrti, an idealist, could introduce as evidence what appear in our minds as the bodily and verbal actions of others. But Matilal adds the following words:

> "Although this argument is not very convincing, it, nevertheless, exploits the weakness of the argument of the opponent, for, the realist

[3] As a matter of course, Dharmakīrti, when adopting the Sautrāntika standpoint, admits the existence of other minds as well as external objects. Cf. *PV* III 68: *siddhañ ca paracaitanyapratipatteḥ pramādvayam / vyāhārādau pravṛtteś ca siddhas tadbhāvaniścayaḥ //*

[4] *SS* 5,2–4: *tshul 'di ni sems tsam la yang mtshungs pas sems tsam du smra bas kyang gzhan gyi sems rjes su dpag par nus te //1// SS* 6,3–5: *de yang shes pa gzhan gyi g-yo ba'i khyad par med par lus dang ngag gi rnam par rig byed du snang ba'i shes pa de lta bu dag yod par ni mi 'dod do //2//* Cf. [2, p. 466].

> is also in the same uncomfortable position when he tries to prove that there are other minds. [9, p. 238]"

The point is that both the realists and the idealists face the same problem: Other minds can never be perceived; if they are imperceptible, then how can we infer them?

In connection with this problem, we have to note the following statement made by Dharmakīrti in his *Pramāṇavārttika* (*PV*) to show that any cognition is self-cognized (*svasaṃvedana*):

> *PV* III 475–476abc: *pratyakṣāñ ca dhiyaṃ dṛṣṭvā tasyāś ceṣṭābhidhādikam // paracittānumānañ ca na syād ātmany adarśanāt /sambandhasya*
>
> We infer other minds after observing a cognition, which is perceived, and activities related to it, such as a bodily or verbal one. This would not be possible [if we did not accept that a cognition has a self-cognitive nature]. For, in that case, we could not observe the relation [between the cognition and such activities] in ourselves.

Here the structure of the inference of other minds as conceived by Dharmakīrti is clearly shown. We can never directly perceive other minds. But we can perceive our own minds, since our minds, which consist in cognition, are self-cognized. Consequently, we can determine in ourselves the causal relationship between our minds and our physical and verbal activities. On the basis of this causal relationship we can infer other minds by seeing activities of others. It is to be noted in passing that as Katsura clearly points out, this type of inference of other minds is classed as the "argument from analogy" for other minds in Western philosophy [6, p. 103].[5]

2.2

However, the question arises: Can Vijñānavādins admit the existence of other minds? If they affirm the existence of other minds, then the affirmation would be inconsistent with their idealistic theory, for accepting the existence of other minds leads to accepting that of external objects.

Unlike Dharmakīrti, Ratnakīrti argues that other minds can never be inferred and denies their existence. His main point is this: while one can observe one's own speech and acts and be aware of one's own mind, one is never aware of the minds of others. Thus, while one might conclude that

[5]For example, Hyslop explains the analogical inference to other minds in Western philosophy as follows: "Other people behave like me in similar circumstances and have the same physico-chemical composition. When I burn myself it hurts and I cry out and wince. When other people are burned they cry out and wince. I can thus infer that they are in pain too. More generally, others are very like me. I know I have beliefs, experiences and emotions. So I am entitled, given how like me they are, to infer that other people also have beliefs, experiences and emotions. [1, p. 172]"

there is a connection between one's physical and verbal acts, on the one hand, and one's mind, on the other, one cannot conclude that there is a universal connection between the physical and verbal acts of others, on the one hand, and their minds, on the other, since one can never observe the minds of others.[6]

But Ratnakīrti also faces an objection when he denies the existence of other minds. According to Buddhists, the non-perception (*anupalabdhi*) of something leads to knowledge of its absence only if the thing in question is, in fact, observable (*dṛśya*). Thus, since a ghost is, in fact, imperceptible (*adṛśya*), failure to perceive it does not warrant concluding that it is absent.[7] Similarly, other minds are, in fact, imperceptible. The question arises: on what grounds can Ratnakīrti conclude that they do not exist? In order to reply to this objection, Ratnakīrti gives the following argument:

> *SD* 148, 25–28: *yad upalabhyamānam yena rūpeṇa na bhāsate na tat tena rūpeṇa sadvyavahārayogyam yathā nīlaṃ pītarūpeṇa; nopalabhyate ca svacittaṃ upalabhyamānaṃ parasantānād bhinne[na] rūpeṇeti bhedasya svacittatādātmyaniṣedhe dṛśyaviśeṣaṇaprayogānapekṣā svabhāvānupalabdhir iyam //*
>
> [*Vyāpti*:] If a thing (X), being perceived, does not appear in a certain form (Y), then the thing (X) cannot be treated as a thing existing in that form (Y). For example, blue, which does not appear in the form of yellow, cannot be treated as a thing existing in the form of yellow.
>
> [*Pakṣadharmatā*:] One's own mind, being perceived [through a self-cognition], does not appear in the form distinct from other minds [which are imperceptible].
>
> [Conclusion: Therefore, one's own mind cannot be treated as distinct from other minds.]
>
> [The logical reason] here is the non-perception of the distinction itself, [which is to be established between one's own mind and other minds] when it is denied that the former is identical with the latter; this logical reason does not require that one should apply the qualifier "perceptibility" [to other minds].

As Inami points out, Ratnakīrti here does not directly prove the non-existence of other minds [2, p. 472]. Since they are imperceptible, their non-existence cannot be proved by inference. Ratnakīrti holds that the absence of the distinction between one's own mind and other minds implies

[6] For further details, cf. [4, 5, 2]. It is noteworthy that Mokṣākaragupta (c. 11th-12th century) is of the opinion that on the assumption that the mind is self-cognized, other minds can also be regarded as perceptible since other persons can perceive their own minds through self-cognition. *TBh* 44,13–14: *svasaṃvedanaṃ hi tatra vyāptigrāhakam / svaparasantānagatasvasaṃvedanamātrāpekṣayā paracittasyāpi dṛśyatvāt* / Cf. [4, p. 108, fn. 289]. On Ratnakīrti's objection to this kind of view, cf. [2, p. 469].

[7] Cf. [7].

the non-existence of other minds. If other minds were existent, one's own mind should be known as distinct from them. But such a distinction never appears in our mind. In Ratnakīrti's view, through a self-cognition one's own mind is perceived in its own form, but not as something distinguished from other minds. Self-cognition permits Dharmakīrti to establish a causal relation of one's mind to one's actions, whereas for Ratnakīrti, self-cognition establishes that no other minds exist except one's own.

3

Let us turn now to the arguments about the inference of other minds which are presented by Prajñākaragupta in his comments on *PV* III 330cd–332ab.[8]

3.1

Prajñākaragupta discusses there the question whether we can infer other minds from bodily actions of others. He brings forward the following case in illustration: one has a feeling such as joy (*sukha*) after seeing blue;[9] the joy gives him a symptom such as gooseflesh (*romaharṣa*), the bristling of the hair of the body.

In order to demonstrate that a number of people see the same external thing, realists should make an inference of other minds as follows: A person (A) is the one who infers the mind of another person (B). When B has a symptom such as gooseflesh, A, seeing it, infers that B has a feeling such as joy, and hence that, as A has the cognition of blue, so B also has the cognition of blue. The inference in question might be formulated as follows:

> Whoever, in a certain context, has gooseflesh has joy preceded by the cognition of blue; Person B has gooseflesh; therefore, Person B has joy preceded by the cognition of blue.

[8] In commenting on *PV* III 330–332, Prajñākaragupta tries to justify the Vijñānavāda thesis that there is no external reality apart from cognition, while responding to objections which Kumārila (c. 600-650) raised in the Nirālambanavāda chapter of his *Ślokavārttika*. We should notice that the main purpose of Prajñākaragupta's arguments here is to reject the existence of external objects.

[9] In the *Tattvasaṃgrahapañjikā* (*TSP*) *Bahirarthaparīkṣā*, Kamalaśīla explains that the situation where more than two persons see the same entity, blue, is the one in which a number of persons see a dancer on the stage (*naṭa*), the moon (*candra*), and a wrestler on the mat (*malla*). *TSP* 692,11–13: *tathā hi naṭacandramallaprekṣāsu na hy ekenaivopalambho nīlādeḥ / nāpi nīlatadupalambhayor ekenaivopalambhaḥ / tathā hi nīlopalambhe 'pi tadupalambhānām anyasantānagatānām anupalambhāt /*; 693,1–3: *na ca naṭacandramallaprakṣāsu kaścij jñānopalambho 'sti yo na jñeyopalambhakaḥ jñeyopalambho vā na jñānopalambhaka iti kuto 'siddhatā /*

Vādirājasūri criticizes Prajñākaragupta's arguments (*PVA* 366–367) in his *Nyāyaviniścayavivaraṇa* (*NVV* I 360–364), where he mentions a female dancer (*nartakī*) instead of blue. *NVV* I 360,13–14: *nartakīṃ paśyatas tadviṣayasya pareṇa parijñāne 'pi tajjñānasyāparijñānāt /*

3.1.1

To begin with, in order to reject the inference mentioned above, Prajñākaragupta says the following:

> *PVA* 366,20–22: *anumānasya sāmānyaviṣayatvasya varṇanāt /*
>
> *sa eva dṛśyate 'nyenety etad eva na sidhyati /*
>
> It is said that inference is concerned [only] with the universal (*sāmānya*). Therefore, it can never be established that one and the same thing is perceived by others.

Buddhist epistemologists argue that what is known by inference is the universal (*sāmānyalakṣaṇa*). Consequently, what we understand through the above-mentioned inference should be joy in general and blue in general. But the joy and blue which are perceived by others should be particular objects (*svalakṣaṇa*). Accordingly, it cannot be established on the basis of this inference that the joy and blue which are perceived by others are the same as those perceived by us.

3.1.2

Next, Prajñākaragupta puts the realists into a dilemma:

> *PVA* 366,22–23: *yathā ca romaharṣādikāryadṛṣṭes tadekatā //721//*
>
> *tathā sukhāder ekatvaṃ tata eva prasidhyati /*
>
> *anyad eva sukhaṃ tasya grāhyam apy anyad astu tat //722//*
>
> As the identity of the [blue which is perceived by A with the blue which is perceived by B] [can be established] on the basis of the experience of an effect such as gooseflesh [on B's body], in the same manner the identity of the joy [which is perceived by A with the joy which is perceived by B] is also established on the basis of the very same [experience of the effect such as gooseflesh on B's body]. If [B's] joy is completely different [from A's joy], [blue] to be grasped [by B] also must be different [from blue to be grasped by A].

If the realists argue that B who is seen to have gooseflesh is known to see the same thing as A sees, then they have to accept the undesirable consequence that A's joy is not distinguished from B's joy. If, on the other hand, they argue, to avoid this consequence ensuing, that A's joy and B's joy are different from each other, then they have to accept that the blue which is perceived by A is different from the blue which is perceived by B.

3.1.3

A is located in one place and B in another. This difference in place between A and B does not provide a basis for the difference between A's joy and B's.

PVA 366,24: *deśabhedāt sukhādīnām anyatvam iti cen matiḥ /*

ekatve deśabhedo 'pi kathaṃ sidhyati tattvataḥ //723//

[Objection:] It can be considered that [A's] joy [and B's] are different from each other because of the difference between A's place and B's.

[Answer:] If [according to your assumption, A's joy and B's are] identical with each other, how can you establish that in reality (*tattvataḥ*) A and B are located in different places?[10]

A's joy can be differentiated from B's joy on the basis of the difference between A and B, which is established by the difference between the places where A and B are located. If A's joy were identical with B's joy, it would have to be said that A and B are identical with each other, and hence that A's place and B's are identical with each other. In a sense a place where a person who has joy is located is a differentiator of the joy.

3.1.4

One might argue that A's joy is different from B's because A's gooseflesh is different from B's. To this objection Prajñākaragupta makes the following argument:

PVA 366,25–26: *anyatvād romaharśādeḥ sukhāder bhinnatā yadi*[11] *//724//*
anyatve grāhyam apy anyad iti kasmān na gṛhyate /

If [you say that A's] joy is different [from B's joy] because [A's] gooseflesh is different [from B's gooseflesh], then why do you not consider that [blue] to be grasped [by A] is also different [from blue to be grasped by B] provided [A's gooseflesh] is different [from B's gooseflesh].

If the realists considered the difference between A's gooseflesh and B's as evidence for the difference between A's joy and B's, then they would have to accept that there is a difference between the blue which is seen by A and the blue which is seen by B. But, in that case, they cannot establish that both of A and B see the same thing.

3.1.5

In addition, from the point of view of the self-cognition theory, Prajñākaragupta says the following:

PVA 366,26–27: *romaharṣādayo 'py asmatsaṃvidantargatā yadi //725//*
kathaṃ tebhyo 'nyasātādipratibhāsagatiḥ[12] *sphuṭā /*

[10] *J* (D134b7; P153b6): ***de nyid*** (em.; *gnyis* DP) ***las*** *zhes bya ba ni yul tha dad pa nyid las so //*

[11] *sukhāder binnatā yadi M*; *sukhasya yadi bhinnatāṃ PVA*.

[12] *tebhyo 'nyasātādi- M*; *te 'nyonyasātādi- PVA*.

> If a symptom such as gooseflesh appears in our own cognition (*asmat-saṃvidantargata*), then how could there be a clear cognition on account of this [gooseflesh etc.] in which the another [person's] joy appears?

What Prajñākaragupta intends to say in this *kārikā* is this: Saying that B's gooseflesh is known by A amounts to saying that B's gooseflesh appears in A's cognition. In this sense it can no longer be said that B's gooseflesh is B's and not A's. Accordingly, it follows that the joy which is inferred from B's gooseflesh is A's joy.

3.1.6

Prajñākaragupta continues to base the argument on the theory of self-cognition:

> *PVA* 366,27–28: *asmatsukhaṃ vināpy asya romaharṣādayo yadi //726// asmadgrāhyam vināpy asya romaharṣādayo na kim /*
>
> If B has a symptom such as gooseflesh even when A has no joy, then how would this not involve the undesirable consequence that B has a symptom like gooseflesh even when A grasps no [blue]?

If the realists accepted that B has gooseflesh even when A does not grasp blue, then they would have to accept that there is no external thing which is seen by both A and B and which brings joy into their minds.

3.1.7

A difference in time also does not afford a basis for the difference of joy.

> *PVA* 366,28–29: *kālabhedena tatrāpi yadi bhedaḥ samiṣyate //727// abhinnasya svarūpeṇa kālabhit kiṃ kariṣyati /*
>
> [Objection:] It can also be accepted on the basis of a difference in time that there is a difference between [A's joy and B's].
>
> [Answer:] The difference in time will have no effect on what is essentially undifferentiated (*abhinna*).

This argument is not so very different from the above-mentioned argument about the differentiation of joy in terms of place. We may say that the joy which occurs at a certain time is different from the joy which occurs at another time. But this does not mean that the joy differs from one time to another; rather, it itself remains constant. What differs is time itself.

3.1.8

Finally, Prajñākaragupta points out that an undesirable consequence would follow if the realists claimed that the blue to be grasped by A should be identical with the blue to be grasped by B.

> *PVA* 366,29: *abhedo 'py astu tatrāpi parokṣo na bhaved asau //728//*
>
> Suppose also that there is the identity of the [blue which is perceived by A with the blue which is perceived by B]. But, in that case, this [cognition of blue which belongs to B] would not be imperceptible [for A].[13]

In the theory of *svasaṃvedana*, blue which is cognized by a cognition is not distinct from the cognition. Therefore, to say that the blue grasped by B is identical with the blue grasped by A is to say that B's cognition of blue is identical with A's cognition of blue. Cognition is self-cognized. Consequently, it follows that the former is perceptible by A, that is, B's mind is perceptible by A.

3.2

Let me summarize the main points that have been made by Prajñākaragupta in his arguments about the inference of other minds from gooseflesh. According to Prajñākaragupta, all that can be known from an inference is a universal fact. However, the mental states of others are particular facts. Therefore, he concudes, one cannot know the mental states of others by inference. He has also discussed how A's joy and B's joy, which are respectively supposed to be preceded by A's cognition of blue and B's cognition of blue, are to be differentiated from each other. In his view, the different places where A and B are located, the different times at which A's joy and B's occur, and the different types of gooseflesh which A and B have cannot account for the difference between A's joy and B's. His serious objection against the inference in question is that if by the inference it were established that the blue grasped by B is identical with the blue grasped by A, the contradiction comes up that other mind is perceptible.

4

Prajñākaragupta discusses not only the inference of other minds from physical activities but also that from verbal activities. It is also interesting to note his arguments about the question of whether we can infer other minds from the verbal actions of others.

4.1

According to Prajñākaragupta, the verbal actions of others also cannot serve as evidence to show that others see the same thing as we see. He says the following:

> *PVA* 366,33–367,1: *yadi pratyakṣān na pratyeti vacanād api naiva pratyeṣyati / tad api svapratibhāsam eva sūcayati / tvatpratibhāsitaṃ*

[13] *Y* (D271b3; P363b8–364a1): *gzung bar bya ba* ***de la yang tha dad pa med par yang*** *'gyur ro // de lta na yang bzung ba* ***'di lkog tu gyur par mi 'gyur ro*** *//*

mama pratibhātīti tenāpi pṛṣṭvaiva[14] *jñātavyaṃ / tata itaretarāśraya-doṣaḥ /*

If [we] cannot know, through a perception, [that others see the same thing as we see], then [we can] certainly not know it from a verbal expression either. The [verbal expression] also indicates precisely that [something] appears in [a hearer's] own mind.[15] He (a speaker)[16] also should understand [that the hearer sees the same thing as he sees], only after asking [the hearer] the question: "Does what appeared in your mind appear in my mind?" Thus, the fallacy of mutual dependence follows.

The point here is as follows. Let blue be before the eyes of two persons A and B. Person A makes the statement: "What appears in my mind is identical with what appears in your mind." In order for this statement to be true, it must be established that what appears in A's mind is identical with what appears in B. It is supposed that this cannot be established through perception. Suppose that in order to establish the truth of the statement of A, A resorts to B's statement: "What appears in my mind is identical with what appears in your mind." Unless this statement of B is true, the truth of the statement of A is not established. How should B establish the truth of B's own statement? Under the given assumption that it cannot be established through perception that A and B see the same blue, B will have to resort to A's statement. Thus there occurs the mutual dependence. It is to be noted in passing that Prajñākaragupta considers that in verbal communication a speaker makes an utterance to convey what appears in the speaker's mind and from the utterance something appears in a hearer's mind.

4.2

Finally, Prajñākaragupta points out that in the conventional world of ours in which we communicate among ourselves through language it is impossible to establish that a number of people see the same thing at a given place and time.

PVA 367,4: *parasparasahāyatvaṃ na taimirikayor dvayoḥ /*
na pratyekam asāmarthye samudāyasya tad yataḥ //730//

A couple of sick persons, who are afflicted by eye-disease (*taimirika*), cannot help each other. For they can have no [ability to see the moon] even if they join together, because neither of them has an ability [to see the moon].

[14] *pṛṣṭvaiva M=NVV*; *vṛthaivaṃ PVA*, *de ltar mthong ba* (**dṛṣṭvaivaṃ*) *T*.
[15] *J* (D135a7; P154a7): ***rang gi snang ba nyid*** *ni nyan pa po'i'o //*
[16] *J* (D135b1; P154a8): *smra ba pos kyang ngo //*

Due to their eye-disease, sick persons see the moon as the double moon. They may have a common belief that the same thing appears in their minds, and may believe that there is in reality the double moon. However, this belief is simply erroneous because the double moon does not exist separately from their minds. In the kārikā cited above, Prajñākaragupta intends to say that even if we can speak of the same thing, it is as if two sick persons suffering from eye-disease spoke of the double moon. Even if two persons believe that they are speaking of the same thing, still, its reality is merely conventional.

5 Conclusion

If external objects did not exist, then how could it be established that a number of people see the same thing at a given place and time? Prajñākaragupta's answer is this: We can never know either from the bodily actions of others or from the verbal actions of others that others see the same thing as we see. What we can know is just what appears in our own mind. For Prajñākaragupta, to question what others see makes sense only in our conventional world. Even if we can speak of the same thing, it is as if two sick persons spoke of the double moon.

Unlike Dharmakīrti, Ratnakīrti holds that self-cognition establishes that no other minds exist except one's own. This view of Ratnakīrti's is essentially identical with that of Prajñākaragupta. What is real is a cognitive fact that a cognition is self-cognized.

Primary Sources

J. = Jayanta, *Pramāṇavārttikālaṃkāraṭīkā*: P 5720. D 4222.

M. = Manuscript B of *PVA*. In: [16].

NVV. = Vādirāja, *Nyāyaviniścayavivaraṇa.* In: [3].

PV. = Dharmakīrti, *Pramāṇavārttika* . In: [10].

PVA. = Prajñākaragupta, *Pramāṇavārttikālaṃkāra* . In: [12].

SD. = Ratnakīrti, *Santānāntaradūṣaṇa.* In: [15], 145-149.

SS. = Dharmakīrti, *Santānāntarasiddhi.* In: [14].

T. = Tibetan translation of *PVA* [12]: P 5719. D 4221.

TBh. = Mokṣākaragupta, *Tarkabhāṣā.* In: [11].

TSP. = Kamalaśīla, *Tattvasaṃgrahapañjikā.* In: [13].

Viṃś. = Vasubandu, *Viṃśatikā Vijñaptimātratāsiddhi.* In: [8].

Y. = Yamāri, *Pramāṇavārttikālaṃkāraṭīkā Supariśuddhā*: P 5723. D 4226.

References

[1] Alec Hyslop. Other Minds. In Edward Craig, editor, *Routledge Encyclopedia of Philosophy*, volume 7. Routledge, London and New York, 1998.

[2] Masahiro Inami. The Problem of Other Minds in the Buddhist Epistemological Tradition. *Journal of Indian Philosophy*, 29(4):465–485, 2001.

[3] Mahendra K. Jain, editor. *Nyāyaviniścayavivaraṇa of Śri Vādirāja Sūri.* Bharatiya Jnanapith, Varanasi, 1944.

[4] Yuichi Kajiyama. Buddhist Solipsism. *Journal of Indian and Bnddhist Studies*, 13(1):465–485, 1965.

[5] Yuichi Kajiyama. Do Other People's Minds Exist? with a Japanese Translation of Ratnakīrti's *Santānāntaredūṣaṇa. Annual Report of the International Research Institute for Advanced Buddhology*, 3:3–35, 2000.

[6] Shoryu Katsura. Dharmakīrti's *santānāntarasiddhi*; Japanese Translation and Synopsis. *The Hiroshima University Studies Faculty of Letters*, 43:102–120, 1983.

[7] Birgit Kellner. Levels of (Im)perceptibility: Dharmottara's Views on the *dṛśya* in *dṛśyānupalabdhi*. In Shoryu Katsura, editor, *Dharmakīrti's Thought and Its Impact on Indian and Tibetan Philosophy: Proceedings of the Third International Dharmakīrti Conference*, pages 193–208. The Hiroshima University Studies Faculty of Letters, 1999.

[8] Sylvain Lévi, editor. *Vijñaptimātratāsiddhi, Deux Traités de Vasubandhu, Viṃśatikā (la Vingtaine) accompagnée d'une Explication en Prose et Triṃśikā (la Trentaine) avec la commentaire de Sthiramati I.* Librairie Ancienne Honors Champion, Paris, 1925.

[9] Bimal Krishna Matilal. *Logic, Language and Reality: Indian Philosophy and Contemporary Issues.* Motilal Banarsidass, Delhi, 1985.

[10] Yusho Miyasaka, editor. *Pramāṇavārttika-kārikā (Sanskrit and Tibetan)*, volume 2 of *Acta Indologica.* Naritasan Shinshoji, Narita, 1971/72.

[11] H.R. Rangaswami Iyengar, editor. *Tarkabhāṣā and Vādasthāna of Mokṣākaragupta and Jitāripāda.* Hindusthan Press, Mysore, 1952.

[12] Rāhula Sāṅkṛtyāyana, editor. *Pramāṇavārttikabhāṣyam or Vārttikālaṅkāraḥ of Prajñākaragupta.* Kashi Prasad Jayaswal Research Institute, Patna, 1953.

[13] Swami Dwarikadas Shastri, editor. *Tattvasaṅgraha of Ācārya Shāntarakṣita with the Commentary 'Pañjikā' of Shrī Kamalashīla.* Bauddha Bharati Series. Varanasi, 1968.

[14] Theodor Stcherbatsky, editor. *Santānāntarasiddhi of Dharmakīrti*, volume 19 of *Bibliotheca Buddhica.* Petrograd, 1916.

[15] Anantalal Thakur, editor. *Ratnakīrti-Nibandhāvaliḥ.* Tibetan Sanskrit Work Series. K.P. Jayaswal Research Institute, Patna, 2nd edition, 1975.

[16] Shigeaki Watanabe, editor. *The Sanskrit Commentaries on the Pramāṇavārttikam from the Rāhula Sāṅkṛtyāyana's Collection of Negatives.* Bihar Research Society, Patna and Narita, 1998.

Marking time

Kamal Lodaya*

The Institute of Mathematical Sciences, Central Institutes of Technology (C.I.T.) Campus, Chennai 600 113, India.

E-mail: kamal@imsc.res.in

Tense logics. The traditional viewpoint of logics of time is as a kind of modal logic, with Kripke models where the accessibility relation is deemed to specify properties particular to time. We call this *tense logic* after a classic survey by John Burgess in the *Handbook of philosophical logic* [10]. We begin by changing the tense logic models to incorporate *duration*.

Next, we discuss the point-based and interval-based versions of time. These were studied in Johan van Benthem's book *The logic of time* and in several papers appearing around the same time: Vilain and Allen, developed an interval algebra [44, 1]; Moszkowski and Manna, as well as Schwartz, Melliar-Smith and Vogt, advocated interval-based reasoning for hardware [32, 36]. The prohibitive complexity of logics which evaluate propositions at intervals was established by Halpern and Shoham [18]. Many fragments have been shown to be undecidable (cf. [28]). Goranko, Montanari, Sciavicco and Bresolin recently showed that a few are decidable by exploiting their resemblance to the point-based logic [38, 6]. Interval logic has made a resurgence, even making it into industry standards like PSL/Sugar: Vardi gives a picture of the history [41].

We expand the discussion by generalizing from durations to arbitrary measurements. Two logics, one point-based and another interval-based, are presented. We sketch a completeness proof for the point-based logic. We also have a brief section on expressive completeness of these logics.

---

*I thank the organizers of the *Logic, Navya-Nyāya and Applications* conference in honour of Bimal Krishna Matilal, January 2007, for inviting me to speak on the occasion, and the hospitality of Jadavpur University where the conference was held. An earlier version of the talk was presented at the workshop on *Advances and Issues in Timed Systems* during FSTTCS XXVI, Kolkata, December 2006. I thank Supratik Chakraborty and Deepak D'Souza for inviting me to speak there, and the Indian Statistical Institute for their hospitality.

Paritosh Pandya and I collaborated itinerantly on a paper on measurement logics, which finally got written [29]. Many of the definitions in the present article arise from that work. As a consequence of his expertise on timed systems, Paritosh had to put up with a dense barrage of questions during the interval I was preparing for the Kolkata talks, towards the end of 2006. At the Matilal conference a little later, Johan van Benthem expressed interest in the development of sampled time models. R. Ramanujam started off a lively discussion on "time" in timed systems while I was writing this article. Sunil Simon enlightened me on the fine points of alternating timed automata. To all of them, thank you.

Mihir K. **Chakraborty**, Benedikt **Löwe**, Madhabendra Nath **Mitra**, Sundar **Sarukkai** (*eds.*). Logic, Navya-Nyāya & Applications. Homage to Bimal Krishna Matilal. College Publications, London, 2008. Studies in Logic 15. pp. 185–203.

Received by the editors: 14 May 2007; 24 February 2008, 19 March 2008.
Accepted for publication: 20 March 2008.

Temporal and dynamic logics. Zohar Manna and Amir Pnueli viewed linear time models as *runs* generated from a finite transition system since they were interested in efficient algorithms for verifying time properties [30]. The Kripke frames were fixed to be the natural numbers, or an initial segment. We shall use the name *temporal logic* for this "informatic" approach to time, as Manna and Pnueli did. This transition from tense logic to temporal logic, with automata theory playing a constructive rôle, is detailed in the chapter by Ian Hodkinson in the second volume of the book *Temporal logic* [24].

A *duration calculus* was developed early on by Zhou Chaochen, Tony Hoare and Anders Ravn to reason about timed systems [11]. The book [12] by Zhou and Michael Hansen is a good reference. Rajeev Alur, David Dill and Tom Henzinger developed the "informatic" approach to duration by extending the Manna-Pnueli temporal logic to timed systems [2, 3].

Again we generalize from durations to arbitrary measurements, and instead of a temporal logic we present a dynamic logic. Decidability is proved for a future fragment, not for arbitrary measurements but only for durations, and only when the models are restricted to be finite.

This article. The purpose of this article is expository: to use these informatic ideas and develop tense and temporal logic afresh, this time with measurement. Many of the definitions and results are new (for instance, we have never seen a dynamic logic with measurement modalities before), but they are small generalizations of what has appeared in the literature.

It is not our aim to survey the field of logics dealing with time. The papers [10, 38, 41] provide many references. The two volumes of *Temporal logic* edited by Gabbay, Hodkinson, Reynolds and Finger offer a reasonably up-to-date compendium of technical details. The articles [17, 21, 40] have a discussion of linguistic details.

1 Duration frames and measurement models

Definition 1.1 (Dutertre). A *duration domain* $(D, +, 0, <)$ is a linearly ordered monoid which is cancellative (if $x + y = x + z$ or $y + x = z + x$ then $y = z$) and zerosumfree (if $x + y = 0$ then $x = y = 0$).

In this article we shall only work with duration domains which are Abelian. Common examples of duration domains are the natural numbers and the nonnegative reals.

Definition 1.2. A *(point) duration frame* $\mathcal{T} = (T, \prec, d)$ is a nonempty linear order $\mathcal{T} = (T, \prec)$ (the underlying *flow of time*) with a symmetric order-preserving *distance function* d from $T \times T$ into a duration domain D.

We shall also define interval duration frames. The general definition follows the one in van Benthem's book [39].

Definition 1.3. An *interval duration frame* $\mathcal{I} = (I, \subset, \ll, d)$ is a nonempty poset $(I, \subset)$ with greatest lower bounds, together with a partial order $\ll$ and a distance function $d : I \to D$ into a duration domain D which are monotonic with respect to $\subset$. That is, if $w \subset x \ll y \supset z$ then $w \ll y$, $d(w) \leq d(x)$ and $d(y) \geq d(z)$.

Given a point frame $\mathcal{T} = (T, \prec, d)$, we can construct an interval frame $\text{Int}(\mathcal{T}) = (I, \subset, \ll, d)$ by letting I be the nonempty convex subsets of T, $\subset$ be inclusion, $x_1 \ll x_2$ iff for every t_1 in x_1, t_2 in x_2, $t_1 \prec t_2$ and $d(x) = d(b, e)$ where b and e are the beginning and ending points (or limit points) of the interval x. This interval frame is also *atomic*: for every x there is $x_1 \subset x$, such that if $x_0 \subset x_1$ then $x_0 = x_1$.

Given an atomic interval frame $\mathcal{I} = (I, \subset, \ll, d)$, we can construct a point frame $\text{Pt}(\mathcal{I}) = (T, \prec, d)$ by letting T be the set of atoms of I, $\prec$ be $\ll$ restricted to T and $d(b, e) = \inf\{d(x) \mid b, e \subset x\}$.

The theorem below was proved for tense frames, but extending it to duration frames is not difficult.

Theorem 1.4 (van Benthem). An atomic interval frame $\mathcal{I}$ is isomorphic to $\text{Int}(\text{Pt}(\mathcal{I}))$.

Let us consider a more specific example. If we take $\mathcal{T}$ to be a strict linear order, we can define its intervals to be the usual "open intervals" $(t_1, t_2) = \{t \mid t_1 \prec t \prec t_2\}$. It is an easy exercise to list the 5 possible point-interval relations[1]. Hamblin [19] and Allen [1] showed that all 13 interval-interval relations are definable using $\subset$ and $\ll$ (the first two below). The converses of these six and the identity relation make up the total.

- (t, u) *during* (v, w) if $v \prec t$ and $u \prec w$,
- (t, u) *before* (v, w) if $u \prec v$.
- (t, u) *overlaps* (v, w) if $t \prec v \prec u \prec w$.
- (t, u) *meets* (v, w) if $u = v$.
- (t, u) *begins* (v, w) if $t = v$ and $u \prec w$.
- (t, u) *ends* (v, w) if $v \prec t$ and $u = w$.

1.1 A signature of measurements

Let Prop be a set of propositions. Let $\Sigma = \{m_1, m_2, \ldots\}$ be a signature of measurement function symbols (of arity 2). The signature Σ always contains the distinguished function ℓ which will be used to measure the length of an interval of time. We shall abbreviate the signature $\{\ell\}$ to ℓ.

[1] Cf. [44]

Definition 1.5. A *measurement model* $M = (\mathcal{T}, \theta)$ is a duration frame with a *behaviour* $\theta : (\text{Prop} \to T \to \{0,1\}) \times (\Sigma \to (T \times T) \to D)$ such that $\theta(\ell)[b,e] = d(b,e)$. An *interval measurement model* is given by $M = (\text{Int}(\mathcal{T}), \theta)$.

A behaviour consists of a valuation, a boolean function of time which we write as $\theta(p)$, together with an interpretation of the measurement signature, with $\theta(m)[b,e]$ giving the value of the measurement function $m \in \Sigma$ on the interval $[b,e]$. The behaviour is defined in this way so that it allows Σ to depend on the propositions: the *Duration calculus* book [12] has examples of measurements $\int p$, which give the total duration for which a proposition p holds in a given interval.

In this article we shall only work with measurement functions which are symmetric. We can impose further conditions on the measurement functions, such as making them additive, order-preserving or anti-order-preserving, as required. Moreover, we require that the measurement ℓ is always interpreted by the distance function.

2 Measurement logics

The formulae of *point measurement logic*, defined below, allow tense modalities and future and past modalities which are simple generalizations of the usual tense modalities to measurement. This logic is a generalization of the *metric tense logic* defined by Burgess [10] and **MTL** defined by Koymans [26], which only dealt with the length signature ℓ.

Throughout this article we shall use χ as a parameter for a set of comparison operations, e.g., Punct $= \{<, =, >, \leq, \geq\}$ is called the set of *punctual* comparisons. The set Eq $= \{=\}$ is the set of *equality* comparisons. The set of *Weak* comparisons is defined so that equality comparisons are not definable in the logic, e.g., $\{\leq, >\}$. This use of parameters is from a paper with Pandya [29].

In the syntax below, the metavariable m gives the value of the function m during the interval of interest. The actual value of m is not accessible in the syntax, but only a *guard*: a comparison of m with a constant c. We use $-m$ to denote that the interval is to be oriented going into the past.

Definition 2.1 (Point measurement logic χ**MTL**$[\Sigma]$).

$$\begin{aligned} \alpha \ ::= \ & p \in \text{Prop} \mid \neg\alpha \mid \alpha \vee \beta \mid \alpha\, \mathcal{U}\, \beta \mid \alpha\, \mathcal{S}\, \beta \mid \\ & \langle -m \sim c\rangle\alpha \mid \langle m \sim c\rangle\alpha, \ m \in \Sigma, \ \sim \in \chi, \ c \in D \end{aligned}$$

Satisfaction is inductively defined as usual.

$$
\begin{array}{l}
M,t \models p \text{ iff } \theta(p)[t] = 1 \\
M,t \models \alpha\,\mathcal{U}\,\beta \text{ iff } \exists v \prec t : M,v \models \beta \text{ and } \forall l : t \prec u \prec v : M,v \models \alpha \\
M,t \models \alpha\,\mathcal{S}\,\beta \text{ iff } \exists r \prec t : M,r \models \beta \text{ and } \forall s : r \prec s \prec t : M,r \models \alpha \\
M,t \models \langle -m \sim c\rangle\alpha \text{ iff } \exists s \prec t : \theta(m)[s,t] \sim c \text{ and } M,s \models \alpha \\
M,t \models \langle m \sim c\rangle\alpha \text{ iff } \exists u \succ t : \theta(m)[t,u] \sim c \text{ and } M,u \models \alpha.
\end{array}
$$

We define the future and past modalities using $\mathcal{U}$ and $\mathcal{S}$; e.g.,

$$\Diamond\alpha \overset{\text{def}}{=} \mathsf{true}\,\mathcal{U}\,\alpha,$$

but they are also definable using the length operators, e.g., $\Diamond\alpha$ is $\langle \ell > 0\rangle\alpha$ or $\langle \ell \geq 0\rangle\alpha$, depending on whether the modality is to be strict or not. We take the comparisons $<, =, >$ as basic and $\leq, \geq$ as abbreviations.

It is also possible to define in the logic until and since operations which specify a measurement comparison. E.g., if the requirement β should occur after a measurement $\geq c$ and α is to hold until then, this can be written $[m < c]\alpha \wedge \langle m = c\rangle(\alpha\,\mathcal{U}\,\beta)$. If the measurement is $\leq c$, the formula can be written as $(\alpha\,\mathcal{U}\,\beta) \wedge \langle m \leq c\rangle\beta$.

Here is an example of reasoning, adapted from Burgess [10].

Suman: Have you heard? Jagan is going to Alabama this September.	$\langle m = 9\rangle jga$
Sameen: He won't get in without a visa. Has he remembered to apply for one?	$\neg\Diamond(jga \wedge \neg\diamondminus jgv)$
Suman: Not yet, as far as I know.	$\neg\diamondminus jav \wedge \neg jav$
Sameen: Visa queues might even take a month to clear. He'll have to do so by July.	$jgv \supset \langle -m \leq 2\rangle jav$ $\therefore \langle m \leq 7\rangle jav.$

Here are some well known axioms for validity of tense logic (cf. [9, 10]), recast into the measurement framework. We mostly provide the future axioms, leaving the reader to supply the mirror image axioms for the past. There are some specific axioms for the comparisons.

$$
\begin{array}{ll}
[m \sim c](\alpha \supset \beta) \supset ([m \sim c]\alpha \supset [m \sim c]\beta), & \\
[-m \sim c](\alpha \supset \beta) \supset ([-m \sim c]\alpha \supset [-m \sim c]\beta) & K \\
\alpha \supset [\ell \sim c]\langle -\ell \sim c\rangle\alpha, \quad \alpha \supset [-\ell \sim c]\langle \ell \sim c\rangle\alpha & \textit{symmetry} \\
\langle m < c_1\rangle\alpha \supset \langle m < c_1 + c_2\rangle\alpha, \;\; \langle m > c_1 + c_2\rangle\alpha \supset \langle m > c_1\rangle\alpha & \textit{monotonicity} \\
\Diamond\alpha \equiv \langle m < c\rangle\alpha \vee \langle m = c\rangle\alpha \vee \langle m > c\rangle\alpha & \textit{linearity}
\end{array}
$$

$\langle \ell = c \rangle \alpha \supset [\ell = c] \alpha$	*unique length*
$\alpha \supset \langle m = 0 \rangle \alpha, \quad \langle \ell = 0 \rangle \alpha \supset \alpha$	*reflexivity*
$\langle m \sim c_1 \rangle \langle m \sim c_2 \rangle \alpha \supset \langle m \sim c_1 + c_2 \rangle \alpha$	*transitivity*
$\langle m \sim c_1 + c_2 \rangle \alpha \supset \langle m \sim c_1 \rangle \langle m \sim c_2 \rangle \alpha$	*density*
$\langle m \leq c_1 \rangle \alpha \wedge \langle m \leq c_1 + c_2 \rangle \beta \supset$	*connectedness*
$\langle m \leq c_1 \rangle (\alpha \wedge \langle m \leq c_1 + c_2 \rangle \beta) \vee \langle m \leq c_1 \rangle (\alpha \wedge \beta) \vee \langle m \leq c_1 \rangle (\beta \wedge \langle m \leq c_1 \rangle \alpha)$	
$\alpha \, \mathcal{U} \, \beta \equiv \beta \vee ((\alpha \wedge \alpha \, \mathcal{U} \, \beta) \, \mathcal{U} \, \beta)$	*until*
$\alpha \, \mathcal{U} \, \mathsf{false} \supset \mathsf{false}$	*unless*

Completeness for the tense fragment is claimed in Burgess [10, § 6.1]. We stretch the claim to the measurement setting below. For completeness of the fragment with equality comparisons and duration domains which are ordered abelian groups, cf. [31].

Claim 2.2. There is a complete axiomatization for $\chi\mathbf{MTL}[\Sigma]$.

A formula mentions finitely many measurement functions $\Sigma_0 \subseteq \Sigma$ and finitely many constants $D_0 \subseteq D$ in finitely many guards. We always include ℓ in Σ_0. The guards implicitly divide the product duration domain $D_0^{|\Sigma_0|}$ into finitely many *regions* $r_1, \ldots, r_n$. E.g., a region might be $5 < \ell < 7, m_1 > 8, m_2 = 3$. The idea of regions is from Alur and Dill [2].

Define for each region r_i, an accessibility relation $\prec_i$ which is *compatible* with the constraints in the region. E.g., the accessibility relation for our example region will ensure that for every formula of the kind $[\ell > 5]\alpha$, $[\ell < 7]\alpha$, $[m_1 > 8]\alpha$ or $[m_2 = 3]\alpha$ in Γ, $\alpha \in \Delta$. Using the connectedness axioms, we can show that at least one of the $\prec_i$ relations will hold between any pair of maximal consistent sets Γ, Δ.

Using these ideas, a Henkin construction can be performed, ensuring that a linear order is maintained. We spell out one detail in the lemma below which provides an maximal consistent set satisfying a future measurement requirement. It illustrates that modalities like

$$\langle 5 < \ell < 7 \wedge m_1 > 8 \wedge m_2 = 3 \rangle \alpha,$$

or even those which check that a measurement lies in an interval such as $\langle m \in [b, e] \rangle \alpha$, are not required for proving completeness.

Lemma 2.3. If a maximal consistent set Γ has $\langle m \sim c \rangle \alpha$ then there is a compatible region r_i and a maximal consistent set $\Delta \succ_i \Gamma$ containing α.

Proof. It is sufficient to show that for some $d \in D_0$, the set of formulae $\Gamma^- = \{\gamma \mid [m \sim c]\gamma \wedge [\ell \sim d]\gamma \wedge \langle \ell \sim d \rangle \alpha \in \Gamma\} \cup \{\alpha\}$ is consistent. The same argument will be repeated for the other measurements in Σ_0, and the resulting consistent set will be expanded to a maximal consistent set Δ

using a Lindenbaum lemma. The comparisons between m and c, ℓ and d and so on constitute the region r_i. Hence $\Delta \succ_i \Gamma$ by construction.

So suppose Γ^- is not consistent. Then it has a finite inconsistent subset whose conjunction we denote by $\widehat{\gamma} \wedge \alpha$. By supposition and the K axiom, $\langle m \sim c\rangle(\widehat{\gamma} \wedge \alpha) \in \Gamma$.

Consider the smallest d_1 in D_0 under the duration order. By the linearity axiom, one of $\langle \ell < d_1\rangle(\widehat{\gamma}\wedge\alpha)$, $\langle \ell = d_1\rangle(\widehat{\gamma}\wedge\alpha)$, $\langle \ell > d_1\rangle(\widehat{\gamma}\wedge\alpha)$ is in Γ. Suppose, e.g., it is not the first two but the third. Then Γ also has $[\ell \leq d_1]\neg(\widehat{\gamma} \wedge \alpha)$.

Now we proceed to the next d_2 in the D_0 ordering. Using monotonicity and linearity, we ask whether $\widehat{\gamma} \wedge \alpha$ lies within the interval (d_1, d_2) or at d_2 or beyond. Continuing in this way, we shall home in on a suitable d in D_0 and arrive at a contradiction with the consistency of Γ. Q.E.D.

2.1 Interval measurement logic

An *interval measurement logic* can also be defined. The logic below was defined in a paper with Pandya [29] and is used here because it matches a first order logic, as will be seen later. As in the case of the point logic, we use χ as a parameter for a set of comparison operations.

Definition 2.4 (Guarded interval measurement logic, χ**GIML**$[\Sigma]$).

$$\begin{aligned} \varphi \quad ::= \quad & \lceil p \rceil,\ p \in \mathrm{Prop} \mid \neg\varphi \mid \varphi \vee \psi \mid \varphi;\psi \mid \\ & \langle -m \sim c\rangle\psi \mid \langle m \sim c\rangle\psi, \quad \sim \in \chi,\ c \in D \end{aligned}$$

The satisfaction relation is inductively defined below. Note that propositions are evaluated at points and lifted to intervals by making them "hereditary" [39].

$$\begin{aligned} M, [b,e] \models \lceil p \rceil \quad & \text{iff} \quad \forall t : b \prec t \prec e : \theta(p)[t] = 1, \\ M, [b,e] \models \varphi;\psi \quad & \text{iff} \quad \exists z : b \prec z \prec e : M, [b,z] \models \varphi \\ & \qquad \text{and } M, [z,e] \models \psi \\ M, [b,e] \models \langle -m \sim c\rangle\psi \quad & \text{iff} \quad b = e \text{ and } \exists z \prec b : \theta(m)[z,b] \sim c \\ & \qquad \text{and } M, [z,b] \models \psi \\ M, [b,e] \models \langle m \sim c\rangle\psi \quad & \text{iff} \quad b = e \text{ and } \exists z \succ e : \theta(m)[e,z] \sim c \\ & \qquad \text{and } M, [e,z] \models \psi \end{aligned}$$

Dutertre gave an axiomatization of first order interval tense logic [13]. Here are some of his axioms which are applicable in a propositional setting. We do not repeat the axioms for the measurement modalities from the point version. The symbol ε stands for the formula $\langle \ell = 0\rangle\mathsf{true}$.

$(\varphi \vee \psi);\chi \supset \varphi;\chi \vee \psi;\chi, \quad \varphi;(\psi \vee \chi) \supset \varphi;\psi \vee \varphi;\chi$ K

$\varepsilon;\varphi \equiv \varphi \equiv \varphi;\varepsilon$ *reflexivity*

$(\varphi;\psi);\chi \equiv \varphi;(\psi;\chi)$ *transitivity*

Dutertre's completeness proof [13] is a first order logic Henkin construction. It needs to be examined to pull out a completeness proof for the quantifier-free version of interval logic that we are considering here.

2.2 Decidability

The decidability of measurement logic depends on the comparisons used. Alur and Henzinger [3] showed that Punct-**MTL**[ℓ] validity is undecidable. Their proof uses Eq comparisons of the form $\ell = c$ for $c > 0$. Weak-**MTL**[ℓ] was shown decidable by Alur, Feder and Henzinger [4].

Theorem 2.5 (Alur, Feder and Henzinger)**.** Validity of Punct-**MTL**[Σ] formulae is undecidable, but for Weak-**MTL**[ℓ] formulae it is decidable.

The algorithmic situation is no better for interval models.

Theorem 2.6 (with Pandya)**.** The validity of Punct-**GIML**[Σ] formulae is not decidable, but it is decidable for Weak-**GIML**[ℓ] formulae.

Proof. Both proofs are by translation. χ**MTL**[Σ] formulae can be coded into χ**GIML**[Σ], yielding the undecidability. The decidability follows from that of the first order fragment Weak-**GF**[ℓ], defined in the next section, which was proved by Hirshfeld and Rabinovich [23]. As we shall see, Weak-**GIML**[ℓ] is expressively complete for this fragment, hence the decidability can be transferred. Q.E.D.

3 Expressive completeness

Kamp [25] introduced a new dimension to tense logic by relating it to the first order theory of linear order with monadic predicates **FO**[$<$]. Specifically, he showed that tense logic with the binary modalities $\mathcal{U}$ (until) and $\mathcal{S}$ (since) has the same expressive power as three-variable first order logic, which in turn is as expressive as full **FO**[$<$]. Kamp's work was extended by Stavi to all linear orders. The first volume of the book *Temporal logic* [16] has a detailed treatment of Kamp's theorem.

Kamp's syntactic techniques were used by Venema [43] to establish an expressiveness result for interval tense logic with respect to three-variable first order logic. Just as Kamp had to, Venema showed that binary "chop" modalities are needed. If propositions are evaluated at points (as in the previous section), this again yields full **FO**[$<$].

To extend these ideas to measurement, observe that the semantics of all the logics we have considered translate into a guarded fragment of first order logics over linear orders extended with measurement functions **FO**[$<, \Sigma$].

Definition 3.1. Let χ be a given set of length comparisons. By $\chi\mathbf{GF}[\Sigma]$, we denote the logic which extends $\mathbf{FO}[<]$ by the χ-*guarded quantifier* $\varphi(t_0) = \exists t(G(t_0, t) \wedge \psi(t_0, t))$, where ψ is a formula with at most two free variables t_0 and t, and the guard G is a boolean combination of comparisons from the set χ.

In earlier work, Hirshfeld and Rabinovich conjectured that such a fragment does not have an expressively complete modal logic. Recently, Pandya and I refuted this conjecture [29]. We use all of Venema's chop modalities.

Theorem 3.2 (with Pandya). An extension of the logic $\chi\mathbf{GIML}[\Sigma]$ is expressively complete for the corresponding guarded fragment $\chi\mathbf{GF}[\Sigma]$.

Hirshfeld and Rabinovich [23] defined a smaller fragment by using a *point guarded quantifier* $\varphi(t_0) = \exists t(G(t_0, t) \wedge \psi(t))$, where ψ is a formula with at most *one* free variable t, and the guard G is an *atomic* comparison. An induction shows that the logic $\chi\mathbf{MTL}[\Sigma]$ is expressively complete with respect to the corresponding point guarded fragment.

4 Discrete models and sampled time

Manna and Pnueli shifted attention to the question of *verification* of satisfaction: given a model M, a point t and a formula α, how do we check whether $M, t \models \alpha$ [30]? This leads to a somewhat trivial-sounding question, how is the model M to be presented to an algorithm?

Let Prop be a finite set of propositions, Σ a finite signature of *additive* measurement functions and D a duration domain. We fix an ordering of the function symbols in the signature Σ beginning with the length ℓ. A model M with a discrete linear order as a frame can be represented as a pair of finite words $v = v_0 v_1 \ldots v_n$ and $w = w_0 w_1 \ldots w_n$, or a pair of infinite words $v = v_0 v_1 \ldots$ and $w = w_0 w_1 \ldots$ over the alphabets $D^{|\Sigma|}$ and $\wp(\text{Prop})$ respectively. Since the Kripke frame ($\mathbf{N}$ or an initial prefix $[0..n]$) is fixed by the words, this "word model" consists only of a behaviour.

Definition 4.1. A *sampled time behaviour* is a pair of words $\theta = (v, w)$, both of the same length, over the alphabets $D^{|\Sigma|}$ and $\wp(\text{Prop})$. If the durations in the first (length) component of v are positive, the underlying flow of time is said to be *monotonic*, otherwise it is said to be *weakly monotonic*.

Sampled measurement models over the signature ℓ using the real numbers as a duration domain were introduced as *timed state sequences* (or *timed words*) by Alur and Dill [2]. They used an alternate definition where time values $(v_0(\ell))(v_0(\ell) + v_1(\ell))(v_0(\ell) + v_1(\ell) + v_2(\ell)) \ldots$ are used in the sampling sequence. Our definition is consistent with time differences being used. The additivity assumption on the signature makes both definitions equivalent. We shall use $\sum_i^j v(m)$ to denote the sum $\sum_{\ell=i+1}^j v_i(m)$, which sums up the measurements over an interval from the differences. Usually, additional constraints are put on infinite behaviours so that time does not converge to a point but diverges to infinity.

An infinite model can be represented as an ω-word if we further assume that such a model is finitely generated, for instance, as an infinite path in a finite transition system. This suggests the *model checking* question: given a finite automaton and a formula α, do all finite/infinite words which belong to the language accepted by the automaton satisfy α? The evaluation point is *anchored* at the beginning to v_0, w_0.

From the earlier work of Büchi, it is easy to see that the model checking and satisfiability questions can be reduced to the language inclusion and emptiness problems for automata [7, 8].[2]

4.1 Measurement logic

While one can define point and interval logics over sampled time behaviours, the absence of the Kripke frame makes the distinctions somewhat arbitrary. Instead one could combine the ideas of both into one system, as Henriksen and Thiagarajan did using a dynamic temporal logic on sequences [22]. We use a propositional dynamic logic with converse.[3]

Our logic generalizes the sampled semantics of **MTL**, given by Alur and Henzinger and the sampled semantics used for duration logics by Pandya [3, 35]. The measurement modality $\langle \mu \rightarrow \pi \rangle \alpha$ says that there is a behaviour conforming to the program π which satisfies the measurement μ, after which the formula α holds. The modality $\langle -\mu \leftarrow \pi \rangle \alpha$ describes the converse behaviour, going into the past from the present point in the behaviour. Since the full power of regular expressions is used here for the programs, this logic is more expressive than the guarded fragment $\chi\mathbf{GF}[\Sigma]$, which has a first order semantics.

Definition 4.2 (Dynamic measurement logic $\chi\mathbf{DML}[\Sigma]$).

$$\begin{array}{lcl} \pi & ::= & \lceil p \rceil,\ p \in \mathrm{Prop} \mid \mathsf{skip} \mid \pi_1 \cup \pi_2 \mid \pi_1;\pi_2 \mid \pi^* \\ \mu & ::= & m \sim c,\ m \in \Sigma,\ \ \sim \in \chi,\ c \in D \\ \alpha & ::= & p \mid \neg\alpha \mid \alpha \vee \beta \mid \langle \mu \rightarrow \pi \rangle \alpha \mid \langle -\mu \leftarrow \pi \rangle \alpha \end{array}$$

Let $\theta = (v, w)$ be a sampled time behaviour. A program π represents a subsequence of the behaviour $(v_i \dots v_j, w_i \dots w_j)$ which is specified by the indices i and j. That this subsequence is part of the relation defined by a

[2] Cf. also [14, 37] in the case of finite words.

[3] Cf. [20] for more details of various dynamic logics.

program π is written as $\theta, [i, j] \models \pi$.

$$\begin{array}{l}
\theta, [i,j] \models \lceil p \rceil \text{ iff } \forall z : i \prec z \prec j : \theta(p)[z] = 1 \\
\theta, [i,j] \models \textsf{skip} \text{ iff } j = i + 1 \\
\theta, [i,j] \models \pi_1 \cup \pi_2 \text{ iff } \theta[i,j] \models \pi_1 \text{ or } \theta, [i,j] \models \pi_2 \\
\theta, [i,j] \models \pi_1 ; \pi_2 \text{ iff } \exists z : i \prec z \prec j : \theta, [i,z] \models \pi_1 \text{ and } \theta, [z,j] \models \pi_2 \\
\theta, [i,j] \models \pi^* \text{ iff } \text{ for some } n \geq 0 \text{ and } i = z_0 \prec z_1 \prec \cdots \prec z_n = j : \\
\qquad \text{for all } \ell : 0 \leq \ell < n : \theta, [z_\ell, z_{\ell+1}] \models \pi
\end{array}$$

A formula α is evaluated at a time and state v_k, w_k in the model, which is specified by its index k.

$$\begin{array}{rcl}
\theta, k \models p & \text{iff} & p \in w_k \\
\theta, k \models \langle m \sim c \rightarrow \pi \rangle \alpha & \text{iff} & \exists \ell \succ k : \left(\sum_k^\ell v(m) \right) \sim c, \\
& & \theta, [k, \ell] \models \pi \text{ and } \theta, \ell \models \alpha \\
\theta, k \models \langle -m \sim c \leftarrow \pi \rangle \alpha & \text{iff} & \exists j \prec k : \left(\sum_j^k v(m) \right) \sim c, \\
& & \theta, [j, k] \models \pi \text{ and } \theta, j \models \alpha
\end{array}$$

5 The finite generation of models

Representing sampled-time models by automata is still not trivial. Alur and Dill [2] defined a *timed automaton* with a finite number of *clocks* for this purpose. They also used an extra finite alphabet of letters.

A *guarded transition* on a letter is a set of *clock constraints* $x \sim c$ and *clock resets* which include the target state for convenience (thus $x.s$ stands for resetting the clock x and going to state s).

The finitely many guarded transitions in a finite timed automaton can now describe unboundedly many change points in a finite or infinite behaviour. Hence the automaton provides a finite generation mechanism for sampled time behaviours.

But there is still a catch. The duration domain D can be, and is usually meant to be, infinite. How is a finite automaton supposed to read a letter belonging to an infinite alphabet?

Assume that all the measurement functions in the signature Σ (which we have already assumed to be additive) are *order-preserving* (as ℓ is) or *anti-order-preserving*. As we saw in an earlier section, the clocks and constants mentioned in the guards of a finite timed automaton implicitly divide the product duration domain into finitely many "regions" over which the automaton remains in the same state with only the clocks ticking away. This enabled Alur and Dill [2] to construct a finite *region automaton* which works on the alphabet of regions (along with the letters) which accepts exactly the "untiming" of the language of the timed automaton. They could decide emptiness of the language of the timed automaton by checking emptiness of the language of the region automaton.

5.1 The formula automaton

What remains is to effect a logic-to-automata translation which reduces the validity of the logic to the emptiness of the language of the automaton. Such a *formula automaton* is implicit in the work of Büchi, Elgot and Trakhtenbrot. Vardi and Wolper constructed an explicit formula automaton for temporal logic [42].

We shall be interested in a line of work initiated by Muller, Saoudi and Schupp, who constructed a succinct *alternating* formula automaton for temporal and dynamic logics [33].[4] Since the languages accepted by timed automata are not closed under complement, alternating timed automata (which include nondeterministic timed automata and for which the languages accepted are closed under complement) are convenient to use as "formula automata" for logics with duration. They were defined in the two papers [27, 34].

A transition in an alternating timed automaton with clocks X and states Q is a positive boolean combination of guards with clock constraints $x \sim c$ and resets $x.s$. A disjunction means that the automaton chooses one of the disjuncts in its move (as in a nondeterministic automaton), but a conjunction means that the automaton works on *all* conjuncts. We shall write $\mathcal{B}^+(Z)$ for the positive boolean combinations over a set Z.

Definition 5.1. An *alternating timed automaton* over an alphabet A and a set of clocks X is a tuple $M = (Q, \delta, q_0, F)$, where Q is a finite set of states, $q_0 \in Q, F \subseteq Q$ are the initial state and the set of final states respectively and $\delta : Q \times A \to \mathcal{B}^+(G(X, Q))$ is the guarded transition function.

Defining the run of such an automaton is tedious. We refer to [34] for the definition. In this paper they construct a 1-clock alternating timed automaton for the future fragment of Punct-**MTL**$[\ell]$. Their construction works only for future formulas and only for finite models. With Pandya, we constructed a 1-clock alternating timed automaton over finite words for a future fragment of Punct-**GIML**$[\ell]$ in which checking lengths is not nested [29]. (This keeps the 1-clock restriction intact.)

Emptiness of the language accepted by an alternating timed automaton restricted to *one* clock was shown to be decidable in the papers of Lasota

[4] There is an exponential blowup in going from an alternating automaton to an ordinary nondeterministic automaton.

and Walukiewicz and Ouaknine and Worrell. With two clocks, the problem is known to be undecidable.

Below we construct an alternating timed automaton with the single clock x working on the alphabet $A = \wp(\mathrm{Prop})$ which accepts exactly the finite models of a *pure future* formula α of Punct-**DML**$[\ell]$. This means that α does not have past subformulas of the kind $\langle -m \sim c \leftarrow \pi \rangle \beta$. To put it differently, we have a propositional dynamic logic without converse.

We assume all negations in α have been pushed inside to the level of literals. The closure of α is defined, based on the ideas of Fischer and Ladner [15] for propositional dynamic logic, as used by Ouaknine and Worrell [34] for Punct-**MTL**$[\ell]$. This is used to build the states of the formula automaton.

Definition 5.2 (Derivatives, closure, formula automaton)**.** For a letter a in A, the *a-derivatives* $\partial\pi/\partial a$ *of a program* π are defined inductively:

- The special program skip^r is an a-derivative of skip for any a.
- $\lceil p \rceil$ has itself and skip^r as a-derivatives if $p \in a$ and false otherwise.
- $\pi_1 \cup \pi_2$ has the a-derivatives of π_1 and π_2 as its a-derivatives.
- $\pi_1; \pi_2$ has $\{q_1; \pi_2 \mid q_1 \in \partial\pi_1/\partial a\}$ as its a-derivatives. A derivative $\mathsf{skip}^r; \pi_2$ is taken to be the same as π_2.
- π^* has $\{\mathsf{skip}^r\} \cup \{q; \pi^* \mid q \in \partial\pi/\partial a\}$ as its a-derivatives.

If q is an a-derivative of π, we define the formula $\langle \mu \to q \rangle \alpha$ to be an a-derivative of $\langle \mu \to \pi \rangle \alpha$.

The *closure* $\mathrm{CL}(\alpha)$ of a formula α contains α, a special *initial copy* α_{init} of α. It is closed under taking subformulas $\gamma = \langle \mu \to \pi \rangle \beta$ with an outermost modality, of a formula already in the closure, and under taking derivatives (of a formula). We also throw in two states true and false. It is a standard dynamic logic exercise to check that the closure of a formula is a finite set.

The *(1-clock alternating timed) formula automaton* of a formula α has $\mathrm{CL}(\alpha)$ as its states. The state α_{init} is the initial state. The $[\mu \to \pi]$ and $\langle \mu \to \mathsf{skip}^r \rangle$ formulas and the formula true are the final states. The transition function is given by the clauses below:

$$\begin{aligned}
\delta(\alpha_{\mathrm{init}}, a) &= x.\delta(\alpha, a) \\
\delta(\gamma_1 \vee \gamma_2, a) &= \delta(\gamma_1, a) \vee \delta(\gamma_2, a) \\
\delta(\gamma_1 \wedge \gamma_2, a) &= \delta(\gamma_1, a) \wedge \delta(\gamma_2, a) \\
\delta(\langle \mu \to \pi \rangle \beta, a) &= \bigvee_{b \in A} \bigvee_{q \in \partial\pi/\partial b} (\langle \mu \to q \rangle \beta \wedge x.\delta(a, b)) \\
\delta([\mu \to \pi] \beta, a) &= \bigwedge_{b \in A} \bigwedge_{q \in \partial\pi/\partial b} ([\mu \to q] \beta \vee x.\delta(a, b)) \\
\delta(\langle \ell \sim c \to \mathsf{skip}^r \rangle \beta, a) &= (x \sim c) \wedge x.\delta(\beta, a)
\end{aligned}$$

$$\delta([\ell \sim c \to \mathsf{skip}^r]\beta, a) = \neg(x \sim c) \vee x.\delta(\beta, a)$$
$$\delta(\neg p, a) = \mathsf{true\ for}\ p \notin a,\ \mathsf{false\ for}\ p \in a$$
$$\delta(p, a) = \mathsf{true\ for}\ p \in a,\ \mathsf{false\ for}\ p \notin a$$

The next theorem is our decidability result. For the reader wondering about its restricted nature, Ouaknine and Worrell showed [34] that **MTL** (and hence our logic) with both past and future modalities is undecidable; the same is true when infinite models are considered.

Theorem 5.3. For the future fragment of Punct-**DML**$[\ell]$ over finite models, model checking and validity are decidable.

Proof. Since the language emptiness and inclusion problems are decidable for one-clock alternating timed automata, it is sufficient to show that the timed language accepted by the formula automaton for α is exactly the finite behaviours where α holds.

Consider a finite behaviour $\theta = (v, w)$ of length n accepted by the formula automaton for α, using the accepting run $u_0 \xrightarrow{v_1,w_1} u_1 \xrightarrow{v_2,w_2} \dots \xrightarrow{v_n,w_n} u_n$. We show for each subformula γ of α and each index i that if the guard $\delta(\gamma, w_{i+1})$ is satisfied in u_i then $\theta, i \models \gamma$. This is shown by structural induction on γ.

The base case, when γ is p or $\neg p$: The guard is satisfied by checking $p \in a$. Correspondingly $\theta, i \models p$ or $\theta, i \models \neg p$.

For the induction step, γ has a modality, say $\gamma = \langle \mu \to \pi \rangle \beta$. If the guard is satisfied at i, there is a derivative $q \in \partial\pi/\partial a$ such that the guard $\delta(\langle \mu \to q \rangle \beta, b)$ is satisfied at $i+1$. Repeating this argument, we arrive at a position j and a derivative where the guard $\langle \mu \to \mathsf{skip}^r \rangle \beta$ is satisfied. Hence $\delta(\beta, w_{j+1})$ is satisfied in u_j and by the induction hypothesis, $\theta, j \models \beta$. At this point, the clock constraint is checked. From the transition function, we see that the clock is not reset going from a modality to its derivative. Hence the entire execution $\theta[i, j]$ of π satisfies the clock constraint, which agrees with the semantics.

Now we do an inner induction on $k = j - i$ to work out $\theta, [i, j] \models \pi$. We shall do this by temporarily forgetting the comparison and arguing that $\theta, k \models \langle \mathsf{true} \to q \rangle \beta$ for a suitable derivative q of π.

For the base case, when $k = 0$ we have just seen that

$$\theta, j \models \langle \mathsf{true} \to \mathsf{skip}^r \rangle \beta.$$

For the inner induction step, consider $i < j$. Suppose the guard $\delta(\gamma, a)$ holds in u_i. Since there is a successor in the behaviour, using the transition function, for some derivative $q \in \partial\pi/\partial a$, the guard $\delta(\langle \mathsf{true} \to q \rangle \beta, b)$ is satisfied at $i+1$. By the induction hypothesis $\theta, i+1 \models \langle \mathsf{true} \to q \rangle \beta$. By the semantics of the logic, $\theta, i \models \langle \mathsf{true} \rightarrow \pi \rangle \beta$. Since we earlier verified that the clock constraint is also satisfied, we finally get that $\theta, i \models \gamma$.

The dual modality can be similarly handled.

By taking $i = 0$ and $\gamma = \alpha$, we have shown that a behaviour accepted by the formula automaton is a model of α. The reverse inclusion follows from the observation that the formula automaton for $\neg\alpha$ is the dual alternating automaton of the one for α and hence accepts the complementary language.

Q.E.D.

6 Remarks

There has been no mention of dense or continuous time in the previous sections, since the logics do not even satisfy basic density axioms, and there is no attempt to deal with limits. The philosopher of time will be disappointed to see how little of the structure of time, or of the nature of its metric topology, is needed to develop a usable logic of measurement.

Bojańczyk, David, Muscholl, Schwentick and Segoufin have abstracted the region construction further by considering the *marked projection* of a *data word* over D^{Σ} to C^{Σ}, where C is a collection of equivalence classes of D [5]. A *data automaton* works as a two-level process: a letter-to-letter *transducer* which outputs an equivalence class for each letter of the input (the marked projection of the data word), and a *class automaton* which works on this information to recognize the language. As might be expected, *data logics* are an abstraction of logics with duration where the structure of a duration domain is replaced by an equivalence relation.

References

[1] James F. Allen. Maintaining Knowledge about Temporal Intervals. *Communications of the Association for Computing Machinery*, 26(11):832–843, 1983.

[2] Rajeev Alur and David L. Dill. A Theory of Timed Automota. *Theoretical Computer Science*, 126(2):183–236, 1994.

[3] Rajeev Alur and Thomas A. Henzinger. Real-time Logics: Complexity and Expressiveness. *Information and Computation*, 104:390–401, 1993.

[4] Rajeev Alur, Tomás Feder, and Thomas A. Henzinger. The Benefits of Relaxing Punctuality. *Journal of the Association for Computing Machinery*, 43(1):116–146, 1996.

[5] Mikolaj Bojańczyk, Anca Muscholl, Thomas Schwentick, Luc Segoufin, and Claire David. Two-Variable Logic on Words with Data. In Lisa O'Conner, editor, *Proceedings of the 21st Annual IEEE Symposium on Logic in Computer Science*, pages 7–16. IEEE Computer Society, 2006.

[6] Davide Bresolin, Angelo Montanari, and Guido Sciavicco. An Optimal Decision Procedure for Right Propositional Neighborhood Logic. *Journal of Automated Reasoning*, 38(1-3):173–199, 2007.

[7] J. Richard Büchi. Weak Second-Order Arithmetic and Finite Automata. *Zeitschrift für Mathematische Logik und Grundlagen der Mathematik*, 6:66–92, 1960.

[8] Julius R. Büchi. On a Decision Method Inrestricted Second-Order Arithmetic. In Ernest Nagel, Patrick Suppes, and Alfred Tarski, editors, *Logic, Methodology, Philosophy and Science. Proceedings of the 1960 International Congress*, pages 1–11. Stanford University Press, 1962.

[9] John P. Burgess. Axioms for Tense Logic, I: "since" and "until", II: Time Periods. *Notre Dame Journal of Formal Logic*, 23(4):367–383, 1982.

[10] John P. Burgess. Basic Tense Logic. In Dov M. Gabbay and Franz Guenthner, editors, *Handbook of Philosophical Logic*, volume II, pages 8–133. D. Reidel, 1984.

[11] Zhou Chaochen, Charles A. R. Hoare, and Anders Ravn. A Calculus of Durations. *Information Processing Letters*, 40(5):269–276, 1991.

[12] Zhou Chaochen and Michael R. Hansen. *Duration Calculus*. Springer, 2004.

[13] Bruno Dutertre. Complete Proof Systems for First Order Interval Temporal Logic. In Dexter Kozen, editor, *Proceedings of the 10th Annual IEEE Symposium on Logic in Computer Science*, pages 36–43. IEEE Computer Society, 1995.

[14] Calvin C. Elgot. Decision Problems of Finite Automata Design and Related Arithmetics. *Transactions of the American Mathematical Society*, 98:21–52, 1961.

[15] Michael J. Fischer and Richard E. Ladner. Propositional Dynamic Logic of Regular Programs. *Journal of Computer and System Sciences*, 18(2):194–211, 1979.

[16] Dov M. Gabbay, Ian Hodkinson, and Mark A. Reynolds. *Temporal Logic: Mathematical Moundations and Computational Aspects*, volume 1. Oxford, 1994.

[17] Antony P. Galton. Time and Change for AI. In Dov M. Gabbay, Christopher J. Hogger, and John A. Robinson, editors, *Handbook of Logic in Artificial Intelligence and Logic Programming. Volume IV*, pages 175–240. Oxford, 1995.

[18] Joseph Y. Halpern and Yoav Shoham. A Propositional Modal Logic of Time Intervals. *Journal of the Association for Computing Machinery*, 38(4):935–962, 1991.

[19] Charles L. Hamblin. Starting and Stopping. *The Monist*, 53:410–425, 1969.

[20] David Harel, Dexter Kozen, and Jerzy Tiuryn. *Dynamic Logic*. MIT Press, 2000.

[21] Patrick J. Hayes. A Catalog of Temporal Theories. Technical Report UIUC-BI-AI-96-01, Beckman Institute, University of Illinois, 1996.

[22] Jesper G. Henriksen and P. S. Thiagarajan. Dynamic Linear Time Temporal Logic. *Annals of Pure and Applied Logic*, 96(1-3):187–207, 1999.

[23] Yoram Hirshfeld and Alexander Rabinovich. Timer Formulas and Decidable Metric Temporal Logic. *Information and Computation*, 198(2):148–178, 2005.

[24] Ian Hodkinson. Temporal Logic and Automata. In Dov M. Gabbay, Mark A. Reynolds, and Marcelo Finger, editors, *Temporal Logic: Mathematical Foundations and Computational aspects. Volume 2*, pages 30–72. Oxford, 2000.

[25] Johan A. W. Kamp. *Tense Logic and the Theory of Linear Order*. PhD thesis, University of California, Los Angeles, 1968.

[26] Ron Koymans. Specifying Real-Time Properties with Metric Temporal Logic. *Real-Time Systems*, 2(4):255–299, 1990.

[27] Slawomir Lasota and Igor Walukiewicz. Alternating Timed Automata. In Vladimiro Sassone, editor, *Proceedings on the Foundations of Software Science and Computation Structures*, volume 3441 of *Lecture Notes in Computer Science*, pages 250–265. Springer, 2005.

[28] Kamal Lodaya. Sharpening the Undecidability of Interval Temporal Logic. In Jifeng He and Masahiko Sato, editors, *Advances in Computing Science. ASIAN 2000. 6th Asian Computing Science Conference Penang, Malaysia, November 25–27, 2000 Proceedings*, volume 1961 of *Lecture Notes in Computer Science*, pages 290–298. Springer, 2000.

[29] Kamal Lodaya and Paritosh K. Pandya. A Dose of Timed Logic, in Guarded Measure. In Eugene Asarin and Patricia Bouyer, editors, *Formal Modeling and Analysis of Timed Systems*, volume 4202 of *Lecture Notes in Computer Science*, pages 260–273. Springer, 2006.

[30] Zohar Manna and Amir Pnueli. *The Temporal Logic of Reactive and Concurrent Systems: Specification.* Springer, 1992.

[31] Angelo Montanari and Maarten de Rijke. Two-Sorted Metric Temporal Logics. *Theoretical Computer Science*, 183(2):187–214, 1997.

[32] Ben C. Moszkowski and Zohar Manna. Reasoning in Interval Temporal Logic. In Edmund M. Clarke and Dexter Kozen, editors, *Proceedings in Logics of Programs*, volume 164 of *Lecture Notes in Computer Science*, pages 371–382, Pittsburgh, 1983. Springer.

[33] David E. Muller, Ahmed Saoudi, and Paul E. Schupp. Weak Alternating Automata Give a Simple Explanation of Why Most Temporal and Dyhamic Logics Are Decidable in Exponential Time. In Yuri Gurevich, editor, *Proceedings, Third Annual Symposium on Logic in Computer Science, 5-8 July 1988, Edinburgh, Scotland, UK*, pages 422–427. IEEE Computer Society, 1988.

[34] Joël Ouaknine and James Worrell. On the Decidability of Metric Temporal Logic. In Prakash Panangaden, editor, *20th IEEE Symposium on Logic in Computer Science (LICS 2005), 26-29 June 2005, Chicago, IL, USA, Proceedings*, pages 188–197. IEEE Computer Society, 2005.

[35] Paritosh K. Pandya. Interval Duration Logic: Expressiveness and Decidability. *Electronic Notes in Theoretical Computer Science*, 65(6), 2002.

[36] Richard L. Schwartz, Peter M. Melliar Smith, and Friedrich H. Vog. An Interval-Based Temporal Logic. In Edmund M. Clarke and Dexter Kozen, editors, *Proceedings in Logics of Programs*, volume 164 of *Lecture Notes in Computer Science*, pages 443–457, Pittsburgh, 1983. Springer.

[37] Boris A. Trakhtenbrot. Finite Automata and the Logic of Monadic Predicates. *Doklady Akademii Nauk*, 140:326–329, 1961.

[38] Valentin Goranko, Angelo Montanari, and Guido Sciavicco. A Road-map of Interval Temporal Logics and Duration Calculi. *Journal of Applied Non-Classical Logics*, 14(1–2):9–54, 2004.

[39] Johan F.A.K. van Benthem. *The Logic of Time.* Reidel, 1983.

[40] Johan F.A.K. van Benthem. Temporal Logic. In Dov M. Gabbay, Christopher J. Hogger, and John A. Robinson, editors, *Handbook of Logic in Artificial Intelligence and Logic Programming. Volume IV*, pages 241–350. Oxford, 1995.

[41] Moshe Y. Vardi. From Church and Prior to PSL. In Orna Grumberg and Helmut Veith, editors, *25 Years of Model Checking. History, Achievements, Perspectives*, volume 5000 of *Lecture Notes in Computer Sciences*, pages 150–171. Springer, 2006.

[42] Moshe Y. Vardi and Pierre Wolper. Reasoning about Infinite Computations. *Information and Computation*, 115(1):1–37, 1994.

[43] Yde Venema. Expressiveness and Completeness of an Interval Tense Logic. *Notre Dame Journal of Formal Logic*, 31(4):529–547, 1990.

[44] Marc B. Vilain. A System for Reasoning About Time. In David L. Waltz, editor, *Proceedings of the National Conference on Artificial Intelligence. Pittsburgh, PA, August 18-20, 1982*, pages 197–201. AAAI Press, 1982.

Sense data and *ākāra*

Shinya Moriyama*

Department of Philosophy, Shinshu University, 3-1-1, Asahi, Matsumoto, Nagano 390-8621, Japan

E-mail: smoriyam@shinshu-u.ac.jp

1 Introduction: A general survey

In this article I am going to compare two epistemological doctrines of two different traditions and periods, doctrines that concern immediate objects of perception and their relation to our common beliefs about material objects. The one is the doctrine of sense data that was propagated by twentieth century analytic philosophers such as Moore, Russell, Price and Ayer. The other is the doctrine of *ākāra* held by the Buddhist epistemologists and logicians Dignāga and Dharmakīrti of the fifth and seventh centuries, respectively. It is well known that the sense data doctrine has several variations, especially with respect to the ontological status of sense data: Some have argued that sense data are mind-dependent entities, while others consider them to be aspects or parts of material objects. The same controversy occurred in classical Indian epistemology with respect to *ākāra*: Some thinkers assumed *ākāra* to be mental, while others held it to belong to the external object. Here, however, I shall deal only with those theories that consider sense data and *ākāra* to be mind-dependent.[1]

Within these limits, one can further notice that the existence of *ākāra* and the existence of sense data are justified through similar arguments.[2] That sense data are different from physical objects is defended by arguments from illusion and hallucination. When one views a straight stick that is half

*I wish to thank John Taber (University of New Mexico), Birgit Kellner (University of Vienna), and Takashi Ikeda (University of Tokyo) for their valuable remarks and suggestions, and Cynthia Peck-Kubaczek for correcting my English. Research for this paper was carried out at the University of Vienna (Austria) within the project *The awareness of the mental in Buddhist philosophical analysis*, funded by the *Fonds zur Förderung der wissenschaftlichen Forschung* (P18758-G03), directed by Birgit Kellner.

[1]As a consequence, in the following I shall translate the term "*ākāra*" as "mental form." Although Dharmakīrti uses the term in two senses, that of *grāhakākāra* (the mental form of grasping, viz. its subjective form) and *grāhyākāra* (the mental form to be grasped, viz. its objective form) in the mind, the present article is mainly concerned with the latter concept. For a detailed study on the notion of *ākāra*, cf. [6, pp. 92–95]. On the basis of early Yogācāra literature, in his study he has translated the term as "phenomenological content" or "mode of appearance." Whether these translations can be used for *ākāra* in Dharmakīrti's texts is, however, still unclear.

[2]This summary is mainly based on Ayer [2, p. 94–104]. The argument from illusion used by sense-data philosophers has been sharply criticized by Austin [1]. For a more detailed survey on sense data, cf. [9].

Mihir K. **Chakraborty**, Benedikt **Löwe**, Madhabendra Nath **Mitra**, Sundar **Sarukkai** (*eds.*). Logic, Navya-Nyāya & Applications. Homage to Bimal Krishna Matilal. College Publications, London, 2008. Studies in Logic 15. pp. 205–216.

Received by the editors: 30 April 2007; 22 May 2008.
Accepted for publication: 20 August 2008.

submerged in water, the stick appears bent. In actual fact, however, the stick is not bent, and thus what we see is an illusion. In this case, one perceives something non-physical (a bent stick). Likewise, we experience hallucinations in which we perceive mental images that have no external objects causing them. The non-physical character of the immediate object of awareness occurring in these cases is then generalised for all cases of sense-perception: the true object of perception is a mental entity that appears directly; this is called a sense datum. Sense-data philosophers have aimed to base all empirical knowledge on such sense-data.

Similarly, in Dharmakīrti's system, *ākāra*, i.e., a mental form, is the immediate object of perception, especially when Dharmakīrti adopts the Sautrāntika position that presupposes the external world. In this position, we do not perceive external objects directly, but rather perceive them through the medium of their mental forms appearing in cognitions. In *Pramāṇavārttika* (*PV*) III 402-406,[3] Dharmakīrti notes that when a person whose vision has been damaged by the *timira*-disease sees light (*pradīpa*), he sees colourful circles (*maṇḍala*) resembling the eye in a peacock's tail. He does not perceive the external object (i.e., the light), but merely a mental form (i.e., circles). This observation is then generalized for all cases: all cognitions contain a mental form to be grasped (*grāhyākāra*) as its own nature.[4]

In spite of the similar reasoning to defend their existence, however, sense data and *ākāra* have different contextual backgrounds: Sense-datum philosophers have introduced the concept of indubitable sense data that justifies empirical knowledge to counter sceptical arguments that question the existence of material objects. In contrast, Dharmakīrti's theory of *ākāra* is not a reaction to sceptical arguments at all. Accordingly, although his discussions, based on the Sautrāntika ontology, relate to our common beliefs of external objects, one finds no attempt to securely ground these beliefs on

[3]According to Tosaki's analysis, this argument is the fifth argument for proving cognition's nature of having two forms, viz. *grāhakākāra* and *grāhyākāra*. In the above argument, Dharmakīrti aims to establish the existence of *grāhyākāra*, but pays no attention to *grāhakākāra*. Cf. [24, pp. 82–85].

[4]Because of these comparable characters, some modern scholars of Buddhism have referred to the doctrine of sense data or used it in their descriptions of the Buddhist theory of perception. Cf. [10, pp. 215–228], [11], [23, pp. 37–66], [4, Chapter 19], and [12]. Of these, [10, pp. 217*sq*] has examined whether the term *pratibhāsa* (appearance) can be considered equivalent to sense data, but rejects this idea, stating that an appearance in a conceptualized illusion "involves a judgment, an interpretation of the datum." However, his examination disregards non-conceptualized illusion as exemplified by the illusion of the net of hair seen by a sufferer of the *timira* eye disease. By its definition, this illusion is free of conceptual constructions (*kalpanā*), including judgments. Thus, as far as the nature of being free of conceptualization or interpretation is concerned, *ākāra* or the (non-conceptualized) appearance of an object in a cognition cannot be differentiated from a sense-datum.

the concept of *ākāra*. This does not necessarily mean, however, that Dharmakīrti was not confronted with similar problems concerning the relationship between internal and external objects. Specifically, while examining the means of valid cognition (*pramāṇa*) and its result (*phala*), he deals with the problem of how an *ākāra* in self-awareness (*svasaṃvedana*) relates to our common belief in external objects. The aim of this article is to examine how Dharmakīrti and his successors attempted to refute Kumārila's attack on Dignāga, viz. that in Dignāga's theory, means and result would incur the fallacy of having different objects (*bhinnārthatva/viṣayabheda*). This will help to clarify contextual distinctions between the theory of *ākāra* and the sense data theory.

2 The problem of *bhinnārthatva/viṣayabheda*

In his *Pramāṇasamuccaya* (*PS*) I 8cd-10, Dignāga presents a detailed examination of the relationship between the means of a valid cognition and its result[5] that entails three significant points which lead to Kumārila's later criticism: (1) the means of valid cognition and its result are identical, (2) not only the object-cognition, but also self-awareness is assumed to be the result, (3) a cognition's having a mental form corresponding to an external object is the means of valid cognition with respect to an external object. Based on these points, Kumārila raises the following problem in his *Ślokavārttika*:

> On the other hand, [the Buddhist claim] that self-awareness is the result is not correct, because this [self-awareness] will be refuted [later[6]]. It is also not correct because if the means of valid cognition is the object-form (*viṣayākāra*) [of the cognition], then [the means of valid cognition and self-awareness] have different objects (*bhinnārthatva*).[7]

According to the commentator Sucarita Miśra, this verse aims to refute the Sautrāntika position that is expressed in *PS* I 9.[8] Although Dignāga's

[5]Cf. [7, pp. 28*sq* & 97–107].

[6]In *ŚV śūnyavāda*, Kumārila refutes Dignāga's theory of self-awareness.

[7]Cf. *ŚV* pratyakṣa 79: *svasaṃvittiphalatvaṃ tu tanniṣedhān na yujyate/ pramāṇe viṣayākāre bhinnārthatvān na yujyate //*

The above translation is based on Taber [21, p. 81]. For the background of the verse, cf. [21, pp. 80–81 & 194–196, fn. 86]. Cf. also *TSP* 1350cd.

[8]Cf. *Kāś* 237.18-25. Here, Sucarita Miśra quotes *PS* I 9 with a different word order and some variants: *viṣayākāra evāsya pramāṇaṃ tena mīyate / svasaṃvittiḥ phalaṃ cātra tadrūpo hy arthaniścayaḥ //*

In this case, *pramāṇa* and *phala* are clearly identical with *viṣayākāra* and *svasaṃvitti*, respectively. *PS* I 9 originally reads as follows: *svasaṃvittiḥ phalaṃ vātra tadrūpo hy arthaniścayaḥ // viṣayākārataivāsya pramāṇaṃ tena mīyate //*

verse and its auto-commentary can be interpreted in another manner, according to Kumārila and his followers, the verse proposes the following schema:

model	prameya	pramāṇa	phala
Dignāga's model	*(bahirartha)*	*viṣayākāra/(-tā)*	*svasaṃvitti*

Since self-awareness is the cognition of a cognition itself, it does not relate to an external object. A means of valid cognition, on the other hand, does relate to an external object. Means and result are therefore concerned, respectively, with two different objects, despite Dignāga's assertion that they are identical. This is the problem of *bhinnārthatva*, as Kumārila points out. When examined closely, the problem actually arises from the dual function of mental forms, which, on one hand, causally depend on external objects, but on the other hand, appear within the mind, according to the *svasaṃvedana* doctrine, being intrinsically aware of itself. If one emphasizes that a mental form depends causally on an external object, an additional explanation is required for the necessity of self-awareness that does not relate to external objects; if one maintains the theory of self-awareness, the means of accessing external objects is closed. Buddhist epistemologists are now in a dilemma between these two alternatives.

3 The causal connection of self-awareness with object-cognition

To solve this problem, Dharmakīrti presents a logical way to connect self-awareness with object-cognition (*arthavid*). Commenting on *PS* I 9cd, he first clarifies the point of Dignāga's argument: even if one accepts an external object to be the object of valid cognition (*prameya*), the experience of the cognition itself (*svānubhava*), viz. self-awareness, is the result of the means of valid cognition. Unlike in Yogācāra idealism, according to which the subjective form in cognition (*grāhakākāra*) is accepted as the means of valid cognition, in this case, something that relates to an external object must be the means of valid cognition, viz. the cognition having the appearance of the object (*arthābhāsatā*).[9] Now a question arises about the

"Alternatively, self-awareness is here the result; for the determination of an [external] object has the nature of this [self-awareness]. The means of valid cognition for this [object] is exactly [cognition's] having the form of an [external] object. [The object] is cognized by means of this [cognition's having the form of an external object]." According to the *Vṛtti*, only the last half of the verse presupposes external objects, and it is unclear which result the means of valid cognition will cause. Thus, it is difficult to say that the entire verse is based on the Sautrāntika ontology. Cf. [7, pp. 28*sq* & 100–106].

[9]Cf. *PV* III 346: *tadārthābhāsataivāsya pramāṇaṃ na tu sann api / grāhakātmā 'parārthatvād bāhyeṣv artheṣv apekṣyate //*

relationship between three items, viz. (1) cognition having the mental form of the object, (2) self-awareness, and (3) object-cognition. This point is addressed in *PV* III 347-350, which Dharmakīrti describes as the consideration of [a cognition's] own nature (*svabhāvacintā*)[10] :

> [The means of valid cognition is *arthābhāsatā*] because, just like this nature of the object (*arthātman*, i.e., the mental form of the object[11]) that has entered (*niviṣṭa*) into a cognition, so is [the object] ascertained from self-awareness (*ātmasaṃvid*) [in the form] that this [object that] has entered [into a cognition] is such. (v. 347) Thus, precisely this [self-awareness] is accepted as object-cognition (*arthasaṃvid*), since the object itself (*arthātman*, i.e., an external object) is not perceived [directly]. The object [-form] that has entered into a cognition is the means for accomplishing (*sādhana*) this [self-awareness], [and] this [self-awareness] is the action (*kriyā*) for this [*sādhana*], (v. 348) because that [self-awareness] appears in the manner in which that [external] object enters [the cognition]. Since the determination of [external] objects (*arthasthiti*) has self-awareness (*svavid*) as [its] nature, [the result] is [generally] accepted to be "object-cognition" (*arthavid*), even though [it] is [actually] self-awareness.(v. 349) Therefore, there is also no *viṣayabheda*. (v. 350a)[12]

Under the premise that one cannot perceive external objects directly, Dharmakīrti elaborates the arising process of perception in the following sequence: (I) the entry of the mental form of an external object into a cognition, (II) the accomplishment of the action of the self-awareness by means of this mental form, and (III) the determination of the external object in accordance with the self-awareness. In this process, the self-awareness plays the role for converting a datum given by an external object to an element that forms our determination of the object, the source of our everyday

"In this case, its (i.e., a cognition's) having the appearance of the object is the means of valid cognition. However, even though the nature of the subjective form exists, [it] does not depend on external objects, since [it] does not have other things [other than *grāhyākāra*] as [its] objects." Cf. [24, p. 31].

[10] *PV* III 350bcd: *svasaṃvedanaṃ phalam / uktaṃ svabhāvacintāyāṃ tādātmyād arthasaṃvidaḥ //*

"In the consideration of [a cognition's] own nature (*svabhāvacintā*), [Dignāga] claimed that self-awareness is the result because object-cognition has this [self-awareness] as [its] nature."

[11] Cf. *PVV* 223.19: ... *vārthasyātmākāra* ... ; *PVP* (D 225a1) : *don bdag nyid don gyi rnam pa'o //*. The same usage of the term arthātman is also found in *PV* III 267a: *arthātmā svātmabhūto*

[12] *PV* III 347-350a: *yasmād yathā niviṣṭo 'sāv arthātmā pratyaye tathā / niścīyate niviṣṭo 'sāv evam ity ātmasaṃvidaḥ //347// ity arthasaṃvit saiveṣṭā yato 'rthātmā na dṛśyate / tasyā buddhiniveśyarthaḥ sādhanaṃ tasya sā kriyā //348// yathā niviśate so 'rthaḥ yataḥ sā prathate tathā / arthasthites tadātmatvāt svavid apy arthavin matā //349// tasmād viṣayabhedo 'pi na*

activity. From the viewpoint of the determination, retrospectively, the self-awareness is conceived to be identical with the object-cognition.

This connection that the determination of an external object presupposes self-awareness, is more clearly presented in a parallel passage in Dharmakīrti's *PVin* I, which contains the additional condition "from the viewpoint of the result" (*kāryatas*).[13] Using this framework, while commenting on *PS* I 9d and its *Vṛtti*, Jinendrabuddhi, a follower of the Dharmakīrti tradition, clarifies the connection as follows:

> [The purpose of Dignāga's statement is that an external object is cognized by means of this *viṣayākāratā*.] For this self-awareness causes the determination of [the external] object (*arthaniścaya*), which is the result of the object-cognition (*arthasaṃvid*). Therefore, [as Dharmakīrti has stated, this self-awareness] should be seen [here], from the viewpoint of the result, as the object-cognition itself — metaphorically. In order to bring out this meaning, [*PS* I 9d and its *Vṛtti*] are stated in this way [by Dignāga]. For, in this manner, there is no *viṣayabheda* between the means of valid cognition and [its] result...[14]

In this account, Jinendrabuddhi distinguishes the object-cognition (*arthasaṃvid*) from the determination of an external object (*arthaniścaya*) and explains that the latter is a common result of both object-cognition and self-awareness. From this viewpoint of the result, its two causes, viz. self-awareness and object-cognition, cannot be distinguished from one another. Therefore, one can understand the term "object-awareness" to be a metaphor for self-awareness. On such a metaphorical level, the means of valid cognition, viz. cognition having the mental form of an external object, and its result, object-cognition, are both related to an external object, and thus, the fallacy of *viṣayabheda* is avoided.[15]

---

[13] *PVin* I 37.4-6: *arthasthiteḥ svasaṃvedanarūpatvāt svavid apīyam arthavid eva kāryato draṣṭavyā.* "Because the determination of an external object has self-awareness as its nature, even if this [cognition as the result] is self-awareness, from the viewpoint of the result, [it] should be considered to be nothing but the object-cognition."

[14] *PSṬ* 73.5-8: *sā hi svasaṃvit, arthasaṃvido yat kāryam arthaniścayaḥ, tat karoti. ata upacāreṇārthasaṃvid eva kāryato draṣṭavyety amum arthaṃ sūcayitum evam uktam. evaṃ hi pramāṇaphalayor viṣayabhedo na bhavati ...* The underlined phrase is a citation of *PVin* I 37.6.

[15] The view that self-awareness is causally connected to the determination of an external object is also applied in Kamalaśīla's commentary on TS 1351cd, where he asserts "object-cognition" (*arthasaṃvitti*) to be the result of self-awareness (*tatkāryatva*). Cf. *TSP* 490.23f.: *nāpi bhinnaviṣayatvaprasaṅgo yuktaḥ, yataḥ svasaṃvittir apy arthasaṃvittir iṣṭā, tatkāryatvāt, na tu tanmayatvena. svasaṃvittes* (em. : *-vittis* ed.) *tu tādrūpyād iti na virodhaḥ.* "The undesirable consequence that [the means of valid cognition and the result] have different objects (*bhinnaviṣayatva*) is also not correct, because the self-awareness [as the result] is also accepted as the object-cognition. [This is] because [object-cognition] is the result of this [self-awareness] (*tatkāryatva*), but not because [object-cognition] consists of this [self-cognition] (*tanmayatva*). However, [to say] 'because the

model	*prameya*	*pramāṇa*	*phala*	*phalaphala*
Jinendrabuddhi's model	*(bahirartha)*	*viṣayākāratā*	*svasaṃvid (=arthasaṃvid)*	*arthaniścaya*

To a certain extent, this causal relationship between self-awareness and object-determination is comparable with the type of sense data theory which assumes that sense data provide our only access to external material objects. This access is explained in two ways: representationalism asserts that material objects are causally connected to sense data, and hence one can infer them from sense data that represent material objects. Phenomenalism, on the other hand, insists that a material object is constructed by these sense data. On the surface, both arguments are applicable to Dharmakīrti's discussion;[16] yet there is an important difference. Unlike sense data, which function only in order to secure the foundation of empirical knowledge, *ākāra* in Dharmakīrti's system is closely related to the theory of self-awareness. According to Dharmakīrti, self-awareness serves to generate our ascertainment of external objects; alternatively, self-awareness distinguishes itself from this ascertainment of external objects. Of these two alternatives, for Dharmakīrti the latter is more important for establishing his final position, Yogācāra idealism.

4 Idealistic interpretation

Still another approach to the problem of *viṣayabheda* reflects this idealistic point of view. Instead of proposing a causal relation between self-awareness and object-cognition, Prajñākaragupta, a commentator on the PV, distinguishes sharply between the two by using the theory of two truths: object-cognition on the conventional level, and self-awareness on the ultimate level. In this manner, in contrast to the causal account that unifies the two possible results by force, Prajñākaragupta aims to separate them from one another in order to make two different *pramāṇa-phala* relationships at two different levels clear. After having introduced the objection concerning *viṣayabheda*,[17] he comments on *PV* III 349 as follows:

self-awareness has the nature of this [object-cognition]' is not contradictory [to the above explanation]"

[16]For instance, commenting on the term *niścīyate* in 347c, Devendrabuddhi glosses it as "inferred" (*rjes su dpog par 'gyur ro*). If one follows this interpretation, what is meant by the verse is similar to the account of representationalism, in which an external object can be inferred from the mental form that is caused by that object.

[17]Cf. *PVABh* 394.17f.: *evaṃ tarhi bāhye 'rthe pramāṇam ākāraḥ, saṃvedanaṃ tu svarūpe phalaṃ pravṛttam iti viṣayabhedaḥ.* "Then, in this manner, the mental form is the means of valid cognition with respect to an external object; yet self-awareness occurs as the result with respect to [cognition's] own nature. Thus, there is [the fallacy of] *viṣayabheda*."

> Ultimately (*paramāthatas*),[18] this [cognition] is self-awareness, and conventionally (*vyavahāratas*) [it is] object-cognition. Therefore, regarding everyday activity, the result [occurs] only with respect to an [external] object (*artha*), and the means of valid cognition [occurs] only with respect to [the same external] object. Therefore, how [could] *viṣayabheda* [occur]? Also regarding the ultimate [perception], the two (i.e., the result and the means of valid cognition) [occur] with respect to the own nature (*svarūpa*) [of cognition, and here there is also no *viṣayabheda*].[19]

A strong emphasis on the difference between an external object (*artha*) and the cognition's own nature (*svarūpa*) constitutes one essential feature of Prajñākaragupta's commentary on *PV* III. For instance, commenting on *PV* III 287, he distinguishes between the two concepts from the viewpoint of their different relationships to the definition of perception: cognition's own nature, which has a clear form (*spaṣṭākāra*), becomes the object of the cognition free of conceptualization (*nirvikalpaka*) and without error (*abhrānta*); the external object, which has an unclear form, on the other hand, relates to the cognition with conceptualization and error.[20] Whereas the former is concerned with self-awareness, the ultimate perception, the latter is concerned with object-cognition, conventional perception, for such an object-cognition presupposes the conceptualization of an external object that differs from cognition's own nature.[21] On the basis of the same kind of distinction, Prajñākaragupta constructs his interpretation of *PV* III 347-350, including the above argument, in which we can find his consistent rejection of any causal relationship between self-awareness and object-cognition.[22] According to his interpretation, before we reach the idealistic understanding that only the self-awareness of a cognition's own nature is

[18] Devendrabuddhi and Manorathanandin also use the concept of *paramārtha* in this context. Cf. *PVP* (D 225a6f): *don dam par 'dir* ***rang rigs yin na yang*** */ 'on kyang cha 'di tsam gyis nye bar btags nas /* ***don rig 'dod****/.* *PVV* 224.6f.: *paramārthataḥ* ***svavid api*** *satī* ***arthavid matā****. svasaṃvedanam evārthavedanam upacārād ucyata iti tādātmyam anayoḥ.*

[19] Cf. *PVABh* 394.22f.: *svavid eveyaṃ paramārthataḥ. vyavahārato 'rthavit. tato vyavahārāpekṣayārtha eva phalam, artha eva pramāṇam iti kuto viṣayabhedaḥ. paramārthāpekṣayāpi svarūpe dvayam api.*

[20] Cf. *PVABh* 331.13f.: *svarūpaṃ tad eva spaṣṭākāram, arthas tu na tathā. tataḥ svarūpe tan nirvikalpakam, arthe tat savikalpakam iti ... svarūpe tad abhrāntam, arthe bhrāntam iti...*

[21] On the basis of this distinction, Prajñākaragupta insists that the two qualifiers in the definition of perception, viz. being free of conceptualization and non-erroneous, indicate the same contents. Cf. *PVABh* 252.29-253.2. For Prajñākaragupta's interpretation of the qualifier *abhrānta* and its theoretical background, including its relation to *artha* and *svarūpa*, cf. [13].

[22] For this reason, Prajñākaragupta's interpretation of *PV* III 347-348ab contains a crucial difference from other commentators' interpretations. Unlike other commentators, he does not construe *ātmasaṃvidaḥ* in 347d with the previous phrase *niviṣṭo 'sāv evam*

real, there is no room for self-awareness in everyday cognition.[23] Only after we understand this ultimate reality can we realize that something we wrongly thought to be object-cognition concerning an external object was nothing but self-awareness concerning cognition's own nature. In this manner, by disconnecting self-awareness from external objects, the fallacy of *viṣayabheda* is avoided.

model	*prameya*	*pramāṇa*	*phala*
Prajñākaragupta's model	*bahirartha* *(jñāna)svarūpa*	*(viṣayākāratā)* *(grāhakākāra)*	*arthasaṃvid* *svasaṃvid*

5 Conclusion

Modern analytical philosophers and Buddhist *pramāṇa* theories attempt to bridge the gap between internal and external objects, that is, between sense data and material objects, or *jñānākāra* and *bāhyārtha*, albeit in different contexts. For modern Cartesian philosophers, this problem is closely connected to their common project of the foundation of empirical knowledge. Whether they adopt representationalism or phenomenalism, indubitable sense data are considered to be a starting point for justifying our common belief in the existence of the material world. In ancient India, on

ity, but with the following verse. Therefore, in contrast to 347abc, in which the determination of an external object through its mental form is explained, 347d-348ab are interpreted as showing self-awareness as the result of perception. Cf. *PVABh* 394.15: *tasmāt svarūpapratyakṣatvād arthasyāsaṃvedanāt svasaṃvedanaṃ phalam.* According to this interpretation, these verses could be translated as follows: "[The means of valid cognition is *arthābhāsatā*] because [an external object] is determined (i.e., conceptualized, cf. *PVABh* 394.9: *arthakalpanā*) [in the form:] 'This has entered in this manner,' just as this nature of the object (i.e., the mental form of the object), which has entered into a cognition. [However, ultimately, self-awareness is the result of perception] because [cognition's] own nature is cognized (*ātmasaṃvidaḥ*). Thus, only this [self-awareness] is accepted as object-cognition since the object itself is not perceived directly."

[23]In the recent article [22], J. Tanizawa has pointed out a tendency towards a kind of direct realism in Dharmakīrti's theory of perception in his distinguishing between two phases of perception: perception of an external object in the first phase and self-awareness in the second phase. If one applies this idea to Prajñākaragupta's above interpretation, the first phase corresponds to the conventional level, and the second, to the ultimate level. If one accepts this division, it must be explained how one perceives an external objects without introducing self-awareness. In this regard, Bhāviveka's *MHK* V 25-26 provides us an example that explains perception purely by means of *arthābhāsatā*: *bibhratā jāyamānena jñānena viṣayābhatām / pramīyate prameyaṃ yat pramāṇaṃ tena tan matam //25// tannirvṛttau ca dṛṣṭatvāt tannirvṛttiḥ phalaṃ matam / anidarśanarūpasya tathaivādhigamo yataḥ //26//*

"An object is cognized by a cognition that arises bearing object-form. Therefore, this [cognition] is accepted as a means of valid cognition. And since [the object] is seen [at the moment] when this [cognition] is accomplished, its accomplishment is accepted to be the result, since an inexpressible nature is apprehended in just this manner." For these verses, see [8, p. 110] and [14] the other hand, Dharmakīrti dealt with a similar problem in the context of defending Dignāga's doctrines of self-awareness and the non-difference between the means of valid cognition and its result. In replying to Kumārila's criticism, which points out the fallacy of *viṣayabheda*, Dharmakīrti explains that self-awareness, which is the result of perceiving an external object through its mental form, causally relates to the cognition of an external object. In this causal explanation, the object-determination that is caused by self-awareness leads us to everyday activities concerning external objects, which are to be appropriated or to be abandoned. However, unlike sense data, which become the basis of empirical knowledge, *ākāra*, i.e., the mental form, cannot alone take on such a role. It is only in combination with self-awareness that mental form can be considered significant for producing the determination of an external object. Moreover, as we have seen in Prajñākaragupta's interpretation, self-awareness is firmly embedded in Yogācāra idealism, where the dichotomy of the internal/external object no longer plays a role. Through philosophical investigation and religious practice of mind, Buddhist *pramāṇa* theorists aimed to reach the state of Mind-only. Therefore, they do not satisfy themselves with sense data, but rather proclaim that self-awareness is the goal to be attained over and above our empirical knowledge.

Primary Sources

Kāś. = Sucarita Miśra, *Kāśikā*, in: [17].

TSP. = Kamalaśīla, *Tattvasaṅgrahapañjikā*, in: [18].

PV III. = Dharmakīrti, *Pramāṇavārttika*, in: [24, Chapter III].

PVABh. = Prajñākaragupta, *Pramāṇavārttikālaṅkārabhāṣya*, in: [15].

PVP. = Devendrabuddhi, **Pramāṇavārttikapañjikā*, *Tshad ma rnam 'grel gyi 'grel pa*, in: [3].

PVV. = Manorathanandin, *Pramāṇavārttikavṛtti*, in: [16].

PVin I. = Dharmakīrti, *Pramāṇaviniścaya*, in: [20, Chapter I] (*pratyakṣa*).

PS. = Dignāga, *Pramāṇasamuccaya (-vṛtti)*, in: [7, Chapter I].

PSṬ. = Jinendrabuddhi, *Pramāṇasamuccayaṭīkā*, in: [19].

MHK V. = Bhāviveka, *Madhyamakahṛdayakārikā* (Chapter V), in: [5].

ŚV. = Kumārila, *Ślokavārttika*, chapter on *pratyakṣa*, in: [21].

References

[1] John L. Austin. *Sense and Sensibilia.* Oxford University Press, London, 1962.

[2] Alfred J. Ayer. *The Problem of Knowledge.* Saint Martin's Press, New York, 1956.

[3] Devendrabuddhi. *Pramāṇavārttikapañjikā.* In Jikido Takasaki, Yasunori Ejima, and Zuihō Yamaguchi, editors, *sDe dge Tibetan Tripiṭaka bsTan 'gyur.* Faculty of Letters, University of Tokyo, Tokyo, 1981. no. 4217, Che 1b1-326b4.

[4] George B. J. Dreyfus. *Recognizing Reality: Dharmakīrti's Philosophy and Its Tibetan Interpretations.* SUNY Press, Albany, 1997.

[5] Yasunori Ejima, editor. *Madhyamakahṛdayakārikā V: Yogācāratattvaviniścayapariccheda of Bhāviveka.* Unpublished.

[6] Paul J. Griffiths. Omniscience in the *Mahāyānasūtrālaṅkāra* and Its Commentaries. *Indo-Iranian Journal,* 33-2:85 120, 1990.

[7] Masaaki Hattori. *Dignāga, On Perception.* Harvard University Press, Cambridge, Massachusetts, 1968.

[8] Paul Hoornaert. An Annotated Translation of *Madhyamakahṛdayakārikā / Tarkajvālā* V. 8-26. *Kanazawadaigaku Bungakubu Ronsyū Kōdōkagaku Tetsugaku-hen,* 20:75–111, 2000.

[9] Michael Huemer. Sense Data. In Edward N. Zalta, editor, *The Stanford Encyclopedia of Philosophy (Summer 2004 Edition).* CSLI, 2004.

[10] Bimal Krishna Matilal. *Logic, Language and Reality: Indian Philosophy and Contemporary Issues.* Motilal Banarsidass, Delhi, 1985.

[11] Bimal Krishna Matilal. *Perception: An Essay on Classical Indian Theories of Knowledge.* Clarendon Press, Oxford, 1986.

[12] Sara L. McClintock. The Role of the 'Given' in the Classification of śāntarakṣita and Kamalaśīla as Svātantrika-Mādhyamikas. In George B. J. Dreyfus and Sara L. McClintock, editors, *The Svātantrika-Prāsaṅgika Distinction,* pages 125–172. Wisdom Publications, Boston, 2003.

[13] Shinya Moriyama. Non-Erroneous Cognition and Direct Awareness. *Indogaku Bukkyōgaku Kenkyū,* 50(2):1001–999, 2002.

[14] Akira Saito. Bhāviveka no shiki-nibun-setsu-hihan. *Indogaku Bukkyōgaku Kenkyū*, 56(2):903–897, 2002.

[15] R. Sāṅkṛtyāyana, editor. *Pramāṇavārttikabhāṣyam or Vārttikālaṅkāraḥ of Prajñākaragupta.* Kashi Prasad Jayaswal Research Institute, Patna, 1953.

[16] Rahula Sāṅkṛtyāyana. Dharmakīrti's Pramāṇavārttika with a commentary by Manorathanandin. *Journal of the Bihar and Orissa Research Society*, 24–26 (Appendix), 1938–1940.

[17] K. Sāṁbāśiva Sāstrī, editor. *Mīmāṁsā Ślokavārttika with the Commentary Kasika of Sucaritamiśra.* CBH Publications, Trivandrum, 1990.

[18] S. D. Shastri, editor. *Tattvasaṅgraha of Ācārya Shāntarakṣita with the Commentary 'Pañjikā'*, volume 1. Bauddha Bharati, Varanasi, 1981.

[19] Ernst Steinkellner, editor. *Jinendrabuddhi's Viśālāmalavatī Pramāṇasamuccayaṭīkā, Chapter 1, Part I: Critical Edition.* China Tibetology Publishing House, Austrian Academy of Science Press, Beijing & Vienna, 2005.

[20] Ernst Steinkellner, editor. *Dharmakīrti's Pramāṇaviniścaya Chapter 1 and 2.* China Tibetology Publishing House, Austrian Academy of Science Press, Beijing & Vienna, 2007.

[21] John Taber. *A Hindu Critique of Buddhist Epistemology.* Routledge-Curzon, London, New York, 2005.

[22] Junzo Tanizawa. Dharmakīrti ni miru bukkyō ronrigakuha no chikakuron no chokusetsujitsuzaironteki keikō. *Indotetsugaku Bukkyōgaku Kenkyū*, 9:17–28, 2002.

[23] Tom J. F. Tillemans. *Materials for the Study of Āryadeva, Dharmapāla and Candrakīrti.* Arbeitskreis für tibetische und buddhistische Studien. Universität Wien, Wien, 1990.

[24] Hiromasa Tosaki. *Bukkyō ninshikiron no kenkyū.* Daitō shuppansha, Tokyo, 1979.

Kauṇḍabhaṭṭa on the *śakyatāvacchedaka* of a meaning of a verb ending

Hideyo Ogawa*

Graduate School of Letters, Hiroshima University, 1-2-3 Kagamiyama, Higashi-Hiroshima 739-8522, Japan

E-mail: hogawa@hiroshima-u.ac.jp

0

In his Editor's Introduction to [13], Daniel H. H. Ingalls said:

> Navya-Nyāya ("The New Method", "The New Logic") exerted for many centuries a profound influence on Indian thought. In metaphysics and epistemology it challenged other schools; its benefits to others in these fields lay in its forcing them to organize their views rationally and systematically in order to oppose the newcomer. Navya-Nyaya logic, on the other hand, being found unassailable, was taken over by others, so that one finds Mīmāṃsakas and Vedāntins coming to use Navya-Nyāya logic even in their diatribes against the Nyāya school. Thus the scholar who would gain a thorough understanding of any school of Indian philosophy since the time of Udayana (eleventh century), or at the very least since the time of Gaṅgeśa, must concern himself with Navya-Nyāya, especially with its logic.

Navya-Nyāya logic was taken over by Pāṇinīyas also. Without a full knowledge of it, Pāṇinian scholars also could not fully understand the Pāṇinian semantics developed by Kauṇḍabhaṭṭa (c. 1610–60) and that developed by Nāgeśa (who flourished between the latter half of the seventeenth century and the first half of the eighteenth century).

In Navya-Nyāya, the reason for using a particular word to denote some object, *bhāva*[1] or *pravṛttinimitta*, is termed *śakyatāvacchedaka* "the limiting property of the denotation' or 'the limitor of the property of being the

*My special thanks are due to Brendan S. Gillon for reading the draft and making a number of helpful suggestions. Professor Bimal Krishna Matilal delivered a lecture on Navya-Nyāya in Hiroshima in 1984. I had the good fortune to attend the lecture. He used as a textbook Mm Maheśa Candra Nyāyaratna's *Brief Notes on the Modern Nyāya System of Philosophy and Its Technical Terms*.

[1]This *bhāva* is the one which forms the meaning condition to introduce *bhāvapratyayas*, mentioned in *A* 5.1.119 *tasya bhāvas tvatalau*. The term *bhāva* means "that by which a word occurs" (*bhavaty aneneti bhāvaḥ*), so that it is synonymous with the term *pravṛttinimitta* "the cause for the occurrence of the word". Cf. [16]. It may be said that the discovery of *pravṛttinimitta* is an epoch-making contribution to the development of Sanskriti semantics.

Mihir K. **Chakraborty**, Benedikt **Löwe**, Madhabendra Nath **Mitra**, Sundar **Sarukkai** (*eds.*). Logic, Navya-Nyāya & Applications. Homage to Bimal Krishna Matilal. College Publications, London, 2008. Studies in Logic 15. pp. 217–234.

Received by the editors: 29 April 2007; 6 June 2008.
Accepted for publication: 20 August 2008.

denotatum (*śakya*)". When it is said: *ghaṭaḥ ghaṭapadaśakyaḥ* "A pot is the denotatum or denotation (*śakya*) of the word *pot*", the Nyāya will restate this utterance as *ghaṭapadaṃ ghaṭatvāvacchinne śakyam* "The word *pot* denotes what is delimited by the property pot-ness". In this case, the pot-ness is described as the delimiting property of what is *śakya*, or the limitor of the property of being a *śakya* (*śakyatāvacchedaka*).[2] Of course, the concept of *śakyatāvacchedaka* is used by later Pāṇinīyas such as Kauṇḍabhaṭṭa to elaborate their theory of semantics.

Now, commenting on *VM* 2, in which Bhaṭṭoji Dīkṣita states that a verb ending (*tiṅ*, *ākhyāta*) denotes the locus (*āśraya*) of an activity (*vyāpāra*) and the locus of the result (*phala*) of the activity, Kauṇḍabhaṭṭa says that the *śakyatāvacchedaka* of the meaning of the verb ending is *āśrayatva* or locusness. Yet he also says, interestingly enough, that this *śakyatāvacchedaka* is essentially identical with the power (*śakti*) to bring an action to accomplishment.[3] The aim of this paper is thus to consider what leads him to bring in

[2]Cf. [13, pp. 26–27]. By using the expression *ghaṭapadaṃ ghaṭatvāvacchinne śakyam*, Matilal tried to explain the concept of *śakyatāvacchedaka*. I have just followed his explanation. But I think it would be better for this purpose to use expressions such as the following: *ghaṭapadaṃ ghaṭatvāvacchinne śaktam*; *ghaṭapadasya ghaṭatvāvacchinne śaktiḥ*; *ghaṭatvāvacchinnaḥ ghaṭapadaśakyaḥ*; *ghaṭatvāvacchinne ghaṭapadasya śakyatā*. Cf. Footnote 3.

[3]The term *śakti* means simply "power, capacity". In the theory of meaning, however, it is used more specifically in the sense of the power or capacity inherent in a word to signify its meaning (*vācakaśakti*) or in the sense of the power or capacity inherent in a meaning to be signified (*vācyaśakti*); accordingly, on the basis of the use of the verb *śak* "be able, be capable" as in the utterances *ayaṃ śabda imam arthaṃ vaktuṃ śaktaḥ* "This word is capable of conveying this meaning" and *ayam artho 'nena śabdena vaktuṃ śakyaḥ* "This meaning is capable of being conveyed by this word", the meaning which can be signified (*vācya*) by a word is called simply *śakya* (*śak-yat*; *A* 3.1.99) and the word which can signify its meaning is called simply *śakta* (*śak-kta*; *A* 3.2.188, *A* 3.4.72).

The relation (*sambandha*) between word and meaning, moreover, is referred to as *śakti* precisely because it is viewed as holding between what can signify and what can be signified. This *śakti* relation is a composite of the property of being what can signify (*śaktatā*) and the property of being what can be signified (*śakyatā*), so that it can be held that the meaning relation resides in a word as the relational abstract signifier-ness (*śaktatā*) and that it resides in a meaning as the relational abstract significand-ness (*śakyatā*). We should notice that a relation resides in its relata (*sambandhin*). To use Bhartṛhari's term, it is *dviṣṭha* "resident in two" (*VP* 3.7.157). We may say, therefore, the following both: the word *pot* is related to the meaning pot by the relation of *śakti* in the form of the relational abstract significand-ness; the meaning pot is related to the word *pot* by the relation of *śakti* in the form of the relational abstract signifier-ness. Cf. [8, pp. 108–114] and [9, pp. 34–50] for a full account of the *śakti* as a meaning relation.

It is to be noted in passing that according to Kauṇḍabhaṭṭa the power inherent in a word to signify its meaning is *bodhakatā* "the property of being what produces the cognition of a given meaning", that is, the power to produce the cognition of a given meaning. *VBhS* on *VM* 2: *tiṅaḥ iti / bodhakatārūpā śaktis tiṅkṣv evety abhipretyedam /* Needless to say, the power inherent in a meaning to be signified by the word may be said to be *bodhyatā* "the property of being what is to be cognized through a word", that is, the power to be cognized through a word.

the concept of power here. What lies behind its introduction here will be shown to be a question concerning the ontological status of *āśrayatva* and Pāṇinīyas' kāraka theory.[4]

1

The second kārikā of the *Vaiyākaraṇamatonmajjana* runs as follows:

> The grammatical tradition declares that a verb (*dhātu*) denotes both an activity and its result, whereas verb endings denote the locus [of the activity] and the locus [of the result of the activity]. The activity is a chief meaning relative to its result, whereas the meaning of the verb endings is a qualifier of the activity.[5]

Pāṇinīyas, like Navya-naiyāyikas, interpret sentences in terms of qualifiers and qualificands (*viśeṣaṇa, viśeṣya*) in a verbal cognition (*śābdabodha*) rendered by a paraphrase (*vivaraṇa*). What Bhaṭṭoji Dīkṣita means to say is lucidly explained by showing the paraphrases which convey the verbal cognitions from the utterances *taṇḍulaṃ pacati caitraḥ* "Caitra is cooking rice" and *taṇḍulaḥ pacyate caitreṇa* "Rice is being cooked by Caitra". The utterances are respectively paraphrased as conveying the following:

> A. *ekataṇḍulāśrayikā yā viklittis tadanukūlaikacaitrābhinnāśrayikā vartamānakālikī bhāvanā /*
>
> "There is an action[6] which leads to the softening located in a single locus, rice; which has a single locus, Caitra; and which occurs at present".
>
> B. *ekacaitrāśrayikā ekataṇḍulābhinnāśrayikā yā viklittis tadanukūlā sāṃpratikī bhāvanā /*
>
> "There is an action which is located in a single agent, Caitra; which leads to the softening located in a single locus, rice; and which occurs at present".[7]

---

[4]There is considerable controversy between Pāṇinīyas and Naiyāyikas as to what the meaning of a verb ending is. According to Naiyāyikas, a verb ending such as *-ti* in *pacati* "... is cooking" denotes an internal, conscious effort (*yatna, kṛti*) and a verb ending such as *-te* in *pacyate* "... is being cooked" denotes a result of an activity such as softening (*viklitti*). If the meaning effort is ascribed to the verb ending *-ti*, the *śakyatāvacchedaka* is the property effort-ness (*yatnatva, kṛtitva*), while if the meaning softening is ascribed to the verb ending *-te*, the *śakyatāvacchedaka* is the property of being softening (*viklittitva*). This is not the place to discuss these points in detail. Cf. [18, pp. 128–157], which contains useful information on the controversy, and also the introduction of [5], which has detailed information on the Navya-Nyāya view about the meaning of a verb ending.

[5]*VM* 2: *phalavyāpārayor dhātur āśraye tu tiṅaḥ smṛtāḥ / phale pradhānaṃ vyāpāras tiṅarthas tu viśeṣaṇam //* For more on this kārikā, cf. [14, pp. 62–75] and [12, pp. 3–5].

[6]According to Bhaṭṭoji Dīkṣita, the terms *vyāpāra, bhāvanā, utpādanā*, and *kriyā* are synonymous with one another. *VM* 5ab: *vyāpāro bhāvanā saivotpādanā saiva ca kriyā /*

[7]Cf. *VBhS* on *VM* 2 and [4, p. 266].

A verb such as *pac* "cook" is considered to denote both an activity and its result. The meanings of a verb ending are an agent (*kartṛ*), an object (*karman*), number (*saṃkhyā*), and time (*kāla*). The principal qualificand (*mukhyaviśeṣya*) of any sentence is considered to be the meaning of a verb (*dhātvartha*), qualified as having certain kārakas participating in it. An activity and its result constitute the meaning of the verb; the latter qualifies the former. Number and time qualify respectively a kāraka and the activity.

An agent is the locus of the activity denoted by a verb, while an object is the locus of the result of the activity; thus the utterance *taṇḍulaṃ pacati caitraḥ* denotes Caitra as the locus of cooking and the rice as the locus of softening which results from it. Further, the denotata of nominal affixes are considered as qualified by the denotata of nominal bases; however, what is denoted by a verb ending qualifies the meaning of a verb. Pāṇinīyas consider that affix and base meanings are related by identity (*abheda*). For example, the agent denoted by *-ti* is identical with the person referred to by *devadatta-* and the object denoted by the accusative ending is identical with what *taṇḍula-* refers to.[8]

2

Under *VM* 2 Kauṇḍabhaṭṭa discusses the meaning of a verb ending, referring to its *śakyatāvacchedaka* as follows:

> [Bhaṭṭoji Dīkṣita says: "The grammatical tradition declares that a verb denotes both an activity and its result, whereas verb endings denote] a locus." What is meant is that verb endings denote the locus of the activity (*vyāpārāśraya*) and the locus of the result (*phalāśraya*). The locus of the result is an object and the locus of the activity is an agent. Of the elements which make up an agent and an object, an activity and its result are to be gotten from a verb, so that, since the elements of the activity and its result are what are to be gotten from an item other than verb endings, the verb endings have no power to denote those elements. [Consequently it is a mere locus that the verb endings have the power to denote.] The *śakyatāvacchedaka* of this meaning is locus-ness. It will be said in the Subarthanirṇaya that this delimitor consists in different specific powers (*tattacchaktiviśeṣarūpa*).[9]

[8] *VBhS* on *VM* 2: *devadattādipadaprayoge tv ākhyātārthakartrādibhis tadarthasyābhedānvayaḥ* / In the case of the utterance *taṇḍulaḥ pacyate caitreṇa*, the object denoted by *-te* is identical with what *taṇḍula-* refers to and the agent denoted by the instrumental ending is identical with what *devadatta-* refers to. *A* 1.4.108 *śeṣe prathamaḥ* says that the verb endings in question are respectively coreferential (*samānādhikaraṇa*) with the co-occurring items *devadatta-* and *taṇḍula-*.

[9] *VBhS* on *VM* 2: *āśraye tv iti phalāśraye vyāpārāśraye cety arthaḥ / phalāśrayaḥ karma vyāpārāśrayaḥ kartā / tatra phalavyāpārayor dhātulabhyatvān na tiṅas tadaṃśe śaktiḥ, anyalabhyatvāt / śakyatāvacchedakaṃ cāśrayatvaṃ tattacchaktiviśeṣarūpam iti*

According to *A* 3.4.69 *laḥ karmaṇi ca bhāve cākarmakebhyaḥ*, a verb ending denotes an agent which is the locus of the activity, as in *pacati*, or an object which is the locus of the result of the activity, as in *pacyate*. On condition that a verb denotes both an activity and its result, it is to be said that the verb ending denotes merely the locus of the activity or of its result. For, if one applies here *ananyalabhyaśabdārthanyāya*, or the rule that a given meaning is assigned to a unit such as a verb ending only if that meaning is not gotten from other items,[10] the activity and its result, which are expressed by the verb, are ruled out of the domain of the denotation of the verb ending.

Thus, after establishing that the denotatum of a verb ending is *āśraya* or locus, Kauṇḍabhaṭṭa goes on to say that the *śakyatāvacchedaka* of this denotatum is locus-ness. According to him, it is important, the locus-ness consists in different specific powers.

What Kauṇḍabhaṭṭa says in the Subarthanirṇaya is as follows:

> [The locus of the result of the activity is an object.] This being the case, furthermore, because an action and its result are gotten from a verb itself, a meaning of an accusative ending is a mere locus, which is not to be gotten from other items. The *śakyatāvacchedaka* is locus-ness, which consists in an unanalyzable power (*akhaṇḍaśaktirūpa*).[11]

Here Kauṇḍabhaṭṭa deals with the meaning of an accusative ending such as *-am* in *taṇḍulaṃ pacati caitraḥ*. The rice serves as object, being the locus of softening which results from the act of cooking. The point he makes is

---

subarthanirṇaye vakṣyate /

Joshi renders the passage *śakyatāvacchedakaṃ cāśrayatvaṃ tattacchaktiviśeṣarūpam iti subarthanirṇaye vakṣyate* as follows: "The property which limits the denotedness [to a *tiṅ* suffix, i.e., which limits the area of denotation of a *tiṅ* suffix] is the property of being a substratum. That this property appears in specific forms as this or that [particular] property [e.g., objecthood, agenthood] will be explained in the section on the meaning of case terminations. [12, p. 10]" In Excursus 2, Joshi gives the following explanation: "It is to forestall this objection that Kauṇḍa Bhaṭṭa claims that the *śakyatāvacchedaka* of *tiṅ* is the property of being a substratum (*aśrayatvam* [*sic*]). Such a property is indivisible and resides in all denotations of *tiṅ* (object or agent) which vary the general area [*sic*], just as the denotations of the verbal root "to cook" vary within the general area of "action favourable to the becoming soft of food". Thus, Kauṇḍa Bhaṭṭa's theory is as simple and neat as the Naiyāyikas. [12, p. 11]" I cannot understand the reason that Joshi makes no mention of *śakti* here. Presumably he misreads the text as *tattadviśeṣarūpam*.

The same passage is translated by Das as follows: "It will be noted subsequently during ascertainment of meaning of a declensional ending that the determinant of denotation is nothing but the state of being a substratum and that it is the particular faculty of denotation (in a word). [6, pp. 174–175]" By the term *śakti* here Kauṇḍabhaṭṭa never means the denotative power of a word.

[10]Cf. [7, Paragraph 80]: text p. 209; translation pp. 70–71.

[11]*VBhS* on *VM* 24: *tathā ca kriyāyāḥ phalasya ca dhātunaiva lābhād ananyalabhya āśraya evārthaḥ, tattvañ cākhaṇḍaśaktirūpam avacchedakam /*

that the meaning of an accusative ending is simply a locus under the same rule mentioned above and that the *śakyatāvacchedaka* of this meaning is the locus-ness which consists in an unanalyzable power.

3

How should we understand Kauṇḍabhaṭṭa's view of the *śakyatāvacchedaka* of the denotatum of the verb ending? In order to consider this question, let us see how Nāgeśa, in his *Vaiyākaraṇasiddhāntamañjūṣā*, explains the above-stated view of Kauṇḍabhaṭṭa about the meaning of the accusative ending. His explanation will be of help in making clear the point made by Kauṇḍabhaṭṭa about the *śakyatāvacchedaka* of the denotatum of the verb ending.

3.1

Nāgeśa discusses the locus-ness there from two points of view: as an analyzable imposed property (*sakhaṇḍopādhi*) and as an unanalyzable imposed property (*akhaṇḍopādhi*).[12] The main question is how the innumerableness of the denotative power of an item which denotes a locus is to be avoided. In order to avoid this difficulty, a certain consecutive property (*anugamakadharma*) has to be found in a denotatum of the item, which is the fundamental premise behind the discussion about this question.

He begins by saying the following:

> [When an accusative ending denotes a locus, *śakyatāvacchedaka* is locus-ness.] And [this] locus-ness is an unanalyzable imposed property; therefore, there is no fault of complexity (*gurutva*) in assuming this to be *śakyatāvacchedaka* [since it is a single entity]. [In addition there is no harm in admitting such an imposed property to be *śakyatāvacchedaka*,] since it has been established that even an imposed property, which suffers from complexity [in comparison with a generic property (*jāti*)], can become *śakyatāvacchedaka*.[13]

Here the view is advanced that when an accusative ending denotes a locus, the *śakyatāvacchedaka* of this denotatum is the locus-ness which is an unanalyzable imposed property. It is important to note that this locus-ness is regarded as a single entity.

[12] I follow the definition of *akhaṇḍopādhi* given by the *Darpaṇa*: An unanalyzable imposed property is the property which is essentially not connected with an entity other than its own locus (*itarapadārthāghaṭitamūrttikadharmarūpa*). If the locus-ness is assumed to be connected with some property which is what is different from the locus of the locus-ness, it is classed as *sakhaṇḍopādhi*. Cf. *Darpaṇa* on *VBhS* and *VM* 24.

[13] *VBhS* on *VM* 5: *śakyatāvacchedakatvasyāpi lakṣyatāvacchedakatvavat guruṇi sambhavāt* / On the point that Navya-naiyāyikas recognize the complexity of the traditional theory explaining their abstract and imposed properties, cf. [10, p. 47, § 1].

VSM 122: *āśrayatvañ ca akhaṇḍopādhiḥ iti na śakyatāvacchedakagauravam / guruṇy api śakyatāvacchedakatvasya nirūpitatvāc ca /*

3.2

Against this view an objection is raised and the answer to the objection is given.

> [Objection] The locus-ness differs as its conditioner (*nirūpaka*) differs, and as its relatum (*sambandhin*) differs. Otherwise it would follow that when the locus-ness conditioned by a pot (*ghaṭāśrayatā*) is grasped, the locus-ness conditioned by a cloth (*paṭāśrayatā*) is grasped. Consequently, on the assumption that locus-ness is subject to differentiation, the innumerableness of the denotative power would have to be assumed [because of the innumerableness of *śakyatāvacchedaka*].
>
> [Answer] The above objection should not be made. When the cloth is grasped, the desirable consequence will ensue [that the locus-ness conditioned by it is grasped]. And, when the cloth is not grasped, there is no fear of the fault [of the innumerableness of the locus-ness since the locus-ness conditioned by the cloth is not grasped]. And in this very way those who assert that inherence (*samavāya*) is one entity, or that a quality (*guṇa*) such as white color is one entity, explain that the locus-ness is *śakyatāvacchedaka*.[14]

It is interesting to note that those who assert that inherence, instanced in different places, is unique or who assert that a quality, instanced in different loci, is unique hold the locus-ness, as an unanalyzable imposed property, to be a consecutive property.

According to Navya-Nyāya, the sentence "x is the locus of y" is translated as "the locus-ness conditioned by y resides in x". The locus-ness is a relational abstract (*sāpekṣadharma*). Moreover, a relational abstract such as the locus-ness is a peculiar kind of relation, what Nyāya calls a *svarūpa* relation (*svarūpasambandha*), which is not different from the relata. If the relation y to x is to be described, the above-mentioned sentence is translated as "y is related to x through the *svarūpa* relation of locus-ness". Through the *svarūpa* relation not only the adjunct (*pratiyogin*) y but also the relation itself is tied to the subjunct (*anuyogin*) x.[15]

A difficulty arises. The locus-ness, as a relational abstract, is particularized by the specification of its locus (x) and conditioner (y), and, as a *svarūpa* relation, it is a particular and hence necessarily differs from one occasion to another, since a *svarūpa* relation is nothing but the selfsame nature of the subjunct or locus.[16] Consequently the locus-ness suffers the

---

[14] *VSM* 122: *na ca āśrayatā nirūpakabhedena sambandhibhedena ca bhinnā, anyathā ghaṭāśrayatādigrahe paṭāśrayatādigrahāpattiḥ iti śaktyānantyam iti vācyam, paṭagraha iṣṭāpattiḥ, tadagrahe ca na doṣaśaṅkā / iyam eva ca samavāyasyaikatvavādināṃ śuklādiguṇānām ekatvavādinān ca gatiḥ /*

[15] Cf. [13, pp. 40–42].

[16] Cf. [13, p. 33].

defect of *ānantya* or innumerableness.[17] If the locus-ness cannot be unique, it cannot serve as a consecutive property. As a result, one cannot avoid the innumerableness of the denotative power of the item which denotes a locus.

Although I cannot identify those who assert that a quality such as white color is one entity, it is certain that in the Nyāya-Vaiśeṣika system inherence is regarded as one entity repeatedly appearing in different cases, and it is on a par with a universal. Thus the point is that as inherence is not subject to particularization by the specification of its adjunct and subjunct, so should also the locus-ness be regarded as unique irrespective of the specification of its locus and conditioner, or its adjunct and subjunct.[18]

3.3

An alternative solution is offered on the assumption that the locus-ness is an analyzable imposed property, which is what is delimited by another property that is a consecutive property. The locus-ness, in this solution, is treated as a property delimited by the property of being locus-ness (*āśrayatātva*).[19]

Nāgeśa adduces two examples: *buddhiviṣayatā* or the property of being an object of a cognition in the case of the denotation of items termed *sarvanāman* such as *tad* "that";[20] and sound-ness (*śabdatva*) in the case of the denotation of the item *ākāśa* "ether".

The demonstrative *tad* can refer to any pot. When a pot is its denotatum, *śakyatāvacchedaka* is the generic property pot-ness. In the same manner, it can refer to any cloth. When a cloth is its denotatum, *śakyatāvacchedaka* is the generic property cloth-ness. In the pot-ness and cloth-ness the property of being an object of a cognition resides. This property, functioning as a consecutive property which should be present in all possible *śakyatāvacchedakas* of the denotation of the demonstrative *tad*, prevents *tad* from having the innumerableness of the denotative power. Thus the

[17]Cf. [13, p. 43]. The commentary *Kiraṇāvalī* on the *Nyāyasiddhāntamuktāvalī* points out the same thing. *Kiraṇāvalī* 297: *navīnair vaiyākaraṇais tu-āśrayamātre eva kartṛkarmākhyātayoḥ śaktiḥ svīkriyate, kṛtyādivyāpāraphalayor dhātunaiva lābhāt, āśrayatvaṃ ca-akhaṇḍopādhir iti tanmate na gauravam / tan na / . . . / kiñca-āśrayatvasya akhaṇḍopādhirūpatve mānābhāvāt, ādhāratārūpasya tasya svarūpasambandharūpatvenānanugatatvāc ca /*

[18]In his *Parīkṣā* on *VBhS* ad *VM* 24 Bhairavamiśra says: *samavāyasya pratiyogyanuyogibhede 'py ekatvavan nirūpakabhede 'pi tad[= āśrayatva]bhedākalpanāt.*

[19]*VSM* 123: *astu vā āśrayatvaṃ nānā, tathāpi tadādau buddhiviṣayatāvacchedakatvavad ākāśapadaśaktau śabdatvavac cāśrayatātvasya śakyatāvacchedakatāvacchedakasyaiva ekatvān na śaktyānantyam /* In his *Vaiyākaraṇasiddhāntalaghumañjūṣā* Nageśa clearly states that the alternative solution is given from the viewpoint that the locus-ness is an analyzable imposed property. *VSLM* 1305–6: (*yat tu*) *phalāśrayaḥ karma tatra phalasya dhātunā lābhād āśrayo dvitīyārthas tatra prakṛtyartho viśeṣaṇam ādheyatayā phalaṃ viśeṣyam, āśrayatvaṃ śakyatāvacchedakam, akhaṇḍopādhirūpam āśrayatātvaṃ vā tadanugamakam /*

[20]*A* 1.1.27 assigns the class name *sarvanāman* to pronominals such as *tad.*

property of being an object of a cognition is properly to be considered as *śakyatāvacchedakatāvacchedaka* or the delimiting property of what is *śakyatāvacchedaka*, the limitor of the property of being a *śakyatāvacchedaka*.[21]

When the item *ākāśa* denotes ether, in addition, *śakyatāvacchedaka* is sound (*śabda*), for the imposed property *ākāśatva* is identical with *śabdāśrayatva* or the property of being the locus of sound, which in turn is identical with the sound.[22] What is referred to as *śabdāśrayatva* is precisely what qualifies the locus. In the Nyāya-Vaiśeṣika system all sounds have the ether as their loci. Accordingly, one has to search for a consecutive property which resides in all sounds. What serves as such a consecutive property is just the generic property sound-ness (*śabdatva*), which is *śakyatāvacchedakatāvacchedaka* in this case.

If it has to be accepted that the locus-ness cannot evade the defect of innumerableness, it is reasonable to posit a consecutive property which is present in all instances of locus-ness. This is the idea underlying the second solution.

3.4

As shown above, Nāgeśa considers the locus-ness either as an unanalyzable imposed property or as an analyzable imposed property. Kauṇḍabhaṭṭa has said that the locus-ness as *śakyatāvacchedaka* consists in an unanalyzable power. It is likely that Nāgeśa discusses the locus-ness simply from the Navya-Nyāya point of view, for in the passages cited above he does not introduce the concept of power.

4

Let us turn now to the question of why Kauṇḍabhaṭṭa describes the locus-ness as consisting in different specific powers or in an unanalyzable power. He evidently approaches from a different angle the question of how to avoid the innumerableness of the denotative power of the item which denotes a

[21] *VBh* on *VM* 51–52ab: *anubhavānurodhāt sarvanāmnāṃ viśiṣyopasthāpakatvam iti sarvasiddham, tac ca yadi buddhiviṣayatvarūpeṇa upasthāpitaghaṭatvapaṭatvaśāliṣu buddhiviṣayavati [read: buddhiviṣayatvavati] śaktaṃ tatpadam ity eva śaktigrahaḥ / buddhiviṣayatvan tu upasthitau anugamakamātram, na tu śakyam iti na tacchābdabodhe bhāsate /* According to Kauṇḍabhaṭṭa the item *tad* denotes things which are called to mind as those which one has in mind (*buddhiviṣaya*) and which are qualified by generic properties such as pot-ness; however, *buddhiviṣayatā* or the property of being a *buddhiviṣaya* is not counted as the denotatum of *tad*.

[22] What Navya-Nyāya calls *tadvattvaṃ tad iti nyāya* is closely linked with the semantics of items ending in *bhāvapratyayas* such as *tva*, *tal* (*-tā*). Generally speaking, if an item is used to refer to a thing known as qualified by x, the *bhāvapratyaya* occurring after the item denotes the qualifier x. *VM* 51: *prayogopādhim āśritya prakṛtyarthaprakāratām / dharmamātraṃ vācyam iti yadvā śabdaparā amī //* Cf. also Footnote 1.

locus. It is important to note that he presupposes Pāṇinīyas' kāraka theory, according to which a kāraka such as an agent and object is the capacity or power (*śakti*, *sāmarthya*) which a thing has to bring an action to accomplishment, or the thing which is the locus of the capacity or power. It goes without saying that in the former case a kāraka is termed a *dharma* "property" of the thing and in the latter case it is termed a *dharmin* "property-possessor".[23]

4.1

In the twenty-fourth kārikā of his *Vaiyākaraṇamatonmajjana* Bhaṭṭoji Dīkṣita says that the meanings of *kārakavibhaktis* are a locus, a point of departure (*avadhi*), and what is intended as a goal (*uddeśya*) and that, alternatively, they are a power (*śakti*).[24] In his *Vaiyākaraṇabhūṣaṇa*, commenting on the kārikā Kauṇḍabhaṭṭa explains that the meaning of a *kārakavibhakti* is a power, which will be useful to see how he views a power.

His exposition starts with the following:

> And further, on the assumption that it is certain in this way that it is such a property as locus-ness which is the denotatum of a *kārakavibhakti*, Bhaṭṭoji Dīkṣita says in *VM* 24: 'Or, the meanings of *kārakavibhaktis* are simply a power (*śaktir eva vā*).'
>
> When he says this, he wishes to imply the following: In the Bhāṣya and other commentaries on sūtras like *A* 2.3.7 *saptamīpañcamyau kārakamadhye*,[25] bearing in mind that what is meant by the term

[23] *VP* 3.7.1: *svāśraye samavetānāṃ tadvad evāśrayāntare / kriyāṇām abhiniṣpattau sāmarthyaṃ sādhanaṃ viduḥ //* ("It is what [Pāṇinīyas from Patañjali onwards] call *sādhana* that is a power (*sāmarthya*) for bringing to accomplishment the act which resides in the same locus as the power itself or the one which in the very same manner resides in a locus different from the one in which the power does.") According to Bhartṛhari, what plays a contributing role in an act is a power (*sāmarthya*), which is treated as *sādhana* in correlation to an act as what is to be brought to accomplishment (*sādhya*). As is suggested by Bhartṛhari's use of the word *viduḥ* 'they consider, call' (*vid*, 3rd pl. pfct.), moreover, this view is firmly rooted in the Pāṇinian tradition. Bhartṛhari developed the view of a *sādhana* as a quality (*guṇa*) into its view as a power, simply following Patañjali who, in answering the question of what a *sādhana* is, had proposed the alternatives of a substance (*dravya*) or a quality and had given preference to a quality.

[24] *VM* 24: *āśrayo 'vadhir uddeśyaḥ sambandhaḥ śaktir eva vā / yathāyathaṃ vibhaktyarthāḥ supāṃ karmeti bhāṣyataḥ //*

[25] This sūtra provides that the locative or the ablative endings occur after an item denoting time or space if it is used with reference to a time or space which comes between two kārakas (*kārakamadhye*). Consider the following utterance: *adya bhuktvā devadatto dvyahe (dvyahād) bhoktā* 'After eating today, Devadatta will eat in two days'. Here one can say that the time involved intervenes between two instances of eating. However, if the term *kāraka* in *A* 2.3.7 denotes a thing, the difficulty arises that the time spoken of in the given utterance does not intervene between two kārakas, since it is the same person Devadatta who eats both times. Therefore, Pāṇinīyas say that *kārakamadhye* in *A* 2.3.7 means 'between two powers'. Cf. [3, p. 251].

> *śakti* 'power' is just such a property which is unanalyzable (*akhaṇḍa*), [Patañjali and other Pāṇinīyas] make the statement that a power is the meaning of a *kārakavibhakti*.[26]
>
> The phrase *ṣaṇṇāṃ kārakavibhaktīnām* 'of six *kārakavibhaktis*' is to be supplied for the expression *śaktir eva vā* in the kārikā, so that the expression gains the meaning that the meanings of six *kārakavibhaktis* are simply a power. The meaning of the genitive ending whose introduction is provided for by *A* 2.3.50 (*śeṣaṣaṣṭhī*), on the other hand, is a relation in general (*sambandhasāmānya*).
>
> The cause for the use of the word *śakti* which denotes powers is the form of the word itself, since it is a word used as a name (*saṃjñāśabda*).[27]

Two points are to be noted here. The first point is that the term *śakti* is used to denote a property such as locus-ness. This can be explained as follows. As said above, Bhaṭṭoji Dīkṣita introduces two views: one view that a *kārakavibhakti* denotes a locus, a point of departure, or what is intended as a goal; and the other view that it denotes a power to bring an action to accomplishment.[28] According to Kauṇḍabhaṭṭa, the former view reflects the assumption that a kāraka is a property possessor and the latter view the assumption that it is a property. For simplicity's sake, let us confine ourselves to the meaning locus. When Caitra serves as agent with respect to the act of cooking, he is said to be the locus of this act on the one hand, and on the other hand he is said to possess the power of functioning as agent with respect to that act.[29] What this undoubtedly suggests is the following:

[26] *VSLM* 1306: *saptamīpañcamyau kārakamadhye ity atra kārakaśabdasya śaktiparatvena śaktiśaktimatoś cābhedena śaktimata eva dvitīyādyarthatāyā bhāṣyādisammatatvāt* / It is to be noted that Nāgeśa, admitting that a power is meant by the term *kāraka* in *A* 2.3.7, argues that a *kārakavibhakti* denotes the possessor of a power (*śaktimat*) because a power and its possessor are ontologically non-distinct from each other.

[27] Bhartṛhari explicitly states that a name-word is used on the basis of its own form. *VP* 2.370: *saṃjñā svarūpam āśritya nimitte sati laukikī / kācit pravartate kācin nimittāsaṃnidhāv api //*

VBh on *VM* 24: *evaṃ cāśrayatvāder eva vācyatve dhruve tad evākhaṇḍaṃ śaktiśabdenocyata iti manasi nidhāya śaktir vibhaktyartha iti saptamīpañcamyau kārakamadhye ityādau bhāṣyādau vyavahriyata iti tad evābhipretyāha-śaktir eva veti / ṣaṇṇāṃ kārakavibhaktīnām iti śeṣaḥ / śeṣaṣaṣṭhyās tu prāguktaṃ sambandhasāmānyam arthaḥ / śaktīnāṃ pravṛttinimittaṃ sa śabda eva, saṃjñāśabdatvāt /*

[28] In general, a locus is the meaning of the accusative, instrumental, and locative endings; a point of departure is the meaning of the ablative ending; what is intended as a goal is the meaning of the dative ending.

[29] In the situation to express which the utterance *devadattas taṇḍulaṃ pacati* is used, it is never odd to say that Caitra has the power of functioning as agent with respect to the act of cooking. When a thing actually plays a role in a given activity, a power is said to be manifested. It is precisely because Caitra can function as agent that he is spoken of as an agent. Similarly, in the very same situation it is entirely fair to say that rice has the power of functioning as object with respect to the same act, since, unless the rice can

The locus is identical with the possessor of the power (*āśraya* = *śaktimat*). In this case the term *āśrayatva* becomes equivalent to the term *śaktimattva*, so that the former can denote the power (*śakti*). For, the locus-ness which is the qualifier of the locus and which is referred to by the term *āśrayatva* is identical with the power which is the qualifier of the locus of the power and which is referred to by the term *śaktimattva*.[30]

The second point is that the term *śakti* is defined as a word used as a name (*saṃjñāśabda*). This is relevant to the point that the power is an unanalyzable property (*akhaṇḍa*). While in the case of a class name such as *go* "cow" the thing appears as qualified by a property which resides in it, say, the generic property cow-ness, in the case of name words such as *Devadatta* the thing appears simply as qualified or distinguished by the name itself. If we accepted the power as qualified by some inherent property such as power-ness (*śaktitva*), we would have to say that the power is an analyzable property. According to Bhartṛhari, a power consists in rendering service to others (*anugrāhin, upakārin*)[31] and hence is of a dependent nature (*paratantra*), so that it should be a quality (*guṇa*) and never that in which a quality resides (*dravya*).[32] Thus it is obvious that by saying that the *śakyatāvacchedaka* of the term *śakti* is its own word-form (*śabdasvarūpa*) itself, Kauṇḍabhaṭṭa intends to ensure unanalyzability for the power. For him, the term *śakti* is comparable to a word which is supposed to denote a generic property and whose *śakyatāvacchedaka* is considered to be the word's own form.

---

be cooked, one cannot have such an utterance.

[30] Cf. Footnote 22.

[31] Bhartṛhari gives the following definition of *sādhana* or *śakti/sāmarthya*. *VP* 3.7.12cd: *yad yadā yadanugrāhi tat tadā tatra sādhanam /* ("When a certain thing x grants a favor (*anugrāhin*) to another thing y, the thing x is a *sādhana* for the thing y.")

[32] *VP* 3.11.7: *paropakāratattvānāṃ svātantryeṇābhidhāyakaḥ / śabdaḥ sarvapadārthānāṃ svadharmād viprakṛṣyate //* ("If a word denotes as something independent (*svātantryeṇa*) whatever in essence serves others, the word used to denote it is alienated from its own property [of being dependent].") According to this kārikā, when things such as a power whose essence lies in rendering service to others (*paropakāratattva*) and hence lies in being dependent on them are denoted as independent things (*svātantryeṇa*) by words of their own, such as *śakti*, their own property of being dependent cannot be touched by those words.

For the concepts of quality and substance here, the following kārikās of the *Vākyapadīya* are to be considered. *VP* 3.4.3: *vastūpalakṣaṇaṃ yatra sarvanāma prayujyate / dravyam ity ucyate so 'rtho bhedyatvena vivakṣitaḥ //* ("That object, with reference to which an item termed *sarvanāman* [such as *tad* 'that'] that refers to an entity is used, is called *dravya* when it is intended to be conveyed as something differentiated."); *VP* 3.5.1: *saṃsargi bhedakaṃ yad yat savyāpāraṃ pratīyate / guṇatvaṃ paratantratvāt tasya śāstra udāhṛtam //* ("Whatever is related [to a certain thing] and differentiates the thing [from others] is regarded as *guṇa* when it activates the function [of differentiating], because it is something dependent. This is what has been illustrated in grammar.")

4.2

Kauṇḍabhaṭṭa continues to adduce the kārikās of the *Vākyapadīya* which discuss number in regard to the power.

> "And Bhartṛhari has said the following:
>
> According to others, there reside in entities six permanent powers to bring an action to accomplishment, which, like a universal, have the difference and non-difference from the entities. (*VP* 3.7.35)
>
> And these powers seem to be unlimited in number because of their differentiation by factors such as a substance and a form. However, the essence of those [different powers] does not go beyond [the essence of] the six powers. (*VP* 3.7.36)
>
> [Or rather,] power is one but is understood in six different ways on the basis of the difference among the causes for the application of kāraka terms.[33] Pāṇinīyas think that it is the power of functioning as agent (*kartṛtva*) which forms the basis for bringing about different expressions such as *karman, karaṇa*. (*VP* 3.7.37)"[34]

On the number of the power to bring an action to accomplishment, Bhartṛhari puts forward two views. In one view, there reside in entities six kinds of powers: the powers of functioning as agent (*kartṛ*), object (*karman*), instrument (*karaṇa*), recipient (*sampradāna*), point of departure (*apādāna*), and locus (*adhikaraṇa*). These kinds of powers seem to differ as substances that are their loci differ and as the forms of the substances differ. But in reality there are only six kinds of powers; a power to bring an action to accomplishment is subsumed under any of these six categories, whatever entity might exert it. For example, the power to cut varies according as it exists in a knife or a sword. And yet, speaking generally, it is of six kinds and no more.

According to another view, which is finally accepted by Bhartṛhari, power is one, assuming six forms according to circumstances. That one power is the power of functioning as agent which is called by different names

[33]For example, when the term *karman* applies to a thing, the thing is that which an agent most wishes to reach (*A* 1.4.49 *kartur īpsitatamaṃ karma*); and, when the term *karaṇa* applies to a thing, the thing is that which most serves to bring about an act (*A* 1.4.42 *sādhakatamaṃ karaṇam*). We may say that to be what an agent most wishes to reach is the cause for the application of the term *karman* and that to be what most serves to bring about an act is the cause for the application of the term *karaṇa*.

[34]*VBh* on *VM* 24: *uktaṃ ca hariṇā-nityāḥ ṣaḍ śaktayo 'nyeṣāṃ bhedābhedasamanvitāḥ / kriyāsaṃsiddhye 'rtheṣu jātivat samavasthitāḥ //* (The edition of the *Vaiyākaraṇabhūṣaṇa* reads the pāda a of this kārikā as *nityāḥ ṣaḍ vyaktayo 'nyeṣāṃ*, which should be amended to read *nityāḥ ṣaḍ śaktayo 'nyeṣām.*) *dravyākārādibhedena tāś cāparimitā iva / dṛśyante tattvam āsāṃ tu ṣaḍ śaktīr nātivartate // nimittabhedād ekaiva bhinnā śaktiḥ pratīyate / ṣoḍhā kartṛtvam evāhus tatpravṛtter nibandhanam //* (The *Vaiyākaraṇabhūṣaṇa* edition reads pāda d as *tatpravṛttinibandhamam.*)

under different circumstances. Whatever power to bring an action to accomplishment is exerted by an entity is subsumed under one category, the category of agency. According to Pāṇinīyas, every karaka is an agent of an action because a kāraka serves no function in a principal action unless it carries out its own activity.[35]

4.3

In addition, Kauṇḍabhaṭṭa goes on further to mention how *A* 2.3.1 *anabhihite*, which is a heading whereby subsequent sūtras introduce vibhaktis, is to be interpreted on the assumption that a kārakavibhakti signifies a power.

> In this view [that the meanings of six *kārakavibhaktis* are a power], *A* 2.3.1 *anabhihite* means: 'when that specific power (*tattacchakti*) is not denoted'. In the meaning of a verb ending (*ākhyāta*) also, a power does exist as its *śakyatāvacchedaka* [because the verb ending denotes a locus which is just what possesses the power], so that grammatical operations are established.[36]

The point made by Kauṇḍabhaṭṭa is this. *A* 2.3.18 *kartṛkaraṇayos tṛtīyā*, for example, is headed by *A* 2.3.1. In the utterance *devadattaḥ pacati* the verb ending *-ti* denotes an agent which is what is delimited by the power of functioning as agent and hence the locus of this power. *A* 2.3.18 provides that the instrumental ending occurs after a nominal base if an agent or instrument, the power of functioning as agent or instrument, is to be denoted. In the given utterance the power of functioning as agent is already denoted by *-ti*, so that the instrumental ending *-ṭā* (*-ina*) does not occur after *devadatta*; instead, the nominative ending ***-su*** occurs after it by *A* 2.3.46. It is important to note here that Kauṇḍabhaṭṭa, saying that a *kārakavibhakti* denotes a power, does not abandon the view that a verb ending denotes the locus of an activity or of its result and that the *śakyatāvacchedaka* of the denotatum of the verb ending is a power. It seems that he holds, as Nāgeśa does, that saying that a *kārakavibhakti* signifies a power amounts to saying that it signifies the possessor of the power, for a power is ontologically non-distinct from its possessor.[37]

5

We have looked carefully at Kauṇḍabhaṭṭa's exposition of the view of Pāṇinīyas that a *kārakavibhakti* denotes a power. We are now in a position to understand what is Kauṇḍabhaṭṭa's theoretical assumption that underlies

[35] *VSLM* 1195: *sarveṣāṃ ca kārakāṇāṃ svasvāvāntarakriyādvārā pradhānakriyāniṣpādakatvam /*

[36] *VBh* on *VM* 24: *etanmate 'nabhihita ity atra tattacchaktyanabhidhāna ity arthaḥ / ākhyātārthe 'py avacchedakatvena śaktir asty eveti kāryavyavasthā /*

[37] Cf. Footnote 26.

his claim that the *śakyatāvacchedaka* of the meaning of a verb ending, locus-ness, is a power.

First of all, in his view, the locus of an activity or its result is identical with that of the power to bring an action to accomplishment (*āśraya* = *śaktimat*). Naturally, it follows from this that what is referred to as *āśrayatva* "locus-ness" is identical with what is referred to as *śaktimattva* "the property of being the possessor of a power" and hence with a power. The locus-ness which is the qualifier of what possesses it is identical with the power which is the qualifier of what possesses it.

As has been pointed out, according to him, the locus-ness consists in different specific powers (*tattacchaktiviśeṣarūpa*) and it consists in an unanalyzable power (*akhaṇḍaśaktirūpa*). The latter point is undoubtedly made, as shown in § 4.1, on the assumption that a power is of a dependent nature. The first point is to be understood as follows.

On the assumption that there are six kinds of kāraka powers, the expression *tattacchaktiviśeṣa* may mean in the given context the power of functioning as agent and that of functioning as object. In *pacati* the verb ending *-ti* denotes an agent who is the locus of the activity of cooking that leads to softening. The meaning locus is to be assigned to the verb ending under the rule *ananyalabhyaśabdārthanyāya*. The *śakyatāvacchedaka* of this meaning is locus-ness, which consists in the power of functioning as agent. As Bhartṛhari says, the power of functioning as agent is one. Similarly in *pacyate* the verb ending *-te* denotes an object which is the locus of softening. The meaning locus alone is assigned to that ending. The *śakyatāvacchedaka* of this meaning is also locus-ness. But this locus-ness consists in the power of functioning as object, which is also one. Even if, as Bhartṛhari maintains, any power to bring an action to accomplishment is reducible to a single power, the power of functioning as agent, it is justifiable that the *śakyatāvacchedaka* of the meaning of the verb ending is the locus-ness which is defined as *tattacchaktiviśeṣarūpa*. For, according to Bhartṛhari, the power of functioning as agent is differentiated into the six kinds of powers. When differentiated by the cause for the application of the term *kartṛ*, the power of functioning as agent appears as the power of functioning as agent; when differentiated by the cause for the application of the term *karman*, it appears as the power of functioning as object. Thus we have to accept that there are six kinds of powers, however they may be derived from the sole power of functioning as agent. We may, therefore, reasonably say the following. When Kauṇḍabhaṭṭa says that the locus-ness which is the *śakyatāvacchedaka* of the denotatum of the verb ending consists in different specific powers, he intends to imply this: The verb ending *-ti* denotes what is delimited by the power of functioning as agent, whereas the verb ending *-te* denotes what is delimited by the power of functioning as object.[38]

What is important is that the power of functioning as agent or object, as such, does not differ from one agent or object to another. Thus according to Kauṇḍabhaṭṭa, if the power of functioning as agent or object is considered as the *śakyatāvacchedaka* of the denotatum of the verb ending, the innumerableness of the denotative power of the verb ending can be avoided on the basis of the singularity of the specific power. It may be said that Pāṇinīyas' traditional view that a kāraka is a power or a power-possessor is skillfully incorporated into Kauṇḍabhaṭṭa's treatment of the *śakyatāvacchedaka* of the meaning of the verb ending. It is quite natural for Kauṇḍabhaṭṭa, who has the Pāṇinian kāraka theory, to take the term *āśrayatva* as referring to a power for the reason that it is equivalent to the term *śaktimattva*.

Primary sources

A. = Pāṇini, *Aṣṭādhyāyī.*

Darpaṇa. = Harivallabha, *Darpaṇa*, in: [17].

Kiraṇāvalī. = Kriṣṇavallabhācārya, Commentary on the *Nyāyasiddhāntamuktāvalī*, in: [15].

Parīkṣā. = Bhairavamiśra, Commentary on the *Vaiyākaraṇabhūṣaṇasāra*, in: [11].

VBh. = Kauṇḍabhaṭṭa, *Vaiyākaraṇabhūṣaṇa*, in: [2].

VBhS. = Kauṇḍabhaṭṭa, *Vaiyākaraṇabhūṣaṇasāra*, in: [17].

VP. = Bhartṛhari, *Vākyapadīya*, in: [19].

VM. = Bhaṭṭoji Dīkṣita, *Vaiyākaraṇ amatonmajjana*, in: [17].

VSLM. = Nāgeśa, *Vaiyākaraṇasiddhāntalaghumañjūṣā*, in: [1].

VSM. = Nāgeśa, *Vaiyākaraṇasiddhāntamañjūṣā*, in: [20].

References

[1] Mādhava-Śāstrī Bhāṇḍāri, Madan Mohan Pāṭhak, and Nityānand Panta Parvatīya. *Vaiyākaraṇa Siddhānta Laghu Mañjūsha by Mahāmahopādhyāya Śrī Nāgeśa Bhaṭṭa.* Chaukhamba, Benares, 1926. with two commentaries, i.e., Kuñjikā of Durbalāchārya and Kalā of Bālam Bhaṭṭa.

[38] *VSM* 123: *karmakaraṇādau śakyatāvacchedakāśrayatvasya tattacchaktirūpasya bhinnatābhyupagamenādoṣāt / anyathā dvitīyādeḥ paryāyatāpatteḥ /*

[2] Manudeva Bhattacharya. *Bṛhadvaiyākaraṇabhuṣaṇam of Śrī Kauṇḍa Bhaṭṭa: A Commentary of Bhaṭṭojidikshita's Vaiyakaraṇamatonmajjanam*, volume 2 of *Harjivandas Prachyavidya Granthamala*. Chaukhamba Amarabharati Prakashan, Varanasi, 1985. edited with 'Rupālī' Notes and Appendix.

[3] George Cardona. Pāṇini's *kārakas*: Agency, Animation and Identity. *Journal of Indian Philosophy*, 2:231–306, 1974.

[4] George Cardona. Paraphrase and Sentence Analysis: Some Indian Views. *Journal of Indian Philosophy*, 3:259–281, 1975.

[5] Krishnendu Chatterjee. *Śiromaṇi's Ākhyāta-Śakti-Vāda: Text with English Translation*. Kishor Vidya Niketan, Varanasi, 1981.

[6] Karunasindhu Das. *A Pāṇinian Approach to Philosophy of Language: Kauṇḍabhaṭṭa's Vaiyākaraṇabhūṣaṇasāra Critically Edited and Translated into English*. Sanskrit Pustak Bhandar, Calcutta, 1990.

[7] Franklin Edgerton. *The Mīmāṅsā Nyāya Prakāśa or Āpadevī: A Treatise on the Mīmāṅsā System by Āpadeva. Translated into English, with an Introduction, Transliterated Sanskrit Text, and Glossarial Index*, volume 36 of *Sri Garib Dass Oriental Series*. Sri Satguru Publications, Delhi, 1986.

[8] Jonardon Ganeri. *Semantic Powers: Meaning and the Means of Knowing in Classical Indian Philosophy*. Clarendon Press, Oxford, 1999.

[9] Jonardon Ganeri. *Artha: Meaning*. Oxford University Press, New Delhi, 2006.

[10] Daniel H. H. Ingalls. *Materials for the Study of Navya-Nyāya Logic*, volume 40 of *Harvard Oriental Series*. Motilal Banarsidass, Delhi, 1988.

[11] Sadāśiva-Śāstrī Joshi. *The Vaiyākaraṇa Bhūṣaṇasāra by M. M. Śrī Kauṇḍabhaṭṭa with the Darpaṇa Commentary by Śrī Harivallabha, the Parīkṣā Commentary by Bhairavamiśra and a Short Commentary by Śrī Kṛṣṇa Mitra with Tiṅarthavādasāra by Śrī Khuddī Jhā Śarmā; edited with Notes, Introduction, etc.*, volume 133 of *Kashi Sanskrit Series*. Chowkhamba, Benares, 1939.

[12] Shivaram-Dattatray Joshi. Kauṇḍa Bhaṭṭa on the Meaning of Sanskrit Verbs (2). *Nagoya Studies in Indian Culture and Buddhism: Saṃbhāṣā*, 16:1–66, 1995.

[13] Bimal Krishna Matilal. *The Navya-Nyāya Doctrine of Negation: The Semantics and Ontology of Negative Statements in Navya-Nyāya Philosophy*, volume 46 of *Harvard Oriental Series*. Harvard University Press, Cambridge, Massachusetts, 1968.

[14] Pradip K. Mazumdar. *The Philosophy of Language: In the Light of Pāṇinian and the Mīmāṃsāka Schools of Indian Philosophy*. Sanskrit Pustak Bhandar, Calcutta, 1977.

[15] Shri Narayancharan Shastri and Shri Swetvaikuntha Shastri. *The Nyayasiddhantamuktavali of Śrī Viśwanātha Panchānan, with the Commentary Kiranāvali by Pt. Śrī Kriśnavallabhācārya*, volume 212 of *Kashi Sanskrit Series*. Chowkhamba, Varanasi, 1972.

[16] Hideyo Ogawa. What is *bhāva*?: A Grammatical Analysis of the Term *bhāva*. *The Annals of the Research Project Center for the Comparative Study of Logic*, 3:107–115, 2005.

[17] Bālakṛṣṇa Pañcholi. *Vaiyākaraṇabhūṣaṇasāra of Śrī Kauṇḍabhaṭṭa, edited with 'Prabhā' Commentary by Pt. Śrī Bālakṛṣṇa Pañcholi and with 'Darpaṇa' Commentary by Śrī Harivallabha Śāstrī*, volume 188 of *Kashi Sanskrit Series*. Chowkhamba, Varanasi, 1969.

[18] Veluri-Subra Rao. *The Philosophy of a Sentence and Its Parts: Śābdabodhadhātunāmapratyayādyarthabodhaviṣayakaḥ prabandhaḥ*. Munshiram Manoharlal Oriental Publishers, New Delhi, 1969.

[19] Wilhelm Rau. *Bhartṛharis Vākyapadīya: Die Mūlakārikās nach den Handschriften herausgegeben und mit einem Pāda-Index versehen*, volume XLII, 4 of *Abhandlungen für die Kunde des Morgenlandes*. Franz Steiner Verlag, Wiesbaden, 1977.

[20] Kapil-Dev Shastri (Kapil Deo Shastri). *Nāgeśa Bhaṭṭa's Vaiyākaraṇasiddhāntamañjūṣā*. Vishal Publications, Kurukshetra, 1985.

On Relating Two Traditions of Logic

Biswambhar Pahi*

Department of Philosophy, University of Rajasthan, Jaipur, 302 004, India
E-mail: bpahi@dataone.in

Logic emerged as a distinct theoretical discipline in ancient India and Greece centuries before the beginning of the Christian era. The wide surface-level gulf separating the logical traditions of ancient Greece and West on the one hand and that of India on the other has served as a deterrent in the search for the unity of Logic as a trans-cultural theoretical discipline. The central concern and the course of development of Logic seem to be determined by the way the notion of theoretical discipline is construed in the intellectual tradition in which the discipline is embedded. The mainstream of western logic has been primarily concerned with the characterization and systematization of valid modes of deductive inference. It began in Greece as a deduction-centered discipline (*nigamana-kendritaśāstra*) and has basically continued to remain so throughout its history. Logic in India though concerned with the problem of validity of inference (*anumāna pramāṇa*) as a mode of justification of knowledge claims, has focused primarily on the relation of pervasion (*vyāpti-kendrita śāstra*). This relation proves to be adequate for characterizing western logical tradition's pivotal notion of valid deductive inference and its underlying relation of logically valid implication. The extensional relation of pervasion (*vyāpti*) can play this role precisely because for any given system of logic such as the classical Propositional Logic defined in a suitable formal language and equipped with an appropriate semantics, the class of all valuations of the underlying formal language can be viewed as a universe of individuals or loci (*dharmin*, *ādhāra*, *adhikaraṇa*) and each well-formed formula can be treated as denoting a property (*dharma*, *ādheya*) having its own truth-set (the set of all valuations each of which makes it true) as its extension. Tautological implication, for example, may be viewed as a relation of pervasion where the property denoted by its antecedent is pervaded by the property denoted by its consequent, just as smoke is pervaded by fire and the property of being a multiple of six is pervaded by the property of being a multiple of three.

The challenging task of making the *Navya-Nyāya System of Logic* accessible to persons trained in the western tradition of Philosophy and Logic was taken up by Daniel H. H. Ingalls in his 1951 pioneering work [20]. His work was continued by a number of competent scholars like Bimal Krishna

*The author is very thankful to the referee for some constructive suggestions on an earlier draft of this paper that was less focused and compact.

Mihir K. **Chakraborty**, Benedikt **Löwe**, Madhabendra Nath **Mitra**, Sundar **Sarukkai** (*eds.*). Logic, Navya-Nyāya & Applications. Homage to Bimal Krishna Matilal. College Publications, London, 2008. Studies in Logic 15. pp. 235–260.

Received by the editors: 5 June 2007; 8 May 2008, 6 June 2008.
Accepted for publication: 10 November 2008.

Matilal, Dinesh Chandra Guha, Jitendra Nath Mohanty, Sibajiban Bhattacharya, Karl H. Potter, Vishwa Nath Jha, Stephen H. Phillips and N. S. Ramanuja Tatacharya. Ingalls dreamt of a day when the two parallel traditions of logic would become mutually accessible. He articulated his vision in his introductory note to Guha's [13] — the year in which he also wrote his Editor's Introduction to Matilal's work [27]. A survey of the work done in this area during the past five and half decades shows that the progress though very notable, has remained confined to making Navya-Nyāya accessible to the western audience. It is evident however that this line of research can neither reinforce the structural strength nor extend the conceptual horizons of Navya-Nyāya. If Ingalls' beautiful dream is to come true we have to work toward making the systems dominating western logical tradition accessible to Navya-Nyāya.

Aristotelian logic continued to constitute the mainstream of western logic almost till the middle of the nineteenth century when important developments in the field of pure mathematics during the preceding three decades triggered a new era marked by the publication of George Boole's [10] in 1847. Boole's algebraic approach to logic was extensively enlarged by W. Stanley Jevons, C. S. Peirce and E. Schröder. The search for the logical foundation of arithmetic led Gottlob Frege to the momentous discovery and axiomatic presentation of a new system of logic in his 1879 work *Begriffsschrift.*[1] The role played by this system, known as *First Order Predicate Logic with Identity* $\mathrm{FPL}_=$, in the formalization of proofs in mathematics and the axiomatic formulations of the various branches of classical mathematics, accounts for its dominant position in western logic. Pahi presents a framework for the conceptual translation of Aristotle's Theory of Syllogisms in terms of notions available in Indian logical tradition [31]. Our primary objective in the present paper is to present the outlines of a framework for the conceptual translation of the fundamental logical and metalogical concepts of $\mathrm{FPL}_=$ in to NN^* which is the same as Navya-Nyāya with a marginally extended ontological basis. The opening section of the paper seeks to account for the divergent courses of development of western and Indian logics on the basis of the concepts of theoretical discipline available in Greek and Indian theoretical traditions. The author's perspective concerning the nature of logic as a theoretical discipline is outlined in the second section. The nature of inferential schemata of Nyāya logic and the characterization problem of the central content-neutral notion of pervasion (*vyāpti*) are taken up in the next two sections. The concluding section is devoted to the paper's main objective of bridge-building. The investigations reported here may be viewed as groundwork for the unattended part of Ingalls' full program.

[1] Cf. [3, Chapter 3].

1 Concepts of Theoretical Discipline and the Development of Logic

In the history of mankind only a very limited number of civilizations have been privileged to experience the pains of giving birth to and nourishing a theoretical tradition. The civilizations of ancient Greece and India do belong to this select group. These two civilizations assigned high priority to theoretical activity. The areas of inquiry focused upon by each were however determined by the ethos of the civilization as a whole A theoretical tradition's admissible modes of justification of knowledge claims (*pramāṇas*) in general and its apparatus of the inferential mode of justification (*anumāna*) in particular appear to be determined by its conception of theoretical discipline (*śāstra*). Evidently theoretical disciplines may take shape and develop without any awareness of problems relating to the building and evaluation of theories. A theoretical tradition may however attain a reflective and critical state where problems concerning the acquisition and organization of knowledge have to be faced in their full generality and resolved. In India it happened at a local level in phonetics and grammar definitely by the fifth century BC Pāṇini's *Aṣṭādhyāyī* (*Aṣṭ*) served as a landmark. Kātyāyana, the author of *Vārtika* (*KV*), and Pātañjali, the author of *Mahābhāsya* (*PM*), were called upon to articulate the nature of the challenge that theory-construction posed in the field of grammars of natural languages. They came up with a theory of grammar construction and evaluation that was manifestly implicit in the grammatical practice of Pāṇini and his predecessors. By the second century AD the problem of building and evaluation of theories was faced and resolved at a more general level by Akṣapāda Gautama in his *Nyāyasūtra* (*AGN*). In ancient Greece the problem was raised in Plato's Academy by the master himself. It was resolved by Aristotle in the form of a fully developed philosophy of science presented in his *An.post.* Plato had inherited the problem of dichotomy of knowledge and true belief (ἐπιστήμη and δόξα) along with the problem of being and becoming from his philosophical ancestors. His philosophical system may be viewed as a sustained effort to resolve these problems.

1.1 The Platonic-Aristotelian Concept of Theoretical Science and the Deduction-centeredness of Western Logic

Plato sought to define scientific knowledge in *Meno* 98a as grounded (tethered) true belief (δόξα). A carpenter may have the true belief that a parallelogram is a rectangle if and only if its diagonals are equal and he may use it to ensure that a table top with equal opposite sides is in fact rectangular. But he cannot claim scientific knowledge of this geometrical truth merely on the ground of its successful application by him. One should be able to demonstrate it from the self-evident first principles of Geometry in order to claim scientific knowledge of it. To ground a true belief in the first principles or to anchor it to the first principles, is the same as to derive it from the indemonstrable basic truths in a finite number of steps. This insight of Plato served as a guiding principle for his most distinguished disciple's foundational investigations. Aristotle's philosophy of science developed in his *An.post.* is a carefully worked out response to Plato's problem concerning the nature of scientific knowledge raised in *Tht.* 210b. The truths of a theoretical discipline are required to be derivable from its self-evident first principles. Thus the Platonic notion of scientific knowledge presupposes the concept of derivation (deduction). Aristotle therefore had to unpack the notion of grounding (derivability) before he could hope to develop a theory of science that would be consistent with Plato's insight concerning the distinction between true belief and scientific knowledge. He met this challenge by successfully developing a theory of deductive inference in his *An.pr.* the groundwork for the theory having been prepared in *Top.* and *Int.* Thus western logic acquired its deduction-centeredness before it even saw the daylight.

1.2 Concepts of Theoretical Discipline in the Indian Tradition

At least two distinct models of theory construction and evaluation are discernible in Indian theoretical tradition. The historically earlier of these two models comes to us from the Indian grammatical tradition and may be called the *Vyākaraṇa Model.* The second model considered here comes to us from Aksāpāda Gautama's *AGN* and may be called the *Nyāya Model.* The pervasion-centeredness of Indian Logic can be accounted for by India's ancient institution of debate (*vāda*) and these two dominant models of theorization

1.2.1 Vyākaraṇa Model: Deductive Organization of Grammatical Knowledge

For the purpose of the present paper it is necessary to distinguish between Pāṇini's deductive model of organization of grammatical knowledge developed in *Aṣṭ* and his method of grammar-building. In contrast with the *Greek model of deductive systematization* developed by geometers beginning with Thales and epitomized in Euclid's monumental work *Elements* [16], the model of deductive systematization used in *Aṣṭ* may be called the *Pāṇinian model* of deductive systematization (PDS). Pāṇini adopted this model with full awareness of the immense challenge he was facing. The morphological component (*pada-vyutpatti bhāga*) of his grammar aims at an empirically adequate and correct deductive theory for generating the body of admissible words (*padas*) in Vedic and classical Sanskrit. The *saṃjñnā* and *vidhi sūtras* serve as definitions and axioms. Taking atomic noun stems (*avyutpanna prātipadika*) and verb stems (*dhātu*) as arguments, the morphological component generates the class of admissible words (*pada*) as values of grammatical operations known as *pratyayas*. The derivational machinery of the morphological component together with the deductive sub-system of the grammar dealing with the morpho-phonemic phenomena known as *sandhi* (*saṃhitā*) permit one to compute the values of the syntactic operations (*pratyayas*) for arbitrarily given arguments from their appropriate domains. The outputs of the word-generating component of the grammar serve as inputs for its sentence generating component (*vākya-vyutpatti-bhāga*) that is based on the theory of cases (*kāraka* theory). It is not necessary for our purpose to go into the details of derivational procedures (*siddhi-prakriyā*) and the methodology of grammar-building. It is a lamentable accident of history that the PDS remained confined to the area of the organization of grammatical knowledge and its immense potential could not be tapped. The model is universal in its scope of application. Compared with the *Greek model of deductive systematization* it has the merit of not being committed to the doctrine of self-evident first principles.

1.2.2 Appraisal of Deductively Organized Grammars

A system of grammar for a language aims at characterizing the informal notion of grammatical correctness of words and sentences (*śabda-sādhutva*) for the language in question. The deductive model of knowledge organization was pressed to extensive service for the first time in Pāṇini (*Aṣṭ*). It was followed by Moggallāna and Hemacandra which present axiomatic grammars for Pāli and Prākṛta (*MS* and *HP*).

An axiomatic system of grammar as a whole has to be treated as the characterization (*lakṣaṇa*) and the body of admissible words and sentences of the language concerned as pre-theoretically presented data (*lakṣya*) to which the system must remain accountable. Katyāyana, the author of *KV*, shows a keen awareness of the empirical adequacy and correctness conditions for grammars. He explicitly formulates the basis of the theoretical appraisal of axiomatized grammars in the following: "*lakṣyalakṣaṇevyākaranam*".[2] Pātañjali, the author of *PM*, in the introductory section of his work is unambiguous about the basic methodological principle that the grammarian has to treat the totality of admissible words and sentences transmitted through inherited texts as well as those available in contemporary literature and *speech of educated native speakers* of the language concerned as given (*lakṣya*). The grammarian is not at liberty to alter the boundary between admissible and inadmissible data. Grammar is descriptive subject only to minimal constraints on the admissibility of data. The evaluation of an axiomatic system of grammar is analogous to the ascertainment of consistency

[2] *PM*, 1.1.1 *Paspaśāhnika*, *KV* 17. Grammar consists of the corpus of admissible words and sentences construed as that which is to be characterized (the *lakṣya*) together with the body of rules (*sūtra*) as the characterization (the *lakṣaṇa*). Cf. [11, 850c, p. 575].

and completeness of an axiomatic system of logic with respect to a semantically delineated body of laws and valid inferences. What is desired is an exact fit between the axiomatic system (the characterization or *lakṣaṇa*) and the given body of admissible words and sentences (the *lakṣya*). An exact fit between *lakṣaṇa* and *lakṣya* calls however for the absence of under-extension (*avyāpti*) which is the condition of adequacy and also for the absence of over-extension (*ativyāpti*) which is the condition of correctness. Katyāyana proposed a number of changes in Pāṇini's system for eliminating some cases of under-extension (*avyāpti*) and over-extension (*ativyāpti*). Clearly, the proposed modifications aimed at achieving an exact fit between the system and the linguistic data. In grammar building too the ideal of exact fit is presupposed in the use of the method of general rule (*utsarga*) and exception (*apavāda*) for getting hold of regularities in linguistic data. Thus the informal notion of pervasion (*vyāpti*) is an indispensable presupposition of the grammarians" model of theory construction and evaluation.

1.3 The Nyāya Model of Theory Construction and Evaluation

The *Vyākaraṇa* Model, being a model of grammar-building and articulation of grammatical knowledge, is *apparently* limited to theoretical investigations in the field of natural languages. Pāṇini relied on purely syntactical notions for giving mathematically precise definitions of an impressive family of terms often not available in ordinary discourse or available with meanings not suitable for his deductive system. He resorted to the technique of listing for defining certain notions such as that of pronoun (*sarvanāma*) and verb (*dhātu*) where general syntactic characterizations were not possible and philosophical definitions would have proved controversial, imprecise and hence of no real use in the building of his deductive system. Knowledge acquisition and organization in the science of medicine (*āyurveda*), astronomy (*jyotirvidyā*), the science of metre (*chandas*), science of State and many other disciplines seemed to pose challenges of a different nature from the ones faced by the grammarian. The *Nyāya Model* of Akṣapāda apparently emerged in response to this methodological need. Akṣapāda's model did not emerge accidentally but rather through design. This is evident from the structure of *AGN* and also from the related comments of Vātsyāyana *VNB*.[3] The articulation of Nyāya Śāstra proceeds through the following three stages: (i) *uddeśa*: enumeration of the basic entity-types (*padārthas*), (ii) *lakṣaṇa* (and *vibhāga*): characterization and classification of the basic entity-types and their subtypes, (iii) *parīksā*: evaluation of the characterizations and classifications undertaken at stage (ii) for adequacy and correctness. The model offers *a program of construction, development and revision of theories in any field by characterization and classification*

[3]Cf. [1, p. 14].

of entity-types (*padārtha-koṭis*). The need for revision may surface at the third stage because of inadequacy of the initial enumeration undertaken at stage one or on grounds of correctness and internal coherence of the resultant network of characterizations and classifications arrived at the end of stage two. The *Nyāya Model* like that of *Vyākaraṇa* provides for revision and development of theories and underlines the crucial role of experience in this process. Details of this model may be found in [30, pp. 20–24] and [31, p. 960].

1.4 The Pervasion-Centeredness (*vyāpti-kendritatva*) of Indian Logic

A screening of the rational appraisal stage of the *Nyāya Model* shows that system-evaluation here, as in the case of the *Vyākaraṇa Model*, is dependent in an essential way on the informal notion of exact fit between characterization (*lakṣaṇa*) and relevant data (*lakṣya*). But the informal notions of exact fit (*anyonyavyāpti*) of characterization (*lakṣaṇa*) and relevant data (*lakṣya*) as well as the related notions of over-extension (*ativyāpti*) and under-extension (*avyāpti*) presuppose the fundamental notion of *vyāpti* (pervasion). We are thus led to the conclusion that Indian tradition's notion of a theoretical discipline remains incompletely explicated without an adequate characterization of the fundamental relation of pervasion (*vyāpti*). It is well known that the schemata of inference developed in the Indian logical tradition are dependent for their validity in an essential way on the relation of pervasion (*vyāpti*). Therefore, the challenge posed by the problem of the correctness of characterizations (*lakṣaṇa*) and that of the validity of inferential cognitions (*anumāna*) are sufficient to account for what we have called the *pervasion-centeredness* (*vyāptikendritatva*) of Indian logic as contrasted with the *deduction-centeredness* (*nigamana-kendritatva*) of Western logic.

2 The Nature of Logic as a Theoretical Discipline

2.1 Aristotelian Logic

The characterization and systematization of valid deductive inferences has been the central concern of western logic since its foundations were laid by Aristotle. An inference has one or more statements called its premises and another called its conclusion. Aristotle states in *Top.* 100a25–27[4] that "a deduction is an argument in which certain things being laid down some thing other than these necessarily comes about through them". In *An.pr.* 24b18–20 he reiterates this with further clarification: "A deduction is a discourse in which, certain things being stated, something other than what is stated follows of necessity from their being so. I mean by the last phrase that it follows because of them, and by this, that no further term is required from

[4]Cf. also *Soph.el.* 165a1–4.

without in order to make the consequence necessary." What we have here is in fact an informal characterization of the validity of deductive inferences in general. Aristotle formulates the general principle that a valid deduction is a truth-preserving operation in the sense that if its premises are true then its conclusion must also be true (*An.pr.* 53b5–25; 57a36–57b4. Consequently, it is impossible for all the premises of a valid inference to be true while its conclusion is false.

Aristotle must have realized, during the long period of what he calls in the concluding sentences of *Soph.el.* as his experimental researches in logic, that a theory of deductive inference can be based only on an appropriate theory of statement forms which in turn can emerge only from a close analysis of relevant discourse. In the fifth chapter of *Int.* he classifies statements under the heads of *simple* and *composite*. In the next chapter of the same work he classifies simple statements under the heads of *affirmative* and *negative* statements. In the seventh chapter of the same work he develops his theory of contradictory and contrary opposition. A simple statement may affirm or deny something either of an individual such as Plato or of a universal such as Athenian. Statements of the first type may be called *singular* and those of the second type may be called *non-singular* or general. Aristotle uses a concatenation such as "XY" of two capital letters "X" and "Y" to symbolize a general categorical statement with the predicate term X and the subject term Y. One may interpose the letters "a', "e', "i" and "o" between the predicate term X and the subject term Y to symbolize respectively the following four familiar types of statements:

1. $X\mathrm{a}Y$: X belongs to (is predicable of) all Y,
2. $X\mathrm{e}Y$: X belongs to (is predicable of) no Y,
3. $X\mathrm{i}Y$: X belongs to (is predicable of) some Y and
4. $X\mathrm{o}Y$: X does not belong to (is not predicable of) some Y.

2.2 Form and Content in Logic: The Dichotomy of Logical and Extra-logical Concepts

Aristotle formulates in *An.pr.* 24b28–30 *truth conditions* for statements of types (1) and (2), known respectively as *universal affirmative* and *universal negative* statements.[5] Truth conditions for their contradictory opposites belonging respectively to types (4) and (3) known as *particular negative* and *particular affirmative* statements are given implicitly. A statement form determines the truth condition of any concrete statement obtainable from it by the usual process of substitution of concrete terms for the letters serving

[5]Cf. also *Top.* VII 5.

as term variables. By the very nature of its function a statement form can not reveal its subject matter and hence can aptly be called *content non-revealing*. Syntactically a simple Aristotelian statement form is a sequence of three letters the first and the third of which are *variables* and the second *a form-denoting constant*. Aristotle's use of variables in the *Analytics* to stand for the constituent terms of the four types of non-singular (general) statements is a deliberate move designed to achieve the separation of a statement's *form* from its *content*. Łukasiewicz observes that it was his commentator Alexander who first realized that letters were used as term variables in syllogisms "in order to show that we get the conclusion not in consequence of the matter of the premisses, but in consequence of their form and combination; the letters are marks of universality and show that such a conclusion will follow always and for any term we may choose" [26, p. 8]. In Aristotle's theory of statement forms of simple general statements the notions of "predicable of all', "predicable of none', "predicable of some" and "not predicable of some" serve as *logical constants*. In the meta-theory of his system of logic he does use the statement connectives of "if-then', "and" in addition to "not". Von Wright, while discussing a particular valid syllogism observes that

> "Since the syllogism expresses a true proposition independent of the meanings of the variables, we shall say that the syllogism expresses truth because of its form and independently of its content ... We shall say that a sentence which expresses truth because of its form and independently of its content, expresses formal or logical truth [45, p. 2]".

Gilbert Ryle while commenting on the enterprise of ancient and modern logicians, aptly observes that the logical constants of their systems show indifference to subject-matter and hence are *topic-neutral* [37, pp. 115–116]. Strawson observes that *indifference to subject matter* is a characteristic feature of logical constants although not all concepts having this characteristic feature are counted by logicians as logical constants [40, p. 60]. The expressions "*content-neutral*" and "*content-independent*" may be used as synonyms of "*topic-neutral*". The stand taken by Strawson and Ryle on the issue is substantiated by the fact that Aristotle places logic in *First Philosophy* or the science of being *qua* being. He raises the issue of investigation into *the starting points of demonstration* and what the mathematicians call *axioms* as different from postulates, in *Metaph.* 996b26–32 and 997a10–14 and offers a well reasoned answer in *Metaph.* IV 3 to the effect that since these truths hold good of all things *qua* being their investigation belongs to the science that studies being *qua* being and not any particular genus of it. He lucidly concludes with the bold observation:

> Evidently then the philosopher, who is studying the nature of all substance, must inquire also into the principles of deduction. (*Metaph.* 1005b6–7)

While settling the issue of logic's place in the field of sciences this however does not demarcate its boundaries within the domain of First Philosophy. Ryle's dichotomy of *formal and informal logics* is pointing precisely at this problem of boundary demarcation.

2.3 The Role of Semantics in the Construction and Study of Logical Systems

Semantical considerations have continued to play an indispensable role in the history of western logic right from its very beginning. This claim can be made without undermining the role of derivational techniques and proof-theory in general. Aristotle's definition of valid deduction was presented above. It is well known that his system admits only the first three figures of traditional logic and the valid moods of traditional logic's fourth figure are accommodated in the first figure. He axiomatized his system by taking the four valid moods of first figure as basic and by deriving all other valid moods from them. Later on he showed that the two valid moods of the first figure known in traditional logic as BARBARA and CELARENT suffice as a basis [8, pp. 53*sq*]. In *An.pr.* 26a1–4 he relies on his previous explanation of the truth conditions for universal affirmative and negative categorical statements to justify his claim of transparent validity of these two basic patterns of deduction. In order to show the completeness of his system he had to ensure that no valid mood has escaped the net of his axiomatic system. It follows from the definition of valid deduction that the two statement forms constituting the premises of a valid mood are inconsistent with the denial of the statement form that is its conclusion. Aristotle makes repeated use of informal interpretations of statement forms by assigning meanings to the term variables in the domain of concrete general terms in order to show the invalidity of inferential moves or the consistency of two or more statement forms. He uniformly applies a general semantical procedure to show the invalidity of each mood not deducible in his system.[6] This general semantical procedure is implicitly announced in *An.pr.* 26a4–10 where he shows that the combination of the premises $A\mathrm{a}B$ and $B\mathrm{e}C$ in the first figure cannot syllogistically yield any conclusion. For this particular case it is sufficient to show by means of two different interpretations that $A\mathrm{a}B$ and $B\mathrm{e}C$ are consistent separately both with $A\mathrm{a}C$ and $A\mathrm{e}C$, because the consistency of $A\mathrm{a}B$, $B\mathrm{e}C$ and $A\mathrm{a}C$ would show that $A\mathrm{o}C$ can not follow as a conclusion and the consistency of $A\mathrm{a}B$, $B\mathrm{e}C$ and $A\mathrm{e}C$ would show that neither can $A\mathrm{i}C$ follow as a conclusion. Since the laws of subaltern are available in

[6] Cf. [32] or [31, pp. 974–975].

his system, it follows that neither can AaC or AeC be derived as conclusions. The underlying general semantical principle can be easily abstracted from the method used in showing the invalidity of the mood under consideration. The preceding observations show the crucial role that semantical considerations play in Aristotle's system of deductive inference.

This is perhaps an appropriate place to note that Kant refers to Aristotelian logic by the term pure general (formal) logic as contrasted with his transcendental logic [23, pp. 17*sq*, 93–95]. The term *Formal Logic* is widely used as an acceptable synonym of the terms *Symbolic Logic and Mathematical Logic*. The reader's attention may, for instance, be drawn to [35, 21, 40, 8, 9] and the title of an international logic periodical *Notre Dame Journal of Formal Logic*. He may also note Körner's comment on [25, p. 43] to the effect that the development and results of modern logic though unforeseen by Kant are entirely compatible with his views on the nature of formal logic as a science.

2.4 Modern Formal Logic

It is a reasonable claim that the mainstream of modern western formal logic in spite of its extensive use of mathematical methods in the construction and investigation of logical systems has remained loyal to the ethos of ancient Greek logic as found in Aristotle's Syllogistic and the propositional logic of the Stoic-Megarian School. Elementary Logic, from a pedagogical perspective, may be thought of as having two parts, one consisting of the more basic and simpler system SL of *classical sentential logic* and the other being the more profound and inclusive system $FPL_=$ of *Predicate Logic with Function Symbols and Identity.* There are two approaches to a logical system, one *derivational* or *proof-theoretic* and the other *semantical or model-theoretic.* We assume here familiarity with these two basic systems in any of their equivalent formulations and the methods used in their meta-logical investigations.[7] In particular, familiarity with the grammars of un-interpreted sentential and first order languages for any axiomatically formulated system S in one such language, familiarity with the basic proof-theoretic notions of axioms, rules of inference, theorems, logical implication, derivability of a sentence from a set of sentences and logical consistency is assumed. Familiarity with the basic semantic notions of *valuations or two-valued interpretations* for such languages, satisfiability and unsatisfiability of sets of sentences, semantic validity of sentences, semantic entailment of one sentence by another and semantic (logical) consequence of a set of sentences is assumed here. Tarski defines the notion of "being a logical consequence of" as the semantic counterpart of the proof-theoretic notion of "being derivable from" [42, XVI]. The definition is uniquely determined

[7] Cf., e.g., [29, 3].

by the forms of the sentences involved independent of their meanings. His original approach to the definition of truth for formalized languages developed in his paper [42, VIII] is widely adopted by logicians to the study of classical sentential and predicate logics.[8] We remind the reader that a valuation is a special kind of function and is a mathematical representation of our intuitive notion of *a logically conceivable context*. Thus, by defining the concept of valuation for a formal language underlying a system such as SL or $\text{FPL}_=$ we in effect determine the universe of all logically conceivable contexts for that system. Valuations for a language underlying SL are usually called *Boolean valuations* and those for a first order language underlying $\text{FPL}_=$ are called *first order valuations* or simply *interpretations*. Familiarity with different proof-theoretic formulations of these systems and metalogical investigations leading to their consistency and completeness results with respect to the standard two-valued semantics is assumed here. Proof-theoretic and model-theoretic techniques originally developed in the meta-theory of classical logic were soon adapted for the metalogical investigations of non-classical logics.

2.5 Logical Constants and Logical Forms of Sentences

The reader is no doubt aware of the fact that the vocabularies of formal languages for SL and $\text{FPL}_=$ always make provision for a special subcategory of symbols called symbols for *logical constants*. These symbols carry the burden of determining the logical forms of sentences of the language under consideration. From an intuitive standpoint the logical constant symbols of such formal languages are intended to stand for *content-neutral* notions as in the case of the quasi-formal Aristotelian system. In case of a formal language for SL the sentential variable symbols, like the term variable symbols in Aristotle's system, carry the burden of conveying *content* either in the form of interpreted statements or for ease of formal semantics their truth values such as true or false, since it is not the precise contents of interpreted statements but rather their truth values which turn out to be relevant for the semantic appraisal of statement forms or inferential patterns of the language. It is clear that the syntactic items usually called *well-formed formulae* (wffs) of such a formal language are intuitively *statement forms* and these syntactic items are *content non-revealing* because of the use of *content-conveying* variables with pre-specified domains of values as in the case of the four familiar types of categorical statement forms of Aristotle's system.

It is well known that the revival of the study of modal logics in the twentieth century was motivated by the search for a theory of implication which would not admit the paradoxical laws of the pure implicational fragment of

[8] Cf., e.g., [3, pp. 317–321].

SL.[9] The systems S1–S5 of C. I. Lewis are based on a sentential language that has negation (N), conjunction (K) and possibility (M) as primitive logical constants. Strict implication (C^*pq) as opposed to material implication (Cpq) is defined as $NMKpNq$. Implication as a relation obtaining between two statements, whether material or strict, has to be construed as a content-neutral notion. Axiomatic bases for the systems S2–S5 in a sentential language with N, K, disjunction (A) and C^* given by Hacking permit us to view these systems as subsystems of SL having content-neutral logical constants, among which C^* unlike C is not truth-functional [14]. It is clear that the statement forms of the underlying sentential language of these systems by their very nature can not reveal content. The system **E** of entailment due to Anderson and Belnap[10] emerged out of the reasonable requirement that in a genuine relation of implication the antecedent should to be relevant to its consequent. This requirement is however not satisfied by strict implication of even the weakest system S1 of Lewis, since laws such as C^*qApNp and C^*KpNpq in addition to other paradoxical ones are available there. The system **E** and related systems of relevant logic family[11] without quantifiers are based in a sentential language with conjunction, disjunction, negation and entailment as logical constants. Whether truth functional or not, negation and entailment have to be treated as content-neutral notions along with conjunction and disjunction. The statement forms of the underlying formal language are naturally content-non-revealing. These observations continue to hold even after quantifiers are added as logical constants. An important family of non-classical logics, known as intermediate logics lying properly beneath SL and containing the Intuitionist sentential logic have also been investigated by logicians during the last fifty years.[12]

The nature and epistemological status of logical constants used in non-classical systems of logic properly contained in the systems SL or $\mathrm{FPL}_=$, make the notion of absolute content-neutrality problematic. For any axiomatic system S of this kind, our notion of content-neutrality needs to be understood only in a sense that is relative to S, for otherwise the claim that two provably non-equivalent systems of this kind represent different logics, becomes vacuous. We recall that while interpreting an arbitrary class of sentences of $\mathrm{FPL}_=$, whether deductively closed or not, we are required to interpret the logical constant symbols in a pre-specified way and are free only to assign to each non-logical symbol occurring in some sentence of the given set and belonging to a particular lexical category, a unique semantic item defined on the basis of the interpretation's domain and appropriate for

[9]Cf. [19, Chapter 12] and [35, pp. 302*sq*].

[10][36]; cf. also [19, pp. 298–301].

[11]Cf. [43].

[12]Cf. [17, pp. 97–105] and [28].

the lexical category in question. If however one entertains the possibility of varying the meanings of the logical constants too then the meaning of the notion of content-neutrality of the constants naturally becomes dependent on the meanings received by the logical constants. While conceding that the division of symbols in a formal language in to logical and extra-logical is not arbitrary, Tarski expresses his reservations concerning the objective basis of the division.[13] The reader's attention was drawn above to the fact that Aristotle did not find it necessary to demarcate the boundaries of logic within the domain of First Philosophy. Strawson concludes his discussion on logical constants with the following perceptive remarks:

> "... it is partly a matter of choice what expressions are to count as logical constants. We can give general criteria of eligibility; but these leave open a certain field within which selection is possible. One can still discuss the logician's reasons for the selection he makes. [40, p. 49]".

Logicians have paid a great deal of attention during the last six decades or so to the construction and investigation of systems in the areas known as Deontic, Tense and Epistemic logics. One may view these as applications of Modal Logics to selected families of philosophically important concepts such as normative, temporal and epistemic, aimed at uncovering their underlying structures.[14] Hintikka views such systems as *explanatory models* aiming at exploring in depth what ordinary discourse involving normative, temporal and epistemic may reveal at the surface level [18]. Usually these systems are based in SL with additional modal axioms suited to the particular area of application. Admittedly when modal operators are pressed to service as logical constants we can not claim for them content-neutrality of the kind the constants of classical logic have. Given the set-theoretic moorings of both the algebraic and possible-world semantics of these logics, it is reasonable to expect that their classically extra-logical subject matter can be represented in appropriate first order theories.

3 Indian Logic

The internal dynamics of Indian theoretical tradition placed pervasion (*vyāpti*) at the centre of logical investigations in India. Its characterization problem however remained unresolved until the logicians of Nyāya School could identify a suitable family of topic-neutral notions known as *pāribhāṣika-padārthas* to serve as a set of well synchronized tools for gaining precision in conceptual analysis in any arbitrarily given domain of investigation. Limitation of space and our main objective of presenting a framework for the

[13] Cf. the remarks on [42, pp. 418–420].

[14] Cf. [19, pp. 301–302, 262] and [18].

conceptual translation of the enterprise of formal logicians in the West into NN*, stand on the way of going into inference as a mode of justification of knowledge claims in Indian philosophy and the history of the characterization problem of the relation of pervasion. The reader is referred to Sharma, Potter, and Bhattacharya.[15] For the same reason it is not possible to go here into to the *topic-neutral nature of the pivotal notions in the apparatus of analysis and disambiguation developed by the Navya-Nyāya logicians* excepting for a few observations which are essential from the point of view of the present paper. The reader is referred to [41, 12, 20, 27, 13, 5, 6, 38, 4].

The dichotomy of attribute (*dharma*) and attribute possessor (*dharmin*) plays a basic role in the ontology of the Nyāya-Vaiśeṣika system. The terms attribute and property are used here as synonymous. These terms do not reveal the ontological categories of the entities denoted by them, because an attribute can be drawn from any admissible ontological category and so can be its possessor. They only reveal the relative semantic roles of the entities denoted by them in a context of predication. These notions are topic-neutral in the sense that they are neither domain nor discipline-specific and are shared by ordinary discourse (*loka*) and theoretical disciplines (*sarvaśāstrasādhāraṇaā*). We may always construe an attribute as a content (a located entity, *ādheya*) and its possessor as its *locus* (*ādhāra*, *adhikaraṇa*) in the analogy of a book and the particular shelf of a bookcase it is in. A located entity always resides in its locus in virtue of some relation, for example the book is in the shelf by a certain kind of physical contact. Such a relation is construed as *regulating* the locus-content complex in question.

The standard schema of predication in Navya-Nyāya is the following: x is y-possessing (y-*vān* x), where y is an attribute (*dharma*) and x is the possessor of the attribute (*dharmin*). We note that the variables x and y can take individuals or shared properties such as universals as values. Since an attribute can always be viewed as a content with the possessor of the attribute in question as its locus and since a locus-content complex must have a unique regulating relation, the predicate *y-possessing* can be represented as an ordered pair (r, y^*) where r is the regulating relation of the locus-content complex and y^* is the generic feature characterizing the attribute y. Thus *every predicate must have two constituents, one relational and another attributive.* For example in the statement "Socrates is armoured" the predicate is to be construed as a pair (r, a^*) where a^* is the generic feature of being an armour and r is a particular kind of physical contact that has to obtain between a suit of armour and a person for us to say that the person is armoured. In the statements "Socrates is running / is arguing / is an Athenian / is a man / is taller than Plato" analogous pairs are to be construed as predicates.

[15] Cf. [39], [33, pp. 179–208], and [34, pp. 69–81].

4 Inferential Schemata

The Nyāya schema of inference with five constituent sentences called *avayavas* along with the Buddhist inferential schema having three constituents emerged out of the ancient Indian tradition of debate. The Nyāya schema, where stock examples serve as variables, is as follows:

(1) *pratijñā* (a thesis to be established by inference): The hill has fire, [p is s-possessing]

(2) *hetu* (the ground on which the claim is made): (since) it has smoke [(since) p is h-possessing],

(3) *udāharaṇa* (the general law and instantiation (*dṛṣṭānta*)): any thing that has smoke has fire also, e.g., the country kitchen [h *is pervaded by* s, as seen for example in d],

(4) *upanaya* (application of the general law to the case in hand): The hill has smoke that is invariably attended by fire [p is h-possessing with h *pervaded by* s],

(5) *nigamana* (the conclusion): therefore, the hill has fire [therefore, p is s-possessing]

In the preceding schema of inference, p, h, s, d, h-possessing and s-possessing are to be treated as term variables. The former four are atomic and the latter two are compound. The compound terms h-possessing and s-possessing are to be interpreted respectively as (r_h, h^*) and (r_s, s^*). We note that the relations r_h and r_s need not be the same. E.g., consider the statement "A zebra is not a horse." The attribute of being a zebra is pervaded by the attribute of being different from any given horse. The relation of an individual zebra to its species is not the same as its being different from every horse. *The relation expressed by "is pervaded by" happens to be the only logical constant that occurs in the schema's third and fourth constituents.*

An attribute-possessor (*dharmin*) is called a *pakṣa* (p) when in an inferential context it is to be shown as possessing a certain featured attribute called *sādhya*(s) on the basis of possessing some other attribute called *hetu* (h) (*sādhana*, ground, basis, reason). A *dṛṣṭānta* (d) (paradigmatic instance) is an attribute-possessor (*dharmin*) which in an inferential context plays the role of possessing the properties serving as *hetu* and *sādhya* or possessing their absences. Since an inferential context may belong either to ordinary discourse or to a theoretical discipline and the concepts of *pakṣa* (locus), *hetu* (ground) and *sādhya* (inferred attribute) are neither discipline specific nor subject-matter specific, the schema of inference presented above is applicable in any domain of discourse.

4.1 On the Relation of Pervasion (vyāpti)

Pervasion (*vyāpti*) is a special kind of relation between two non-empty i.e., instantiated (*prasiddha*) properties (*dharmas*). The relation holds between two properties (*dharmas*) A and B if and only if there is at least one individual x (a *dharmin*) that possesses both A and B and there is no individual that possesses A while failing to possess B. In such a case we say that A is the pervaded (*vyāpya, gamaka, sādhana*) and B is the pervader (*vyāpaka, gamya, sādhya*). Thus pervasion is a relation that can hold between two co-occurring properties when certain additional conditions are satisfied such as in the case of any biological species and its genus. For the Navya-Nyāya definition of pervasion the reader is referred to [34, p. 176] and [6, pp. 109–114]. The Navya-Nyāya logicians are careful to use in the definition of pervasion only indisputably topic-neutral notions from their general apparatus of analysis and disambiguation. Since the properties functioning as terms of this relation can pertain to any arbitrarily given domain of objects, the relation of pervasion is obviously topic-neutral like the relations of identity and difference. Implicit in the Navya-Nyāya definition of pervasion is a set of truth-conditions for the statement form "A is pervaded by B". Also implicit in the definitions of topic-neutral notions in the Navya-Nyāya apparatus of analysis and disambiguation are truth-conditions for statement-forms such as "x is (is not) a locus of A" and "A co-occurs with B".

4.2 A Set-theoretic Look at the Relation of Pervasion (*Vyāpti*)

The relation of pervasion (*vyāpti*) is clearly reflexive and transitive. Reflexive and transitive relations are called quasi-orderings. Reflexive, anti-symmetric and transitive relations are called partial orderings. It is known from the theory of ordering relations[16] that every quasi-ordering induces a partial ordering in the quotient set of its original domain under the equivalence relation obtained by making the quasi-ordering go both ways. Given any nonempty domain of objects and the quasi-ordering relation of pervasion (*vyāpti*) among the properties defined in the domain we can define a relation of *co-pervasion* among the properties of the given domain by requiring that pervasion go both ways. This relation of co-pervasion (*anyonya-vyāpti*) is easily seen to be an equivalence relation. The quotient set of the universe of properties consists of classes of co-pervasive properties. Since all co-pervasive properties have the same extension, i.e., are possessed by precisely the same set of objects in the original domain, each compartment which is in fact a class of co-pervasive properties can be associated with a unique subset of the original domain of objects. The partial ordering induced by the relation of pervasion in the quotient set of the uni-

[16] Cf. [7, pp. 4*sq*].

verse of properties under the equivalence relation of co-pervasion, can be identified with the subset relation defined in the universe of all subjects of the original domain of objects. By this process of abstraction all universal properties (*kevalānvayi-dharmas*) in a domain, though different from each other in meaning, will have the same extension, namely the entire domain under consideration. Similarly, if we admit empty properties (*aprasiddha-dharmas*) all such properties will turn out to be co-pervasive and hence will have the empty set as their extension.

5 Accessing Western Formal Logic from NN*

A framework for the conceptual translation of the basic logical and metalogical concepts of western formal logic can be prepared provided one undertakes an initial reconstruction of the inherited Nyāya-Vaiśeṣika ontology in consistency with the indispensable methodological, epistemological and ontological guiding principles of the system as argued for in [30] and then presses the Navya-Nyāya apparatus of analysis and disambiguation i.e., its well-knit family of *pāribhāṣika-padārthas* to service.

In order to remain consistent with its own basic methodological, epistemological and ontological principles and in order to sustain its theory of part and whole (*avayava-avayavi-siddhānta*) the Nyāya-Vaiśeṣika system needs to grant ontological status to aggregates (*samudāya*) as distinct from their constituent elements (*samudāyin*). A case for admitting aggregates as an independent category of entities in Nyāya-Vaiśeṣika ontology is made out in [30, pp. 223–228]. Once this bold step is taken, Cantor's theory of sets becomes accessible to Navya-Nyāya. In particular, the theory of binary relations and functions can be pressed to service to explore the full conceptual potential of Navya-Nyāya.

The doctrine of part and whole (*avayava-avayavi-siddhānta*) is characteristic of Nyāya-Vaiśeṣika ontology. Wholes are structured aggregates of their parts. The configuration of physical contacts among the parts known as the shape (*ākṛti*, *saṃsthāna*, *vyūha*) is the non-inherent cause (*asamavāyi-kāranṇa*) of the whole and its analysis calls for pairs of parts, their precise positions and their mutual contacts in a given system of reference. The structure has the aggregate of parts as its support or locus and not any single part. Therefore the Nyāya-Vaiśeṣika theory of wholes and parts can not be made intelligible without admitting in to the system aggregates as legitimate objects (*padārthas*) whose entity-hood though presupposing the entity-hoods of their members, can not be analyzed solely in terms of them.

Wholes such as physical bodies and chemical molecules are very special kinds of structured aggregates. Not all aggregates with structures qualify as wholes. For example the constellation Great Bear has the shape of a question mark, but it does not qualify as a whole. Although the concept of shape, configuration or structure (*ākṛti*, *saṃsthāna*, *vyūha*) was introduced into the Nyāya-Vaiśeṣika system in the semantical context of the denotations of words, it was too rich a notion to remain confined within the walls of semantics. It soon found an application in the Nyāya-Vaiśeṣika theory of whole and part and is destined to play a crucial role in the foundations of mathematics from a Nyāya-Vaiśeṣika perspective.

Although Navya-Nyāya operates primarily at the level of the intensions of terms there are a number of contexts such as the correctness of characterizations and the mutual pervasion of properties (*samaniyatatva*, *anyonyavyāpti*) where consideration of the extensions of properties is unavoidable. The methodological policy of selective extensional analysis is not inconsistent with the foundational principles of the Nyāya-Vaiśeṣika system. A philosophical system needs to respond to problems in the foundations of mathematics and the special sciences. How can one make sense of a mathematical structure such as the field of Real Numbers or of a Relational Structure (a model) in general from within the conceptual framework of Nyāya-Vaiśeṣika and Navya-Nyāya? Can one afford to pretend that they are just not there, mumble that no one can match mathematicians when it comes to making of myths and hope to get away with it?

In consistency with its methodological principle of the law of parsimony and economy in theory (*lāghavanyāya* and *śāstralāghava*), Navya-Nyāya ought to recognize the empty set as the extension of each vacuous property (*aprasiddha-dharma*). Not every expression denoting a vacuous attribute wears its vacuous-ness on its face like "sterile woman's son (*bandhyāputra*)" or "square-circle". Consider for example the expressions "a common divisor of two integers (not both of which are zero) that does not divide their greatest common divisor", "a common multiple of two integers (not both of which are zero) that is not divisible by their least positive common multiple" and "a cardinal number greater than the power of the class of all positive integers and smaller than the power of the class of all real numbers". It does take some number-theoretic reasoning to show that there cannot be any instance of the first two properties and the third one too can have no instance because of the continuum hypothesis. It is clear that an atomic nominal stem (*avyutpanna prātipadika*) cannot stand for a vacuous attribute and that only derived nominal expressions can fail to denote. Since the expression "vacuous attribute (*aprasiddha-dharma*)" is itself nonvacuous it cannot be without a denotatum. On grounds of economy we may admit a unique entity as the denotatum of all vacuous nominal expressions and call it the empty set. Every attribute can be looked upon as pervading the vacuous attribute, unless one insists on the condition of co-presence as indispensable for pervasion. There is no point in blocking such innocuous cases of pervasion if simplicity in theory can be secured by conceding their legitimacy. In the characterization of pervasion based on non-deviation (*avyabhicaritatva*)[17] when the probandum (*sādhya*) happens to be a universally present property, it is true that no locus can be qualified by the absence of the probandum and consequently the expression "a locus of probandum's absence (*sādhyābhāvavat*)" is a vacuous attribute. However the principle of generosity of interpretation requires that in such a case we take *sādhyābhāvadvṛttitvam* to be saying that a vacuous attribute is pervaded by every attribute.

One more step needs to be taken in way of preparation. An attribute (*dharma*) is called instantiated (*prasiddha*), uninstantiated or vacuous (*aprasiddha*), uniquely instantiated (*ekavṛttika*), many-seated (*anekavṛttika*) or global (*kevalānvayī*) according as it is possessed by at least one entity (*padārtha*), by no entity, by exactly one entity, by many entities or by every entity. This Nyāya-Vaiśeṣika scheme of classification of properties on the basis of their extensions in the entire ontological system can be treated as remaining applicable to any nonempty aggregate of entities of its reconstructed ontology. Such a step of making these concepts domain-relative will permit us to handle with ease properties which are universal, instantiated, many-seated, uniquely instantiated or uninstantiated in any nonempty domain of discourse such as the domain of natural numbers or that of integers.

After these preliminary considerations we are in a position to present the outlines of a scheme for the conceptual translation of the fundamental logical and metalogical notions of western formal logic in to NN*. A system S of formal logic in the mainstream of western tradition aims at the characterization of logical truth, implication, consequence, consistency, inconsistency, dependence and independence. In view of its theoretical objective, it can only be based on a strategically selected family of content-neutral (global) notions usually called logical constants. Formal logic, whether western or Indian, aims at *universal applicability* of its results and consequently must abstain from any kind of content-dependence as the price for securing it. It cannot get off the ground without a theory of statement forms. A logical system S_F based on a family F of content-neutral notions is fully determined by its class V_F of all valuations. Statement forms, from the perspective of NN*, may be viewed as paraphrased structures of determinate cognitions and hence are sharable properties of cognitions. It is a matter of great theoretical convenience that these structures can be represented as particular kinds of sequences of artificial languages having mathematically precise grammars. We may view valuations as loci or possessors of properties (*dharmin, adhikarana*) and statement forms as properties (*dharma, ādheya, contents or located entities*) which may reside in these loci. A state-

[17] Cf. [34, p. 171] and [20, p. 86].

ment form resides in a valuation if and only if the valuation assigns it the value true. Otherwise the valuation assigns it the value false and we say that it is qualified by the absence of the statement form. In the latter case only we say that the denial of the given statement form resides in it.

If we view the valuations of a system as constituting the individuals of a domain and statement-forms as properties which may either hold good or not of these individuals, then for any given statement-form α the class $\mathrm{Tr}(\alpha)$ of all valuations each of which makes α true, i.e, its truth-set, can be seen as its extension. This would permit us to view logically valid statement-forms as universally present properties (*kevalānvayi-dharmas*) in the universe V_F of all valuations. Similarly a logically inconsistent statement-form may be viewed as an attribute possessed by no valuation (*aprasiddha-dharma*). A logically consistent statement form corresponds to an instantiated attribute (*prasiddha-dharma*). Logical consistency of a body of statement forms becomes the same as locus-sharing (*sāmānādhikaraṇya*) of a set of properties and logical-inconsistency becomes failure to share a locus (*asāmānādhikaraṇya*). Logical-implication can be translated as pervasion (*vyāpti*) of the property denoted by the antecedent by the property denoted by the consequent of a conditional statement form. This proposed scheme of translation is applicable to any system of logic with a well defined model theory (semantics) and in particular to the systems SL and $\mathrm{FPL}_{=}$. The Navya-Nyāya topic-neutral notions of property (*dharma*), locus of properties (*dharmin*), relation (*sambandha*),identity (*abheda*), difference (*bheda*), absence (*abhāva*), conjunction (*ubhayatva*) and alternation (*anyataratva*)[18] along with the notions of a property's having an instance (*prasiddhi*), its being present everywhere (*kevalānvayitva*) understood in a sense that is relative to any nonempty domain, as well as the notion of the co-presence of arbitrarily many properties (*sāmānādhikaraṇya*) are adequate for interpreting First Order Logic with Identity in NN*.

Deductive systemization has always played and continues to play a dominant and indispensable role in the sector of exact sciences of western theoretical tradition. The deductive model of knowledge-organization is rightly prized because of its precision and economy. As pointed out earlier the PDS, though accidentally confined to the organization of grammatical knowledge only, is inherently universal in its scope of application. Kātyāyana's profound methodological insight formulated in *KV* 17 that was quoted above in § 1.2.2 is evidently applicable to any domain of theoretical enquiry where deductive systemization is adopted. The body of truths pertaining to the domain under investigation would constitute the *lakṣya* and a deductive system would be a candidate for a *lakṣaṇa*. An exact fit between the two is the best that the builder of the deductive system can hope for and achieve

[18] Cf. [20, pp. 63–65].

unless the domain of truths has the queer character of not being exhaustible by axiomatic techniques. It is true that the logical apparatus underlying the PDS is informal and intuitive. It can be formalized in First order Predicate Logic with Identity and hence also in NN*. The reader should be reminded that the imposing deductive structure of Euclid's *Elements* [16] was not better off until modern formal logic was pressed to service. Since the framework of conceptual translation outlined here makes western formal logic accessible to NN*, the PDS and NN* together make the sector of exact sciences of the West accessible from Indian theoretical tradition.

Primary Sources

AGN. Akṣapāda-Gautama, *Nyāyasūtra*, in: [1].

An.post. = Aristotle, *Analytica posteriora*, in: [2, Vol. I].

An.pr. = Aristotle, *Analytica priora*, in: [2, Vol. I].

Aṣṭ. = Pāṇini, *Aṣṭādhyāyī*, in: [22].

HP. = Hemacandra, *Prākrta-Vyākaranam*, in: [44].

KV. = Kātyāyana, *Vārtika*, printed in the edition listed for *PM.*

Int. = Aristotle, *De Interpretatione*, in: [2, Vol. I].

Meno. = Plato, *Meno*, in: [15].

Metaph. = Aristotle, *Metaphysica*, in: [2, Vol. II].

PM. = Pātañjali, *Mahābhāsya*, Rohtak, Haryana, 1961–1964. Contains *KV.*

Soph.el. = Aristotle, *De Sophisticis Elenchis*, in: [2, Vol. I].

MS. = Moggallāna, *Sūtrapātha*, in: [24, pp. 339–430].

Tht. = Plato, *Theatetus*, in: [15].

Top. = Aristotle, *Topica*, in: [2, Vol. I].

VNB. = Vātsyāyana, Commentary *Nyāya Bhāsya*, in [1].

Bibliography

[1] Akṣapāda-Gautama. *Nyāyasūtra with Vātsyāyana's commentary Nyāya Bhāsya and Viśvanātha's Vṛtti*, volume 91 of *Anandashrama Sanskrit Series*. Anandashrama Press, Pune, 1923.

[2] Jonathan Barnes, editor. *The Complete Works of Aristotle*. Princeton University Press, Princeton, New Jersey, 1985.

[3] Evert W. Beth. *Foundations of Mathematics*. North Holland Publishing Company, Amsterdam, 1959.

[4] Srimohan Bhattacharya and Dinesh-Chandra Bhattacharya. *Bhāratīya Darśanakośa*, volume I. Sanskrit College, Calcutta, 1978.

[5] Sibajiban Bhattacharyya. *Gadadhara's Theory of Objectivity, Part One*. Indian Council of Philosophical Research, New Delhi, 1990.

[6] Sibajiban Bhattacharyya. *Gangesa's Theory of Indeterminate Perception, Part One*. Indian Council of Philosophical Research, New Delhi, 1996.

[7] Garrett Birkhoff. *Lattice Theory*. American Mathematical Society, Providence, 1961.

[8] Innocentius M. Bocheński. *Ancient Formal Logic*. North-Holland Publishing Company, Amsterdam, 1957.

[9] Innocentius M. Bocheński. *A History of Formal Logic*. University of Notre Dame Press, Notre Dame, 1997. Translated and edited by Ivo Thomas.

[10] George Boole. *The Mathematical Analysis of Logic. Being an Essay towards a Calculus of Deductive Reasoning*. Macmillan, Berkeley, & Macmillan, 1847.

[11] George Cardona. *Pāṇini: His Work And its Traditions. Volume One: Background and Introduction*. Motilal Banarsidass Publishers, 1997.

[12] Ramesh Chandra Das, editor. *Maheśa Chandra Nyāyaratna, Navya-Nyāya-Bhāsāpradīpa*. Department of Philosophy, Utkal University, Bhubaneswar, 2006.

[13] Dinesh C. Guha. *Navya-Nyāya System of Logic: Some Basic Theories and Techniques*. Bharatiya Vidya Prakasan, Varanasi, 1968.

[14] Ian Hacking. What is Strict Implication? *Journal of Symbolic Logic*, 28:51–71, 1963.

[15] Edith Hamilton and Huntington Cairns, editors. *The Collected Dialogues of Plato*, volume 71 of *Bollingen Series*. Pantheon Books, New York, 1961.

[16] Thomas L. Heath, editor. *Euclid, Elements*. Dover Publications, New York, 1956.

[17] Arend Heyting. *Intuitionism*. North Holland Publishing Company, Amsterdam, 1966.

[18] Jakko Hintikka. *Models for Modalities*. D. Reidel Publishing Company, Dordrecht, 1969.

[19] George E. Hughes and Maxwell J. Cresswell. *An Introduction to Modal Logic*. Methuen and Co. Ltd, London, 1968.

[20] Daniel H. H. Ingalls. *Materials for the Study of Navya-Nyāya Logic*, volume 40 of *Harvard Oriental Series*. Harvard University Press, Cambridge Massachusetts, 1951.

[21] Richard C. Jeffrey. *Formal Logic: Its Scope and Limits*. Mc Graw-Hill Book Company, New York, 1967.

[22] Brahmadatta Jijnasu, editor. *Aṣṭādhyāyī-Bhāsya-Prathamāvṛtti*. Amritsar, Sonipat, 1974.

[23] Immanuel Kant. *Critique of Pure Reason*. Macmillan & Co Ltd., London, 1961. Translated by Norman Kemp Smith.

[24] Bhiksu Jagadisa Kasyapa, editor. *Palimahavyākarana*. Motilal Banarsidas, Delhi, 2000.

[25] Stephen Körner. *Kant*. Penguin Books Ltd., 1960.

[26] Jan Łukasiewicz. *Aristotle's Syllogistic*. Oxford University Press, London, 2nd edition, 1957.

[27] Bimal Krishna Matilal. *The Navya-Nyāya Doctrine of Negation: The Semantics and Ontology of Negative Statements in Navya-Nyāya Philosophy*, volume 46 of *Harvard Oriental Series*. Harvard University Press, Cambridge, Massachusetts, 1968.

[28] Craig G. McKay. The Decidability of Certain Intermediate Propositional Logics. *Journal of Symbolic Logic*, 33:258–264, 1968.

[29] Elliott Mendelson. *Introduction to Mathematical Logic*. D. Van Nostrand Company Inc., New York, 2nd edition, 1964.

[30] Biswambhar Pahi. *Vaiśeṣika Padārthavyavasthā kā Paddhatimūlaka Vimarśa*. Department of Philosophy, University of Rajasthan, Jaipur, 2000.

[31] Biswambhar Pahi. Formal Logic in Ancient India and Greece. In Govind Chandra Pande, editor, *History of Science, Philosophy and Culture in Indian Civilization. Volume 1, Part 4*, pages 956–993. Centre for studies in civilizations, New Delhi, 2007.

[32] Biswambhar Pahi and N. N. Vyas. On Aristotle's Method of Invalidating Syllogistic Moods. In Biswambhar Pahi, editor, *Studies in Formal Logic*, pages 14–22. Department of Philosophy, University of Rajasthan, Jaipur, 1993.

[33] Karl H. Potter, editor. *Encyclopedia of Indian Philosophy. Volume 2: The Tradition of Nyāya-Vaiśesika up to Gaṅgeśa*. Motilal BanarsiDass, Delhi, 1977.

[34] Karl H. Potter and Sibajiban Bhattacarya, editors. *Encyclopedia of Indian Philosophy. Volume 6: Indian Philososophical Analysis: Nyāya-Vaiśeṣika from Gaṅgeśa to Raghunātha Śiromaṇi*. Motilal BanarsiDass, Delhi, 1993.

[35] Arthur N. Prior. *Formal Logic*. Oxford University Press, London, 2nd edition, 1962.

[36] Alan Ross Anderson and Nuel D. Belnap Jr. The Pure Calculus of Entailment. *Journal of Symbolic Logic*, 27:19–52, 1962.

[37] Gilbert Ryle. Formal and Informal Logic. In Gilbert Ryle, editor, *Dilemmas*, pages 111–129, Cambridge, 1956. Cambridge University Press.

[38] Vasudeva Abhyankara Sastri, editor. *Bhimacharya Jhalakikar, Nyāya-kośa or Dictionary of Technical Terms of Indian Philosophy*. Bhandarkar Institute, Pune, 1928.

[39] Braj N. Sharma. *Bhāratīya darśan me anumāna*. Madhya Pradesh Hindi Grantha Academy, Bhopal, 1973.

[40] Peter F. Strawson. *Introduction to Logical Theory*. Methuen & Co. Ltd., London, 1960.

[41] Kalipada Tarkacharya, editor. *Maheśa Chandra Nyāyaratna, Navya-Nyāya-Bhāsāpradīpa*. Sanskrit College, Calcutta, 1973.

[42] Alfred Tarski. *Logic, Semantics, Metamathematics.* Oxford University Press, 1956. Translated by J. H. Woodger.

[43] Alsdair Urquhart. Semantics for Relevant Logics. *Journal of Symbolic Logic*, 37:159–169, 1972.

[44] P.L. Vaidya, editor. *Prākrta-Vyākaranam with Prakāśikā Auto-Commentary*, volume 60 of *Bombay Sanskrit and Prakrit Series.* Bhandarkar Oriental Research Institute, Bombay, 1958.

[45] Georg H. von Wright. *Form and Content in Logic. An Inaugural Lecture delivered on 26 May 1949 in the University of Cambridge.* Cambridge University Press, 1949.

Reasoning *in* games

R. Ramanujam and Sunil Simon

The Institute of Mathematical Sciences, Central Institutes of Technology (C.I.T.) Campus, Chennai 600 113, India

E-mail: {jam,sunils}@imsc.res.in

1 Introduction

A game can be thought of as any situation where there are multiple players, each having a number of *strategies* available which he can choose to follow, with a preference ordering on the possible outcomes, which in turn are determined by the strategies chosen by the players. Conflicts arise among players (who can be individuals or abstract entities) when they attach different values to an outcome. Players might be in direct conflict with each other or a group of players might try and cooperate to achieve a common goal.

This abstract definition turns out to be very robust and enables social interactions from a wide range of fields to be theoretically modelled as a game. A few examples include companies adopting marketing strategies to win over customers, candidates adopting campaigning plans in an election, biological species trying to pass their respective genes to future generations. A comprehensive collection of problems from various fields being modelled as games can be found in [31].

Game theory tries to analyse situations where there are elements of conflict and cooperation among rational agents. The ultimate aim of the theory is to predict the behaviour of rational agents and prescribe a plan of action that needs to be adopted when faced with a strategic decision making situation. The theory therefore consists of the modelling part as well as the various solution concepts which try to predict the behaviour of such agents and prescribe what rational players should do. The effectiveness of a particular solution concept depends on how precise and effective the prescription turns out to be.

There are some fundamental problems in coming up with such a theory. Most real world interactions are extremely complex and modelling the complete process as a game may not be feasible. The usual approach to overcome this trouble is to consider an abstraction of the situation and to model this abstract setting as a game. Even though all the constituent elements of the situation cannot be preserved, the abstraction tries to retain the most relevant ones. The other challenge is due to the fact that game theory assumes that all players are *rational* whereas in many real world interactions, people often tend to act irrationally.

Mihir K. **Chakraborty**, Benedikt **Löwe**, Madhabendra Nath **Mitra**, Sundar **Sarukkai** (*eds.*). Logic, Navya-Nyāya & Applications. Homage to Bimal Krishna Matilal. College Publications, London, 2008. Studies in Logic 15. pp. 261–285.

Received by the editors: 14 May 2007; 15 March 2008.
Accepted for publication: 13 April 2008.

Games can be represented in various ways depending on the amount of strategic details that need to be preserved during the abstraction process. The two popular methods of representation are the strategic form (or normal form) which results in "small" games and the extensive form used to represent "large" games where the game structure is presented explicitly.[1]

This article, which is mainly an expository account, is organised as follows. We begin with strategic form games and then outline two approaches to reason about large, complex games. One works with algebraic structure in a large game, and the other with graphical structure. We then try and motivate the necessity to reason about strategies rather than be content with reasoning about games. We present a syntax for strategy specifications (similar to the algebraic structure for games) to describe partially known strategies on graphical games, and show how notions like equilibria may be studied in such a setting.

Strategic form games

Consider the classic situation of two children wanting to divide a piece of cake among themselves. The solution is to let one child divide the cake and let the other choose which piece he wants. Each child wants to maximise the size of his piece, and therefore this process ensures fair division. The first child cannot complain that the cake was divided unevenly and the second child cannot object since he has the piece of his choice. This is a very simple example of a game where two players have conflicting interests and each player is trying to maximize his payoff. The final outcome of the division depends on how well each child can anticipate the reaction of the other and this makes the situation game theoretic.

A game can be presented by specifying the players, the strategies available to each player and the payoff for each player. In the case of a two person game, this can be presented efficiently in a matrix form. For instance the cake cutting game can be represented using the matrix shown in Figure 1. We will refer to the players as *cutter* and *chooser*. Here both players have two strategies, each can choose to cut the cake evenly or to make one piece bigger than the other, which corresponds to picking one of the rows of the matrix. Chooser can choose the bigger piece or the smaller piece, which corresponds to picking one of the columns of the matrix. The outcome for the cutter, after both the players choose their strategies, is the corresponding entry in the matrix. For instance, if the cutter chooses to make one piece bigger and the chooser picks the bigger piece, then the outcome will be that the smaller piece goes to the cutter (bottom left cell). The chooser's outcome is the complement of the cutter's. An equivalent

[1]Note that "small" and "large" are informal notions relating to the typical number of moves in such games.

	Choose bigger piece	Choose smaller piece
Cut the cake evenly	Half of the cake	Half of the cake
Make one piece bigger	Small piece	Big piece

FIGURE 1.

	Choose bigger piece	Choose smaller piece
Cut the cake evenly	0	0
Make one piece bigger	-1	1

FIGURE 2.

representation of the game can be obtained by replacing the outcomes with numbers representing *payoffs* as shown in Figure 2.

The cake cutting game captures the situation of pure conflict, where cutter's gain is chooser's loss and vice-versa. Such games are called *zero-sum* or *win-loss* games. If the cutter had the option of choosing any of the four available outcomes, he would prefer to have the big piece. However, he realizes that expecting this outcome is highly unrealistic. He knows that if he were to make one piece bigger, then the chooser will pick the bigger piece leaving him with the remaining smaller one. If he divides evenly, then he will end up with half of the cake. The cutter's choice is really between the smaller piece and half of the cake. Therefore he will choose to take half of the cake (top left cell) by making an even split of the cake. This amount is the maximum row minimum and is referred to as the *maximin*.

Now consider a variation of this game where the chooser is required to announce his choice (big or small piece) before the cake is cut. This does not change the situation, the chooser would still choose a bigger piece irrespective of how the cutter divides the cake. i.e., the chooser looks for the minimum column maximum (*minimax*) value, which happens to be the top left cell. In this example, the maximin value and the minimax value both happen to be the top left cell. For a game when the maximin value and the minimax value is identical, the outcome is called the *saddle point.* When a game has a saddle point it is the expected rational play since either player cannot unilaterally improve his payoff. A win-loss game is said to be *determined* if a saddle point exists.

Formally a two player zero sum game where player 1 has m strategies and player 2 has n strategies can be represented by an $m \times n$ array A, where the (i, j)th entry $a_{i,j}$ represents the payoff of player 1 when he chooses the strategy i and player 2 picks strategy j. The payoff for player 2 for the corresponding entry is $-1 \times a_{i,j}$. Note that non zero sum payoffs can easily be represented by replacing each matrix entry by a tuple of payoffs for each player.

	Heads	Tails
Heads	1	-1
Tails	-1	1

FIGURE 3. Matching pennies

Unfortunately not all games have saddle points. One of the simplest examples is the game of "Matching pennies" depicted in Figure 3. In this game two players simultaneously place a penny (heads or tails up). When both the pennies match, player 1 gets to keep both. If the pennies do not match, then player 2 gets to keep both. Its easy to see from the payoff matrix that maximin is -1 whereas minimax is 1. It is well known that the best way of playing matching pennies is to play heads with probability half and tails with probability half. This amounts to a *mixed strategy* rather than a *pure strategy* of picking an action with absolute certainty. The minimax theorem asserts that for all two player zero sum games, there is a rational outcome in mixed strategies [35].

The theory can be extended from zero sum objectives to non zero sum objectives with more than just two players. In this case the outcome of the game will specify a payoff for each of the players. The commonly used solution concept in this context is that of Nash equilibrium which corresponds to a profile of strategies, one for each player which satisfies the property that no player gains by unilaterally deviating from his equilibrium strategy. John Nash [22] formulated this notion of equilibrium for multiplayer non zero sum games and proved the analogue of the min-max theorem for such games. The result states that for all finite multiplayer games, there exists a mixed strategy (Nash) equilibrium profile.

Much of the mathematical theory developed for games talks about existence of equilibrium and does not shed light on how the players should go about playing the game. For two person zero sum games, one can show that the maximin theorem is equivalent to the LP (linear programming) duality problem. Therefore construction of optimal strategies is possible using linear programming techniques [36]. For two person non zero-sum games, optimal strategies can be constructed using techniques for solving the linear complementarity problem as shown in [18]. For a multi-player game, Nash's theorem talks of existence of equilibrium but it is not known how to actually construct the equilibrium strategy.

2 Reasoning about games

Strategic form games give a highly abstracted presentation of a game. The representation typically assumes "small" games where the structure of the strategy (individual moves which build up to form the strategy) is absent (or abstracted away). In the context of pure strategies, the above mentioned existence theorems dictate which strategy a player should employ in the game. However, we also need to analyse larger games where the players' actions are part of the representation. We now address reasoning in such a context.

2.1 Game logics

One natural way is to consider a large game as being built up structurally from small atomic games by means of composition. This suggests an algebraic structure in games, and one line of work in game logics proceeds by imposing a program-like compositional structure on games.

Program logics like the propositional dynamic logic (PDL) have been developed to reason about programs [13]. The idea here is to model programs as being constructed using operations like sequential composition, iteration, etc. on simple atomic programs. This compositional approach in program reasoning has been successful in the analysis and verification of programs, especially in giving us insights into the expressive power of various programming constructs. The natural extension to this methodology is to come up with a dynamic logic to reason about multi-agent programs and protocols. Game logic introduced by Parikh in [23] addresses this issue. Game logic (GL) is a generalisation of PDL for reasoning about determined two person games.

Syntax

Let the two players be denoted as player 1 and player 2. Like PDL, the language of GL consists of two sorts, games and propositions. Let Γ_0 be a set of atomic games and P a set of atomic propositions. The set of GL-games Γ and the set of GL-formulas Φ is built from the following syntax:

$$\begin{aligned} \Gamma &:= g \mid \gamma_1;\gamma_2 \mid \gamma_1 \cup \gamma_2 \mid \gamma^* \mid \gamma^d \\ \Phi &:= p \mid \neg\varphi \mid \varphi_1 \wedge \varphi_2 \mid \langle\gamma\rangle\varphi \end{aligned}$$

where $p \in P$ and $g \in \Gamma_0$. Let $[\gamma]\varphi := \neg\langle\gamma\rangle\neg\varphi$ and $\gamma_1 \cap \gamma_2 := (\gamma_1^d \cup \gamma_2^d)^d$.

The formula $\langle\gamma\rangle\varphi$ asserts that player 1 has a strategy in game γ to ensure φ and $[\gamma]\varphi$ expresses that player 1 does not have a strategy to ensure $\neg\varphi$, which by determinacy is equivalent to the fact that player 2 has a strategy to ensure φ. The intuitive definition of composite games are as follows: $\gamma_1;\gamma_2$ is the game where γ_1 is played first followed by γ_2, $\gamma_1 \cup \gamma_2$ is the game where player 1 moves first and decides whether to play γ_1 or γ_2 and then the chosen game is played. In the iterated game γ^*, player 1 can choose how often to play γ (possibly zero times). He need not declare in advance how many times γ needs to be played, but is required to eventually stop. The dual game γ^d is same as playing the game γ with the roles interchanged. The formal semantics is given below.

Semantics

A game model $M = ((S, \{E_g \mid g \in \Gamma_0\}), V)$ where S is a set of states, $V : P \to 2^S$ is the valuation function and $E_g : S \to 2^{2^S}$ is a collection of *effectivity functions* which are monotonic, i.e., $X \in E_g(s)$ and $X \subseteq X'$ imply $X' \in E_g(s)$. The idea is that $X \in E_g(s)$ holds whenever player 1 has a strategy in game g to achieve X.

The truth of a formula φ in a model M at a state s (denoted $M, s \models \varphi$) is defined as follows:

$$\begin{array}{lll} M, s \models p & \text{iff} & s \in V(p) \\ M, s \models \neg\varphi & \text{iff} & M, s \not\models \varphi \\ M, s \models \varphi_1 \wedge \varphi_2 & \text{iff} & M, s \models \varphi_1 \text{ or } M, s \models \varphi_2 \\ M, s \models \langle\gamma\rangle\varphi & \text{iff} & \varphi^M \in E_\gamma(s) \end{array}$$

where $\varphi^M = \{s \in S \mid M, s \models \varphi\}$. The effectivity function E_γ is defined inductively for non-atomic games as follows. Let $E_\gamma(Y) = \{s \in S \mid Y \in E_\gamma(s)\}$. Then

$$\begin{aligned} E_{\gamma_1;\gamma_2}(Y) &= E_{\gamma_1}(E_{\gamma_2}(Y)) \\ E_{\gamma_1 \cup \gamma_2}(Y) &= E_{\gamma_1}(Y) \cup E_{\gamma_2}(Y) \\ E_{\gamma^d}(Y) &= \overline{E_\gamma(\overline{Y})} \\ E_{\gamma^*}(Y) &= \mu X.Y \cup E_\gamma(X) \end{aligned}$$

where μ denotes the least fixpoint operator. It can be shown that the monotonicity of E_g is preserved under the game operations and therefore the least fixpoint $\mu X.Y \cup E_\gamma(X)$ always exists.

Since game logic was designed to reason about multi-agent programs, the modelling approach is quite different from traditional game theoretic notions. Pauly in [24] presents a semantics for Game logic which is closer to the standard game-theoretic approach.

Satisfiability and model checking are fundamental decision problems associated with any logic. For Game logic, the following theorems show that both are decidable.

Theorem 2.1 (Parikh; [23]). The satisfiability problem for Game Logic is in EXPTIME.

Theorem 2.2. Given a Game Logic formula φ and a finite game model M, model checking can be done in time $\mathcal{O}(|M|^{\mathrm{ad}(\varphi)+1} \cdot |\varphi|)$ where $\mathrm{ad}(\varphi)$ is the alternation depth of φ.

Proof. A proof of this theorem can be found in [25, Theorem 6.21]. Q.E.D.

As shown in [23], it is possible to interpret Game logic over Kripke structures. Over Kripke structures, Game logic can be embedded into μ-calculus [16]. Whether Game logic is a proper fragment of the μ-calculus is not known. It is quite conceivable that model checking for Game logic is easier than model checking for the full μ-calculus. However, Berwanger in [3] shows that this is not the case.

One of the main open problems in Game logic is to give a complete axiomatization of valid formulas of the logic. Parikh in [23] proposed an axiom system and conjectured that it is complete, unfortunately no proof of this has been given so far. For the dual free fragment of Game logic, a complete axiomatization is presented in [23].

In Game logic, starting with simple atomic games, one can construct large complex games using operators like composition and union. Due to the presence of the Box-Diamond duality $\langle\gamma\rangle\varphi \equiv \neg[\gamma]\neg\varphi$, it is easy to see that the games constructed remain determined. The compositional syntax of Game logic presents an algebra for game construction. Rather than look at arbitrarily large games, this approach gives us a way of systematically studying complex games in a structured manner and to also look at their algebraic properties. One should however note that the emphasis in this approach is to reason about games, to study the structure of games with interesting properties and definability conditions.

2.2 Graphical games

Graphs are another convenient way of representing large games in such a way that the structure of the game is preserved. The nodes of the graph are game positions and edges represent player moves that are enabled. In this article we consider only *turn based games*: these are games where at any position a single player moves. This can be modelled by having every game position (except for leaf nodes) being assigned to a particular player. A play is then just a path (a sequence of vertex and edge labels) in the graph. Traditional games like chess, bridge, backgammon etc. have a set of rules associated with them which specifies the legal moves of each player. Such games can be easily transformed into graph games where the game positions and actions are derived from the rules specified. A graphical game therefore consists of a game arena (the game graph) along with a winning condition. Formally we can define it as follows:

Game Arena

Let $\Lambda = \{1, 2, \ldots, n\}$ be a finite set of players and $\Sigma = \{a_1, a_2, \ldots, a_m\}$ be a finite set of action symbols, which represent moves of players. For a graph $G = (W, \longrightarrow)$ with vertex set W and edge relation $\longrightarrow: W \times \Sigma \to W$, let the set of successors of $s \in W$ be defined as $\vec{s} = \{s' \in W \mid s \xrightarrow{a} s'$ for some $a \in \Sigma\}$. A node $s \in W$ is a *terminal* node if $\vec{s} = \varnothing$. A **game arena** is a graph $\mathcal{G} = (W, \longrightarrow, s_0)$ with $W = \bigcup_{i \in \Lambda} W^i \cup \{W^{\mathsf{leaf}}\}$. For $i \in \Lambda$, W^i is the set of *game positions* for player i and W^{leaf} is the set of terminal game positions. s_0 is the initial node of the game and the transition function $\longrightarrow: (W \times \Sigma) \to W$ is a partial function also called the move function. In an arena, the play of a game can be viewed as placing a token on s_0. If player i owns the game position s_0 (i.e $s_0 \in W^i$), then she picks an action 'a' which is enabled for her at s_0 and moves the token to s' where $s_0 \xrightarrow{a} s'$. The game then continues from s'. Formally, a play in $\mathcal{G}$ is a (possibly infinite) path $\rho : s_0 a_0 s_1 a_1 \cdots$ where we have for all j that $s_j \xrightarrow{a_j} s_{j+1}$. Let Plays denote the set of all plays in the arena.

The arena $\mathcal{G}$ as defined above merely describes the rules by which the game progresses. More interesting are the objectives of the players, which specify the game outcomes. We assume that each player has a preference relation over the set of plays. Let $\preceq^i \subseteq (\text{Plays} \times \text{Plays})$ be a complete, reflexive, transitive binary relation denoting the preference relation of player i for $i \in \Lambda$. Then the game G is given as, $G = (\mathcal{G}, \{\preceq^i\}_{i \in \Lambda})$.

Determinacy for reachability games

We first consider the case of games (on possibly infinite graphs) where there are two players (i.e., $\Lambda = \{1, 2\}$) with strictly conflicting objectives. Win-loss objectives can be presented in a very simple way by just specifying the set of winning plays for a player (say player 1) instead of giving the explicit preference relation for both the players. The simplest winning condition is the reachability condition which specifies a play to be winning for player 1 if a game position in a specific set of good game positions is reached at least once.

The first step in analysing such a game is to check if determinacy holds. Unlike in Game Logic, where determinacy can be presented as a formula, showing determinacy directly using game-theoretic techniques is quite non-trivial. Determinacy for reachability games however can be shown quite easily using a technique similar to backward induction [17] on extensive form game trees. The idea is to inductively build the set of game positions U from which player 1 has a winning strategy. Initially we take U to be the set of all good game positions specified by the reachability condition and at any stage expand this set by its *attractor set* [39] which is basically the set of all game positions from where player 1 can force a visit into some vertex of U in finitely many steps.

Determinacy for regular objectives

When we consider **infinite plays**, more interesting general winning conditions (than reachability) can be considered. For instance, a infinite play is said to be winning for player 1 if a specific set of game positions is visited during the play *infinitely often*. This is referred to as a Büchi condition. Alternatively, several such sets may be given and we may insist that the set of all infinitely often visited positions in a winning play should figure among the given ones. This is called the Muller condition. Such conditions broadly come under the category of ω-regular objectives [10]. Parity objectives, whereby we associate a finite set of numbers to label game positions and determine winning by considering the parity of (say) the highest visited number, neatly generalize the abstractions studied in this manner.

For games with ω-regular objectives, determinacy follows from a very general result due to Martin [20] which states that all Borel games (a class containing regular objectives) are determined. Adopting this technique however results in winning strategies which in general need to keep track of the entire history of the play and therefore not implementable by finite state machines. Of particular interest are the following two types of strategies:

- Positional (memoryless) strategies: These are strategies for which the next move depends only on the current game position and not on the entire history of play.

- Finite memory strategies: These are strategies where the dependence of the next move to the history of the play can be kept track of by a finite set of states.

Both positional and finite memory strategies can be implemented using finite state automata where the state space of the automaton corresponds to the memory required by the strategy. In particular a positional strategy can be implemented by an automaton with a single state.

For a game with regular winning condition given by the Muller condition, Gurevich and Harrington show that finite memory strategies suffice for winning [11]. In the case of parity games, the existence of memoryless winning strategy was shown by Emerson and Jutla [7].

Applications to automata theory

Establishing positional or finite memory determinacy for a class of games is only a first step in the analysis of those games. For the determinacy theorem to be useful, it is also crucial that we are able to construct the winning strategy. For games played on a finite game arena, we can strengthen the determinacy result from an existence result to one where the winning strategy can be effectively constructed. The *Büchi-Landweber theorem* [5] states that for games played on finite graphs the set of "winning" game positions for each of the players, along with the respective winning strategy can be effectively computed. McNaughton [21] presents a simpler constructive proof for Muller games played on finite game arena where he gives an exponential time algorithm to compute the finite memory winning strategy. Since finite memory strategies can be implemented using finite state automata, the above mentioned theorems imply that for two player zero sum games played on a finite game arena with an ω-regular winning condition, the game is determined and the winning strategy can be synthesized as a finite state automaton.

The techniques developed in the analysis of infinite two player zero sum graphical games have been used extensively in areas outside game theory especially in automata theory and to show the decidability of various modal logics and monadic second order logics. For instance, it has been shown that the model checking problem for μ-calculus is equivalent to deciding the winner in a parity game via a linear time reduction [8, 37]. Along with the result in [3] (mentioned in § 2.1) this also implies that model checking Game logic is not easier than solving parity games. The closure under complementation of automata on infinite trees is another consequence of the determinacy theorem for parity games as shown in [11]. This gives an elegant proof of the difficult part of Rabin's theorem which shows the decidability of monadic second-order theory of the infinite binary tree [26].

A detailed exposition on the applications of techniques developed for infinite games in automata theory and logic can be found in [10].

Overlapping objectives

Infinite games on graphs have been extensively studied in the two player zero sum setting. It makes sense to also look at multi-player non zero-sum games on graphs. Since objectives need not be strictly conflicting, each player can have a preference relation inducing an ordering over the set of valid plays. The game is specified by presenting the game arena along with the preference relation for each player. The notion of equilibrium remains the same as seen in § 1. However, it is no longer clear how to construct an equilibrium strategy profile for a game in general. For games where the objectives of each player is specified by an omega regular condition, the existence of Nash equilibrium is shown in [6]. Ummels in [32] shows the existence of subgame perfect equilibrium for such games.

There is also the question of rational behaviour when we consider games which are not strictly competitive. In the case of finite games, the assumption of rational behaviour has led to the classical concept of *iterated admissibility*, which is based on the well studied notion of weak dominance of strategies. A strategy μ_1 of a player is said to dominate strategy μ_2 if against any choice of strategies of the other players, μ_1 performs at least as well as μ_2 and there are cases when μ_1 performs strictly better than μ_2. As a consequence of rationality, when a player takes into account all strategies of the other players, she will avoid playing dominated strategies. Each player eliminates from her set of strategies those which are dominated. Since rationality is common knowledge each player knows which strategies his opponents eliminated, and as a result he might discover that some of his remaining strategies are dominated when taking into account the new set of possible strategies by the opponents. This leads to further elimination. For games with finite strategy spaces it is easy to see that this process stabilises after a finite number of iterations. A solution concept like the Nash equilibrium predicting the outcome of the game should only involve strategies that survive iterated elimination since those are the only strategies a rational player will need to reason about.

For infinite non zero-sum multi-player games, since it is not clear how to come up with an equilibrium strategy profile, we need some methods to prune down the strategy space that needs to be considered for equilibrium outcomes. This can be achieved by generalising the concept of iterated admissibility to infinite games, since any equilibrium strategy is required to be iteratively admissible. However, the generalisation is not very obvious as the elimination process might not even terminate. Berwanger in [4] studies the question of rational behaviour in this context, and shows that in the case of ω-regular games, the iteration always terminates after a finite number of steps and that the set of iteratively admissible strategies is itself regular.

3 Reasoning in games

The pattern of reasoning about games presented in the previous section consists of trying to find when games are determined and characterising the type of winning strategy that needs to be employed. Throughout the discussion so far, strategies are assumed to be complete plans which prescribe a unique action for every possible scenario. Therefore coming up with a winning strategy requires the entire game graph to be explored and analysed. But this may be a tall order: even when the game is finite, the state space could be so large that exploring all possibilities might be computationally infeasible.

A classic example of such a game is the game of chess. Zermelo showed in [38] that chess is determined, i.e., either there exists a pure strategy for one of the two players (white or black) guaranteeing that she will always win or each one of the two players has a strategy guaranteeing at least a draw. However, neither do we know which of the three alternatives is the correct one, nor a winning strategy. For games like Hex, it is known that the first player can force a win but nonetheless a winning strategy is not known [9]. Connect four is yet another game which has been shown to be determined [1]. Theoretically a finite game like chess or hex is not very interesting since in principle, the winning strategy can be found out in a finite amount of time. The winning strategy is positional and therefore can be presented as a finite state automaton as well.

Unfortunately these results are of no help in advising a player on how to play in an actual game. The situation gets worse in the case of games with overlapping objectives. In general, such games can have multiple Nash equilibria and even if we forget about the computational issues, it still leaves the problem of which equilibrium the players should try to attain. Harsanyi and Selten in [15] develop an equilibrium selection theory where a unique Nash equilibrium is selected. However, due to the complexity associated with the theory, it is not clear if players would actually employ this in order get advice on how to play. In such situations rather than be content with reasoning *about games* using the functional notion of strategies, one needs to reason *about strategies*. Strategies need to be compared with each other to check which ensures better outcome, and their structure needs to be explicitly analysed. Moreover the strategy employed by a player may well depend on her knowledge of or belief regarding the strategies followed by other players.

This is a departure from the classical solution concepts in game theory where the emphasis is on figuring out what happens if a player deviates from the equilibrium strategy. Since specifying the complete strategy may not be possible, one needs to look at partial specifications of strategies and try to compose such specifications in some manner. Heuristics for instance, are extensively used in many of the chess playing programs (such as Crafty and GNU Chess). Listed below are some of them [19, 29]:

- Alpha-beta pruning: This is employed to reduce the number of possibilities evaluated in a search tree by the min-max procedure. It stops evaluating a move completely when it finds the existence of at least one witness which shows that the move is inferior to earlier examined ones.

- The killer move heuristic: Alpha-beta pruning is most efficient when the best moves are considered first. The killer move heuristics tries to guess the best move. The idea being that a move which is good from a different but similar position might also be a good move in the current position.

- Quiescence search: Due to the computational restrictions there is a limit to the number of moves that a machine can search ahead. Humans on the other hand are good at pattern matching and might be able to identify board positions which are interesting and search deeper only on a particular path. Quiescence search tries to emulate this behaviour by making the computer search "interesting" positions to a greater depth than the other positions.

It is quite evident that these heuristics are basically partially specified strategies. A library of such specifications is developed and during the course of play, the actual strategy is built up by composing various partial strategies. Checkers is another game where strong heuristics based game playing programs are available. By performing extensive strategy analysis using computers it was recently shown that perfect play in checkers will result in a draw [30].

Aumann and Dreze [2] make a strong case for the focus of game theory to shift from equilibrium computation to questions of how rational players should play. For zero sum games, the value of the game is unique and rational players will play to achieve this value. However, in the case of non zero sum games as mentioned above, multiple Nash equilibria can exist. This implies that players cannot extract an advice as to which strategy to employ from the equilibrium values. According to Aumann and Dreze, for a game to be well defined, it is also necessary that players have an expectation on what the other players will do. In estimating how the others will play, a rational player should take into account that others are estimating how he will play. The interactive element is crucial and a rational player should then play so as to maximize his utility, given how he thinks the others will play. The strategy specifications we introduce below are in the same spirit, since such a specification will be interactive in the sense of [2].

We look at multi-player non-zero sum graphical games played on finite game arena. Our approach is to combine the techniques presented above to do reasoning *in* games rather than reason about games. We propose a syntax for building strategies, thereby using the techniques developed for graphical games and the ideas in Game logics for reasoning about the strategies in games rather than reasoning about the games themselves. In this work, the emphasis is on coming up with techniques which can advise the players on how to go about playing the game and not on showing existence results that game theory is well known for. Since this requires that we explicitly analyse the structure of the game, graphical games are natural models for our purpose.

In [33], van Benthem uses dynamic logic to describe games as well as strategies and in [14] and [34], van der Hoek and co-authors develop logics for strategic reasoning and equilibrium concepts. This work is close to ours in spirit; however our point of departure is in bringing logical structure into strategies rather than treating strategies as atomic.

We use the graphical game models as defined in § 2.2. For ease of presentation, the technical machinery is developed only for two player games, but the analysis carries over to n-player games where $n > 2$. For convenience we also restrict our attention to finite plays. For this purpose we assume that Σ has a special exit action and that the game arena has a unique terminal node denoted by leaf. For an arena $\mathcal{G} = (W, \longrightarrow, s_0)$, we assume that the transition function satisfies the following property:

- For all $s, s' \in W$ such that $s' \stackrel{x}{\longrightarrow} s'$, $s' = \mathsf{leaf}$ iff $x = \mathsf{exit}$.

Let $\bar{\imath} = 2$ when $i = 1$ and $\bar{\imath} = 1$ when $i = 2$.

Strategies and equilibrium

Let $\mathcal{G}_T$ denote the tree unfolding of the arena $\mathcal{G}$. A strategy for player 1, $\mu = (W_\mu, \longrightarrow_\mu, s_0)$ is a maximal connected subtree of $\mathcal{G}_T$ where for each player 1 node, there is a unique outgoing edge and for the other player every move is included. That is, for $s \in W_\mu$ the edge relation satisfies the following property:

- if $s \in W_\mu^1$ then there exists a unique $a \in \Sigma$ such that $s \stackrel{a}{\longrightarrow}_\mu s'$, where we have $s \stackrel{a}{\longrightarrow}_T s'$.
- if $s \in W_\mu^2$, then for each s' such that $s \stackrel{a}{\longrightarrow}_T s'$, we have $s \stackrel{a}{\longrightarrow}_\mu s'$.

Let Ω^i denote the set of all strategies of Player i in $\mathcal{G}$, for $i = 1, 2$. A strategy profile $\langle \mu, \tau \rangle$ defines a unique path ρ_μ^τ in the game $\mathcal{G}$. This path constitutes a valid *play* if it is of the form $s_0 a_0 \cdots a_{n-1} s_n$ where $s_n = \mathsf{leaf}$. The notion of best response and equilibrium can be defined as follows.

- μ is the best response for τ iff ρ_μ^τ constitutes a valid play and $\forall \mu' \in \Omega_1$ such that $\rho_{\mu'}^\tau$ is a play we have $\rho_{\mu'}^\tau \preceq^1 \rho_\mu^\tau$.
- Symmetric definition for τ.
- $\langle \mu, \tau \rangle$ is a Nash equilibrium iff μ is the best response for τ and τ is the best response for μ.

The natural algorithmic questions that are of interest include:

- Given a strategy τ of player 2, what is the best response for player 1?
- Given a strategy profile $\langle \mu, \tau \rangle$, is it a Nash equilibrium?
- Does the game possess a Nash equilibrium?

Clearly, if we can answer the first question, we can answer the second as well. In any case, to study these questions algorithmically, we need to be able to present the preferences of players' and their strategies in a finite fashion. We do this by presenting the strategies and preference relations of players using finite state automata as shown below.

Advice Automata

In this article, we restrict our attention to *bounded memory* strategies, which can be represented using finite state automata. We think of these as advice automata, in the sense that they constitute an advice for the player to consult at a node. Since our objective is to work with strategies specified by their properties, it makes sense to see them as automata which "accept" a set of strategies.

For a game graph $\mathcal{G}$, a nondeterministic advice automaton for player i is a tuple $\mathcal{A} = (Q, \delta, o, I)$ where Q is the set of states, $I \subseteq Q$ is the set of initial states, $\delta : Q \times W \times \Sigma \to 2^Q$ is the transition relation, and $o : Q \times W^i \to \Sigma$, is the output or advice function.

The language accepted by the automaton is a set of strategies of player i. Given a strategy $\mu = (W_\mu, \longrightarrow_\mu, s_0)$ of player i, a run of $\mathcal{A}$ on μ is a Q-labelled tree $T = (W_\mu, \longrightarrow_\mu, \lambda)$, where λ maps each tree node to a state in Q as follows: $\lambda(s_0) \in I$, and for any s_k where $s_k \stackrel{a}{\longrightarrow}_\mu s'_k$, we have $\lambda(s'_k) \in \delta(\lambda(s_k), s_k, a_k)$.

A Q-labelled tree T is accepted by $\mathcal{A}$ if for every tree node $s \in W^i_\mu$, if $s \stackrel{a}{\longrightarrow}_T s'$ then $o(\lambda(s)) = a$. A strategy μ is accepted by $\mathcal{A}$ if there exists an accepting run of $\mathcal{A}$ on μ. It is easy to see that any bounded memory strategy can be represented using a *deterministic* advice automaton.

Evaluation Automata

The preferences of players can also be presented as a finite state automaton which runs over plays. Let B be a finite state automaton with final states being F. We fix a set of colours C with a preference relation $\lhd^i$ for each player over this set along with a function which maps a final state to each colour in C. The preference relation induces a natural preference ordering over plays by considering the final state reached at the end of the play (note that all plays are finite by definition). The purpose of the evaluation automaton running on a game arena $\mathcal{G}$ can be thought of as checking for certain properties of paths in the arena and providing an appropriate classification. We will use $\mathcal{E}$ to denote an evaluation automaton. Given $\mathcal{E}$ with the set of colours C, for each player i we can always build a set of classical win-loss evaluation automata, one for each colour $c \in C$ where the new automaton wins on all colours at least as preffered as c. We will use $\mathcal{E}^i_c$ to denote such win-loss automata.

4 Strategy specification

We now give a syntax to specify strategies in a structured manner. The atomic case specifies, for a player, what conditions she tests for before making a move. We can associate with the game graph a set of observables for each player. One elegant method then, is to state the conditions to be checked as a past time formula of a simple tense logic over the observables. The structured strategy specifications are then built from atomic ones using connectives. We crucially use an implication of the form: "if the opponent is apparently playing a strategy π then play σ".

Below, for any countable set X, let Past(X) be sets of formulas given by the following syntax:

$$\psi \in \text{Past}(X) := x \in X \mid \neg\psi \mid \psi_1 \vee \psi_2 \mid \diamond\!\!\!-\psi.$$

Syntax

Let $P^i = \{p_0^i, p_1^i, \ldots\}$ be a countable set of observables for $i \in \{1, 2\}$ and let $P = P^1 \cup P^2$.

The syntax is given by:

$$\text{Strat}^i(P^i) := \mathsf{null} \mid [\psi \mapsto a]^i \mid \sigma_1 + \sigma_2 \mid \sigma_1 \cdot \sigma_2 \mid \pi \Rightarrow \sigma$$

where $\pi \in \text{Strat}^{\bar{\imath}}(P^1 \cap P^2)$ and $\psi \in \text{Past}(P^i)$.

Semantics

Given any sequence $\xi = t_0 t_1 \cdots t_m$, $V : \{t_0, \cdots, t_m\} \to 2^X$, and k such that $0 \leq k \leq m$, the truth of a past formula $\psi \in \text{Past}(X)$ at k, denoted $\xi, k \models \psi$ can be defined as follows:

- $\xi, k \models p$ iff $p \in V(s_k)$.
- $\xi, k \models \neg\psi$ iff $\xi, k \not\models \psi$.
- $\xi, k \models \psi_1 \vee \psi_2$ iff $\xi, k \models \psi_1$ or $\xi, k \models \psi_2$.
- $\xi, k \models \diamond\!\!\!-\psi$ iff there exists a $j : 0 \leq j \leq k$ such that $\xi, j \models \psi$.

We consider the game arena $\mathcal{G}$ along with a valuation function for the observables $V : W \to 2^P$. Given a strategy μ of player i and a node $s \in \mu$, let $\rho_s : s_0 a_0 s_1 \cdots s_m = s$ be the unique path in μ from the root node to s. For a strategy specification $\sigma \in \text{Strat}^i(P^i)$, we define when μ conforms to σ (denoted $\mu \models_i \sigma$) as follows:

- $\mu \models_i \sigma$ iff for all player i nodes $s \in \mu$, we have $\rho_s, s \models_i \sigma$.

where we define $\rho_s, s_j \models_i \sigma$ for any s_j in ρ_s as,

- $\rho_s, s_j \models_i \mathsf{null}$ for all ρ_s, s_j.
- $\rho_s, s_j \models_i [\psi \mapsto a]^i$ iff $\rho_s, s_j \models \psi$ implies $\text{out}_{\rho_s}(s_j) = a$.
- $\rho_s, s_j \models_i \sigma_1 + \sigma_2$ iff $\rho_s, s_j \models_i \sigma_1$ or $\rho_s, s_j \models_i \sigma_2$.

- $\rho_s, s_j \models_i \sigma_1 \cdot \sigma_2$ iff $\rho_s, s_j \models_i \sigma_1$ and $\rho_s, s_j \models_i \sigma_2$.
- $\rho_s, s_j \models_i \pi \Rightarrow \sigma$ iff for all player $\bar{\imath}$ nodes $s_k \in \rho_s$ such that $k \leq j$, if $\rho_s, s_k \models_{\bar{\imath}} \pi$ then $\rho_s, s_j \models_i \sigma$.

Above, $\pi \in \text{Strat}^{\bar{\imath}}(P^1 \cap P^2)$, $\psi \in \text{Past}(P^i)$, and for all $i : 0 \leq i < m$, $\text{out}_{\rho_s}(s_i) = a_i$ and $\text{out}_{\rho_s}(s)$ is the unique outgoing edge in μ at s.

The following lemma relates structured strategy specifications to advice automata.

Lemma 4.1. Given a player $i \in \{1, 2\}$ and a strategy specification σ, we can construct an advice automaton $\mathcal{A}_\sigma$ such that $\mu \in \text{Lang}(\mathcal{A}_\sigma)$ iff $\mu \models_i \sigma$.

Proof. We proceed by induction on the structure of σ. We construct automata for atomic strategies and compose them for complex strategies. The states of the automaton consists of sets of subformulas of the past time formulas appearing in σ. Note that the strategy is implemented principally by the output function of the advice automaton.

($\sigma \equiv [\psi \mapsto a]$): The automaton works as follows. The automaton keeps track of past formulas satisfied along a play as game positions are traversed and that the valuation respects the constraints generated for satisfying ψ. The automaton also guesses a move at every step and checks that this is indeed a when ψ holds; in such a case this is the output of the automaton.

($\sigma \equiv \sigma_1 \cdot \sigma_2$): By induction hypothesis there exists $\mathcal{A}_{\sigma_1} = (Q_{\sigma_1}, \delta_{\sigma_1}, o_{\sigma_1}, I_{\sigma_1})$ and $\mathcal{A}_{\sigma_2} = (Q_{\sigma_2}, \delta_{\sigma_2}, o_{\sigma_2}, I_{\sigma_2})$ which accept all strategies satisfying σ_1 and σ_2 respectively. To obtain an automaton which accepts all strategies which satisfy $\sigma_1 \cdot \sigma_2$ we just need to take the product of $\mathcal{A}_{\sigma_1}$ and $\mathcal{A}_{\sigma_2}$.

($\sigma \equiv \sigma_1 + \sigma_2$): We take $\mathcal{A}_\sigma$ to be the disjoint union of $\mathcal{A}_{\sigma_1}$ and $\mathcal{A}_{\sigma_2}$. Since the automaton is nondeterministic with multiple initial states, we retain the intial states of both $\mathcal{A}_{\sigma_1}$ and $\mathcal{A}_{\sigma_2}$. If a run starts in an initial state of $\mathcal{A}_{\sigma_1}$ then it will never cross over into the state space of $\mathcal{A}_{\sigma_2}$ and vice versa.

($\sigma \equiv \pi \Rightarrow \sigma'$): By induction hypothesis there exists $\mathcal{A}_\pi = (Q_\pi, \delta_\pi, o_\pi, I_\pi)$ which accepts all player 2 strategies satisfying π and $\mathcal{A}_{\sigma'} = (Q_{\sigma'}, \delta_{\sigma'}, o_{\sigma'}, I_{\sigma'})$ which accepts all player 1 strategies satisfying σ'. The automaton $\mathcal{A}_\sigma$ has the product states of $\mathcal{A}_\pi$ and $\mathcal{A}_{\sigma'}$ as its states along with a special state q_{free}. The automaton keeps simulating both $\mathcal{A}_\pi$, $\mathcal{A}_{\sigma'}$ and keeps checking if the path violates the advice given by $\mathcal{A}_\pi$, if so it moves into state q_{free} from which point onwards it is "free" to produce any advice. Till π is violated, it is forced to follow the transitions of $\mathcal{A}_{\sigma'}$.

Q.E.D.

For a strategy specification σ, the size of the advice automaton $\mathcal{A}_\sigma$ constructed using the above procedure will be exponential in the size of σ.

5 Comparing strategy specifications

A strategy specification denotes a set of strategies satisfying certain propeties rather than a single strategy and therefore the notion of strategy comparison needs to be re-examined in the new setting. Let C be the set of colours used to classify the runs appropriately by the evaluation automaton and $\lhd^i$ the preference ordering of player i. For a player $\bar{\imath}$ strategy specification π and player i specifications σ and σ', we have various possible definitions as to when σ is better than σ'. Given below are just a few of the possible definitions:

- σ is better than σ' if as long as player $\bar{\imath}$ conforms to π, if there is a $c' \in C$ and a strategy for player i which conforms to σ' ensuring condition c', then there also exists a $c \in C$ where $c' \lhd^i c$ and a strategy for player i which conforms to σ ensuring condition c.

- σ is better than σ' if as long as player $\bar{\imath}$ conforms to π, if for all strategies of player i, which conforms to σ' there is a $c' \in C$ such that the strategy ensures c' then for all strategies which conform to σ, there exists $c \in C$ such that the strategy ensures c where $c' \lhd^i c$.

Having chosen an appropriate notion for comparison, we say that σ is the best response to π if for all σ', we have σ is better (according to that notion) than σ'. A strategy specification pair (σ, π) constitutes an equilibrium if σ is the best response to π and π is the best response to σ.

To algorithmically compare strategies, we first need to be able to decide the following questions. Let σ and π be strategy specifications for player i and player $\bar{\imath}$ and $\mathcal{E}_c^i$ a win-loss evaluation automaton for player i.

- Does player i have a strategy conforming to σ which ensures a valid play that is winning for i with respect to $\mathcal{E}_c^i$, as long as player $\bar{\imath}$ is playing a strategy conforming to π (abbreviated as $\exists\sigma, \forall\pi : \mathcal{E}_c^i$)?

- Is it the case that for all strategies of player i conforming to σ, as long as player $\bar{\imath}$ is playing a strategy conforming to π, the result will be a valid play which is winning for i with respect to $\mathcal{E}_c^i$ (abbreviated as $\forall\sigma, \forall\pi : \mathcal{E}_c^i$)?

We call this the *verification* question. The *synthesis* question is given π and $\mathcal{E}_c^i$ to construct a strategy as a deterministic advice automaton $\mathcal{A}^i$ such that $\mathcal{A}^i, \forall\pi : \mathcal{E}_c^i$ holds (since $\mathcal{A}^i$ is deterministic, we can avoid the quantification).

Theorem 5.1. (Ramanujam-Simon; [28]) Over finite game graphs with Muller objectives,

- The verification problem is decidable.
- The synthesis question is solvable.

These results also enable us to check for a specification σ if it is the best response to the opponent's specification π and to synthesise an advice automaton which is the best response to the opponent's specification π.

A simple logic to reason about structured strategies is presented in [27]. The two main constructs of the logic are:

- $(\sigma)_i : a$ which says that the action a is enabled by the specification σ for player i at a game position.
- $\sigma \leadsto_i \beta$ which asserts that player i can play according to σ and "ensure" β. In other words, for an i node, there exists a choice of action enabled by σ which achieves β. For an $\bar{\imath}$ node, all actions result in β.

The construct $\sigma \leadsto_i \beta$ formalises in a logical framework the backward induction technique. In [27] a complete axiomatization of this logic is presented as well. The truth checking problem for this logic can also be shown to be decidable [28].

6 Example

Probably the best way to illustrate the notion of strategy specification is to look at heuristics used in large games like chess, go, checkers, etc. A heuristic strategy is basically a partial specification, since it involves checking local properties like patterns on the board and specifying actions when certain conditions hold. Heuristics are usually employed when the game graph being analysed is too large for a functional strategy to be specified. Below, we look at a few heuristics applied in chess. Instead of writing explicit formulas we employ a verbal description for convenience. However, it will be clear that the corresponding strategy specifications can be formally presented.

Chess

Fork

Fork or *double attack* are moves that attack two enemy targets simultaneously. Double attacks can be brought about mostly by knight, queen, bishop and pawn. The joy of attacking by pawn is that any two pieces (even if they are defended) are fine since pawn is the least valuable. Checking if a double attack by a pawn is possible is a local check, one just needs to look at the current game position. We can consider this to be an atomic proposition. Therefore we can have a specification as follows.

- If a pawn double attack is possible then play the action resulting in the fork.

Notice that we did not specify a condition of the form "if a pawn is on f2 and the opponent rook and knight are on e5 and g5 respectively then move f2-f4". This would constitute a specific advice which will be part of a functional strategy and not a generic one reflecting the abstract properties of states. In particular this functional strategy would conform to our generic specification mentioned above.

A very common forking piece is the knight because of its unique pattern of movement. The knight is roughly comparable in value to a bishop and is less valuable than a rook or a queen. We can effectively implement a double attack by knight if the attacked pieces are undefended or more valuable (even if it is defended). Therefore the specification will now have an extra conjunct to check these conditions.

- If a knight double attack is available and (the target pieces are not guarded or more valuable) then play the action resulting in the fork.

A queen can also bring about a double attack due to its almost unrestricted movement ability. A queen may sometimes be sacrificed for a checkmate, however it is not usually worthwhile to attack any defended piece with a queen. Therefore a queen double attack is usually implemented only if both target pieces are unguarded or if one target piece is unguarded and the other is the king. We can modify the specification as follows.

- If a queen double attack is available and both target pieces are not guarded then play the action resulting in the fork.
- If a queen double attack is available and (one target piece is not guarded and the other is the king) then play the action resulting in the fork.

The forking strategy itself can be expressed as a specification. For instance a property required to successfully fork with a knight is that the knight and all its targets are placed on squares of the same colour before the move (this is because any time a knight moves, it ends up in a different coloured square). One defence against double attack is to defend the "forking square" (the square used by opponent for double attack). Since in the specification syntax, we can also model responses to opponent's strategy we can make assertions of the form:

- If the opponent is trying to double attack using a knight then defend the forking square.

Pin

A pin occurs when one of the pieces is attacking the enemy king with some other enemy piece blocking its way. In this situation the blocking piece cannot move since its movement will expose the king. The most important consequence of this is that the pinned piece can be attacked. One way to protect the pinned piece is to move other pieces in to defend it. The existence of a pin is again a local property which can be checked by examining the board. A strategy which tries to save a pinned piece can be specified as follows.

- If a piece has been pinned by the opponent then defend the pinned piece.

Admittedly, the heuristics considered here are quite simplified. This is just to give a brief overview of the kind of reasoning that is possible. Usually the tactics used involve multiple moves; however it is not difficult to see that this merely increases the technical details involved in the specification.

7 Discussion

An important aspect which has not been touched upon in this account is the notion of coalitions, and looking at strategic properties by which a coalition can bring about a certain outcome. Reasoning about coalitions in game logic has been studied extensively by Pauly [25].

The work we have presented here on structured strategies can (in a broad sense) be compared to the notion of imperfect information. In classical game theory, since players are assumed to be rational, imperfect information arises due lack of knowledge regarding opponents' moves. Here we are dealing with a situation where the lack of knowledge is with respect to strategies rather than the moves made in the history of the play. This line of work is particularly applicable when we do not make the assumption of common knowledge of rationality (CKR). CKR assumes that a player knows all strategies that are available to him as well as his opponents. As mentioned in the previous sections, it could very well be the case that the the game is too large to explicitly analyse all strategies. In this situation, players will tend to act irrationally. However, if we know that the opponents are of a certain "type" and the kind of strategies they employ, then this information can be explicitly used in the strategic response of the player.

Another interesting line of work would be to bring in the notion of expectation into formal strategic reasoning as, for instance, advocated by [2]. This is lacking in Game logic as well. In the current approach the only information that a player has about his opponent is what he has seen in the past history of play, which is unsatisfactory. Players typically begin with some expectation of the kind of strategy that the opponent plays and revise this expectation depending on what they see in the history of the play. Such problems are extensively studied in classical game theory literature where Bayesian revision of priors is a standard technique. Logical analysis of a similar kind, but using more abstract notions like "likelihood" [12], need to be explored in depth.

References

[1] Victor Allis. A Knowledge Based Approach of Connect Four. Master's thesis, Vrije Universiteit Amsterdam, 1998.

[2] Robert J. Aumann and Jacques H. Dreze. When All Is Said and Done, How Should You Play and What Should You Expect? Technical Report CORE Discussion Paper 2005/21, Catholic University of Louvain, Center for Operations Research and Econometrics (CORE), 2005.

[3] Dietmar Berwanger. Game Logic Is Strong Enough For Parity Games. *Studia Logica*, 75(2):205–219, 2003.

[4] Dietmar Berwanger. Admissibility in Infinite Games. In Wolfgang Thomas and Pascal Weil, editors, *Proceedings of the Symposium on Theoretical Aspects of Computer Science*, volume 4393 of *Lecture Notes in Computer Science*, pages 188–199. Springer, 2007.

[5] Juluis R. Büchi and Lawrence H. Landweber. Solving Sequential Conditions by Finite-State Strategies. *Transactions of the American Mathematical Society*, 138:295–311, 1969.

[6] Krishnendu Chatterjee, Marcin Jurdzinski, and Rupak Majumdar. On Nash Equilibria in Stochastic Games. In Jerzy Marcinkowski and Andrzej Tarlecki, editors, *Proceedings of the 13th Annual Conference of the European Association for Computer Science Logic*, volume 3210 of *Lecture Notes in Computer Science*, pages 26–40. Springer, 2004.

[7] Ernest A. Emerson and Charanjit S. Jutla. Tree Automata, μ-calculus and Determinacy. In *Proceedings of the 32nd IEEE Symposium on Foundations of Computer Science*, pages 368–377. IEEE Computer Society Press, 1991.

[8] Ernst A. Emerson, Charanjit S. Jutla, and A. Prasad Sistla. On Model-Checking for Fragments of μ-calculus. In Costas Courcoubetis, editor,

Proceedings of the 5th International Conference on Computer Aided Verification, CAV'93, volume 697 of *Lecture Notes in Computer Science*, pages 385–396. Springer, 1993.

[9] David Gale. The Game of Hex and Brouwer Fixed-Point Theorem. *The American Mathematical Monthly*, 86:818–827, 1979.

[10] Erich Grädel, Wolfgang Thomas, and Thomas Wilke, editors. *Automata, Logics and Infinite Games*, volume 2500 of *Lecture Notes in Computer Science*. Springer, 2002.

[11] Yuri Gurevich and Leo Harrington. Trees, Automata and Games. In *Proceedings of the 14th Annual Association for Computing Machinery Symposium on Theory of Computing*, pages 60–65. Association for Computing Machinery Press, 1982.

[12] Joseph Y. Halpern and Michael O. Rabin. A logic to Reason about Likelihood. *Artificial Intelligence*, 32:379–405, 1987.

[13] David Harel, Dexter Kozen, and Jerzy Tiuryn. *Dynamic Logic*. MIT Press, 2000.

[14] Paul Harrenstein, Wiebe van der Hoek, John-Jules Meyer, and Cees Witteven. A Modal Characterization of Nash Equilibrium. *Fundamenta Informaticae*, 57(2–4):281–321, 2003.

[15] John C. Harsanyi and Reinhard Selten. *A General Theory of Equilibrium Selection in Games*. MIT Press, 1987.

[16] Dexter Kozen. Results on the Propositional μ-calculus. *Theoretical Computer Science*, 27:333–354, 1983.

[17] Harold W. Kuhn. Extensive Games and the Problem of Information. In Harold W. Kuhn and Albert W. Tucker, editors, *Contributions to the Theory of Games*, volume 2, pages 193–216. Princeton University Press, 1953.

[18] Carlton E. Lemke and Joseph T. Howson Jr. Equilibrium Points of Bimatrix Games. *Journal of the Society of Industrial and Applied Mathematics*, 12:413–423, 1964.

[19] David N. L. Levy. *How Computers Play Chess*. W.H. Freeman & Co., 1990.

[20] Donald A. Martin. Borel Determinacy. *Annals of Mathematics*, 102:363–371, 1975.

[21] Robert McNaughton. Infinite Games Played on Finite Graphs. *Annals of Pure and Applied Logic*, 65:149–184, 1993.

[22] John F. Nash. Equilibrium Points in n-Person Games. *Proceedings of the National Academy of Sciences*, 36:89–93, 1950.

[23] Rohit Parikh. The Logic of Games and Its Applications. *Annals of Discrete Mathematics*, 24:111–140, 1985.

[24] Marc Pauly. Game Logic for Game Theorists. Technical report, CWI Amsterdam, 2000.

[25] Marc Pauly. *Logic for Social Software.* PhD thesis, Universiteit van Amsterdam, 2001. ILLC Publications DS-2001-10.

[26] Micheal O. Rabin. Decidability of Second-Order Theories and Automata on Infinite Trees. *Transactions of the American Mathematical Society*, 141:1–35, 1969.

[27] R. Ramanujam and Sunil Simon. Axioms for Composite Strategies. In Giacomo Bonanno, Wiebe van der Hoek, and Michael Wooldridge, editors, *Proceedings of the Seventh Conference On Logic and the Foundations of Game and Decision Theory, LOFT 06, 13th–15th July, 2006, University of Liverpool, UK*, pages 189–198. University of Liverpool, 2006.

[28] R. Ramanujam and Sunil Simon. Structured strategies in games on graphs. In Eric Grädel, Jörg Flum, and Thomas Wilke, editors, *Logic and Automata: History and Perspectives*, volume 2 of *Texts in Logic and Games*, pages 567–587. Amsterdam University Press, 2007.

[29] Stuart J. Russell and Peter Norvig. *Artificial Intelligence: A Modern Approach.* Prentice Hall, 2002.

[30] Jonathan Schaeffer, Neil Burch, Yngvi Björnsson, Akihiro Kishimoto, Martin Müller, Robert Lake, Paul Lu, and Steve Sutphen. Checkers is Solved. *Science*, 317:1518–1522, 2007.

[31] Philip D. Straffin. *Game Theory and Strategy.* The Mathematical Association of America, 1993.

[32] Michael Ummels. Rational Behaviour and Strategy Construction in Infinite Multiplayer Games. In S. Arun Kumar and Naveen Garg, editors, *Proceedings of the 26th International Conference on Foundations of Software Technology and Theoretical Computer Science*, volume 4337 of *Lecture Notes in Computer Science*, pages 212–223. Springer, 2006.

[33] Johan F.A.K. van Benthem. Games in Dynamic Epistemic Logic. *Bulletin of Economic Research*, 53(4):219–248, 2001.

[34] Wiebe van der Hoek, Wojtek Jamroga, and Michael Wooldridge. A logic for Strategic Reasoning. In Michal Pechoucek, Donald Steiner, and Simon Thompson, editors, *Proceedings of the Fourth International Joint Conference on Autonomous Agents and Multi-Agent Systems*, pages 157–164, 2005.

[35] John. von Neumann and Oskar Morgenstern. *Theory of Games and Economic Behaviour*. Princeton University Press, 1947.

[36] Bernhard von Stengel. Computing Equilibria for Two-Person Games. In Robert J. Aumann and Sergiu Hart, editors, *Handbook of Game Theory*, volume 3, pages 1723–1759. North-Holland, 2002.

[37] Thomas Wilke. Alternating Tree Automata, Parity Games, and Modal μ-Calculus. *Bulletin of the Belgian Mathematical Society*, 8(2), 2001.

[38] Ernst Zermelo. Über eine Anwendung der Mengenlehre auf die Theorie des Schachspiels. In E. W. Hobson and A. E. H. Love, editors, *Proceedings of the Fifth International Congress of Mathematicians, Cambridge 1912, Volume 2*, pages 501–504. Cambridge University Press, 1913.

[39] Wieslaw Zielonka. Infinite Games on Finitely Coloured Graphs with Applications to Automata on Infinite Trees. *Theoretical Computer Science*, 200(1-2):135–183, 1998.

A Semiotic Interpretation of Indian Logic

Sundar Sarukkai*

National Institute of Advanced Studies, Indian Institute of Science Campus, Bangalore 560012, India

E-mail: sarukkai1@yahoo.com

Matilal's constant endeavour to make ancient Indian philosophy a living tradition has significantly influenced many philosophers. One way to do what Matilal so effectively did is to take the traditions outside their strict historical and cultural boundaries, and engage them in a dialogue with other, new philosophical traditions. This paper attempts to do something similar with a generally ignored theme in Indian logic, the theme of semiotics. One of Matilal's essays on Indian logic has the word semiotics in its title but he does not seem to have explored this relation in detail.[1]

This paper argues that Indian logic can be usefully interpreted through the concerns of semiotics, a tradition that has a long history in western thought. At one level, the connection is obvious. The centrality of the idea of "sign" as the most significant entity in Indian logic must alert us to the potential semiotic world of this logic. By tracing the concerns of Indian logic along the contours of semiotics we can understand this logic not necessarily in terms of formal logic or in contrast to Aristotelian logic but in entirely new terms. Both the early Nyāya as well as the Buddhist systems were essentially engaged with questions of signs and their interpretation. Western traditions too have engaged seriously with the relation between signs and logic. Moving from Aristotle to Augustine and then on to Bacon, Ockham, Leibniz and later on to Peirce, we notice a sustained engagement with the idea of sign and its relation to logic by these thinkers. These attempts to understand logic through semiotics share some striking similarities with ancient Indian logic, including the emphasis placed by both Indian and western traditions on epistemology and cognition as part of the logical enterprise.

When Indian logical systems were available to the scholars in the West, the earliest and most common responses to them were dismissive in nature.[2] There are two issues that were influential in such responses to Indian logic. The claim that Indian logic was not logic was based on the observation that the use of empirical examples as part of the deductive structure negated the

*Thanks to two anonymous reviewers for their useful suggestions.

[1]In his [24], Matilal has a short essay on the semiotic conception in Indian logic, all of which is part of the material in his paper [26]. Unfortunately, he does not expand on the possible semiotic interpretation of Indian logic.

[2]For a brief summary of such responses, cf. [14, pp. 13–15].

Mihir K. **Chakraborty**, Benedikt **Löwe**, Madhabendra Nath **Mitra**, Sundar **Sarukkai** (*eds.*). Logic, Navya-Nyāya & Applications. Homage to Bimal Krishna Matilal. College Publications, London, 2008. Studies in Logic 15. pp. 287–304.

Received by the editors: 30 April 2007; 24 April 2008, 23 June 2008.
Accepted for publication: 20 August 2008.

universality associated with logic and that the logical process was described in terms of cognition and cognitive episodes. Keeping the empirical as an element of the logical seemingly went against the basic tenet of western logic and understanding the logical in terms of cognition suggested that the distinction between the psychological and the logical —a distinction around which some of the most influential debates on logic have occurred— had not been accomplished in Indian logic. Matilal and Mohanty have responded effectively to the charge of psychologising.[3] I have elsewhere discussed a different interpretation of the use of the example as exemplifying a particular structure of scientific explanation, namely, the deductive-nomological model of scientific explanation [36, pp. 194–208].

There are typically two different ways of responding to the charge that Indian logic is not logic at all. One is to understand what the structure of Indian logic *really* is and the other is to approach the problem from the perspectives of western logic. There has been much written from the former perspective and Matilal has been instrumental in generating a nuanced understanding of Indian logical systems. The latter approach is more problematic. Where such an approach exists, it largely consists in trying to rewrite Indian logic in formal terms.[4] Matilal has himself illustrated this possibility but such rewriting only generates more questions, particularly as to what such a rewriting accomplishes. If we grant that we can rewrite statements in Indian logic in formal terms with formal operations defined on them does it mean that Indian logic is formal? Or could it be that there is something in Indian logic that resists such formalisation?

What I shall do in this paper is to approach Indian logic from a specific western perspective. I shall not do this by attempting to show how Indian logical systems can be formalised and/or rewritten in symbolic form. There are two distinct strands in my approach in this paper. One, I shall illustrate how western logic, particularly in medieval times, shared a conceptual space with Indian logic, especially as far as the relations between logic and empiricism, as well as with cognition, are concerned. Two, I shall draw upon the semiotic understanding of logic in the West in order to exhibit the similarities with Indian logic.

Modern logic is fundamentally concerned with symbols and the actions performed on them. Although Indian logic was not traditionally presented in terms of symbolic writing, there is a fundamental relation between this

[3] Cf. [26, pp. 14–18] and [28, pp. 100–132].

[4] Cf. the papers [7, 5, 25] in [13]. I do not intend to negate the importance of formalization of Indian logic. However, prior to formalisation there is a philosophical problem related to the very nature of symbolic reduction. When seen through the semiotic enterprise, we can see that the problem confronting the Indian logician is precisely the conditions under which a symbol can come to stand for something else. The concluding paragraphs of this paper addresses this issue in more detail.

logic and the notion of a sign/symbol. In fact, as I shall argue later on, the concerns about the nature of the sign dictates the structure of this logic. The relation between logic and sign in the Indian tradition is quite clear. Inferring the presence of fire from seeing smoke is a common example not only in Indian philosophy but also in ancient Greek philosophy. An analysis of inference of fire from seeing smoke is based on the recognition that smoke is a *sign* that actually indicates the presence of something else. The Indian logicians extend this standing-for relation to include non-material signs. Thus, we have reason (for a particular inference) itself being understood as a sign. This relation between sign and logic matures in the Buddhist formulation as propounded by Dignāga (c. 400–480 AD).[5] In this formulation, the idea of logical sign plays a central role.

Dignāga turns the question of logic into a question of semiotics. Inference by its very nature is related to signs. Thus, logic primarily becomes an attempt to clarify what kinds of valid signs are possible and how justified inferences are possible from consideration of these signs. There is yet another peculiarity in his formulation, and this has to do with the use of "sign", "reason" and "evidence" as synonyms. Smoke is the sign which indicates the presence of fire. Smoke is the evidence for believing that there is fire and smoke is also the reason for coming to the conclusion that there is fire. Thus, as Matilal notes, sign, reason and evidence are terms that are often used interchangeably in Indian logic [26, p. 5]. Dignāga's theory of inference sets out a structure of inference based on the nature of the sign, thereby defining when a sign can properly stand for another [18]. He formulated the "triple nature of the sign", three conditions which a sign must fulfil in order that it leads to valid inference [26, p. 6].

1. It should be present in the case (object) under consideration.
2. It should be present in a *similar* case or a homologue.
3. It should not be present in any *dissimilar* case, any heterologue.

To summarize the meaning of the above conditions: a sign which is present in a locus signifies another property of the locus. To have a degree of certainty about this signification, we need to find similar cases where the sign and the signified occur and also dissimilar cases. The occurrence of the sign and signified together is seen as illustrating a relation between them, the relation of invariable concomitance or pervasion.

As mentioned earlier, the sign is not only a material sign like smoke. For the Indian logicians, "reason" is also a "sign". For example, the fact that a pot is produced is reason enough to infer that it is non-eternal. Production is a sign which stands for something else, namely, non-eternality. How

[5]Cf. [26] and [18] for a comprehensive discussion on these topics.

justified are we in believing that this sign 'being produced' indeed stands for "non-eternality"? This question is at the heart of Indian logic: how can we be certain that a particular sign indeed stands (and will continue to do so) for a particular signified? Answering this question is the task of logic as far as these logicians were concerned.

This method of formulating logic is essentially concerned with understanding the nature of signs and the relation between a sign and its signified, thus placing Indian logic firmly within the tradition of semiotics. Moreover, viewing logic through the perspective of semiotics negates many of the pseudo-problems afflicting the study of Indian logic: the question as to whether Indian logic is inductive or deductive, the problematic role of the example in Indian "syllogisms", the claim that Indian logic mixes logic and epistemology, and so on.

Understanding logic through semiotics is not uncommon. In fact, it can be argued that without engaging with semiotics it is impossible to understand the special characteristics of logic, particularly modern logic. Invoking semiotics also allows us to explore the relation between mathematics and logic by analyzing the way symbols are used in both these disciplines [38]. Most importantly, western logic itself has had a long and sustained relation between logic and semiotics, a relation often overlooked in contemporary readings of logic. Thus, to understand the relation between Indian and western logic, it is useful to first begin with the common ground that both of them share — the semiotic impulse.

Sign and logic in western thought

It might not be an exaggeration to claim that the formulation of the idea of signs is common to human thought in all civilizations. The suggestion that humans are fundamentally semiotic animals is perhaps not misplaced.[6] The basic idea of a sign lies in the possibility of something standing for another. Something is signified by a sign and there is also a relation of signification. Words constitute a simple example. A sign can be understood in many ways. For example, Eco points to the following ways: in opposition to *figurae* and *seme*, as difference, as identity, as inferential, as encoding and so on.[7] The inferential model of signs has immediate correlation with logic but the other ways of understanding sign also figure in the way signs are used in logic.

[6] For a discussion on related topics, cf. [8].

[7] Cf. [11, Chapter 1]. (In the common usages of sign, including in Matilal's use of it in reference to Indian logic, the sign is on a par with the signifier. In this paper, in order to maintain continuity with the common usage of "sign", I use the word sign not only as a relation but also as a signifier.)

The word sign is derived from *signum*, originally σημεῖον, which was often a synonym of τεκμήριον, and was used to mean proof, clue and symptom [11, p. 26]. These meanings share a common semantic space with the ideas of sign, reason and evidence, which are, as we have seen earlier, used in various ways in Indian logic. In the western tradition, the Stoics had the "first and most thorough sign theory every produced" and among the examples of inference, the smoke-fire inference was the "most elementary type of recollectable sign [11, pp. 213*sq*]". Eco notes that the Stoic model of sign is an inferential model of p implying q, "where the variables are neither physical realities nor events, but the propositions that express the events. A column of smoke is not a sign unless the interpreter sees the event as the true antecedent of a hypothetical reasoning (*if* there is smoke ...) which is related by inference (more or less necessary) to its consequent (... *then* there is fire) [11, p. 31]." The sign is not the material sign of a particular column of smoke but is a type standing for smoke. In comparison to Indian logic, we might say that this is a sign removed twice, since the type smoke stands for a particular column of smoke which is the sign for fire (as in Indian logic, although it should be noted that there are disagreements among different schools on what the object of inference could be[8]). Furthermore, the inferences studied by the Stoics were not concerned with the epistemological relation between the terms in the inference, although Aristotle distinguished between necessary and weak signs based on epistemological concerns.

This detour into history should remind us, as Bochenski [6] does so effectively, that the meaning of logic was not clearly specified even in Aristotle. Bochenski points out a difference beween laws and rules, both of which are applicable in logic. Laws are those which can have a truth value whereas rules can only be correct but not true or false. The Stoics' formulation of the rule of *modus ponendo ponens* "allows for a complete translation of a logic stated in terms of laws into one formulated as a set of rules [6, p. 278]". For Bochenski, this possibility is important since laws are about ontology and logic, understood as a set of rules, claims independence from ontological concerns. He also notes that in Aristotle's writings, there are many logics which can be distinguished. For example, the "dialectical" mode in the *Topics* and the formal logical mode in the *Analytics* — the former is a set of rules while the latter is a system of laws. The Stoics however primarily viewed logic as dialectics, thereby not considering ontology in their logic. Even their logic of propositions, which should be an exemplar of formal logic, is still "conceived as being a set of rules for arguing [6, p. 282]".[9] This view of logic as dialectics should remind us of Matilal's work on the tradition of debate and its influence on Indian logic [26]. Furthermore, Bochenski's ar-

[8]Cf. [23, pp. 58–68] on the "objects" of inference.

[9]Cf. also [22].

gument that logic and ontology cannot be mutually separated is supported by examples not only from the Greek tradition but also the Indian schools, particularly the Nyāya and the Buddhist schools.[10]

The relation between logic and ontology, hidden for the most part, is also indicative of the essential connection between logic and semiotics. In the western tradition, it is most clearly seen in the history of the development of logic, particularly as far as the analysis of signs is concerned.

The views of Augustine (354–430 AD) on signs and logic were most influential till medieval times. For Augustine a sign was "something that shows itself to the senses and something other than itself to the mind [27]".[11] The relationship present in this description is triadic, relating "sign of something to some mind". Note the explicit invocation of the mind in describing the action of signs, a presence that will manifest itself in different ways over the centuries. Augustine also classified signs into two: natural and given signs.[12] As an example of the natural sign, he uses the example of smoke and fire. An important contribution of Augustine was in making a distinction between natural signs (those which have in some sense a natural relation between the sign and signified) and conventional signs and yet placing them within a general category of signs. One can see a similar preoccupation among the Indian logicians. For Augustine, signs have a "fundamental epistemic function". This view of signs has important consequences for our understanding of signs and their relation to logic. Augustine's view of sign was central to his theory of language that goes back to the earlier Greeks.

It is also interesting to note that a constant ambiguity stalks the notion of sign: there is one understanding of sign as an argument —an enthymematic proposition— and another view of sign as "semiotic object", a noun or a category that "subsumes nouns and other signs [9]". It is the role of sign as an argument that was under attack and by the Renaissance one can notice the bringing together of these two descriptions.

One of the most important contributions in the western semiotic tradition is by Roger Bacon (1214–1293 AD).[13] I mention his work also because of a curious similarity with the Indian logic tradition. Bacon classified signs in different ways such as those signifying through inference, concomitance and consequence. He also classified those signs which do so necessarily as follows: signifying something present, signifying something past and signifying something future. Here are some examples from his classification: from seeing large extremities we infer strength and this is the case of "signifying

[10] Cf. also [4].

[11] Cf. also [19, 21] for more on Augustine's theory of signs.

[12] Cf. [2], and for references within for Augustine's theory of signs.

[13] E.g., cf. [20].

something present"; from lactation we can infer birth of a child and this is the case of "signifying something past and so on [27]".

Matilal's detailed description of the Nyāya classification of signs allows us to note a similarity with Bacon's three-fold classification. The early Nyāya also had a three-fold classification of signs.[14] The first kind classifies inferences in which the effect is inferred from perceiving the cause [23, p. 30]. The idea of cause in this case is captured in the phrase "as before". This kind of inference classifies inferences based on a prior nature. An example of this kind is the inference that it will rain because there is a cloud. One infers so because this is known from earlier instances. Here, the inference is of the effect from perception of a presumed cause.

The second kind of inference is based on "rest will be alike". Matilal notes four different subtypes of inference under this category as classified by the Nyāya school. One example is the inference that all drops of seawater are salty from tasting just one drop of it. The second subtype is the inference of cause from effect and one example is the inference that it has rained because the river is full and flowing swiftly. The third subtype is "remainder", namely, inference by "elimination of alternatives". This explains inference which we reach by eliminating other possible alternatives rather than infer "directly". And finally, the fourth subtype, gives the example of inferring the whole from the part; the example being the inference of a whole cow from seeing only its parts.

The third kind of inference deals with examples such as inference that there is water nearby because wild geese are present; inferring the taste of fruit from seeing its colour; inferring specific taste from specific smell. In all these examples, there is no cause-effect relationship.

Although we notice some similarity between the classifications of Bacon and the Indian schools (including Caraka), we should note that there is a fundamental difference in the reasons that catalysed such a classification. As for Augustine, the primary motivation for Bacon in analyzing signs was to provide "foundations for the semantics of spoken language [27]". Such does not seem to be the primary motivation for the Indian logicians when they classify and analyse inference through the study of signs.

There are many reasons for this difference in orientation. Primary among them is the fact that complex theories of language were part of all the Indian philosophical schools. In the Indian philosophical traditions, philosophy of language was highly developed right from the beginning.[15] Thus, Indian logic arose in a culture which already possessed complex philosophies of language. The question of arbitrariness of symbols is one such important issue. The relation between word and object can be natural or arbitrary. In the

[14]For more on Indian logic, cf. [23, 42, 16, 30].
[15]E.g., cf. [40, 15].

Indian systems, both these views are held. Grammarians and Mīmāmsakas, for example, held that the word-object relation is fixed. Naiyāyikas and the Buddhists, who are the dominant contributors to logic, argued that the word-object relation is arbitrary.

There were many theories of meaning which were available to the Indian philosophers. In particular, the schools were well aware of the conventionalist theory of meaning. These philosophers were also well aware of the possibility of the arbitrary nature of signs, particularly because of the *apoha* doctrine of language held by the Buddhists, a view that understood meaning as based on difference [26]. Furthermore, this view of language was essential to logic since Dignāga's formulation draws upon the *apoha* theory [40]. It was also very clear for Indian philosophers such as those belonging to the Nyāya tradition that words function as signs standing for something else. Although Mīmāmsakas subscribed to a naturalistic description of words and meaning, the philosophers associated with the logical school, namely, Naiyāyikas and Buddhists, didn't do so. In fact, I think it is reasonable to argue that the stringent conditions on a valid sign may actually be a reflection of the problems of arbitrary connection between words and what they stand for. Since philosophy of language was one of the pillars of ancient Indian thought, the influence of these theories of language on logic might have succeeded in making the conditions on signs more rigorous than it perhaps otherwise would have been!

Logic and cognition

It has been claimed that Indian logic should not be granted the status of logic since it is not propositional in character but episodic in nature. The episodic nature arises from the description of inference through cognitive episodes. Basing logic on cognitive episodes seems at first view to negate the universality and the formal nature of logic, and to explicitly psychologize it. However, the problem is much more complex than it might first seem. One of the best ways of addressing this complexity is actually to analyse western logic's long engagement with cognition. Given that there was such a tradition in the West, a dismissal of the "logical" status of Indian logic because of its episodic nature might be a bit hasty.

In the western tradition, an enduring relation between cognition and logic can be found.[16] Even in the earlier approaches to the study of signs

[16] For a quaint discussion on psychology and logic, cf. [32]. Dewey [10] summarises different types of logic — one of which is "empirical logic" and another is "psychological logic"! In [3], Bhattacharya offers a sustained discussion of the relation between logic and psychology, including a rebuttal of many common arguments against psychology in relation to logic. The relation between psychology and logic has also become subject matter for cognitive science. Van Lambalgen [41] begins with an analysis of the relation between logic and the psychology of reasoning, and argues that logical reasoning is an

we can notice the explicit role of the mind. A sign, as we saw earlier with respect to Augustine, is triadic — a sign of something to some mind. The problem of what words refer to also engages with the mental domain — e.g., the view that words stand for mental aspects and not the object. But this explicit reckoning of the mental with respect to signs (and therefore logic) becomes prominent with Ockham and his view of the "mentalization of sign". As Meier-Oeser notes in [27], with Ockham "sign occupies center state in logic." Following Ockham, logic was understood to be exclusively concerned with signs. These were primarily mental signs. The idea of mentalization of sign meant that signification is possible only with some kind of intentionality. We should note that such a position was dominantly held following Ockham till the early 16th century. One of the important consequences of this position was that it differentiated between signs so as to identify what was special to logical signs or signs in logic. Not all signs are logical signs. Signs in logic had to stand in a relation of "aptness" — so, a sign has to "be apt to stand for the thing it makes come into cognition [27]".

The similarity in this western view and that in Indian logic must be noted. Because the Indians had complex theories of language which included an understanding of the arbitrary nature of the relation between words and objects, they were aware of the fact that logical signs had to be special in some sense. Thus, they first had to look for ways to choose those signs from a large set of signs and this restricted set was the set of logical signs. One of the defining criterion for this choice was that the signs stand in some apt relation — e.g., the relations of identity and causality. The explicit invocation of the activity of sign in its capacity to make the thing "come into cognition" mirrors the general view of the Indian philosophical schools.

There is an important corollary to understanding logical signs in this manner. Almost all the schools of logic following Ockham recognized the primary role of epistemology in logic. Such an attitude towards logic is well captured by the view that a sign was defined by its "capability to act in an epistemologically efficient way on a cognitive power [27]". Note the emphasis on both epistemology and cognition as being intrinsic to logic.

It was only later, around the 16th century, that the written sign was freed from its subordination to the vocal sign (cf. [27]). This allowed a direct relation between the mental and the written without being mediated by the spoken. An important consequence of this was that the written sign was generalized without having to be grounded in the spoken, thus leading to the possibility of meaninglessness and arbitrariness of symbols. Such a view proved to be of great influence in the development of both mathematics and logic.

---

exaptation in contrast to evolutionary explanations.

There is an important difference between symbols and words that needs to be mentioned here. Symbols are not based on the model of language, although they share the nature of arbitrariness with words. Rather, they are concerned with exhibiting two features: one, the distinction between the sign and what it stands for, and two, the possibility of what Leibniz calls *characteristica universalis* which will in some sense remove the arbitrariness in symbolic relations [12, p. 5]. The arbitrary nature of the sign is only in its creation whereas for the Indian logicians the logical sign must have some necessary connection with the signified. In the case of Dharmakīrti, for example, the necessary relations are through identity and causal relation.[17] Thus, there is a reason for our recognition of something as a valid sign. The question of validity of signs itself is quite special to Indian logicians, one which immediately negates arbitrary signs. The basic point is that while there can be a sign which can, in principle, stand for anything, the Indian logicians were concerned about finding the subset of these signs which have a special, natural relation with the signified. Since their logic was responsive to the concerns of language, arbitrary signs, for example, linguistic symbols, were already accepted into the system of signifiers. The synonymous use of sign, reason and evidence also points to the problem of viewing signs as being completely arbitrary.

Arbitrary symbols in certain Indian traditions are exemplified by words. But the idea of a symbol as discussed by Leibniz and others is somewhat different from the arbitrary nature of words. However, the idea of arbitrary symbol has an expanded interpretation, one which can be analysed by distinguishing between arbitrary symbols which can be both like words and not-words, implying thereby that there is a notion of symbol which differentiates between word-symbol and non-word-symbol. Arbitrary symbols can be classified in two ways with respect to meaning. Words, although arbitrary, are filled with meaning. Symbols, as used in logic and mathematics, do not have an associated semantic world like the words.[18] So the relevant question that we need to consider is whether we can have symbols which are arbitrary but do not carry a space of meaning with them. It is important to note that the *meaninglessness* of symbols is important to make a transition into the logical and mathematical symbolical domain, and that this mode of arbitrary symbolisation is different from the arbitrary nature of linguistic words as signs.

[17] Dharmakīrti was a Buddhist logician after Dignāga (mentioned in the earlier part of this paper). Dharmakīrti formulated three types of inferences — those based on identity, causality and non-perception. For more on this, cf. [26, 36, 31].

[18] This is so even for those like Boole who thought that symbols once created have fixed meaning. The problem is that meaning in these symbols is not similar to meaning in words. In fact, the potentiality of symbols to take on a variety of roles and meaning is what makes the use of arbitrary symbols so appealing.

From some of the defining characteristics of western logic till the 16th century — the importance of signs in logic, the attempt to isolate a subgroup of signs which exemplified a logical character, the relation of logic to cognition which is made explicit through the relation of sign to cognition, an epistemological component essential to logic — it is clear that western logic had a very different conception of logic than is usually propounded these days. That these characteristics are also manifested in Indian logic must be cause for some further reflection on the true nature of Indian logic.

Peirce and Indian logic

The development of modern logic with its new found freedom through written symbols meant that cognition and epistemology as part of the activity of logic were no longer explicitly acknowledged. But logic's direct relation to signs was recaptured by Peirce in his influential analysis of logic. Peirce's claim that "logic is nothing else than the general theory of signs" is an important statement relating logic and the larger symbolic world. There are various issues that arise from Peirce's detailed classification of signs. In particular, it allows us to consider some interesting comparative issues between Peirce and the Buddhist logicians, Dignāga and Dharmakīrti. Buchler in his introduction to Peirce's work notes that Peirce's path-breaking contribution is his "conception of logic as the philosophy of communication, or theory of signs [29, p. xii]". He also says that the "conception of logic as semiotic opens broad, new possibilities". Arguably, we can well understand the aims of Indian logic alongside the approach towards logic and signs by Peirce. Peirce's ideas about signs share a common conceptual space with Dignāga and other Indian logicians. Therefore, it seems reasonable to claim that the ancient and medieval Indian logicians who based their logic on the nature of signs understood the essence of logic primarily as what in the western tradition came to be called as semiotics.

Peirce offered a very detailed classification of signs. Peirce begins by defining sign, in a way similar to Dignāga, as "something which stands to somebody or something in some respect or capacity". There are three elements to a sign: the creation of another sign in the mind, the sign standing for an object, and the presence of an idea in reference to which the sign stands for the object. The second element of the sign, namely its capacity to stand for some other object, is what Peirce calls logic. Thus, "logic proper is the formal science of the conditions of the truth of representations [29, p. 99]". There are three types of sign for Peirce, what he calls "three trichotomies". The better known classification of signs by Peirce are the three types of sign under the second trichotomy. These three types are the icon, index and symbol. This extremely short summary does no justice to

Peirce's rich ideas about sign. I mention these points here only in order to ground a different, semiotic interpretation of Indian logic.

To motivate such a comparative study, consider one simple example. We have already seen Dignāga's formulation of the triple condition of logical sign. Is this formulation an indication of the possibility of logic as semiotics? Firstly, Dignāga and Peirce are both interested in valid logical conclusions and judgements. Both of them see the sign as the path towards judgements of the logical kind. Both of them have a broad view of signs, ranging from material signifiers such as smoke to words and concepts. As a theory of signs, Peirce's classification is much more detailed whereas as a theory of logical sign, Dignāga's conditions do more than Peirce's analysis. For example, Peirce's idea of similarity as used in iconic signs is ambiguous whereas this is exactly what the similarity condition in Dignāga's theory tries to answer. In Indian logic, the sign is used synonymously with reason and evidence. The idea of reason is already inherent in the meaning of a sign since a sign is a sign of something else and it is conceivable that there is a reason for this connection. The question for the Indian logicians consisted in knowing whether the sign "really" stood for the thing which it was supposed to stand for. Therefore, this involved understanding the reason why one sign comes to stand for another. This could be psychological (by seeing concomitance, for example) or social (linguistic conventions, for instance), yet part of the doubt about inference comes from doubt about the origins of the relation between sign and the signified object. The conditions of similarity and dissimilarity are also attempts to clarify this relation as well as understand the original impulse for making the connection in the first place.

Dharmakīrti's three types of inference, the ones based on identity, causality and non-perception, can be seen as a classification that explains why some signs come to stand for another. Identity is based on similarity and is actually a more comprehensive definition of icon as compared to Peirce. When we say that an oak tree is a tree, our inference is based on a perception of some similarities. In general, it would seem that our "perception" or inference of universals, such as say cowhood, is based on recognition of similar characteristics and therefore signs in such an inference function as icons.[19]

The causal type, with smoke and fire as example, is illustrative of indexical signs. Smoke is an index, which refers to a fire in that location. Smoke and fire are associated through contiguity, and smoke obeys all the characteristics of an index which Peirce describes as follows:

> First, that they have no significant resemblance to their objects; second, that they refer to individuals, single units, single collections of

[19] Cf. [39] for an interesting and extended analysis of icons.

> units, or single continua; third, that they direct the attention to their objects by blind compulsion [29, p. 108].

Causal signs are just one type of indexical signs. The question is whether Dharmakīrti's second type can be extended to indexicals in general rather than being restricted only to causal signs? Or equivalently whether Peirce's large set of indexical signs need to be pared only to causal ones?

The above discussion about Peirce and other semioticians is only to highlight the importance of re-looking at Indian logic through other frameworks. The dominant mode of understanding Indian logic in comparison to "formal logic" has led to needless debates about its status as logic. A fresh look at the Indian logical systems through the semiotic prism illustrates in what sense it is logical and equally importantly in what sense logic is concerned with semiotics.

In [17], Gerow attempts a comparative study of Peirce in the context of Indian philosophy. Firstly, he finds in Mīmāmsa the closest similarity with Peirce's classification of icon, index and symbol. His discussion focuses more on issues of language, and in particular, the questions concerning word, reference and meaning. But the real distinction he finds is in the idea of the symbol as formulated by Peirce. Gerow's question is: "where is the Indian 'symbol'?" The fundamental point about the symbol lies in the role of the "interpretant" (in Peirce's sense) who interprets the symbol. Drawing from poetics, Gerow suggests that the *dhvani* can function in the role of the Peircean symbol although there are problems in such an interpretation. However, what is surprising is that Gerow does not engage with the formulations of Indian logic (and related theories of language, especially since Nyaya and Buddhists have a different take on language as compared to the Mīmāmsakas) to explore this relationship. The discussion in this paper is one way to approach this comparative study.

I should like to suggest here that the semiotic reading of Indian logic necessitates a more careful look at the meaning of a symbol, particularly as it is used in symbolic logic and mathematics. It is the case that there is a lack of philosophical clarity on the meaning and use of symbols in logic. Indeed, there is a great need to actually understand the exact role of symbols and symbolic manipulation that are so central to modern logics. A similar question can be addressed to mathematics. In recent times, there has been more sustained effort in trying to understand the use of symbols in mathematics, which includes analyzing specific writing strategies of symbols in mathematics which have deep epistemological consequences.[20]

Let me conclude with one such reflection on the nature of the symbol. As mentioned earlier, a primary concern of the Indian logician was about the

[20] Cf. [35, 33, 34] for a more detailed discussion on this topic.

relation of necessity, both logical and "contingent" necessity.[21] Arbitrary symbolization —here I mean choosing something to arbitrarily stand for another such as choosing A to stand for "men"— is not of much interest to these logicians because words in language do that job anyway. (In this context, we need to ask what *really* differentiates A from "men" as linguistic markers.) Moreover, the question is: what in the nature of symbols resists the creation of meaning that is not based on convention? That is, is it possible that an arbitrary symbol —through use or through knowledge— becomes a "natural" sign? And if so, then how do we analyse this new character of the symbol?

Let me illustrate this shift from the arbitrary to the "natural" with a simple example from mathematics. Mathematics is essentially concerned with symbolic manipulation of various kinds. However, the way mathematics uses its symbols should point us to a more complex definition of a symbol. For example, the way mathematics writes its symbols —what I have elsewhere referred to as "alphabetization"— indicates how meaning is encoded into the symbols themselves [35]. Furthermore, it is often the case that symbols lose their arbitrary sense and get associated with specific meanings — that is, they get "naturalized". From being arbitrary symbols they become "necessary" signs. Applied mathematics is filled with such shifts in meaning. In physics, it is often the case that one discovers physical properties merely by finding an appropriate pattern in the mathematical description. For example, whenever a term of the form ab^2 is found in an equation there is an interpretative possibility that a stands for the mass based on a prior meaning of kinetic energy which is symbolized in a similar way [35, 37].

Once the shift away from the arbitrary to the necessary happens, then it is the task of the logician to discover rules that will validate this necessary relation. Dignaga's conditions are precisely an attempt to do this. The universality of his rules can be noted when we compare his formulation to how experimental interpretations are done in modern physics. Experimental physics has an essential engagement with inferences. In a typical experiment, what the experimenter sees are a set of signs from which she has to infer the existence of some entity or property. For example, the presence of the electron can be inferred only through certain signs. These signs necessarily correspond to certain properties or entities — such a necessary connection between sign and signified is essential for science to be effective. And such a necessary relation is given by an appropriate scientific

[21] In using "contingent" necessity I am following Armstrong's use of this term in the context of scientific laws. Cf. [1]. It is possible and fruitful to understand one of the most important terms in Indian logic —*vyāpti*— in terms of contingent necessity and in terms of a lawlike structure.

theory. We can now understand Dignaga's three conditions for a logical sign as exemplifying the experimental ideal of replicability and the importance of null-experiments [36]. At the foundational level, the concerns of Indian logic and that of modern science are related to each other through this semiotic enterprise. Thus, the semiotic reading of Indian logic not only allows a dialogue with contemporary philosophy but it also poses a new set of questions to modern logic, particularly on the nature of the symbol.

Bibliography

[1] David M. Armstrong. *What Is a Law of Nature?* Cambridge University Press, Cambridge, 1983.

[2] Brigitte M. Bedos Rezak. Medieval Identity: A Sign and a Concept. *American Historical Review*, 105(5):1489–1533, 2000.

[3] Sibajiban Bhattacharyya. The Concept of Logic. *Philosophy and Phenomenological Research*, 18(3):326–340, 1958.

[4] Sibajiban Bhattacharyya. Logic and Ontology. In Sibajiban Bhattacharyya, editor, *Doubt, Belief and Knowledge*, pages 113–120. Indian Council of Philosophical Research, New Delhi, 1987.

[5] Sibajiban Bhattacharyya. Some Aspects of the Navya-Nyāya Theory of Inference. In Jonardon Ganeri, editor, *Indian Logic: A Reader*, pages 162–181. Curzon Press, Amsterdam, 1997.

[6] Innocentius M. Bocheński. Logic and Ontology. *Philosophy East and West*, 24(3):275–292, 1974.

[7] Innocentius M. Bocheński. The Indian Variety of Logic. In Jonardon Ganeri, editor, *Indian Logic: A Reader*, pages 117–150. Curzon Press, Amsterdam, 1997.

[8] John Deely. *What Distinguishes Human Understanding?* St. Augustine's Press, South Bend, Indiana, 2002.

[9] Marie-Lucie Demonet. Natural Inference and the Science of Signs in the Renaissance. *South Central Review*, 10:76–99, 1993.

[10] John Dewey. Notes Upon Logical Topics. *The Journal of Philosophy, Psychology and Scientific Methods*, 1(3):57–62, 1904.

[11] Umberto Eco. *Semiotics and the Philosophy of Language*. Macmillan Press, London, 1984.

[12] Massimo Ferrari. The Concept of Symbol from Leibniz to Cassirer. In Massimo Ferrari and Ion-Olimpiu Stamatescu, editors, *Symbol and Physical Knowledge: On the Conceptual Structure of Physics*, pages 3–32. Springer, Berlin, 2002.

[13] Jonardon Ganeri, editor. *Indian Logic: A Reader*. Curzon Press, Amsterdam, 1997.

[14] Jonardon Ganeri. Introduction: Indian Logic and the Colonization of Reason. In Jonardon Ganeri, editor, *Indian Logic: A Reader*, pages 1–25. Curzon Press, Amsterdam, 1997.

[15] Jonardon Ganeri. *Artha: Meaning*. Oxford University Press, New Delhi, 2006.

[16] Mrinal K. Gangopadhyay. *Indian Logic in Its Sources: On Validity of Inference*. Munshiram Manoharlal, New Delhi, 1984.

[17] Edwin Gerow. Language and Symbol in Indian Semiotics. *Philosophy East and West*, 34(3):245–260, 1984.

[18] Richard Hayes. *Dignaga on the Interpretation of Signs*. Kluwer, Dordrecht, 1988.

[19] Darrell Jackson. The Theory of Signs in St. Augustine's *De doctrina christiana*. *Revue des Études Augustiniennes*, 15:9–49, 1969.

[20] Thomas Maloney. The Semiotics of Roger Bacon. *Medieval Studies*, 45:120–154, 1983.

[21] Robert Markus. St. Augustine on Signs. *Phronesis*, 2:60–83, 1957.

[22] Benson Mates. Stoic Logic and the Text of Sextus Empiricus. *The American Journal of Philology*, 70(3):290–298, 1949.

[23] Bimal Krishna Matilal. *Logic, Language and Reality: Indian Philosophy and Contemporary Issues*. Motilal Banarsidass, Delhi, 1985.

[24] Bimal Krishna Matilal. *The Word and the World: India's Contribution to the Study of Language*. Oxford University Press, Delhi, 1990.

[25] Bimal Krishna Matilal. Introducing Indian Logic. In Jonardon Ganeri, editor, *Indian Logic: A Reader*, pages 183–215. Curzon Press, Amsterdam, 1997.

[26] Bimal Krishna Matilal. *The Character of Logic in India*. Suny Series in Indian Thought, Texts and Studies. Clarendon Press, Albany, 1998.

[27] Stephan Meier Oeser. Medieval Semiotics. In Edward N. Zalta, editor, *The Stanford Encyclopedia of Philosophy (Winter 2003 Edition)*. CSLI, 2003.

[28] Jintendra N. Mohanty. *Reason and Tradition in Indian Thought: An Essay on the Nature of Indian Philosophical Thinking*. Clarendon Press, Oxford, 1992.

[29] Charles S. Peirce. *Philosophical Writings of Peirce*. Dover Publications, New York, 1955.

[30] Stephen Phillips. *Classical Indian Metaphysics*. Motilal Banarasidass, Delhi, 1997.

[31] Rajendra Prasad. *Dharmakirti's Theory of Inference: Revaluation and Reconstruction*. Oxford University Press, Delhi, 2002.

[32] David G. Ritchie. The Relation of Logic to Psychology. *Philosophical Review*, 5:585–600, 1996.

[33] Brian Rotman. *Ad Infinitum: The Ghost in Turing's Machine*. Stanford University Press, Stanford, 1993.

[34] Brian Rotman. Mathematical Writing, Thinking, and Virtual Reality. In Paul Ernest, editor, *Mathematics, Education and Philosophy*, pages 76–86. The Falmer Press, London, 1994.

[35] Sundar Sarukkai. *Translating the World: Science and Language*. University Press of America, Lanham, 2002.

[36] Sundar Sarukkai. *Indian Philosophy and Philosophy of Science*. CSC/Motilal Banarsidass, New Delhi, 2005.

[37] Sundar Sarukkai. Revisiting the 'Unreasonable Effectiveness' of Mathematics. *Current Science*, 88:414–423, 2005.

[38] Sundar Sarukkai. The Use of Symbols in Mathematics and Logic. In Giandomenico Sica, editor, *Essays on the Foundations of Mathematics and Logic*, pages 389–544. Polimetrica, Monza, 2005.

[39] Thomas A. Sebeok. Iconicity. *Modern Language Notes*, 91:1427–1456, 1976.

[40] Mark Siderits. *Indian Philosophy of Language*. Kluwer, Dordrecht, 1991.

[41] Michiel van Lambalgen. Evolutionary Considerations on Logical Reasoning. In Dag Westerståhl, editor, *Proceedings of Twelfth International Conference of Logic, Methodology and Philosophy of Science*, Oviedo, 2003. University Press.

[42] Satis C. Vidyabhusana. *A History of Indian Logic: Ancient, Mediaeval and Modern Schools.* Motilal Banarasidass, Calcutta, 1920.